D1591255

CHRISTIANITY
and the
ROMAN
EMPIRE

CHRISTIANITY
and the
ROMAN
EMPIRE

Background Texts

Ralph Martin Novak Jr.

TRINITY PRESS INTERNATIONAL
Harrisburg, Pennsylvania

BR
167
.N69
2001

Scripture Quotations are from the Revised Standard Version of the Bible, copyright 1946, 1952, 1971 by the Division of Christian Education of the National Council of the churches of Christ in the U.S.A. Used by permission. All rights reserved.

Copyright © 2001 Ralph Martin Novak Jr.

All rights reserved. No part of this book may be reproduced, stored in a retrieval system, or transmitted in any form or by any means, electronic, mechanical, including photocopying, recording, or otherwise, without the written permission of the publisher, Trinity Press International.

Trinity Press International, P.O. Box 1321, Harrisburg, PA 17105

Trinity Press International is a division of the Morehouse Group.

Cover design: Thomas Castanzo

Library of Congress Cataloging-in-Publication Data
Novak, Ralph Martin.
    Christianity and the Roman Empire : background texts / Ralph Martin Novak, Jr.
        p. cm.
    Includes bibliographical references (p.) and index.
    ISBN 1-56338-347-0 (alk. paper)
        1. Church history—Primitive and early church, ca. 30-600—Sources. I. Title.

    BR167 .N69 2001
    270.1—dc21   00-046688

Printed in the United States of America

01 02 03 04 05 06   10 9 8 7 6 5 4 3 2 1

Truth, which is simple and one, does not admit of variety.

POPE LEO I "THE GREAT"
BISHOP OF ROME, 440–461 C.E.

What is Truth?

PONTIUS PILATE
ROMAN PREFECT OF JUDAEA, 26–36 C.E.

CONTENTS

FOREWORD

This book traces its origins to an adult Christian education course entitled "The Roman Empire's Perspective of Christianity" that I taught at St. Matthew's Episcopal Church in Austin, Texas in the fall of 1996. In planning that course I decided at an early stage to rely heavily on readings in the ancient texts. That decision was in part the result of the training I had received from a series of outstanding history professors at Rice University and the University of Chicago, but it also grew out of my perceptions of the people likely to take the course. I anticipated that most of the class would, aside from their familiarity with the New Testament, know little about early Christian history other than as presented by the popular press and Hollywood movies—sources of information better known for dramatic flair and license than understanding or accuracy. For precisely that reason I did not want my class to be just another lecture course. I wanted my students to develop a basic foundation in Christian history and learn how to evaluate the merits of conflicting historical interpretations, so that they would be equipped to pursue sound independent study long after my course had ended. This meant that I would have to introduce the class to the primary sources and guide them in developing a logical approach to the study of the sources. Unfortunately, I could not locate a good primary source book that dealt with early Christian history in an orderly fashion at the non-specialist level, and so I put such materials together myself. Those original materials have grown and evolved over the years, but I have always kept in mind that original target audience: the non-specialist adult who, though perhaps having little formal training in historical study, is willing to learn and apply logic to the primary sources to build a solid foundation in Christian history.

The reader will see that many of the ancient texts reproduced here are radiant with emotion and energy that the centuries cannot diminish. A primary goal of my narrative, therefore, has been to direct the reader along the path of the majority historical consensus without being so intrusive as to obscure the majesty and power of the texts themselves. Whenever I had choices to make concerning the direction and scope of the narrative, in most instances I chose to simplify and summarize rather than to expound at greater length. I have also tried to present the materials in such a way that this book could serve as both a useful adjunct to the work of other scholars in the field and as a stand-alone account for the non-specialist reader. In preparing footnotes I have intentionally attempted to refer to eminent historians whose works are still widely available in the marketplace, in the hope that the interested reader, who may have neither the time nor the inclination to track down the most current specialist literature, will nonetheless be able to pursue further profitable study through the local library or bookseller.

Sound history must be made available to the non-specialist in an accessible and understandable manner, or else the study of history will eventually be reduced to a mere elitist intellectual pursuit and its value lost to the greater part of the modern world. I will be immensely satisfied if both the non-specialist reader and the professional historian find this book a useful tool for learning and teaching.

There are a great many people I wish to thank for their help in the making of this book. Some are distant in time and place, like my professors Floyd Seyward Lear and Katherine Fischer Drew of Rice University and Stewart Irvin Oost of the University of Chicago, who by shaping me in their ancient history classes helped shaped this book. Other people have been of more immediate assistance. Mikail M. McIntosh-Doty and the rest of the staff of The Booher Library of the Episcopal Seminary of the Southwest in Austin, Texas have provided tremendous help and assistance over the years, both in locating materials and in patiently listening to stories concerning my research. Maritta Terrell and Joann Gunlock have spent many hours assisting with word-processing, preparing correspondence, and listening to yet more stories about the ancient texts. Charlsa Stark and Kathleen Davis Niendorff edited and commented on several of the early chapters of the manuscript and provided invaluable assistance in preparing the all important "proposal to publishers." Kathleen Davis Niendorff also acted as agent for this book, and without her persistence, energy, and knowledge of the publishing field, I do not believe that this book would ever have made it to print. Richel Rivers and Amy Brueggeman read and commented on the manuscript at various stages of the writing process. James Barnes and Jennifer Davis helped work on ideas for the book cover design. Amy Tuvell provided critical last minute assistance in locating copyright holders for permissions as the typesetting deadline for the manuscript loomed close. Henry Carrigan of Trinity Press provided guidance and needed encouragement throughout the editing process, and I am grateful to Henry, Lois Sibley, and the rest of the people at Trinity Press International for their work and their faith in this book. Most of all, I wish to thank those members of St. Matthew's Episcopal Church, All Saints' Episcopal Church, and University Christian Church in Austin, Texas who attended my classes over the years and by their interest, questions, criticisms, and comments made this book far better than I could have accomplished on my own.

This book is dedicated to my grandparents, parents, and children.

Ralph Martin Novak, Jr.
November 10, 2000
Austin, Texas

DATES OF SIGNIFICANT EVENTS
AND PRIMARY SOURCES

ca. 6–5 B.C.E. Birth of Jesus
ca. 30–33 C.E. Crucifixion of Jesus
50–51   Hearing of Paul before Gallio
61   Transport of Paul to Rome for trial
64   Nero's persecution of the Christians after the Great Fire of Rome
66–70   First Jewish War with Rome
95–96   Domitian's persecution
ca. 108   Letters of Ignatius
111   Pliny's Letter to the Emperor Trajan
124–125   Hadrian's Rescript to the Proconsul of Asia
155   Justin Martyr's First Apology
ca. 156   Martyrdom of Polycarp
177–180   Local persecutions during reign of Marcus Aurelius
177   Letter of the Gallican Churches
ca. 178   Celsus writes *True Doctrine*
180   *Acts of the Scillitan Martyrs*
197–212   Tertullian's writings
ca. 200   Epitaph of Avircius
203   *Martyrdom of Perpetua*
240s   Origen writes Against *Celsus*
248   Thousandth anniversary of the founding of the City of Rome
249–251   Persecution of Decius
257–260   Persecution of Valerian
260   *Edict of Toleration* by Gallienus
270s   Porphyry writes *Against the Christians*
late third Porphyry writes *Philosophy From Oracles*
century
303–311   The "Great Persecution" under Diocletian and the tetrarchs
311   Galerius's *Edict of Toleration*, ending the "Great Persecution"
314   *Edict of Milan*, recognizing Christianity as a licensed religion
324   Constantine I becomes sole emperor of Rome
361–363   Julian the Apostate attempts to revive paganism
384   Symmachus's Appeal concerning the Senate's Altar of Victory
388   Ambrose's Letter to Theodosius concerning the Synagogue at Callinicum
390   Ambrose's conflict with Theodosius concerning the massacre at Thessalonica
391   Theodosius's Edict prohibiting pagan worship in the temples
391–392   Seizure of the Serapeum in Alexandria; assault on Apamea's Temple
394   Theodosius's military victory over Eugenius
415   Destruction of Alexandria's Jewish Quarter; the murder of Hypatia

1 | A BRIEF INTRODUCTION TO HISTORICAL METHOD

HISTORY IS A JOURNEY INTO OTHERNESS. SURELY IT HAS AS MUCH RIGHT TO HELP
US OVERCOME OUR LIMITATIONS AS TO MAKE US FEEL AT HOME WITH THEM.
—PAUL VEYNE.[1]

C hristianity's rise to dominance in the Roman Empire during the first four centuries C.E. is the pivotal development in Western history and profoundly influenced the later direction of world history. Yet for all that has been written on the early history of Christianity, the sources of this history are widely scattered, difficult to find, and generally unknown to a layperson. The purpose of this book is to assemble these ancient texts into a single continuous account of the political and social relationships among Christians, the Roman government, and the peoples of the Roman Empire during these crucial four centuries.

Most of the ancient texts reproduced in this book are taken from literary sources. This is not meant to denigrate the importance of the extant archaeological materials, which are often essential to supplement or correct the conclusions one would draw solely from the literary sources.[2] However, the literary sources do provide a most convenient and useful introduction to our subject if understood in their proper context. A proper understanding of basic historical methodology and its application to written materials will, therefore, greatly enhance our appreciation of these literary sources.

Historical methodology is based upon the application of the rules of logic and deductive reasoning to the available evidence, but the proper application of these rules requires an understanding of the cultural and historical context of the evidence. The essential starting point in studying an ancient text is the effort to understand the perspective, motives, and biases of the author that underlie the words of the text. At minimum, this involves asking five fundamental questions of any given text:

> 1. *Who is speaking?* Who is the author of the text? What are the author's personal and cultural biases, and how do these biases affect the author's statements?

---

1. Philippe Aries and Gearge Duby, (eds.), "A History of Private Life," Vol. 1 *From Pagan Rome to Byzantium.* Paul Veyne (ed.), Arthur Goldhammer, trans. (Cambridge: Harvard University Press, 1987), 2.

2. For example, archeological studies indicate that the role of Christianity in the everyday life of Rome's North African provinces during the late fourth century C.E. was much smaller than the writings of St. Augustine suggest. For a discussion of the distortions to the historical record caused by the dominance of Christian perspectives in the surviving literature of late antiquity and the Middle Ages, see Ramsay MacMullen in *Christianity & Paganism in the Fourth to Eighth Centuries* (New Haven: Yale University Press, 1997), 1–6 and the accompanying notes.

2. *What is the author saying?* Every text must be read carefully to determine what facts, attitudes, and biases are expressed, implied, and/or assumed by the author. The reader must also learn to distinguish between the author's statements of fact and the author's interpretations of fact.

3. *What is the author's source for his or her statements of fact?* How does the author know of what he or she writes? Is the author's information first-hand or second-hand in nature? If second-hand, what are the author's sources for the information and how reliable are these sources?

4. *How does the author's intended audience influence the text's content and perspectives?* Authors invariably select and shape their materials for presentation to a specific audience and this has an obvious influence on the scope, content, and perspectives of the text. Less obvious, but equally important, is that an author will typically omit from his or her text material seen as inappropriate, offensive, or of little interest to the intended audience. Such omissions can gravely distort the overall accuracy of historical analysis based solely on the written text itself. For example, the great majority of ancient writers passed over without mention the cares and concerns of women, the poor, and slaves, even though collectively those groups constituted all but a tiny fraction of the total population of the ancient world. Such omissions tell the modern historian much about the values and perspectives of both the literary class that produced the surviving ancient texts and the intended audience for those texts, and serve as warnings to the modern reader against accepting ancient literary works as full and accurate representations of the past.

5. *What is the author's purpose in making the statements?* Every author has a purpose when he or she takes the trouble to write materials intended for distribution to other people. What is the author's purpose, and how does it influence his or her statements?

Closely related to the issue of understanding the author's personal context is the issue of understanding the larger social and cultural context of the author and the text. While modern Europeans and Americans have many cultural, historical, and linguistic ties to the world of the Roman Empire, there are significant cultural differences between modern Western industrial societies and the agricultural societies characteristic of the Mediterranean region during the Roman Empire. Those ancient agricultural societies were typically organized around the fundamental principles of kinship and politics, and, contrary to modern industrial cultures, religious, social, and economic institutions were but subsets of these two larger systems. Moreover, many of these ancient cultures placed great emphasis on systems of social relationships, such as the client-patron system of Rome, which are without close parallels in modern industrial societies. Even in instances where ancient social institutions seem to have parallels in modern cultures, such as Roman slavery and American slavery, closer inspection reveals fundamental differences between the ancient and the modern institutions.

An understanding of the significant cultural differences that underlie the ancient literary sources brings home the true meaning of Paul Veyne's observation at the beginning of this chapter: history is indeed a journey into otherness. The modern reader simply cannot interpret an ancient text in the light of his or her own cultural values and biases and have any realistic hope of fully understanding the meaning of the text. Rather, an ancient text must first be analyzed and interpreted in the light of the author's own values and culture and only afterward can a modern perspective be applied to the text.[3] Because of the personal biases and perspectives each reader brings to an ancient text, it takes a conscious and persistent effort to remember to seek the author's perspective before interpreting the material from one's own perspective. If the modern reader fails to acknowledge and deal with these historical and cultural differences, then the reader's understanding will be at best egocentric:

> Our judgments of value are characteristically dependent on attitudes peculiar to our own place and time. If we universalize these attitudes, as though they were Platonic realities, and assume that they have a validity for all time, we turn history into a mirror which is of significance to us only insofar as we may perceive in it what appear to be foreshadowings of ourselves arising from reconstructions of the evidence based on our own values. And when this happens, history, although it may seem to flatter us with the consoling message "Thou art the fairest of all," becomes merely an instrument for the cultivation of our own prejudices. We learn nothing from it that we could not learn from the world around us.[4]

At its worst, the reader's understanding will simply be wrong:

> Not to ask "What do they mean now?" is to refuse to deal with the fundamental intention of the texts, which were certainly written to inform, inspire, challenge, and convict. Not to ask "What did they mean then?" is to run the risk that the answer to the former question will be fantasy.[5]

In addition to these general concerns about understanding the historical and cultural context of the ancient texts, the reader needs to be aware of the specific cultural factors and historical problems applicable to Graeco-Roman written materials of the first four centuries C.E. These issues include the following:

Multiple Translations. Translating an ancient document always introduces the possibility of altering the meaning of the text. An added complication is that many ancient documents have survived only in a language other than the language of the

---

3. See the discussion of this issue by Norman F. Cantor and Richard I. Schneider in *How to Study History* (Wheeling, Ill.: Harlan Davidson, 1967), 41–44.

4. D. W. Robertson, Jr., *A Preface to Chaucer* (Princeton: Princeton University Press, 1962), 3.

5. University of the South, Sewanee School of Theology, Swanee, TN: *Course Catalogue* 1995–96.

original text. For example, there are many instances in which an original Latin text was translated into Greek, or vice versa, and only the second text has survived. This obviously creates problems where the exact wording of the text is critical to understanding its meaning.

Cultural Attitudes Concerning History's Purpose. In studying ancient texts, one finds that while ancient writers appreciated the entertainment value of a good story, relatively little value was placed on the mere preservation of "historical facts" for their own sake. Instead, most ancient writers believed that the primary purpose and goal of historical writing was to illustrate and preserve lessons useful for the moral and intellectual edification of the individual. Thus, neither Christian nor pagan writers were overly concerned with the niceties of "historical accuracy" in a modern sense, particularly when a clever or pointed quotation or moral lesson could be illustrated, or manufactured, from the materials at hand. The great freedom with which many ancient writers adapted their materials to achieve such goals contrasts sharply with the expectations of historical accuracy many modern laypersons presume for the texts.

Christian Forgeries. While preserving the texts of original historical documents was not a high priority among ancient authors, various writers did on occasion search out and quote the texts of important letters, statutes, treaties, and treatises and in such a manner preserved many valuable historical documents for the modern historian. This is particularly true of certain fourth-century C.E. Christian writers such as Lactantius and Eusebius, who collectively preserved many important documents on early Christian history. Unfortunately, however, many other Christians forged documents wholesale, usually with attribution to a figure of authority, when a text was needed for theological or political purposes. These Christian forgeries began at a very early period—the Apostle Paul wrote that letters were being forged in his name during his own lifetime (2 Thessalonians 2:1)—and only grew worse with the passing centuries. The historian Robin Lane Fox has written

> In the period c.400–600 "aggressive forgeries" added false letters to the collection of almost every early Christian letter writer. These fake texts of theology helped to enlist the great authorities of the past on this or that side of a contemporary schism or unorthodoxy. An expert in Church history [Robert M. Grant] has aptly concluded "Under such circumstances the preservation of any authentic texts seems almost miraculous. The needs of dogmatic theology were undisturbed by much historical sense. [By c.600], they had resulted in a distortion of the historical materials on which theology was supposedly built. The absence of any understanding of historical development allowed genuine and false documents to be so thoroughly mixed that they would not be disentangled for more than a millennium." A critical history of Christian

thought could not possibly begin to have been written until after 1500 because of forgeries by Christians themselves.[6]

In general, this book omits most materials generally acknowledged by modern historians to be forgeries, and where a serious dispute exists concerning the authenticity of any particular text, mention of the issue is made in the narrative or a footnote.[7]

Cultural Convention Concerning Attribution. Closely related to the problem of forgeries is the question of the attribution of a work. It was a not uncommon custom in both Classical and Hellenistic Greek society for a student to honor his or her teacher by attributing the student's own work to the teacher. Thus, when a student wrote that "X taught so and so," it is often difficult today to determine what "X" actually taught and what is independent work by the student being attributed to "X." This tradition carried over into the period of the Roman Empire. For this reason it can be difficult for a modern historian to distinguish a well-meaning attribution from an outright forgery. The historian James H. Charlesworth has described seven different types of "attribution" applicable to ancient texts: (i) writings not by an author, but probably containing some of his own thoughts; (ii) writings by someone who was influenced by another person to whom the work is attributed; (iii) writings influenced by the earlier works of another author to whom the work is assigned; (iv) writings attributed to an individual but actually deriving from a circle or school surrounding that individual; (v) Christian writings attributed by their authors to an Old Testament personality; (vi) once anonymous writings now correctly or incorrectly attributed to an individual; and (vii) writings that intentionally try to deceive the reader into thinking that the author is someone else.[8] These attribution issues obviously affect the relative weight and reliability of statements found in a text of uncertain authorship.

Literary Convention Concerning Speeches. Because ancient peoples had no mechanical means of recording the spoken word, it was difficult for them to create accurate records of speeches. The clearest expression of both the problem and the "solution" adopted by ancient writers was given by Thucydides (ca. 460–400 B.C.E.), one of the greatest of the ancient historians, in his *History of the Peloponnesian War*:

> I have found it difficult to remember the precise words used in the speeches which I listened to myself and my various informants have experienced the

---

6. Robin Lane Fox, *The Unauthorized Version: Truth and Fiction in the Bible* (New York: Alfred A. Knopf, 1991), 153–54.
7. See, for example, the discussion concerning the Rescript of Antoninus Pius in chapter 3, at page 66.
8. James H. Charlesworth, "Pseudo-Epigraphy," *Encyclopedia of Early Christianity*, Everett Ferguson (ed.) (New York: Garland Publishing, Inc., 1990), 765–67, at 766.

same difficulty; so my method has been, while keeping as closely as possible to the general sense of the words that were actually used, to make the speakers say what, in my opinion, was called for by each situation.[9]

Because of these difficulties, from at least the fourth century B.C.E. it became customary for speakers to issue, after the fact, written copies of important speeches, but it also became customary for the speaker to rewrite the speech as "he wished he had given it." Many ancient historians adopted more or less the same convention, reproducing speeches "as they should have been given," that is, with the content the historian considered appropriate for the occasion and often reworded to meet the rhetorical standards of the historian's day. Over time, this practice evolved into a distinct literary genre in which ancient writers would recreate famous speeches in their entirety as a display of the writer's own rhetorical skills, without any regard for "historical accuracy."[10] The general consensus of modern historians is that many speeches found in the ancient sources are the wholesale creation of the respective authors of the written works in which the speeches appear and that even in those instances where an ancient author attempted to reproduce accurately the actual words of the speaker there may be substantial differences between the original speech and the written report of the speech. Thus, the "facts" set forth in speeches must be evaluated and handled carefully by the modern historian.

The "Big Lie". Ancient authors were not always hesitant to tell a whopper of a story, if it served the author's literary, political, social, or theological purpose. Such a technique can be quite effective, as demonstrated by the career of Adolf Hitler, who wrote:

> [people] more readily fall victims to the big lie than the small lie, since they themselves often tell small lies in little matters, but would be ashamed to resort to large-scale falsehoods. It would never come into their heads to fabricate colossal untruths and they would not believe that others could have the impudence to distort the truth so infamously. ... The grossly impudent lie always leaves traces behind it, even after it has been nailed down. [11]

The "grossly impudent lie" can usually be detected by reference to the other pertinent evidence, and the historian's job is not to be misled or wrongly influenced by such statements in the sources.

---

9. Thucydides, *History of the Peloponnesian War* I.22, translated by Rex Warner (Baltimore: Viking Penguin, 1980), 47.

10. More or less the same rhetorical convention was accepted with respect to the descriptions of famous battles, which is one reason why so few reliable details are known about many significant ancient battles.

11. Adolf Hitler, *Mein Kampf* I.10, translated by James Murphy (London: Hurst and Blackett, Ltd., 1939).

Once the historian understands the evidence in its social and cultural context, the historian can proceed with the orderly application of logic and deductive reasoning to the evidence. A full discussion of such methods is beyond the scope of this chapter, but some of these principles of logic and reason have over the years been distilled into "rules of thumb," which will be useful to the modern reader in his or her analysis of the ancient texts:

1. William of Occam (ca. 1280–1349 C.E.) promulgated what is known today as "Occam's Razor": "*Entia non sunt multiplicanda praeter necessitatem*"— "Entities are not to be multiplied beyond necessity." In other words, a historian does not invent acts or events to resolve problems when there are explanations that do not require such inventions. As a corollary to this rule, if a problem admits of two or more possible answers, one should choose the simplest and least complicated answer as more likely to be correct. Although not infallible, Occam's Razor is a useful tool for avoiding the endless swamps of improbability and tortured reasoning so beloved by conspiracy theorists and the like.

2. Arguing from the silence of the sources is not good practice. This is particularly true of ancient history, where so much material has been lost over the centuries. However, there is a distinction between an absence of evidence and a meaningful silence in the extant evidence, as demonstrated by Sir Arthur Conan Doyle in *The Adventure of Silver Blaze*:[12]

Inspector Gregory: Is there any other point to which you would wish to draw my attention?

Sherlock Holmes   To the curious incident of the dog in the night-time.

Inspector Gregory: The dog did nothing in the night-time.

Sherlock Holmes: That was the curious incident.

The silence of the watch dog was a physical fact from which necessary and obvious deductions could be made; in this case, that the watch dog must have recognized the thief since the dog did not bark while the theft occurred. This is not the same as silence resulting from the absence of evidence.

3. An admission against interest is strong evidence for the truth of a statement. This is a generally accepted rule of evidence in law as well as in history. Most people write to advance a particular point of view. Thus, a statement that contradicts the author's point of view usually indicates that the author could not deny the truth of the statement, for otherwise the author would not have repeated it. However, that does not mean that the admission is necessarily true, just that the author thought it true.

---

12. Arthur Conan Doyle, *The Original Illustrated Sherlock Holmes* (Secaucus: Castle Books, 1981), 196–97.

4. A good historian is always aware that no matter how strong the evidence may appear on any point, there is never absolute certainty. Historians bring their personal biases and subjectivity to the interpretation of the available evidence, which is always incomplete and fragmentary. Historians do not study or reconstruct "reality" with anything even approximating the "objectivity" of a mathematician or a physicist.

5. Not all questions can be resolved from the extant evidence. The easiest way to get into trouble as a historian is to stretch an argument too far to reach a conclusion for which there is simply insufficient evidence.

6. Common sense and an understanding of human nature will take one a long way, if one has not already pre-determined the final outcome.

Good historical methodology requires considering all the evidence without a predetermined outcome in mind. To avoid shaping the interpretation of the evidence to reach a predetermined result, the historian must be aware of the personal biases and presumptions of truth that he or she brings to bear on the interpretation of the evidence. No historian can totally eliminate his or her own subjective beliefs and attitudes from the analysis of the evidence. The best the historian can do is to be aware of the problem and attempt to control it. The methodological advantage of analyzing the extant evidence by applying logic and deductive reasoning is that other individuals may use the same methods to evaluate both the evidence and the historian's interpretation of the evidence. As a result, meaningful distinctions and value judgments can be made: "historian A's interpretation is better reasoned and more logical than historian B's interpretation." On this basis, the advancement of historical knowledge is possible.

E. P. Sanders has addressed this problem of personal bias and presumptions of truth in his own research into the historical Jesus:

. . . some may claim special privilege for the gospel material on the ground that it is revealed. The believer *knows* that Jesus was raised, that his miracles were truly supernatural, and so on. This special revelation means that the ordinary canons of critical investigation cannot be applied. Perhaps the erroneous nature of this insidious form of obscurantism (*we* know secrets which you cannot know) may best be shown by pointing to its logical consequence. The person who argues this way when it comes to knowledge about Jesus may apply the same argument to any number of issues. The Bible says that the world was created in six days. Does this then give the believer access to cosmological information which should supplant the evidence of astronomy, geology, archaeology, chemistry and physics? A few will argue that it does. This chapter is clearly not for them: they are at a level of fundamentalism which is beyond reasonable argumentation. Many others, however, will grant to science free rein in its own domain, but will want a protective wall built around their portrait of Jesus, which they will see as based on revelation. A sufficiently detailed exploration would show that what is revealed to one person is not to another: that the appeal to "revelation" about Jesus as a historical figure usually masks entirely human biases, individual preferences and wishful thinking. The academic historian may have biases and presuppositions, but they can be exposed by people using the same critical tools, and thus progress can be made towards sound historical knowledge. The appeal to revelation as the ground of historical information essentially denies the possibility of learning, and that is an extremely unfortunate denial. Those who are tempted to look for a protective wall are urged not to do so, but to be genuinely open to investigation which leads to historical knowledge and insight. The historian, in any case, whatever her or his theological beliefs, has no choice but to soldier on. Academic study has its own rules, and one of them is that nothing is exempt from scrutiny and verification.[13]

The same point was made by Clement of Alexandria (Titus Flavius Clemens, ca. 150–215 C.E.), head of the Christian catechetical school in Alexandria, Egypt, in approximately 200 C.E.:

> If our faith. . . is such that it is destroyed by force of argument, then let it be destroyed; for it will have been proved that we do not possess the truth.[14]

The faith of the historian lies in following the evidence wherever it will lead, rather than requiring the evidence to go where the historian desires.

---

13. E. P. Sanders and Margaret Davies, *Studying The Synoptic Gospels* (Harrisburg: Trinity Press International, 1989), 303–304. Emphasis is that of Sanders and Davies.
14. Clement of Alexandria, *Miscellanies* 6.10.

2 | THE EAGLE AND THE CROSS: THE FIRST CENTURY C.E.

The exact year of the birth of Jesus of Nazareth is not known, but most historians believe that His birth occurred some time between 10 B.C.E. and 4 B.C.E.[1] Such a date falls roughly in the middle of the reign of Gaius Octavius, the founder and first emperor of the Roman Empire. Octavius, who is better known today by the name of Augustus or Caesar Augustus, was the nephew and adopted son of Julius Caesar. Octavius had come to power by winning the more or less continuous civil war for control of the Roman state that had begun in 49 B.C.E. with the conflict between Julius Caesar and Pompey the Great and had ended in 31 B.C.E. with Octavius's decisive defeat of Marcus Antony and Cleopatra at the battle of Actium.

One of Octavius's strengths was his political astuteness and it was his desire to avoid the fate of Julius Caesar, who had been assassinated by senators who feared that Caesar desired to be king over the Romans, that led Octavius to seek a political basis other than mere military might to govern Rome in the years after Actium. Using the leverage provided by his unchallenged military strength, Octavius maneuvered over a number of years to consolidate control of the Roman state in his person while avoiding the appearance of a dictatorship. A key step in this reordering of the Roman state took place in 27 B.C.E., when in a carefully managed piece of political theater Octavius surrendered his powers to the Roman Senate only to have the senate immediately bestow many of the same powers on him again as a "voluntary" gesture of gratitude for his service to the Roman people. In this way Octavius could plausibly claim to have restored the Roman Republic and rule by the senate, but in fact the many offices and powers the senate granted to Octavius, while individually consistent with prior practice during the Roman Republic, were collectively an unprecedented concentration of governmental power and authority in one man. Many Romans of course recognized the reality of Octavius's position, but there was a widespread sense of true gratitude toward Octavius for his moderation in victory after the civil wars, and so it was that in 27 B.C.E. the senate also bestowed on Octavius the title of "Augustus," or "revered one," that was used by all later Roman emperors.[2]

---

1. See Appendix E for a discussion of the sources pertinent to the determination of Jesus' year of birth.

2. Octavius himself, in keeping with his program of maintaining the facade of Republican government, preferred the title of "Princeps," which implied only that he was first among equals.

Rome's transition from an oligarchic republic to an empire governed by a single individual was greatly aided by the fact that Octavius lived for forty-four years after his victory at Actium, a reign so long that by his death most peoples of the Roman Empire had no personal experience with any form of Roman government other than rule by Octavius with the assistance of members of his immediate family. Moreover, during his later years Octavius spent so much effort attempting to orchestrate the succession to the throne by one relative or another, most of whom inconveniently died as Octavius lived on, that when Octavius finally died in 14 C.E. and his stepson Tiberius succeeded to the emperor's position, hereditary succession must have been seen by most of the Empire's population as the normal and expected mode of transferring imperial power. The concept of hereditary succession had strong support within the Roman army and so the practice continued after Tiberius, as the subsequent emperors Caligula (37–41 C.E.), Claudius (41–54 C.E.), and Nero (54–68 C.E.) were all related to Octavius in one way or another.

The family dynasty founded by Octavius ended with the death of Nero in 68 C.E. In 69 C.E., the "year of the four emperors," the Roman general Vespasian won a brief civil war among various Roman army commanders for succession to the vacant throne. Vespasian founded what is now known as the Flavian dynasty, as he was succeeded as emperor by his sons Titus (79–81 C.E.) and Domitian (81–96 C.E.). Vespasian proved to be a capable ruler and the Roman Empire prospered during his reign. His son Titus was also very popular, although his reign was too short to indicate clearly whether he would have been a successful ruler. Domitian, however, governed autocratically and displayed increasingly megalomaniac tendencies over the years, which led to his murder in 96 C.E.

In the confusion that followed Domitian's assassination, the Roman Senate attempted to preempt the Roman military commanders in the selection of the next emperor by moving quickly to name one of its own as emperor, a well-respected but elderly senator named Nerva. The Roman generals were apparently reluctant to risk the outbreak of civil war over succession as had followed Nero's death as they did not take action to block Nerva's assumption of the throne (96–98 C.E.). The Praetorian Guard of Rome, however, soon became unruly and threatening towards the new emperor and neither Nerva nor the senate had sufficient strength to assert firm control over the Praetorians. In 97 C.E., Nerva moved to secure his position by adopting the prominent general Trajan as his son and successor. Trajan (98–117 C.E.) quickly brought the Praetorian Guard under control and when Nerva died the next year Trajan succeeded to the emperor's position without contest.

The civil war after Nero's death and Nerva's adoption of a military commander as successor are evidence that, as during the reign of Octavius, the Roman emperor's power was ultimately based upon his control of the Roman legions. While there were political conflicts between the emperors and senators throughout the first century C.E., by the end of the century the senate and the senatorial order no longer constituted a serious challenge to the concepts of one man rule and hereditary succession to the throne. Rather, by that time Rome's senatorial order was more concerned that the emperor respect the dignity and privileges of the senate and use its members to assist in the governing the Empire.

The first century of rule by emperors was generally a period of military success and geographical expansion for Rome. While Rome did not attempt to re-occupy the province of Germania, that portion of modern Germany lying between the Elbe and the Rhine Rivers, lost during the later years of Octavius's reign, the emperors after Octavius expanded Roman rule into the English Isles, the Balkans, the Arabian Peninsula, and northwest Africa, and strengthened Rome's frontier defenses along the Rhine and Danube River to the north and the Persian frontier to the east. Aside from the brief civil war after Nero's death, the most significant military conflict within the territories of the Roman Empire after Augustus's death was the massive Jewish rebellion in Palestine known as the "First Jewish War," which Rome brutally suppressed after four years of fighting (66–70 C.E.). The outcome of the First Jewish War had significant implications for the growth of the Christian faith.

THE EARLIEST NON-GOSPEL SOURCES FOR CHRISTIAN HISTORY

While Jesus was born during the reign of Augustus, Jesus' ministry was conducted entirely during the reign of Augustus's successor Tiberius (14–37 C.E.). As with the year of Jesus' birth, the exact years of Jesus' ministry during Tiberius's reign are uncertain, but the evidence indicates that Jesus' ministry consisted of a two- or three-year period that ended with his crucifixion sometime between 30 and 33 C.E.[3] Under the leadership of the twelve apostles, James, Paul, and other leaders, the new Christian faith continued to grow after Jesus' death, but relatively little is known about the details of Christianity's growth during the reigns of Caligula (37–41 C.E.), Claudius (41–54 C.E.), and Nero (54–68 C.E.) because the extant sources for the first thirty or so years of Christianity are limited. Among the most important of these sources are the letters of Paul the Apostle and the Acts of the Apostles, which pertain to or describe events between Jesus' crucifixion in 30/33 C.E. and 63 or 64 C.E. The history of Christianity during the subsequent Flavian dynasty (69–96 C.E.) is even more obscure because there are even fewer relevant sources for that period.

What evidence does exist has been interpreted to indicate that, notwithstanding the efforts of the first few generations of Christian leaders, the absolute number of Christians in the Roman Empire during the first century C.E. was very small. Estimates for the number of Christians by 100 C.E. range from as low as 7,500[4] to upwards of 50,000[5] out of the approximately sixty million

---

3. See Appendix E for a discussion of the sources pertinent to the determination of the dates of Jesus' ministry and death.

4. Rodney Stark, *The Rise of Christianity* (Princeton: Princeton University Press, 1996), 6–7.

5. Robert L. Wilken, *The Christians as the Romans Saw Them* (New Haven: Yale University Press, 1984), 31.

inhabitants of the Roman Empire. The small number of Christians is a likely factor behind the paucity of contemporary historical sources on Christianity during the first century, as it appears that there were simply too few Christians to attract the attention of the social and political elite of the Roman Empire who wrote the contemporary histories and literary works. The only apparent references by first-century Jews to either Jesus or Christians are two short passages in Josephus (Selections 2.2 and 2.13) and the prayer benediction instituted by Gamaliel II (Selection 2.19). The earliest Roman references to Christianity date to approximately 110–120 C.E., in works written by Tacitus (Selection 2.15), Suetonius (Selection 2.16 and possibly Selection 2.6), and Pliny the Younger (Selection 3.3.). Aside from these Jewish and Roman sources, there appears to be only one other contemporary reference to first-century Christianity by a non-Christian, a letter written by a Syrian sometime between 70 and 100 C.E. (Selection 2.21).

The earliest surviving Roman authors to mention Christianity—Tacitus, Pliny the Younger, and Suetonius—each seems to have performed imperial service in provinces where Christians had conducted extensive missionary work during the first century C.E. Tacitus served as proconsul of Asia, a Roman province located in the area of modern southwestern Turkey, during the years 112–113 C.E., and Asia, with its principal city of Ephesus, was the site of extensive missionary work by Paul and other Christians during the first century C.E. While it is uncertain whether Tacitus wrote his famous account of Nero's persecution of Christians before or after this proconsulship, Tacitus's extremely critical attitude toward Christians (Selection 2.15) would suggest that he had some personal familiarity with Christians and their beliefs and it is tempting to speculate that this familiarity was the result of contacts in Asia during his proconsulship. Pliny the Younger, a close friend of Tacitus, served as the special imperial legate of the Emperor Trajan to the neighboring provinces of Bithynia and Pontus, located in modern northwestern Turkey, during the period of approximately 110–112 C.E., and while Bithynia and Pontus were not areas visited by the Apostle Paul, we know from Pliny's famous exchange of letters with the Emperor Trajan (Selection 3.3) that during his mission Pliny personally interrogated members of an active Christian community. There is reason to believe that Suetonius was a member of Pliny's personal staff during this mission,[6] and if so then Suetonius presumably also had contact with these same Christians. As with Tacitus, it may be that any such contacts influenced Suetonius to mention Christians in his later historical writings.

While the non-Christian sources on Christianity during the first seventy or eighty years of its existence are quite brief, these materials do indicate that even when the Jewish or Roman authors were aware of the early Christians, they did

---

6. See, e.g., Pliny, *Letters* 3.8 and 10.94; Michael Grant, *The Ancient Historians* (New York: Barnes & Noble, 1970), 330; and *The Oxford Classical Dictionary* (Oxford: Oxford University Press, 1996), "Suetonius," 1451–52.

not consider Christianity sufficiently important to devote much time to describing it. Typical in this regard is the following passage by Tacitus.

2.1 Tacitus, *The Histories* 5.9 (ca. 106 C.E., concerning events ca. 63 B.C.E.–37 C.E.)

The first Roman to subdue the Jews and set foot in their temple by right of conquest was Gnaeus Pompey; thereafter it was a matter of common knowledge that there were no representations of the gods within, but that the place was empty and the secret shrine contained nothing. The walls of Jerusalem were razed, but the temple remained standing. Later, in the time of our civil wars, when these eastern provinces had fallen into the hands of Mark Antony, the Parthian prince, Pacorus, seized Judaea, but he was slain by Publius Ventidius, and the Parthians were thrown back across the Euphrates: the Jews were subdued by Gaius Sosius. Antony gave the throne to Herod, and Augustus, after his victory, increased his power. After Herod's death, a certain Simon assumed the name of king without waiting for Caesar's decision. He, however, was put to death by Quintilius Varus, the governor of Syria; the Jews were repressed; and the kingdom was divided into three parts and given to Herod's sons. Under Tiberius all was quiet.

Tacitus was quite aware that Christianity had originated in Palestine during the reign of Tiberius, but here, in his great history of Rome's emperors and legions, Tacitus did not treat Christianity as being worthy of mention in his account of the difficulties Rome encountered in maintaining control over Palestine during the period of approximately 63 B.C.E. to 37 C.E.

The same attitude is found in the earliest Jewish historical work to mention either Jesus or the Christians, the *Jewish Antiquities* of Josephus, which was published in 93 or 94 C.E. Even though Josephus wrote from the perspective of some sixty years after Jesus' death, Josephus devoted more space in his history of the Jewish people to John the Baptist than to Jesus and dealt with Jesus and his followers in only the two short passages reproduced below at Selections 2.2 and 2.13. From the modern historian's perspective, even more unfortunate than the brevity of Josephus's references is that the text of the most important passage was altered in antiquity and has come down to us in two versions.

2.2 Josephus, *Jewish Antiquities* 18.63–64 (ca. 93 or 94 C.E.)
Western Vulgate Version

About this time [following Pontius Pilate's seizure of the temple treasury funds to build a new aquaduct for Jerusalem] there lived Jesus, a wise man, if indeed one ought to call him a man. For he was one who wrought surprising feats and was a teacher of such people as accept the truth gladly. He won over many Jews and many of the Greeks. He was the Messiah. When Pilate, upon hearing him accused by men of the highest standing among us, had condemned him to be crucified, those who had in the first place come to love him did not cease. On the third day he appeared to them restored to life, for the prophets of God had prophesied these and countless other marvelous things about him. And the tribe of the Christians, so called after him, has still to this day not disappeared.

Arabic Version as preserved in a tenth-century manuscript of *Universal History* 8.3, by the sixth century Syrian churchman Agapius (Mahboub of Menbidj):

At this time there was a wise man who was called Jesus. And his conduct was good, and [he] was known to be virtuous. And many people from among the Jews and the other nations became his disciples. Pilate condemned him to be crucified and to die. And those who had become his disciples did not abandon his discipleship. They reported that he had appeared to them three days after his crucifixion and that he was alive; accordingly, he was perhaps the Messiah concerning whom the prophets have recounted wonders.

Even prior to the publication of the Arabic manuscript of *Universal History* by Shlomo Pines in 1971,[7] a wide variety of circumstantial evidence had led most modern historians to doubt the authenticity of the Western Vulgate text of Josephus. The earliest example of the Western Vulgate text is found in Eusebius of Caesarea's *Ecclesiastical History* 1.11.7–8 (ca. 311–323 C.E.). The historian Louis H. Feldman has noted that at least eleven church fathers living before or contemporaneously with Eusebius cited Josephus in their works but did not cite this particular passage and that five of the six church fathers, including Augustine, living in the century after Eusebius who cited Josephus also never referred to this passage.[8] It is difficult to believe that all of these early church fathers would have passed over without comment a passage by the famous Jewish historian Josephus describing Jesus as the Messiah if the passage were in fact in their texts of Josephus. Moreover, Jerome (345–420 C.E.), the sole early church father after Eusebius to refer to this passage,[9] quoted the text of Josephus as reading that "Jesus was believed [*credebatur*] to be the Messiah." Other strong evidence of tampering with the original text of Josephus is found in two works of the great Christian scholar Origen (185–254 C.E.). In *Against Celsus* 1.47, Origen wrote, "For Josephus in the eighteenth book of the *Jewish Antiquities* bears witness that John was a baptist and promised purification to people who were baptized. The same author, although he did not believe in

---

7. Shlomo Pines, *An Arabic Version of the Testimonium Flavianum and Its Implications* (Jerusalem: Israel Academy of Sciences and Humanities, 1971), 70.

8. Louis H. Feldman and Gohei Hata (eds.), *Josephus, Judaism and Christianity* (Detroit: Wayne State University Press, 1987), 57.

9. Jerome, *De viris illustribus* 13.14.

Jesus as Christ, sought for the cause of the fall of Jerusalem and the destruction of the Temple." Similarly, Origen, while discussing Josephus's account of the trial of James by the Sanhedrin, wrote, "and wonderful it is that while he [Josephus] did not receive Jesus for Christ, he did nevertheless bear witness that James was so righteous a man." [*Commentary on Matthew* 10.17] These two passages obviously indicate that the text of Josephus available to Origen, who wrote some seventy years before Eusebius, did not contain any reference to Jesus being the Messiah. In view of this literary evidence and the alternative text found in the Arabic manuscript, the majority consensus among historians today is that while Josephus did refer to Jesus at this point in *Jewish Antiquities*, the surviving passage is not the original form of Josephus's text.

Although historians agree that the original text of Josephus has been altered, they have engaged in lengthy and often bitter arguments about the proper reconstruction of the wording of the original text.[10] However, one would probably not stray too far from the sense of the original text by simply dropping what appear to be the obvious Christian interpolations in the Vulgate text and substituting the second and sixth sentences of the Arabic manuscript version for the second and sixth sentences of the Vulgate version, leaving the following:

> About this time there lived Jesus, a wise man. And his conduct was good, and [he] was known to be virtuous. He won over many Jews and many of the Greeks. When Pilate, upon hearing him accused by men of the highest standing among us, had condemned him to be crucified, those who had in the first place come to love [him] did not cease. They reported that he had appeared to them three days after his crucifixion and that he was alive. And the tribe of the Christians, so called after him, has still up to now not disappeared.

The Western Vulgate version of Josephus's text was regarded by medieval Christians as very important testimony by a first-century Jew as to the messiahship of Jesus, and it was probably because of the weight given this passage that an unknown Christian copied the passage from *Jewish Antiquities* into the text of Josephus's *The Jewish War* and there greatly expanded the text.

2.3 Josephus, *The Jewish War* 2.9.3 (Slavonic Manuscript Tradition) (Interpolations to the text, according to Eisler's edition, are shown in brackets.)

> At that time there appeared a man, if it is permissible to call him a man. His nature [and form] were human, but his appearance [was something] more than [that] of a man; [notwithstanding his works were divine]. He worked miracles wonderful and mighty. [Therefore

---

10. Many of the suggested reconstructions for the text are set forth and discussed by Gerd Theissen and Annette Merz, *The Historical Jesus* (Minneapolis: Fortress Press, 1998), 65–74.

it is impossible for me to call him a man]; but again, if I look at the nature which he shared with all, I will not call him an angel. And everything whatsoever he wrought through an invisible power, he wrought by word and command. Some said of him, "Our first law-giver is risen from the dead and hath performed many healings and arts," while others thought that he was sent from God. Howbeit in many things he disobeyed the Law and kept not the Sabbath accord-ing to [our] fathers' customs. Yet, on the other hand, he did nothing shameful; nor [did he do anything] with aid of hands, but by word alone did he provide everything. And many of the multitude fol-lowed after him and hearkened to his teaching; and many souls were in commotion, thinking that thereby the Jewish tribes might free themselves from Roman hands. Now it was his custom in general to sojourn over against the city upon the Mount of Olives; and there, too, he bestowed his healings upon the people.

And there assembled unto him of ministers one hundred and fifty, and a multitude of the people. Now when they saw his power, that he accomplished whatsoever he would by [a] word, and when they had made known to him their will, that he should enter into the city and cut down the Roman troops and Pilate, and rule over us, he disdained us not.

And when thereafter knowledge of it came to the Jewish leaders, they assembled together with the high-priest and spake: "We are powerless and [too] weak to withstand the Romans. Seeing, more-over, that the bow is bent, we will go and communicate to Pilate what we have heard, and shall be clear of trouble, lest he hear [it] from others, and we be robbed of our substance and ourselves slaughtered and our children scattered." And they went and communicated [it] to Pilate. And he sent and had many of the multitude slain. And he had the Wonder-worker brought up, and after instituting an inquiry concerning him, he pronounced judgment: "He is [a benefactor, not] a malefactor, [nor] a rebel, [nor] covetous of kingship." [And he let him go; for he had healed his dying wife.]

[And he went to his wonted place and did his wonted works. And when more people again assembled round him, he glorified himself through his actions more than all. The teachers of the Law were over-come with envy, and gave thirty talents to Pilate, in order that he should put him to death. And he took (it) and gave them liberty to execute their will themselves.] And they laid hands on him and cru-cified him contrary to the law of [their] fathers."*

*The Rumanian text of Josephus reads: "according to the law of the emperors."

Josephus's *Jewish Antiquities* appears to be the only surviving first-century C.E. Jewish reference to the crucifixion of Jesus, as there is a general consensus among historians that the scattered references to Jesus in early rabbinic writings either date from no earlier than the second century C.E. or were later insertions into first-century C.E. texts.[11] Of these various rabbinical writings, one of the more significant texts dates to the early second century C.E.

2.4 A Rabbinic Account Of The Death Of Jesus (Babylonian Talmud Sanhedrin 43a, second century C.E.)

On the Sabbath of the Passover festival Yeshu [Jesus] the Nazarene was hanged. For forty days before execution took place, a herald went forth and cried: "Here is Yeshu the Nazarene, who is going forth to be stoned because he practiced sorcery and enticed Israel to apostasy. Anyone who can say anything in his favor, let him come forth and plead on his behalf." But since nothing was brought forth in his favor, he was hanged on the eve of Passover. . . .

This text presents Jesus as a blasphemer who "enticed Israel to apostasy" and was duly punished by being stoned to death and afterwards hung on a cross. (Stoning, the traditional Jewish punishment for blasphemy, was the fate of Jesus' brother James. See Selection 2.13, below.) The reference to a forty-day opportunity for anyone to come forth to defend Jesus has no certain explanation, but it may have been intended to counter Christian accusations that Jesus was unfairly tried and executed in too quick a proceeding. While the text as a whole appears to be a second-century Jewish response to Christian accounts of Jesus' trial and crucifixion rather than an independent account of those events, curiously, this Jewish account makes no mention of any Roman involvement in Jesus' execution and the time of the execution ("the eve of Passover") corresponds to the date given in the Gospel of John, rather than the date indicated by the Synoptic Gospels.[12]

During the years after Jesus' crucifixion, the members of the new "Jesus Movement," or "The Way" as it was known to its adherents,[13] began to spread through Judaea and the neighboring provinces of the Roman Empire. One of the earliest known direct contacts between Christian missionaries and Roman imperial officials occurred about 46–48 C.E., when the Apostle Paul had an audience with Sergius Paulus, the Roman governor of Cyprus.

2.5 The Acts Of The Apostles 13:4–12 (written ca. 80–85 C.E.)

So, being sent out by the Holy Spirit, they went down to Seleucia; and from there they sailed to Cyprus. When they arrived at Salamis, they proclaimed the word of God in the synagogues of the Jews. And they had John to assist them. When they had gone through the whole island as far as Paphos, they came upon a certain magician, a Jewish

---

11. See the discussion of these rabbinic passages in Gerd Theissen and Annette Merz, *The Historical Jesus* (Minneapolis: Fortress Press, 1998), 74–76 and John P. Meier, *A Marginal Jew* Vol. 1 (New York: Doubleday, 1991), 93–98.

12. See the discussion of this point in Appendix E, pages 303–5.

13. See, e.g., Acts 24:22.

false prophet, named Bar-Jesus. He was with the proconsul, Sergius Paulus, a man of intelligence, who summoned Barnabas and Saul and sought to hear the word of God. But Elymas the magician (for that is the meaning of his name) withstood them, seeking to turn away the proconsul from the faith. But Saul, who is also called Paul, filled with the Holy Spirit, looked intently at him and said, "You son of the devil, you enemy of all righteousness, full of all deceit and villainy, will you not stop making crooked the straight paths of the Lord? And now, behold, the hand of the Lord is upon you, and you shall be blind and unable to see the sun for a time." Immediately mist and darkness fell upon him and he went about seeking people to lead him by the hand. Then the proconsul believed, when he saw what had occurred, for he was astonished at the teaching of the Lord.

Acts depicts the proconsul Sergius Paulus as having been convinced of the truth of Christianity by the demonstrated power of the Christian God and not by the teachings of Jesus. This emphasis on the power of the Christian God would be a key part of the Christian message to pagans and Jews during the first four centuries C.E.:

We are sometimes told that the unique attractiveness of the central figure of Christianity as presented in the Synoptic Gospels was a primary factor in the success of Christianity. I believe this idea to be a product of nineteenth-century idealism and humanitarianism. In early Christian literature those aspects of the Gospel picture which are now most prominent in homiletic writing are not stressed, and all the emphasis is on the superhuman qualities of Jesus, as foreshadowed by prophecy and shown by miracle and Resurrection and teaching, and not on his winning humanity. He is a savior rather than a pattern, and the Christian way of life is something made possible by Christ the Lord through the community rather than something arising from imitation of Jesus. The central idea is that of divinity brought into humanity to complete the plan of salvation, not that of perfect humanity manifested as an inspiration; it is *Deus de deo* rather than *Ecce homo*. The personal attractiveness of Jesus had done much to gather the first disciples, though even then the impression of power was probably more important than the impression of love: thereafter the only human qualities which proved effective were those of individual Christian teachers and disciples.[14]

Soon after Paul's meeting with Sergius Paulus there was another incident that may have involved Roman officials taking administrative action against members of an early Christian community.

---

14. A. D. Nock, *Conversion: The Old and The New in Religion from Alexander the Great to Augustine of Hippo* (London: Oxford University Press, 1933, 1961), 210.

2.6 Suetonius, *Life of Claudius* 25.4 (ca. 122 C.E.)
> Since the Jews constantly made disturbances at the instigation of Chrestus, he [the emperor Claudius] expelled them from Rome.

Claudius's expulsion of the Jews from Rome is generally dated to 49 C.E.[15] The issue raised by this passage is whether "Chrestus" is to be understood as referring to Christ and thus by implication indicating that at this early date there was a sufficiently active Christian community in Rome to create some conflict or turmoil with the local Jewish community, which came to the attention of the Roman authorities. In support of this interpretation is that fact that the late second-century C.E. Christian writer Tertullian wrote that the Romans sometimes mispronounced "Christianus" as "Chrestianus," a word derived from the Greek "chrestos," meaning "good."[16] However, "Chrestus" was a relatively common name in antiquity.[17] Moreover, Suetonius clearly named "Christians" as a distinct social/religious group in his *Life of Nero* (Selection 2.16, below) and thus it is not clear why he would use the term "Chrestus" here, if he meant either Christ or a Christian community. If this text does refer to an actual incident between the Christians and Jews of Rome, then Suetonius's source material was presumably vague or confused as to both the relationship between Christians and Jews at this early date and the time of the death of Jesus (who was crucified at least five years before the reign of Claudius) since Suetonius did not make the connection between Chrestus and the Christians.

Claudius's expulsion of the Jews from the city of Rome is mentioned in The Acts of the Apostles and thus it provides an important chronological reference for Paul's career.

2.7 The Acts Of The Apostles 18:1–2 (ca. 80–85 C.E.)
> After this he [Paul] left Athens and went to Corinth. And he found a Jew named Aquila, a native of Pontus, lately come from Italy with his wife Priscilla, because Claudius had commanded all the Jews to leave Rome.

Sometime after meeting Aquila and Priscilla in Corinth, Paul was brought up on charges before the Roman governor of Greece ("Achaea") by the local Jewish leaders.

2.8 The Acts Of The Apostles 18:12–16 (ca. 80–85 C.E.)
> But when Gallio was proconsul of Achaea, the Jews made a united attack upon Paul and brought him before the tribunal, saying, "This man is persuading men to worship God contrary to the law." But when Paul was about to open his mouth, Gallio said to the Jews, "If it were a matter of wrongdoing or vicious crime, I should have reason

15. The fifth-century C.E. Christian Orosius wrote that Claudius expelled the Jews in the ninth year of his reign, which ran from January 24, 49 C.E. to January 23, 50 C.E. *Seven Books of History Against the Pagans*, 7.6.
16. Tertullian, *Apology* 3.5, written ca. 197–98 C.E.
17. See the discussion of this point in Stephen Benko, *Pagan Rome and the Early Christians* (Bloomington: Indiana University Press, 1986), 18–19 and note 44.

to bear with you, O Jews; but since it is a matter of questions about words and names and your own law, see to it yourselves; I refuse to be a judge of these things." And he drove them from the tribunal.

As a result of the discovery of the following inscription at the Temple of Apollo in Delphi, Greece, we can roughly compute the years during which Lucius Annaeanus Junius Gallio, brother of the famous Roman philosopher Seneca, was proconsul in Achaea.

2.9 The Gallio Inscription At Delphi *Sylloge Inscriptionum Graecarum* 801D (third ed.)

> Tiberius [Claudius] Caesar Augustus Germanicus [Pontifex Maximus, in his tribunician] power [year 12, acclaimed Emperor for] the 26th time, father of the country, [consul for the 5th time, censor, sends greeting to the city of Delphi] I have for long been zealous for the city of Delphi [and favorable to it from the] beginning, and I have always observed the cult of the [Phythian] Apollo, [but with regard to] the present stories, and those quarrels of the citizens of which [a report has been made by Lucius] Junius Gallio my friend, and [pro]consul [of Achaea]. . .

From other inscriptions, we know that Claudius was first acclaimed emperor (*imperator*) on January 25, 41 C.E., that he was acclaimed for the 22nd, 23rd, and 24th times in his eleventh year of rule, and that his 27th acclamation occurred no later than August 1, 52 C.E., his twelfth year of rule.[18] While the dates of the 25th and 26th acclamations are not known, they could not have occurred before late 51 C.E. and must have been prior to August 1, 52 C.E., when Claudius was acclaimed for the 27th time. We also know that Claudius held the tribunician power for the 12th time from January 25, 52 C.E. through January 24, 53 C.E.[19] The Delphi inscription must therefore refer to an event sometime between January 25 and August 1 of 52 C.E.

During Claudius's reign, a proconsul such as Gallio normally left the city of Rome in mid-April to assume his post by the late spring or early summer of the year, usually for a term of one year but occasionally for two years.[20] Because the Delphi inscription refers to an event that could have occurred as late as June or July of 52 C.E., it is not certain whether Gallio was then serving a year of office that ran from the late spring or early summer of 51 C.E. through late spring or

---

18. See C.K. Barrett (ed.), *The New Testament Background* (New York: Harper San Francisco, 1987), 52 and note l.2, and Jack Finegan, *Handbook of Biblical Chronology* (Peabody, Mass.: Hendrickson, 1998), 392–94. The dedicatory inscription on the Claudian Aqueduct in Rome gives a date of August 1, 52 C.E. and states that Claudius was then imperator for the 27th time and holder of the tribunician power for the 12th time.

19. See Jack Finegan, *Handbook of Biblical Chronology* (Peabody: Hendrickson Publishers, 1998), 90–91, 392.

20. The third century C.E. Roman historian Cassius Dio wrote that Claudius required governors to leave for their provinces before the middle of April and that his governors normally only served for one year. *Roman History* 60.11.6, 17.3, 25.6.

early summer of 52 C.E., or from the late spring or early summer of 52 C.E. through late spring or early summer of 53 C.E. Moreover, we do not know whether Gallio served one or two years as proconsul of Achaea or whether Paul's trial occurred early or late in Gallio's proconsulship. Thus, the possible range of dates for Gallio's proconsulship, and hence for Paul's trial, runs from the late spring of 50 C.E. at the earliest (on the assumption that the Delphi inscription dates to early 52 C.E., during the second year of a two-year proconsulship) to the early summer of 54 C.E. at the latest (on the assumption that the Delphi inscription dates to the late spring or early summer of 52 C.E., during the first year of a two-year proconsulship for Gallio).[21]

The median of this range is 52 C.E., but a slightly earlier date of late 50 or 51 C.E. for Paul's trial is indicated by the Acts account of the circumstances surrounding the trial. Acts 18:2 states that when Paul arrived in Corinth he met Aquila and Priscilla, who had "recently" come to Corinth because of Claudius's expulsion of the Jews from Rome in 49 C.E.[22] Acts 18:11 states that Paul lived in Corinth for eighteen months. Acts 18:18 states that Paul remained in Corinth "many days" after the Gallio trial before departing the city, presumably at the end of the eighteen months mentioned in Acts 18:11. These texts help establish a range of possible dates for Paul's stay in Corinth when related to the 49 C.E. date for Claudius's expulsion of the Jews. If Claudius's edict were issued in January of 49 C.E. and Paul came to Corinth and met Aquila and Priscilla, within six or so months of the edict, then an eighteen-month stay in Corinth would indicate that Paul's trial must have occurred sometime after late spring of 50 C.E. and "many days" before January of 51 C.E., since Gallio assumed office no earlier than the spring of 50 C.E. under any dating of the Delphi inscription. If Claudius's edict were issued in December of 49 C.E., then under the same assumptions Paul arrived in Corinth by the summer of 50 C.E. and his trial must have occurred "many days" prior to January of 52 C.E. Thus, 50 or 51 C.E. seem the most likely dates for Paul's trial.

The Acts account of Paul's appearance before Gallio indicates that the Roman proconsul did not understand Christianity to be anything other than a sect of Judaism.[23] While many modern Christians seem to believe that Christians and Jews were sharply separate and distinct groups from the earliest days of the Christian movement, the consensus of modern historians is that during the first century C.E. most Christians perceived themselves as more or

---

21. While this analysis was independently developed by the author, it closely parallels the arguments of F. J. F. Jackson and Kirsopp Lake in *The Beginnings of Christianity* (Grand Rapids: Baker Book House, 1966), V.459–64.

22. The fifth century C.E. Christian Orosius wrote that Claudius expelled the Jews in the ninth year of his reign, which is known to have run from January 24, 49 C.E. to January 23, 50 C.E. *Seven Books of History Against the Pagans*, 7.6.

23. The reader may refer to Acts 21:27–40, 23:6–10, and 23:12–35 for similar New Testament accounts describing the refusal of Roman officials to intervene in a "Jewish" dispute and/or Roman intervention to protect Paul from Jewish mobs.

less a part of Judaism. Indeed, it is easy to believe that most first-century Jewish converts to Christianity saw themselves simply as Jews who believed that the Messiah prophesied by the Jewish Scripture had come, in contrast to those Jews who believed that the Messiah was still to come. The divergence of the two faiths widened with the growing importance of the gentile-oriented churches founded by the Apostle Paul and other missionaries. The tension between Christians and Jews in Palestine itself during the first century C.E. apparently increased significantly after the First Jewish War (66–70 C.E.), when the system of worship based on the Second Temple was destroyed and the newly prominent rabbis sought to maintain a stricter religious discipline among the surviving faithful. However, the more or less final break between Judaism and Christianity does not appear to have occurred until approximately 130–150 C.E., a time when Christian separateness was marked by both increasingly distinct doctrine and the general Christian refusal to aid Jews in the Second Jewish War against Roman rule (ca. 132–135 C.E.). The degree of separation between the two faiths should not be overemphasized, however, as for the next several centuries many Christians continued to move freely in and out of worship within the Jewish synagogues, a fact of great concern to the Christian bishops and emperors of the fourth century C.E.

THE DEATHS OF THE APOSTLES JAMES, PAUL, AND PETER

Claudius was succeeded as emperor by Nero (54–68 C.E.). The sources on Christianity during Nero's reign are extremely significant because, among other matters, they describe the arrest of Paul, the execution of the Apostle James, and the earliest known Roman persecution of the Christian church. Even prior to these events, however, there was an earlier incident that some have interpreted to indicate that Christianity had penetrated into at least one family of the Roman governing elite.

> 2.10 Tacitus, *Annals of Imperial Rome* 13.32 (ca. 110 C.E.)
> These events date to ca. 57 C.E.
>> Pomponia Graecina, a woman of high family, married to Aulus Plautius—whose ovation after the British campaign I recorded earlier—and now arraigned for alien superstition, was left to the jurisdiction of her husband. Following the ancient custom, he held the inquiry, which was to determine the fate and fame of his wife, before a family council, and announced her innocent. Pomponia was a woman destined to long life and to continuous grief: for after Julia, the daughter of Drusus, had been done to death by the treachery of Messalina, she survived forty years, dressed in perpetual mourning and lost in perpetual sorrow; and a constancy unpunished under the Empire of Claudius became later a title to glory.

Some historians have suggested that this "alien superstition" was Christianity, connecting the "constancy unpunished," which "became later a title to glory," to the fact that archaeologists have discovered in the Catacombs of

Callistus in the city of Rome burial vaults with Christian inscriptions honoring the Pomponia clan and a "Pomponius Graecinus." However, the most recent archaeological studies indicate that these Christian burial vaults date from the mid-second century C.E. at the earliest and thus could not be related to this Pomponia Graecina.[24] If the "alien superstition" were in fact Christianity, then the text indicates the disrepute with which Christian belief was held among the Roman upper classes during this period: Aulus Plautius invoked "ancient custom" to convene a private family inquiry rather than suffer the embarrassment of a public inquiry into his wife's religious beliefs.

At approximately the same time as the inquiry into Pomponia Graecina's "alien superstition," the Jewish leaders in Jerusalem attempted to silence once and for all the Apostle Paul, but the plot miscarried and Paul was taken into Roman custody and eventually transported to Rome.

> 2.11 The Acts Of The Apostles 23:12–13, 16–17, 23–34; 24:1, 22–23, 26–27 (ca. 80–85 C.E.) These events date to ca. 58–60 C.E.
>
> [23] When it was day, the Jews made a plot and bound themselves by an oath neither to eat nor drink till they had killed Paul. There were more than forty who made this conspiracy. . . . Now the son of Paul's sister heard of their ambush; so he went and entered the barracks and told Paul. And Paul called one of the centurions and said, "Take this young man to the tribune; for he has something to tell him." So he took him and brought him to the tribune. . . . Then he [the tribune] called two of the centurions and said, "At the third hour of the night get ready two hundred soldiers with seventy horsemen and two hundred spear men to go as far as Caesarea. Also provide mounts for Paul to ride, and bring him safely to Felix the governor." And he wrote a letter to this effect: "Claudius Lysias to his Excellency the governor Felix, greetings. This man [Paul] was seized by the Jews, and was about to be killed by them, when I came upon them with the soldiers and rescued him, having learned that he was a Roman citizen. And desiring to know the charge on which they accused him, I brought him down to their council. I found that he was accused about questions of their law, but charged with nothing deserving death or imprisonment. And when it was disclosed to me that there would be a plot against the man, I sent him to you at once, ordering his accusers also to state before you what they have against him." So the soldiers, according to their instructions, took Paul and brought him by night to Antipatris. And on the morrow they returned to the barracks, leaving the horsemen to go on with him. When they came to Caesarea and delivered the letter to the governor, they presented Paul also before him. . . .

24. W. H. C. Frend, *Martyrdom and Persecution in the Early Church* (New York: University Press, 1965), 216–17.

²⁴ And after five days the high priest Ananias came down with some elders and a spokesman, one Tertullus. They laid before the governor their case against Paul. . . . But Felix, having a rather accurate knowledge of the Way, put them off, saying, "When Lysias the tribune comes down, I will decide your case." Then he gave orders to the centurion that he should be kept in custody but should have some liberty, and that none of his friends should be prevented from attending to his needs. . . . At the same time he [Felix] hoped that money would be given him by Paul. So he sent for him often and conversed with him. But when two years had elapsed, Felix was succeeded by Porcius Festus; and desiring to do the Jews a favor, Felix left Paul in prison.

Most historians believe that Felix was procurator of Judaea from 52–60 C.E. and that the text of Acts means that Paul was under arrest from 58–60 C.E. However, a few historians have argued that the "two years" mentioned in Acts 24 refers to the term of Felix's office and not to the period of Paul's arrest.²⁵ Under this minority view, Paul was under arrest from approximately 52 to 54 C.E. and the dates given below for the subsequent events described in The Acts of the Apostles would be adjusted forward by approximately six years.

2.12 The Acts Of The Apostles 25:13–21, 25-26; 27:1 (concerning events ca. 60 or 61 C.E.) and 28:16, 30 (concerning events ca. 61–63 C.E.)

²⁵˒¹³ Now when some days had passed, Agrippa the king and Bernice arrived at Caesarea to welcome Festus [the new Roman governor]. And as they stayed there many days, Festus laid Paul's case before the king, saying, "There is a man left prisoner by Felix, and when I was at Jerusalem, the chief priests and the elders of the Jews gave information about him, asking for sentence against him. I answered them that it was not the custom of the Romans to give up any one before the accused met the accusers face to face, and had opportunity to make his defense concerning the charge laid against him. When therefore they came together here, I made no delay, but on the next day took my seat on the tribunal and ordered the man to be brought in. When the accusers stood up, they brought no charge in his case of such evils as I supposed; but they had certain points of dispute with him about their own superstition and about one Jesus, who was dead, but whom Paul asserted to be alive. Being at a loss how to investigate these questions I asked whether he wished to go to Jerusalem and be tried there regarding them. But when Paul had appealed to be kept in custody for the decision of the Emperor, I commanded him to be held until I could send him to Caesar. . . .

25. For the arguments in favor of the minority view, see Marta Sordi, *The Christians and the Roman Empire* (Norman: University of Oklahoma Press, 1986), 35 note 3.

²⁵·²⁵ But I found that he had done nothing deserving death; and as he himself appealed to the Emperor, I decided to send him [to Rome]. But I have nothing definite to write to my lord about him. . . .

²⁷·¹ And when it was decided that we should sail for Italy, they delivered Paul and some other prisoners to a centurion of the Augustan cohort, named Julius. . . .

²⁸·¹⁶ And when we came into Rome, Paul was allowed to stay by himself, with the soldier that guarded him. . . . And he lived there two whole years at his own expense, and welcomed all who came to him, preaching the kingdom of God and teaching about the Lord Jesus Christ quite openly and unhindered.

While Paul was in Rome awaiting trial, the Jewish leaders in Jerusalem took advantage of the sudden death of the Roman governor Porcius Festus in 62 C.E. to move against the Apostle James, the brother of Jesus and the leader of the Christian community in Jerusalem, before the new Roman governor Albinus could arrive to assume the post.

2.13 Josephus, *Jewish Antiquities* 20.200 (ca. 93 or 94 C.E.)
. . . Ananus thought that he had a favorable opportunity because Festus was dead and Albinus was still on the way. And so he convened the judges of the Sanhedrin and brought before them a man named James, the brother of Jesus who was called the Christ, and certain others. He accused them of having transgressed the law and delivered them up to be stoned. Those of the inhabitants of the city who were considered the most fair-minded and who were strict in observance of the law were offended at this.

Apparently within one or two years after the death of James, the Apostles Paul and Peter were tried and executed in the city of Rome by the Roman authorities. The deaths of James, Paul, and Peter within such a short time must have been a stunning blow to the early Christian communities, but no contemporary Christian account of these deaths has survived. The earliest known reference to the deaths of Peter and Paul appears in a Christian letter written about thirty years after the fact.

2.14 The Letter Of The Church Of Rome To The Church Of Corinth, commonly called *Clement's First Letter* 5.1–7 (ca. 95 C.E.)
⁵ . . . . Let us come to the heroes nearest our own times. Let us take the noble examples of our own generation. By reason of rivalry and envy the greatest and most righteous pillars were persecuted, and battled to the death. Let us set before our eyes the noble apostles: Peter, who by reason of wicked jealousy, not only once or twice but frequently endured suffering and thus, bearing his witness, went to the glorious place which he merited. By reason of rivalry and contention Paul

showed how to win the prize for patient endurance. Seven times he was in chains; he was exiled, stoned, became a herald in East and West, and won the noble renown which his faith merited. To the whole world he taught righteousness, and reaching the limits [or "goal"—*terma*] of the West he bore his witness before rulers. And so, released from this world, he was taken up into the holy place and became the greatest example of patient endurance.

The statement that Paul reached "the limits of the West" has been interpreted by some to mean that Paul carried out his expressed intent to visit Spain (Romans 15:24) and that accordingly Paul must have been released from his first imprisonment in Rome and arrested a second time after the mission to Spain. However, there is no first-century evidence other than this passage for the belief that Paul traveled to Spain and here the Latin *terma* might better be translated as "goal" rather than "limits." Certainly the city of Rome would fit the statement that Paul had reached "the goal of the West" and would better fit the immediately following "bore his witness before rulers."[26]

While the Letter of the Church in Rome referred to the deaths of Paul and Peter, it did not actually describe the time, place, or manner of their deaths. In fact, there are no contemporary accounts of the circumstances of either Paul's or Peter's death. The earliest known sources for the Christian traditions that Paul was beheaded and Peter was crucified upside down are *The Acts of Paul* and *The Acts of Peter*, both of which are mid- to late-second-century C.E. works, ultimately rejected by the orthodox Christian church as apocryphal or heretical. However, it is rather curious that the traditions concerning the deaths of Peter and Paul would have been preserved by orthodox Christians while the Acts containing the traditions were rejected, if the traditions first appeared in these two Acts. It may be that these Acts are simply by historical accident the earliest surviving written accounts of oral traditions derived from the Christians of the city of Rome.

The uncertain nature of the surviving information concerning the deaths of Paul and Peter means that even the years of their deaths are uncertain. Because Acts 28:30 is silent about Paul's fate after he had spent two years awaiting trial in Rome, many historians believe that Paul was tried and executed by the Roman authorities about 63 or 64 C.E. and accept the second-century C.E. Christian tradition that Peter was executed at more or less the same time.[27] A date of 63 or 64 C.E. for Paul's death would support the suspicion of many historians that Paul's trial involved an examination of his Christian beliefs, and that these beliefs were a factor in the earliest known Roman persecution of a Christian community,

---

26. E. P. Sanders, *Paul* (Oxford: Oxford University Press, 1991), 16.

27. See, e.g., Howard Clark Kee, *Understanding the New Testament* (Englewood Cliffs: Prentice-Hall, Inc., fourth ed. 1983), 295. Most of the relevant sources are summarized in Jack Finegan, *Handbook of Biblical Chronology* (Peabody, Mass.: Hendrickson, 1998), 374–89.

that which occurred under the emperor Nero (54–68 C.E.) in the city of Rome after a great fire destroyed much of the city in the summer of 64 C.E.

2.15 Tacitus, *Annals of Imperial Rome* 15.44 (ca. 110 C.E.)

So far, the precautions taken were suggested by human prudence; now means were sought for appeasing deity, and application was made to the Sibyline books; at the injunction of which public prayers were offered to Vulcan, Ceres and Proserpine, while Juno was propitiated by the matrons, first in the Capitol, then at the nearest point of the sea-shore, where water was drawn for sprinkling the temple and image of the goddess. Ritual banquets and all-night vigils were celebrated by women in the married state. But neither human help, nor imperial munificence, nor all the modes of placating Heaven, could stifle scandal or dispel the belief that the fire had taken place by order. Therefore, to scotch the rumor, Nero substituted [*subdidit*—literally, "falsely accused"] as culprits and punished with the utmost refinements of cruelty, a class of men, loathed for their vices, whom the crowd styled Christians. Christus, the founder of the name, had undergone the death penalty in the reign of Tiberius, by sentence of the procurator Pontius Pilate,[28] and the pernicious superstition [*superstitio*] was checked for the moment, only to break out once more, not merely in Judaea, the home of the disease, but even in the capital itself [Rome], where all things horrible or shameful in the world collect and find a vogue. First, then, the confessed members of the sect were arrested; next, on their disclosures, vast numbers were convicted, not so much on the count of arson as for hatred of the human race. And derision accompanied their end: they were covered with wild beasts' skins and torn to death by dogs; or they were fastened on crosses, and, when daylight failed were burned to serve as lamps by night. Nero had offered his Gardens for the spectacle, and gave an exhibition in his Circus, mixing with the crowd in the habit of a charioteer, or mounted on his car. Hence, in spite of a guilt which had earned the most exemplary punishment, there arose a sentiment of pity, due to the impression that they were being sacrificed not for the welfare of the state but to the ferocity of a single man.

While some of the hostility expressed toward Christians clearly reflects Tacitus's own attitudes, the passage does indicate that only thirty years after the founding of their faith Christians were so notoriously unpopular among Rome's urban masses that Nero could attempt to use the Christians as a scapegoat for

---

28. This is the only extant reference to Pontius Pilate in pagan Roman literary sources, although Pilate's governorship of Judaea is described in some length by Josephus, and archaeologists have found in Germany and Israel inscriptions bearing Pilate's name.

the Great Fire of Rome. Unfortunately, Tacitus does not describe the exact "vices" of the Christians other than their "hatred of mankind" and none of the other more or less contemporary ancient sources are more specific on this question. As a result, historians are reduced to explaining the unpopularity of Christians at this early date either by extrapolating from the known cultural and religious attitudes of Rome and its subject peoples as to how Christians "must have" been perceived or by reading back into the first-century accounts the second-century allegations that Christians refused to worship the traditional pagan gods and engaged in cannibalism, sexual promiscuity, magical practices, and the like. Although many of these theories are logical extrapolations of the later evidence, they must remain to some extent mere speculation, and it would certainly be preferable to have more contemporary evidence on this question.

The forms of punishment Nero inflicted on the Christians may not have been mere random acts of brutality, but rather may have reflected formal criminal charges of arson and/or the practice of magic. The penalties specified by Roman law for both magicians and arsonists included being burned alive and crucifixion, and arsonists might also be thrown to wild beasts.[29] While charges of arson would certainly be understandable in the context of Nero's desire to find scape-goats for the Great Fire, an accusation that the Christians were magicians as well as arsonists would be consistent with one of the possible translations of "*malefica*" in the following passage from Suetonius's *Life of Nero*.

2.16 Suetonius, *Life of Nero*, 16.2 (ca. 122 C.E.)
During his [Nero's] reign many abuses were severely punished and put down, and no fewer new laws were made: a limit was set to expenditures; the public banquets were confined to a distribution of food; the sale of any kind of cooked viands in the taverns was for-bidden, with the exception of pulse and vegetables, whereas before every sort of dainty was exposed for sale. Punishment was inflicted on the Christians, a class of men given to a new and mischievous superstition [*superstitiones novae ac maleficae*]. He put an end to the diversions of the chariot drivers, who from immunity of long standing claimed the right of ranging at large and amusing themselves by cheating and robbing people. The pantomimic actors and their par-tisans were banished from the city.

"*Malefica*" means injurious, evil-doing, wicked, criminal, but it can also carry connotations of magical practices and sorcery. Thus, an alternative translation of

---

29. The "Cornelian Law Concerning Assassins and Poisoners" promulgated by Sulla in 81 B.C.E. provided that magicians were to be crucified or burned alive and the people who associ-ated with them were to be burnt publicly. Gaius, writing on "The Law of the Twelve Tables," Book IV, prescribed death by fire to arsonists, and Ulpianus, in "The Duty of Proconsuls," Book VIII, prescribed throwing arsonists "of low rank" to wild beasts.

this passage is, "a new superstition that involved the practice of magic."[30] Either translation would be consistent with the low regard that Suetonius, like Tacitus, had for Christians, whom he associated in his text with charioteers and pantomime actors, groups regarded by the Romans as the dregs of society. While a reader might assume that the phrase "punishment was inflicted on the Christians" is an oblique reference to Nero's persecution after the Great Fire, it is rather curious that Suetonius did not expressly mention the persecution in association with the Great Fire, if that were in fact his meaning, since elsewhere in his history Suetonius expressly accused Nero of being responsible for the Great Fire.[31] A more explicit assertion that Nero persecuted Christians as the perpetrators of the Great Fire is found in the work of the early fifth-century Christian historian Sulpicius Severus.

> 2.17 Sulpicius Severus (ca. 360–420 C.E.), *Chronicle* 2.29 (ca. 400 C.E.)
> In the meantime, the number of the Christians being now very large, it happened that Rome was destroyed by fire, while Nero was stationed at Antium. But the opinion of all cast the odium of causing the fire upon the emperor, and he was believed in this way to have sought for the glory of building a new city. And in fact Nero could not, by any means he tried, escape from the charge that the fire had been caused by his orders. He therefore turned the accusation against the Christians, and the most cruel tortures were accordingly inflicted upon the innocent. Nay, even new kinds of death were invented, so that, being covered in the skins of wild beasts, they perished by being devoured by dogs, while many were crucified or slain by fire, and not a few were set apart for this purpose, that, when the day came to a close, they should be consumed to serve for light during the night. In this way, cruelty first began to be manifested against the Christians. Afterwards, too, their religion was prohibited by laws which were enacted; and by edicts openly set forth it was proclaimed unlawful to be a Christian. At that time Paul and Peter were condemned to death, the former being beheaded with a sword, while Peter suffered crucifixion.

The bulk of this text appears to be derived from the account of Tacitus (Selection 2.15), but it adds the intriguing detail that it was at this time that Christianity was formally outlawed by the Roman authorities. The legal basis for the Roman persecution of Christians is a contentious issue in early Christian history and is discussed in the next chapter.

CHRISTIANITY AFTER THE FIRST JEWISH WAR

In 66 C.E., just two years after the Great Fire of Rome, the Jews of Palestine

---

30. See the discussion of this point in Stephen Benko, *Pagan Rome and the Early Christians* (Bloomington: Indiana University Press, 1984), 20–21.
31. *Life of Nero* 38.

erupted into a full scale revolt against Roman rule. Although the Jewish forces inflicted a serious initial defeat on the local Roman forces, Rome quickly mounted a counter-offensive and methodically reoccupied the countryside, driving the Jewish armies and civilians into Jerusalem. At this point, the Roman armies paused in response to first the rebellion against the Emperor Nero and then to the outbreak of a Roman civil war over the succession to the throne after Nero's death. The commander of the Roman army in Palestine, Vespasian, ultimately triumphed in the civil war and became emperor in 69 C.E. The final reduction of Jerusalem was thus left to his son Titus, who captured the city in the early fall of 70 C.E.

> 2.18 Josephus, *The Jewish War* 6.403–408, 414–418, 420–421; 7.1–4 (Aramaic ca. 73 C.E.; Greek ca. 75–76 C.E.)
>
> [6.403] The Romans, now masters of the walls, planted their standards on the towers, and with clapping of hands and jubilation raised a paean in honor of their victory. They had found the end of the war a much lighter task than the beginning; indeed they could hardly believe that they had surmounted the last wall without bloodshed, and, seeing none to oppose them, were truly perplexed. Pouring into the alleys, sword in hand, they massacred indiscriminately all whom they met, and burnt the houses with all who had taken refuge within. Often in the course of their raids, on entering the houses for loot, they would find whole families dead and the rooms filled with the victims of the famine, and then, shuddering at the sight, retire empty handed. Yet, while they pitied those who had thus perished, they had no similar feelings for the living, but, running everyone through who fell in their way, they choked the alleys with corpses and deluged the whole city with blood, insomuch that many of the fires were extinguished by the gory stream. Towards evening they ceased slaughtering, but when night fell the fire gained the mastery, and the dawn of the eighth day of the month Gorpiaeus [circa September 26, 70 C.E.] broke upon Jerusalem in flames. . . .
>
> [414] Since the soldiers were now growing weary of slaughter, though numerous survivors still came to light, Caesar [Titus] issued orders to kill only those who were found in arms and offered resistance, and to make prisoners of the rest. The troops, in addition to those specified in their instructions, slew the old and feeble; while those in the prime of life and serviceable they drove together into the temple and shut them up in the court of the women. Caesar appointed one of his freedmen as their guard, and his friend Fronto to adjudicate upon the lot appropriate to each. Fronto put to death all the seditious and brigands, information being given by them against each other; he selected the tallest and most handsome of the youth and reserved them for the triumph; of the rest, those over seventeen years of age he sent in chains to the works in Egypt, while multitudes were presented by

Titus to the various provinces, to be destroyed in the theaters by
sword or by wild beasts; those under seventeen were sold. . . .

[420] The total number of prisoners taken throughout the entire war
amounted to ninety-seven thousand and of those who perished
during the siege, from first to last, to one million one hundred thousand. Of these the greater number were of Jewish blood, but not
natives of the place; for, having assembled from every part of the
country for the feast of unleavened bread, they found themselves
suddenly enveloped in the war, with the result that this over-crowding
produced first pestilence, and later the added and more rapid
scourge of famine. . . .

[7.1] The army now having no victims either for slaughter or plunder,
through lack of all objects on which to vent their rage—for they would
assuredly never have desisted through a desire to spare anything so
long as there was work to be done—Caesar ordered the whole city
and the temple to be razed to the ground, leaving only the loftiest
of the towers—Phasael, Hippicus, and Mariamme—and the portion
of the wall enclosing the city on the west; the latter as an encamp-
ment for the garrison that was to remain, and the towers to indicate to posterity the nature of the city and of the strong defenses
which had yet yielded to Roman prowess. All the rest of the wall
encompassing the city was so completely leveled to the ground as
to leave future visitors to the spot no ground for believing that it
had ever been inhabited. Such was the end to which the frenzy of
revolutionaries brought Jerusalem, that splendid city of world-
wide renown.

The First Jewish War profoundly affected the nature and direction of
Christianity's growth. Many, if not all, of the Christian churches founded in
Palestine by the twelve apostles were apparently destroyed during the war, as at
this time these churches essentially disappear from the historical record.[32] Many
historians believe that with the destruction of these communities the written
records and many of the oral traditions of the earliest Christian communities
were lost or confused, as seen in the loss of essentially all information about
Jesus' life before his ministry; the historical errors found in Luke and Acts;[33] the
significant discrepancies as to chronology, places, and events concerning Jesus'
ministry found in the four Gospels; and the absence of contemporaneous information about the time or circumstances of the deaths of Peter, Paul, and most of
the twelve apostles. The destruction of the Jewish-oriented Christian churches
founded by the apostles undoubtedly facilitated the eventual supremacy within

---

32. W. H. C. Frend, *Martyrdom and Persecution in the Early Church* (New York: University
Press, 1965), 178–80.

33. See, e.g., the discussion found in Appendix E at pages 292–97.

Christianity of the gentile-oriented Christian churches founded by the Apostle Paul and others.[34]

The political and social turmoil in Palestine that led to and followed the First Jewish War also influenced the relationship between Christians and the Roman government. Relations between Rome and the Jews deteriorated sharply before the outbreak of the war, and during and after the war Rome inflicted massive punishment on the Jews, so there were good reasons for Christians to distinguish their communities from the "disloyal" Jewish population. The desire of Christians to emphasize their loyalty to Rome and their differences from Jews is reflected in the Gospels, which consistently depicted Christians as being distinct from Jews and claimed that in every instance in which any Roman official examined Christians and their faith, the official found no evidence of crime or wrongdoing among the Christians or their leaders. See, for example, Matthew's account of Pilate's examination of Jesus, Act's account of Paul's appearance before Gallio at Selection 2.8, Paul's rescue by the Tribune Lysias at Selection 2.11, and Paul's examination by Festus at Selection 2.12.[35] Further, after the war many of the surviving Jews and Christians began dispersing throughout the Roman Empire. The dispersal of Christian survivors would have facilitated the spread of Christianity throughout the Roman world more broadly and more quickly than might otherwise have occurred simply through missionary efforts.

Unfortunately, sources concerning the nature of the relations between Jews and Christians in the decades after the First Jewish War are few and fragmentary. Such evidence would be extremely useful for understanding the manner in which Christianity grew apart from Judaism during this period. It does appear that the Jewish survivors saw the disastrous loss of the war and the destruction of the Second Temple as the result of the Jewish people having abandoned the proper worship of God. From that perspective, it is easy to understand why pious Jews might name the Christians as the people who had fallen away from the proper worship of God. One of the few contemporary sources touching upon this issue is the Gospel of John (ca. 95 C.E.), which many historians believe superimposes various details and perspectives of Jewish-Christian relations during the late first century C.E. on to the story of Jesus' ministry.[36] Passages in John seem to indicate that after the First Jewish War the leaders of the surviving Jewish

---

34 W. H. C. Frend, *Martyrdom and Persecution in the Early Church* (New York: University Press, 1965), 177–78.

35 The majority of modern scholars believe that while the Gospel of Mark may possibly have been written before the First Jewish War, the Gospels of Matthew and Luke were clearly written after the war. See, for example, E. P. Sanders and Margaret Davies, *Studying the Synoptic Gospels* (Philadelphia: Trinity Press International, 1989), 16–20; John P. Meier, *A Marginal Jew* (New York: Doubleday, 1991), 43–44; Raymond E. Brown *The Death of the Messiah* (New York: Doubleday, 1994), 45–46, 236–37; Bart D. Ehrman, *The New Testament: A Historical Introduction to the Early Christian Writings* (New York: Oxford University Press, 2000), 43.

36. See, for example, Raymond E. Brown, *The Community of the Beloved Disciple* (New York: Paulist, 1979).

communities took rigorous measures against those Christians who continued
to participate in the services and community of the synagogue.[37] It is in this
context that one must interpret the revisions to the form of the Twelfth
Benediction (one of the Eighteen Benedictions used in the liturgy of the Jewish
synagogue) that Gamaliel II of Jerusalem ordered about 85 C.E.[38]

> 2.19 The Twelfth Benediction (ca. 85 C.E.)
>> For the apostates let there be no hope, and the dominion of arro-
>> gance do Thou speedily root out in our days, and let the Nazarenes
>> and the heretics perish as in a moment, let them be blotted out of the
>> book of the living, and let them not be written with the righteous.
>> Blessed art Thou, O Lord, who humblest the arrogant.

Gamaliel II ordered that the Benedictions be recited three times a day as part
of Jewish worship and the Twelfth Benediction evidently continued in use for
centuries. The Christian bishop Epiphanius (fourth century C.E.) wrote that in
his time Christians were cursed three times a day in the synagogues of Palestine.[39]

The inclusion of the revised Twelfth Benediction into the worship service
must have had the effect of excluding Christians from synagogue services.[40]
However, a Christian text known as the Didache, a portion of which seems to
date from the last third of the first century C.E., indicates that Christian forms
of worship continued to reflect a close relationship to Jewish ceremonies.

> 2.20 The Didache 6.3–15.4 (portion of text quoted dates to late first cen-
> tury C.E.[41])
>> The Lord's Teaching to the Heathen by the Twelve Apostles:
>> [6] . . . .Now about food: undertake what you can. But keep strictly away
>> from what is offered to idols, for that implies worshipping dead gods.
>> [7] Now about baptism: this is how to baptize. Give public instruction
>> on all these points, and then baptize in running water, "in the name
>> of the Father and of the Son and of the Holy Spirit." [Matthew 28:19]
>> If you do not have running water, baptize in some other. If you can-
>> not in cold, then in warm. If you have neither, then pour water on the
>> head three times "in the name of the Father, Son, and Holy Spirit."
>> Before the baptism, moreover, the one who baptizes and the one

---

37. See, for example, Raymond E. Brown, *The Community of the Beloved Disciple* (New York:
Paulist , 1979), 40–43.

38. Some historians reject the belief that the Twelfth Benediction was ever modified to include
a curse of the Christians. See, for example, N. T. Wright, *The New Testament and the People of God*
(Minneapolis: Fortress Press, 1992), 164–65 and the sources cited therein.

39. *Panarion* 29.9.2.

40. W. H. C. Frend, *Martyrdom and Persecution in the Early Church* (New York: University
Press, 1965), 179 and the sources cited therein.

41. The date and place of origin of the Didache is one of the most disputed issues in early
Christian literature. The earliest certain quotation of the Didache is from the early third century
C.E., but historians agree that the material comes from a much earlier period of church history. The
Didache was once dated as early as 70–90 C.E., but now parts of the text are dated to the second

being baptized must fast, and any others who can. And you must tell the one being baptized to fast for one or two days beforehand.

[8] Your fasts must not be identical with those of the hypocrites. [i.e., the Jews] They fast on Mondays and Thursdays; but you should fast on Wednesdays and Fridays.

You must not pray like the hypocrites, but pray as follows as the Lord bid us in his gospel: "Our Father in heaven, hallowed be your name; your Kingdom come; your will be done on earth as it is in heaven; give us today our bread for the morrow; and forgive us our debts as we forgive our debtors. And do not lead us into temptation, but save us from the evil one, for yours is the power and the glory forever."[42]

You should pray in this way three times a day.

[9] Now about the Eucharist. This is how to give thanks: First in connection with the cup: "We thank you, our Father, for the holy vine of David, your child, which you have revealed through Jesus, your child. To you be glory forever."

Then in connection with the piece [broken off the loaf]: "We thank you, our Father, for the life and knowledge which you have revealed through Jesus, your child. To you be glory forever. As this piece was scattered over the hills and then was brought together and made one, so let your Church be brought together from the ends of the earth into your kingdom. For yours is the glory and the power through Jesus Christ forever."

You must not let anyone eat or drink of your Eucharist except those baptized in the Lord's name. For in reference to this the Lord said, "Do not give what is sacred to dogs." [Matthew 7:6]

[10] After you have finished your meal, say grace [or, "give thanks"] in this way: "We thank you, holy Father, for your sacred name which you have

century C.E. because chapters 1 through 5 are derived from Mandate 2.4–6 of *The Shepherd of Hermas*, (ca. 140–150 C.E.), and chapter 16.2 is derived from section 4.9 of *The Letter of Barnabas* (ca. 100–130 C.E.). Other portions of the Didache reflect a knowledge of the Gospel of Matthew and thus would have to have been composed after that Gospel, which is generally dated to approximately 80 or 85 C.E. In its present form, the Didache appears to be a mid-second-century combination of two different documents: chapters 1–5 are a second-century C.E. form of catechism in which some Christian sayings were inserted, and chapters 6–15 are an early manual of church order, perhaps from Syria, dating to the late first century C.E.

42. This is the oldest extant recital of the Lord's Prayer outside of the Gospels. Compare this text to Matthew 6:9–13 RSV: "Our Father who art in heaven. Hallowed be thy name. Thy kingdom come. Thy will be done, on earth as it is in heaven. Give us this day our daily bread; and forgive us our debts as we also have forgiven our debtors; and lead us not into temptation, but deliver us from evil" and Luke 11:2–4 (RSV): "Father, hallowed be thy name. Thy kingdom come. Give us each day our daily bread; and forgive us our sins, for we ourselves forgive everyone who is indebted to us; and lead us not into temptation." The Didache prayer is evidently derived from either the Gospel of Matthew or that Gospel's source, and not from the Gospel of Luke, as it follows the longer text of Matthew.

lodged in our hearts, and for the knowledge and faith and immortality which you have revealed through Jesus, your child. To you be glory forever. Almighty Master, you have created everything for the sake of your name, and have given men food and drink to enjoy that they may thank you. But to us you have given spiritual food and drink and eternal life through Jesus, your child. Above all, we thank you that you are mighty. To you be glory forever. Remember, Lord, your Church, to save it from all evil and to make it perfect by your love. Make it holy and gather it together from the four winds into your Kingdom which you have made ready for it. For yours is the power and the glory forever. Let Grace come and let this world pass away. Hosanna to the God of David. If anyone is holy, let him come. If not, let him repent. Our Lord, come! Amen."

In the case of prophets, however, you should let them give thanks in their own way.

[11] Now, you should welcome anyone who comes your way and teaches you all we have been saying. But if the teacher proves himself a renegade and by teaching otherwise contradicts all this, pay no attention to him. But if his teaching furthers the Lord's righteousness and knowledge, welcome him as the Lord.

Now about the apostles and prophets: act in line with the gospel precept. [Matthew 10.40–41] Welcome every apostle on arriving, as if he were the Lord. But he must not stay beyond one day. In case of necessity, however, the next day too. If he stays three days, he is a false prophet. On departing, an apostle must not accept anything save sufficient food to carry him till his next lodging. If he asks for money, he is a false prophet.

While a prophet is making ecstatic utterances, you must not test or examine him. For "every sin will be forgiven," but this sin "will not be forgiven." [Matthew 12.31] However, not everybody making ecstatic utterances is a prophet, but only if he behaves like the Lord. It is by their conduct that the false prophet and the [true] prophet can be distinguished. For instance, if a prophet marks out a table in the Spirit, he must not eat from it. If he does, he is a false prophet. Again, every prophet who teaches the truth but fails to practice what he preaches is a false prophet. But every attested and genuine prophet who acts with a view to symbolizing the mystery of the Church, and does not teach you to do all he does, must not be judged by you. His judgment rests with God. For the ancient prophets too acted in this way. But if someone says in the Spirit, "Give me money, or something else," you must not heed him. However, if he tells you to give for others in need, no one must condemn him.

[12] Everyone who comes to you in the name of the Lord must be welcomed. Afterward, when you have tested him, you will find out about

him, for you have insight into right and wrong. If it is a traveler who arrives, help him all you can. But he must not stay with you more than two days, or, if necessary, three. If he wants to settle with you and is an artisan, he must work for his living. If, however, he has no trade, use your judgment in taking steps for him to live with you as a Christian without being idle. If he refuses to do this, he is trading on Christ. You must be on your guard against such people.

[13] Every genuine prophet who wants to settle with you "has a right to his support." [Matthew 10.10] Similarly, a genuine teacher himself, just like a "workman, has a right to his support." [Id.] Hence take all the first fruits of vintage and harvest, and of cattle and sheep, and give these first fruits to the prophets. For they are your high priests. If, however, you have no prophet, give them to the poor. If you make bread, take the first fruits and give in accordance with the precept. [Deuteronomy 18.3–5] Similarly, when you open a jar of wine or oil, take the first fruits and give them to the prophets. Indeed, of money, clothes, and of all your possessions, take such first fruits as you think right, and give in accordance with the precept.

[14] On every Lord's Day—his special day—[literally, "On every Lord's Day of the Lord"] come together and break bread and give thanks, first confessing your sins so that your sacrifice may be pure. Anyone at variance with his neighbors must not join you, until they are reconciled, lest your sacrifice be defiled. For it was of this sacrifice that the Lord said, "Always and everywhere offer me a pure sacrifice; for I am a great King, says the Lord, and my name is marveled at by the nations." [Malachi 1.11,14]

[15] You must, then, elect for yourselves bishops and deacons who are a credit to the Lord, men who are gentle, generous, faithful and well tried. For their ministry to you is identical with that of the prophets and teachers. You must not, therefore, despise them, for along with the prophets and teachers they enjoy a place of honor among you.

Furthermore, do not reprove each other angrily, but quietly, as you find it in the gospel. Moreover, if anyone has wronged his neighbor, nobody must speak to him, and he must not hear a word from you, until he repents. Say your prayers, give your charity, and do everything just as you find it in the gospel of our Lord. . . .

The eucharistic prayers in the Didache are modeled on the Jewish forms for grace before and after meals and indicate that this part of the text dates to a time when the Eucharist was still celebrated as part of a real meal. In the late first century C.E., the hierarchy of the congregation was apparently still relatively ill-defined, as the text refers only to bishops and deacons, without mention of presbyters, and wandering prophets still hold positions of respect and authority. Of even greater interest, however, is the fact that the Didache reflects a Christian eucharistic practice wholly unrelated to the gospel accounts of the

Last Supper and the few references to Jesus in the text do not emphasize his relationship with God or state that a relationship with Jesus is necessary for salvation. Clearly this is a text meant for a Christian community whose beliefs are much closer to Judaism than to Christianity as practiced only a generation or two later, in the mid-second century C.E.

It was at approximately the same time as the earliest portion of the Didache was composed and Jewish leaders were instituting measures against Jewish Christians after the First Jewish War that the earliest extant pagan reference to Jesus was written. The following passage is from a letter written by Mara bar Sarapion of Samosata, Syria while under Roman arrest. Although the exact date of the letter is uncertain, the oblique reference to the First Jewish War indicates that the letter was written after 70 C.E.

> 2.21 Mara Bar Sarapion (active last third of the first century C.E.), *Letter to his Son* (after 70 C.E.)
> . . . What good did it do the Athenians to kill Socrates, for which deed they were punished with famine and pestilence? What did it avail the Samians to burn Pythagoras, since their country was entirely buried under sand in one moment? Or what did it avail the Jews to kill their wise king, since their kingdom was taken away from them from that time on? God justly avenged these three wise men. The Athenians died of famine, the Samians were flooded by the sea, the Jews were slaughtered and driven from their kingdom, everywhere living in the dispersion. Socrates is not dead, thanks to Plato; nor Pythagoras, because of Hera's statute. Nor is the wise king, because of the new law which he has given.

Because Sarapion was a pagan (he refers to "our gods" elsewhere in the letter), it is not surprising that the letter treats Jesus as a mere man and a lawgiver and not as the resurrected Son of God. The letter does seem to indicate some familiarity with Christian teachings, however, as the statement that the Jews were responsible for the death of Jesus and that the destruction of their nation by the Romans was punishment for this deed reflected the early Christian perspective presented in, for example, Matthew 22:7 and 27:25.

THE EMPEROR DOMITIAN AND THE CHRISTIANS

There are few relatively contemporary sources for Christian history during the latter third of the first century C.E. Because most of the surviving materials on this period were written at least a century or more afterwards, it is often difficult to separate fact from the later Christian legends that grew up around the history of the early church. Among the most interesting of the Christian accounts of this period is Eusebius of Caesarea's (ca. 260–340 C.E.) description of a purported persecution of Christians under the Emperor Domitian (81–96 C.E.).

> 2.22 Eusebius, *Ecclesiastical History* 3.17–18 (ca. 311–323 C.E.)
> [17] When Domitian had given many proofs of his great cruelty and had put to death without any reasonable trial no small number of men

distinguished at Rome by family and career, and had punished without cause myriads of other notable men by banishment and confiscation of their property, he finally showed himself the successor of Nero's campaign of hostility to God. He was the second to promote persecution against us, though his father, Vespasian, had planned no evil against us. [18] At this time [ca. 95 C.E.], the story goes, the Apostle and Evangelist John was still alive, and was condemned to live in the island of Patmos for his witness to the divine word. At any rate Irenaeus, writing about the number of the name ascribed to the anti-Christ in the so-called Apocalypse of John, states this about John in so many words in the fifth book against heresies: "But if it had been necessary to announce his name plainly at the present time, it would have been spoken by him who saw the apocalypse. For it was not seen long ago but almost in our own time, at the end of the reign of Domitian."

The teaching of our faith shone so brilliantly in the days described that even writers foreign to our belief did not hesitate to commit to their narratives the persecutions and the martyrdoms in it, and they even indicated the time accurately, relating that in the fifteenth year of Domitian, Flavia Domitilla, who was the niece of Flavius Clemens, one of the consuls at Rome at that time, was banished with many others to the island of Pontia as testimony to Christ.

Most historians believe that Eusebius's source for the purported Domitian persecution of Christians was the pagan chronicler Bruttius, whose work has been lost. However, in another part of his history Eusebius preserved a passage by a second-century C.E. Christian bishop, which also supported the assertion that there was a persecution of Christians under Domitian.

2.23 Melito, Bishop of Sardis (died ca. 190 C.E.), *To Antoninus* (Eusebius *Ecclesiastical History* 4.26.9)
> The only emperors who were ever persuaded by malicious men to slander our teachings were Nero and Domitian, and from them arose the lie, and the unreasonable custom of falsely accusing Christians.

The historical problem with the assertion of persecution under Domitian is that the Roman historians Suetonius and Cassius Dio both wrote that Domitian's persecution was directed at Jews, not Christians.

2.24 Suetonius, *Life of Domitian* 12.2 (ca. 122 C.E.)
> [12] Besides other taxes, that on the Jews was levied with the utmost rigor, and those were prosecuted who without publicly acknowledging that faith yet lived as Jews, as well as those who concealed their origin and did not pay the tribute levied upon their people.[43] I recall being present in my youth when the person of a man ninety years old

---

43. People who adopted Jewish monotheism without adopting Jewish custom were called "God Fearers." See, for example, Acts 10:2 and 10:22 concerning the centurion Cornelius (a

was examined before the procurator and a very crowded court, to see whether he was circumcised.

2.25 Cassius Dio, *Roman History* 67.14[44] (ca. 214–226 C.E.)
And the same year [95 C.E.], Domitian slew, along with many others, Flavius Clemens the consul, although he was a cousin and had to wife Flavia Domitilla, who was also a relative of the emperor. The charge brought against them both was that of atheism, a charge on which many others who drifted in Jewish ways were condemned. Some of these were put to death, and the rest were at least deprived of their property. Domitilla was merely banished to Pandataria. But Glabrio, who had been Trajan's colleague in the consulship, was put to death, having been accused of the same crimes as most of the others, and, in particular, of fighting as a gladiator with wild beasts.

Roman History 68.1–2[45] (written ca. 214–226 C.E.)
After Domitian, the Romans appointed Nerva Cocceius emperor [96 C.E.]. Because of the hatred felt for Domitian, his images, many of which were of silver and many of gold, were melted down; and from this source large amounts of money were obtained. The arches, too, of which a very great number were being erected to this one man, were torn down. Nerva also released all who were on trial for *maiestas* [treason] and restored the exiles; moreover, he put to death all the slaves and the freedmen who had conspired against their masters and allowed that class of persons to lodge no complaint whatever against their masters; and no persons were permitted to accuse anybody of *maiestas* or of adopting the Jewish mode of life.

In light of the accounts of Cassius Dio and Suetonius, historians are divided over whether to accept the Christian tradition of a persecution by Domitian.[46] Part of this reluctance stems from the fact that Eusebius preserved other traditions about the Christian Church during the reign of Domitian, which seem rather outlandish.

2.26 Eusebius of Caesarea, *Ecclesiastical History* 3.19–20 (ca. 311–323 C.E.)
   [19] The same Domitian gave orders for the execution of those of the

man "who feared God") and Paul's statement at Acts 13:16, "Men of Israel, and you that fear God, listen." By refusing circumcision, which would make them legally "Sons of Abraham," they avoided liability for the tax on Jews. See Appendix A for a discussion of the Roman tax on Jews.

44. The original text of book 67 has not survived. This passage is from a summary composed by a later scribe.

45. The original text of book 68 has not survived. This passage is from a summary composed by a later scribe.

46. The debate over this issue is discussed at, e.g., Marta Sordi, *The Christians and the Roman Empire* (Norman: University of Oklahoma Press, 1986), 43–53; Robin Lane Fox, *Pagans and Christians* (New York: Alfred A. Knopf, Inc., 1989), 433 and notes; and N. T. Wright, *The New Testament and the People of God* (Minneapolis: Fortress Press, 1992), 355–56.

family of David and an ancient story goes that some heretics accused the grandsons of Judas (who is said to have been the brother, according to the flesh, of the Savior), saying that they were of the family of David and related to the Christ himself. Hegesippus (ca. 175–180 C.E.) relates this exactly as follows:

[20] "Now there still survived of the family of the Lord grandsons of Judas, who was said to have been his brother according to the flesh, and they were [accused] as being of the family of David. These the officer brought to Domitian Caesar, for, like Herod, he was afraid of the coming of the Christ. He asked them if they were of the house of David and they admitted it. Then he asked them how much property they had, or how much money they controlled, and they said that all they possessed was nine thousand denarii between them, the half belonging to each, and they stated that they did not possess this in money but that it was the valuation of only thirty-nine plethra of ground on which they paid taxes and lived on it by their own work." They then showed him their hands, adducing as testimony of their labor the hardness of their bodies, and the tough skin which had been embossed on their hands from their incessant work. They were asked concerning the Christ and his kingdom, its nature, origin, and time of appearance, and explained that it was neither of the world nor earthly, but heavenly and angelic, and it would be at the end of the world, when he would come in glory to judge the living and the dead and to reward every man according to his deeds. At this Domitian did not condemn them at all, but despised them as simple folk, released them, and decreed an end to the persecution against the church. But when they were released they were the leaders of the churches, both for their testimony and for their relation to the Lord, and remained alive in the peace which ensued until Trajan. Hegesippus tells this; moreover, Tertullian also has made similar mention of Domitian: "Domitian also once tried to do the same as he, for he was a Nero in cruelty, but, I believe, inasmuch as he had some sense, he stopped at once and recalled those whom he had banished."

After Domitian had reigned fifteen years, Nerva succeeded. The sentences of Domitian were annulled, and the Roman Senate decreed the return of those who had been unjustly banished and the restoration of their property. Those who committed the story of those times to writing relate it. At that time, too, the story of the ancient Christians relates that the Apostle John, after his banishment to the island, took up his abode at Ephesus. . . .

There is no evidence to indicate that the Emperor Domitian ever visited Judea, and there is no hint of a search for the descendants of David in any of the other sources on Domitian's reign.[47] The reference to the Apostle John, however, is part of a larger tradition preserved by Eusebius and other Christian writers to the effect that the Apostle John lived a very long life and died in Ephesus.

> 2.27 Eusebius of Caesarea, *Ecclesiastical History* 3.23 (ca. 311–323 C.E.)
>
> [23] At this time that very disciple whom Jesus loved, John, at once Apostle and Evangelist, still remained alive in Asia and administered the churches there, for after the death of Domitian [96 C.E.], he had returned from his banishment on the island. And that he remained alive until this time may fully be confirmed by two witnesses, and these ought to be trustworthy for they represent the orthodoxy of the church, no less persons than Irenaeus [writing ca. 180 C.E.] and Clement of Alexandria [writing ca. 200 C.E.]. The former of these writes in one place in the second of his books *Against the Heresies*, as follows: "And all the presbyters who had been associated in Asia with John, the disciple of the Lord, bear witness to his tradition, for he remained with them until the times of Trajan." And in the third book of the same work he makes the same statement as follows: "Now the Church at Ephesus was founded by Paul, but John stayed there until the time of Trajan, and it is a true witness of the tradition of the Apostles."

While this tradition concerning the Apostle John has been widely accepted by both ancient and modern Christians, some historians reject the tradition and argue that John the Apostle has been confused with a "John the Presbyter" of Ephesus mentioned by Papias and several other early Christian authors.[48]

In examining the fragmentary sources on Christianity during the first century C.E., one is struck by the sense that the early Christians, who are generally regarded by modern Christians as being the most righteous, gentle, and loving of people, were by the end of the first century C.E. generally regarded as the worst sort of people by both Jews and Romans. Moreover, while the Roman sources, with the possible exception of Tacitus's description of Nero's persecution, indicate that the Romans did not generally perceive Christianity as distinct from Judaism until the very late first century or early second century C.E. at the earliest, once the Romans became of aware of the distinction they were not at all pleased with what they learned about the new faith. The Roman repugnance and contempt for Christianity becomes even more explicit in the more numerous sources from the second century.

---

47. Robin Lane Fox, at *Pagans and Christians* (New York: Alfred A. Knopf, Inc., 1989), 433, regards Eusebius's report as "strange" but does not entirely rule it out. Marta Sordi, at *The Christians and the Roman Empire* (Norman: University of Oklahoma Press, 1986), 39–41, accepts the basics of the report, but believes that Hegesippus has erroneously attributed the events to Domitian's reign and that the events actually occurred under Titus.

48. See Eusebius, *Ecclesiastical History* 3.39.1–7 and the discussion by Robin Lane Fox, *The Unauthorized Version* (New York: Alfred A. Knopf, 1992), 208 and the sources cited therein.

3 | A CENTURY OF MARTYRS:
3 | THE SECOND CENTURY C.E.

N erva (96–98 C.E.), Trajan (98–117 C.E.), Hadrian (117–135 C.E.),
Antoninus Pius (135–161 C.E.), and Marcus Aurelius (161–180 C.E.) are
known today as the "Five Good Emperors," and the Romans themselves saw the
period of 96–180 C.E. as the golden age of their Empire. It was during this
period that the Roman Empire achieved its maximum physical extent, as
Roman legions under the emperor Trajan occupied Dacia, in modern
Romania, portions of Scotland and Wales, and the Mesopotamian River Valley
down to the Gulf of Persia. The period of 96–180 C.E. was also a time of general peace and prosperity within the Roman Empire. The provinces in particular enjoyed an increased prosperity as a result of the new roads and ports, the
increasing urbanization, and the growth of industry and trade that accompanied the general peace, the Pax Romana, enforced by the Romans throughout
the Mediterranean world.

Notwithstanding the Roman Empire's military successes and general pros-
perity during this period, however, historians also perceive the second century
C.E. as a time when the limitations of Roman power became more apparent.
The most obvious of these limitations was the increasing military difficulties
Rome encountered on its frontiers. Shortly after Trajan's death in 117 C.E.,
Hadrian abandoned Trajan's conquests in the southern Mesopotamian River
Valley as indefensible and withdrew from central Scotland to a more defensible
line in northern England, where he built the fortifications known as "Hadrian's
Wall." While Rome's frontiers were mostly quiet during the reigns of Hadrian
and Antoninus Pius, Marcus Aurelius spent almost his entire reign campaigning against barbarian tribes along the Danube River, while his generals fought
the Persian Empire. The frontiers were mostly quiet during the reign of Marcus
Aurelius's son Commodus (180–192 C.E.), but during the following period of
the Severian emperors (193–235 C.E.) there was again significant warfare along
the Roman frontiers.

Serious social and economic problems within the Roman Empire also grew
worse during the second century C.E. The Roman Empire's population growth
had already begun to stagnate when during Marcus Aurelius' reign legions
returning from a victorious campaign against the Persian Empire brought back
a plague which spread quickly through the provinces and killed millions of
people. As a result of the increased military expenditures for the frontier wars

and the declining population during the latter part of the second century C.E., the taxes and obligatory services Rome imposed on the provinces began to bear more heavily on the subject peoples. The rich and politically powerful were generally able to shift the bulk of these increased obligations onto the lower orders of society, thus widening the already extraordinary social and economic divisions between the rich and the poor in the Roman world.

It should be acknowledged that even cumulatively the difficulties Rome faced over the course of the second century C.E. constituted only a slow erosion of its strength and not a catastrophic failure. Moreover, during the second century C.E. Rome made real progress in integrating the many disparate local ruling classes of the provinces into a single political and cultural whole. But if the second century was a peaceful and prosperous time for many, it was also a time of increasing discontent among many in Rome's empire, as demonstrated by the increasing social banditry and anti-Roman literary works such as the Book of Revelation and the pagan Acts of the Pagan Martyrs. Rome's failure to address and resolve its military and social problems during a period of relative strength would allow these problems to become urgent during the third and fourth centuries C.E., when Rome had fewer resources at its disposal.

One circumstance that facilitated the peace and prosperity of the second century C.E. was that upon the death of each of the Five Good Emperors a new emperor succeeded to power without significant contest. The means for peaceful transfer of the emperor's power grew out of what was initially an ad hoc effort by a weak emperor to preserve his throne. After Nerva's selection as emperor by the senate in 96 C.E., he was forced to adopt the prominent Roman general Trajan as his son and successor in order to counter the threat to his rule posed by the Praetorian Guard. This measure was successful in that Trajan suppressed the Praetorian threat, and when Nerva died a natural death in 98 C.E., Trajan succeeded to the emperor's position without conflict. The practice of adopting and grooming a successor during the emperor's lifetime continued thereafter, as Trajan adopted Hadrian, Hadrian adopted Antoninus Pius, and Antoninus Pius adopted Marcus Aurelius. In each instance, the emperor gave the chosen successor meaningful experience and position during the emperor's own lifetime.

There were significant advantages to the practice of adopting and grooming a successor to the throne. Adoption allowed for the selection and training of a qualified individual while still satisfying the Roman cultural preference for family-based succession. The practice also served to discourage contested successions, since the chosen individual already enjoyed at least partial authority over the civil administration and the legions when the emperor died. A fortuitous aspect of the adoption practice was that none of the first four of the five Good Emperors had living sons of their own. Marcus Aurelius, the first of the five with a surviving son, abandoned the practice and arranged for his own son Commodus (180–192 C.E.) to become emperor.

Commodus proved to be an unpopular ruler and he was assassinated in 192 C.E., which led to a civil war over the succession. The victor in the war was Septimus Severus (193–211 C.E.), who established a Severian dynasty based upon biological succession, not adoption for merit. After the last emperor of the Severian dynasty was assassinated in 235 C.E., the next fifty years saw almost continuous rebellion and civil war among Rome's generals as the mechanisms of legitimate succession to the emperor's position essentially collapsed.

It is estimated that by the end of the second century C.E. Christians numbered only about 220,000 out of the 60 million inhabitants of the Roman Empire.[1] Over the course of the century the organization of both the individual churches and the churches as a collective grew more structured and hierarchical. The increasing emphasis on organization and concentration of authority was a response to the practical needs arising from the realization that the churches had to be prepared to go forward for an indefinite length of time until the return of Jesus, now acknowledged to be coming much later than Paul and the apostles had anticipated; the challenges posed by increasingly frequent persecution of the churches; and the need for discipline in the face of the doctrinal disputes among the various Christian communities.

Among these changes, the growth of the power and authority of the bishops was of particular significance. The bishop ("overseer") was originally merely the presiding officer of an individual church's council of elders ("presbyters"). Because essentially all of the cultures of the Graeco-Roman world were hierarchical and patriarchal, a gradual increase over time of the bishop's authority might have been reasonably expected as the natural result of the local Christian communities adopting modes and structures of authority that paralleled the predominant cultural values. However, the bishop's authority was also strengthened by the increasing acceptance within the Christian communities of the doctrine of apostolic succession. This doctrine taught that the original twelve apostles had held a unique spiritual authority, which had been passed solely to their hand-picked successors and that in turn this authority had passed to the duly selected successors of these individuals, and so on down through the generations. The result, according to the doctrine, was that only bishops who could trace an unbroken line of succession back to the Twelve Apostles could rightfully exercise authority in the church, administer valid sacraments, or appoint other bishops. Whereas in the first century C.E., the leaders of the individual Christian churches seem to have been appointed and removed by the congregations, and authority was based on the individual's demonstrated faith, social position, and/or communion with the Holy Spirit, by the end of the second century C.E. a self-appointed and self-perpetuating clergy held the only legitimate authority in many Christian communities. As part of this growth of clerical authority, over the course of the century the bishops, presbyters, and deacons became salaried officers and more clearly distinguished

1. Rodney Stark, *The Rise of Christianity* (Princeton: Princeton University Press, 1996), 6–7.

from the lay members, who gradually ceased to participate actively in either the administration of church affairs or the performance of worship services.

CHRISTIANS AND THE EMPEROR TRAJAN

Eusebius, in relating Hegesippus's account of the emperor Domitian's interrogation of the great-nephews of Jesus (Selection 2.25), stated that after their release these great-nephews "remained alive in the peace which ensued until Trajan." While the rather fragmentary evidence does not suggest that Trajan (98–117 C.E.) ordered any general persecution of Christians, there are a number of sources that indicate that localized persecutions took place during his reign.

> 3.1 Eusebius of Caesarea, *Ecclesiastical History* 3.32.1–2 (ca. 311–323 C.E.)
> After Nero and Domitian tradition says that under the Emperor [Trajan] whose times we are now describing persecution was raised against us sporadically, in some cities, from popular risings. We have learnt that in it Symeon, the son of Clopas, whom we showed to have been the second bishop of the church in Jerusalem, ended his life in martyrdom. The witness for this is that same Hegesippus, of whom we have already quoted several passages. After speaking of certain heretics he goes on to explain how Symeon was at this time [ca. 106 or 107 C.E.] accused by them and for many days was tortured in various manners for being a Christian, to the great astonishment of the judge and those with him, until he suffered an end like that of the Lord.

Very shortly after Symeon of Jerusalem was martyred, Ignatius, the bishop of Antioch, was arrested and sent to Rome for execution in 108 C.E.[2] On the journey to Rome, Ignatius's guards allowed him to receive representatives from various local churches along the route and to send letters to these and other churches. Seven of these letters have survived.

> 3.2 Ignatius (died ca. 108 C.E.), *Epistle to the Romans* 4.1, 5.1–2 (ca. 108 C.E.)
> [4] I am corresponding with all the churches and bidding them all realize that I am voluntarily dying for God—if, that is, you do not interfere. I plead with you, do not do me an unseasonable kindness. Let me be fodder for wild beats—that is how I can get to God. I am God's wheat and I am being ground by the teeth of wild beasts to make a pure loaf for Christ. . . .
> [5] Even now as a prisoner, I am learning to forgo my own wishes. All the way from Syria to Rome I am fighting with wild beasts, by land and sea, night and day, chained as I am to ten leopards (I mean to a detachment of soldiers), who only get the worse the better you treat them. But by their injustice, I am becoming a better disciple, "though

---

2. The most commonly accepted date for Ignatius's martyrdom is 108 C.E., given by Eusebius. However, John Malalas, writing ca. 600 C.E., dated Ignatius's arrest to Trajan's visit to Antioch in 115 C.E.

not for that reason am I acquitted." [1 *Corinthians* 4.4] What a thrill I shall have from the wild beasts that are ready for me! I hope that they will make short work of me.

Epistle to The Philadelphians 10.1–2 (c.108 C.E.)

Thanks to your prayers and to the love that you have for me in Christ Jesus, news has reached me that the church at Antioch in Syria is at peace. Consequently, it would be a nice thing for you, as a church of God, to elect a deacon to go there on a mission, as God's representative, and at a formal service to congratulate them and glorify the Name. He who is privileged to perform such a ministry will enjoy the blessing of Jesus Christ, and you too will win glory. If you really want to do this for God's honor, it is not impossible, just as some of the churches in the vicinity have already sent bishops; others presbyters and deacons.

Just three or four years after Ignatius traveled to Rome and his martyrdom, a senior Roman official named Pliny the Younger (ca. 61–113 C.E.) wrote the emperor Trajan concerning "the Christian problem" in the provinces of Bithynia and Pontus, in the area of modern northwestern Turkey. Pliny's letter and the emperor Trajan's reply are perhaps the most important non-Christian texts on Christianity during its first two centuries, as the letters set forth what would become the official policy of the Roman Empire toward Christians throughout the second century and provide a precious view of the organization and forms of worship of an early Christian community.

3.3 Pliny The Younger, *Letters of Pliny*, 10.96 and 97 (ca. 111 C.E.)
Pliny to the Emperor Trajan:
It is with me, sir, an established custom to refer to you all matters on which I am in doubt; for who indeed is better able either to guide my uncertainty or instruct my ignorance? I have never been present at any trials of the Christians; therefore I do not know the methods or the limits to be observed either in examining or punishing them. Nor have my hesitations been slight, as to whether any difference is to be made on account of age, or no distinction allowed between the youngest and the adult; whether repentance admits to a pardon, or if a man has been once a Christian it avails him nothing to recant; whether the mere profession of the name itself, albeit without crimes, or only the crimes associated with the name, are punishable.
In the meanwhile, the method I have observed towards those who have been denounced to me as Christians is this: I asked them personally whether they were Christians; if they confessed it, I repeated the question a second and a third time, adding the threat of capital punishment; those who persisted, I ordered to be executed. I could at least feel no doubt that whatever the nature of their creed might be, pertinacity and inflexible obstinacy deserved chastisement. There

were others also possessed with the same infatuation, but being citizens of Rome, I added them to the list of persons to be sent to the City for trial.

These accusations spread—as is usually the case—from the mere fact of the matter being investigated and several forms of accusations came to light. A pamphlet was put out, without any signature, accusing a large number of persons by name. I thought it proper to discharge those who denied they were, or had ever been, Christians, who repeated after me an invocation to the gods, and offered adoration, with wine and incense, to your statute, which I had ordered to be brought for that purpose, together with those of the gods, and who finally cursed Christ—none of which acts it is said, those who are really Christians can be forced into performing. Others who were named by an informer at first confessed themselves Christians, and then denied it; true, they had been of the persuasion but they had quitted it, some three or more years ago—some even twenty years ago. They all worshiped your statute and the images of the gods, and cursed Christ.

They affirmed, however, the whole of their guilt, or their error, was that they were in the habit of meeting on a certain fixed day before it was light, when they sang in alternate verses songs to Christ, as to a god, and bound themselves by solemn oath, not to commit any wicked deeds, fraud, theft, or adultery, never to falsify their word, nor deny a trust when they should be called upon to deliver it up. After which it was their custom to separate, and then later reassemble to partake of food—but food of an ordinary and innocent kind. Even this practice, however, they had abandoned after the publication of my edict, by which, according to your orders, I had forbidden political associations [*hetaerias*]. I judged it so much the more necessary to seek the truth, with the assistance of torture, from two female slaves, who were styled deaconesses; but I could discover nothing more than depraved and excessive superstition.

I therefore adjourned the proceedings, and betook myself at once to your counsel. For the matter seemed to me well worth referring to you, because of the numbers endangered. Persons of all ages and classes, and of both sexes are, and will be, called into danger. Not only are the towns, but also the villages and rural districts are infected through contact with this wretched superstition; it seems possible, however, to check and cure it. It is certain at least that the temples, which had been almost deserted, begin now to be frequented; and the sacred festivals, after a long intermission, are again revived; while there is a general demand for sacrificial animals, which for some time past have met with but few purchasers. From this it is easy to imagine what multitudes may be reclaimed, if a door be left open to repentance.

The Emperor Trajan to Pliny:
You have followed the right course of procedure, my dear Secundus, in investigating the cases of those brought before you as Christians. It is not possible to lay down any general rule which can be applied as the fixed standard in all cases of this nature. No search should be made for these people; if they are brought before you and found guilty, they must be punished; with the restriction, however, that when the party denies himself to be a Christian, and shall give proof that he is not, by offering prayers to our gods, he shall be pardoned on the ground of repentance, even though he may have formerly incurred suspicion. But pamphlets without the accuser's name subscribed must not be admitted in evidence against anyone: that is the worst of precedents, and not in accord with the spirit of our age.

Pliny is one of the earliest known Roman officials to have shown any serious interest in learning about Christian belief and customs,[3] and his exchange of letters with Trajan contains the earliest Roman description of Christian worship services and ethical teachings. As a youth, Pliny was raised by his uncle Pliny the Elder, the greatest encyclopedist of the Roman Empire, and so it is not surprising that Pliny took an interest in the beliefs and rites of a strange new religious cult. Pliny's general position and status within Roman society can be seen in a memorial stele to Pliny found by archaeologists:

3.4 Pliny's Memorial Stele *Corpus Inscriptionum Latinarum* 5.2 (Berlin 1877) no. 5262
Gaius Plinius Caecilius Secundus, son of Lucius of the tribe Oufentina, consul; augur; praetorian commissioner with full consular power for the province of Pontus and Bithynia, sent to that province in accordance with the Senate's decree by the Emperor Nerva Trajan Augustus, victor over Germany and Dacia, the Father of his Country; curator of the bed and banks of the Tiber and sewers of Rome; official of the Treasury of Saturn; official of the military Treasury; praetor; tribune of the people; quaestor of the Emperor; commissioner for the Roman equestrians; military tribune of the Third Gallic Legion; magistrate on the board of Ten; left by will public baths at a cost of [...] and an additional 300,000 sesterces for furnishing them, with interest on 200,000 for their upkeep [...] and also to his city capital of 1,866,666 2/3 sesterces to support a hundred of his freedmen, and subsequently to provide an annual dinner for the people of

3. Acts contains two other early instances of Roman officials demonstrating an interest in Christian belief. Acts 13:4–12 (Selection 2.5) describes a meeting between Paul and Sergio Paulus, the Roman governor of Cyprus, and many historians suspect that the "most excellent Theophilus" to whom Acts is addressed was a high Roman official, since the only other use of "most excellent" in Acts is with reference to the Roman governor of Judaea.

the city [...] Likewise in his lifetime he gave 500,000 sesterces for the maintenance of boys and girls of the city, and also 100,000 for the upkeep of the library. . . .

It is indicative of the fundamental differences between modern Western culture and Roman culture that Pliny, a man of obvious social standing, education, and wealth who was concerned for the welfare of orphans and his freedmen and a generous contributor to public projects, could nonetheless summarily execute Christian provincial subjects for disrespect to his person and position ("pertinacity and inflexible obstinacy") even though he found no evidence of other crimes during his investigation.

The approach of Pliny and Trajan to the "Christian problem" seems to have been based on the belief that Christianity, while certainly a system of religious belief so reprehensible as to justify capital punishment for its mere profession, was not so serious a threat to Rome as to justify the social disruption that would result from searching out the Christians. Such a conclusion must admittedly interpret Pliny's statements as to the great numbers of Christians as mere literary license, but it is difficult to believe that Pliny would have suggested or Trajan would have adopted a passive approach if the "dangerous" Christians were really so numerous in Bithynia and Pontus as to be a meaningful threat to public order. Trajan's pragmatic response, which balanced the principle of Roman political supremacy against the desire not to cause unnecessary social turmoil, was not strictly logical, as was observed by the later Christian writer Tertullian (ca. 155–220 C.E.).

3.5 Tertullian, *Apology* 2.6–9 (ca. 197 C.E.)
And yet we find it is forbidden even to hunt us down. For when Plinius Secundus was governing his province and had condemned some Christians and driven others from their steadfastness, and still the sheer numbers concerned worried him as to what he ought to do thereafter, he consulted the Emperor Trajan. He asserted that, apart from an obstinacy that refused to sacrifice, he had learnt nothing about the Christian mysteries—nothing beyond meetings before dawn to sing to Christ and to God, and to band themselves together in discipline, forbidding murder, adultery, dishonesty, treachery, and the other crimes. Trajan replied in a rescript that men of this kind were not to be sought out, but if they were brought before Pliny they must be punished. What a decision, how inevitably entangled! He says they must not be sought out, implying that they are innocent; and he orders them to be punished, implying they are guilty. He spares them and he rages against them, he pretends not to see and punishes. Why cheat yourself with your judgment? If you condemn them, why not hunt them down? If you do not hunt them down, why not also acquit them? To track down bandits through all the provinces is a duty assigned by lot to the garrisons. Against those guilty of treason,

against public enemies, every man is a soldier; inquiry is extended to confederates, to accessories. The Christian alone may not be hunted down; but he may be haled before the magistrate; as if hunting down led to anything but haling to the court. So you condemn a man when haled to court—a man whom nobody wished to be sought out, who (I suppose) really has not deserved punishment because, he is guilty, but because, forbidden to be looked for, he was found!

THE LEGAL BASIS FOR THE PERSECUTION OF CHRISTIANS

The letters of Pliny and Trajan indicate that less than a century after the beginning of the Christian religion the Roman authorities treated the mere profession of Christianity as a capital offense. How this came about is one of the most important questions in the history of Christianity's relationship to the larger Graeco-Roman world.

Some historians have argued that the early trials of Christians were conducted by the Roman governors pursuant to a governor's inherent police power to maintain the public order, but this does not explain why the Christians were seen as a danger to the public order. Indeed, Pliny's letter explicitly stated that he discovered no criminal acts in his investigation, only an "excessive and depraved superstition." Moreover, it is difficult to believe that the Roman governors would have been interested in conducting any hearing, much less a capital trial, concerning the religious disputes of provincial subjects unless there were an official policy encouraging such investigations. Recall, for example, that the Roman governor Gallio refused to even hear the complaint of the Jews against Paul once he determined that the dispute involved religious beliefs (Selection 2.8). Thus, other historians have argued that there must have been a formal imperial edict against profession of the Christian faith. Pliny's statement that he was unfamiliar with the proper procedures to be followed because he had never attended any trials of the Christians could be interpreted to suggest that there was a more regular procedure than the ad hoc exercise of a governor's police power. However, Pliny was an experienced, knowledgeable lawyer and a senior member of Rome's governing elite, so his inquiry to Trajan concerning the proper procedures to be followed suggests that there was no officially promulgated policy or procedure. This latter view is strongly supported by Trajan's response to Pliny, which expressly stated that no fixed procedure could be prescribed for dealing with the Christians.

Even if this latter point is true, however, it still does not address why or when the profession of Christianity became a capital offense. Here the fragmentary nature of the evidence on Christianity in the first century C.E. creates a number of problems. There is no contemporary evidence concerning any Roman trials of Christians between Tacitus's account of Nero's persecution in 64 C.E. and Pliny's letter. Moreover, the relatively contemporary sources on Christianity in the first century C.E. did not explicitly address why Christians were unpopular, except for the statements of Tacitus and Suetonius that Christians deserved punishment for their "hatred of mankind" and "mischievous superstition."[4] However, these statements may reflect the attitudes of second-century Romans being read back into the first-century events. The significant clue as to why Christianity became a capital offense would seem to be found in the one question of Pliny that Trajan chose to answer. Pliny asked if repentance by a Christian would justify pardon, and Trajan responded "that when the party denies himself to be a Christian, and shall give proof that he is not, by offering prayers to our gods, he shall be pardoned on the ground of repentance, even though he may have formerly incurred suspicion." In the context of the two letters, the act of repentance, the offering of sacrifice to the Roman gods, was intended both to distinguish the Christian from the non-Christian and to allow the Christian to earn pardon by rectifying the refusal to honor the gods which constituted the offense in the first place.

To understand why the Christian refusal to pay homage to the Roman gods would rise to the level of a capital offense, one must understand that the Romans, like essentially all other Mediterranean peoples of the time, recognized no meaningful distinction between religion and politics. Roman literature is filled with assertions that their political and military success was directly dependent upon, and a sign of, the favor of the gods, which had been earned through Rome's careful and diligent efforts to propitiate the gods. Conversely, the same sources also emphasized that the failure to maintain such observances would inevitably provoke the gods to punish Rome.[5] Related to this was the Roman belief, shared by other ancient peoples, including the Jews, in the concept of a divine "trial by battle" in which the various gods proved their relative strength through the earthly victories of their respective followers. From the perspective of both the Romans and their subject peoples, the refusal to honor the Roman gods, particularly if such refusal were based on the worship of a competing god, as with the Christians, was a more or less explicit rejection of and challenge to Roman sovereignty. Thus, religious opposition to the Roman gods would cause the Romans to suspect political opposition to Roman rule that might lead to open revolt, if an opportunity arose. This is precisely the situation reflected at the start of the First Jewish War, when the decision of the Jewish Temple officials in 66 C.E. to stop offering sacrifices to God on behalf of the Roman emperors was understood by both the Romans and the Jews to be the functional equivalent of a Jewish declaration of war against Rome (See Selection A–6 in Appendix A.). That the Romans saw the Christian refusal to honor the Roman gods as a political as well as a religious statement becomes clearer in the later second- and third-century C.E. sources, where the key issue at the trials of the Christians was invariably the demand that the Christians sacrifice to the Roman emperor as well as to the Roman gods.

---

4. See selections 2.15 and 2.16.

5. Robin Lane Fox, *Pagans and Christians* (New York: Alfred A. Knopf, Inc. 1986), 425–26; Jo Ann Shelton, *As the Romans Did* (New York: Oxford University Press, 1988), 360–61, 371–73.

Still unresolved, however, is the issue of exactly when the proscription of the Christian faith was first adopted. While Christians were persecuted under Nero as the scapegoats for the Great Fire and the Apostles Paul and Peter were executed about the same time, there is no relatively contemporary evidence that Nero made the profession of Christianity per se a capital offense at that time. (However, the early fifth century C.E. Christian account of the persecution found in the *Chronicle* of Sulpicius Severus states that the formal prosecution of Christianity began under Nero after the Great Fire.) If we examine the extant sources concerning the acts of the emperors after Nero, we find no clearer evidence on point. Eusebius wrote that the emperor Vespasian (69–79 C.E.) did not persecute Christians during his reign (Selection 2.21). There is no evidence to indicate that either Titus (79–81 C.E.) or Nerva (96–98 C.E.) adopted such a policy during their short reigns. Thus, it appears that after Nero only the emperors Domitian (81–96 C.E.) and Trajan (98–117 C.E.) could be the possible originators of such a policy. There was a Christian tradition that Domitian persecuted the faith and if such a persecution did occur it might have been either the cause or the result of a proscription of Christianity. Further, while there were at least localized persecutions of Christians during Trajan's reign, Trajan's response to Pliny, with its emphasis on restricting searches and encouraging pardon, seems more of pro forma reaffirmation of an existing practice than the follow-through of an emperor who instituted the policy in question. Also, we noted in chapter 2 that the Christian authors of various of the first-century New Testament Gospels and The Acts of the Apostles took great care to assert that Christians were loyal to Rome and that any Roman official who had examined Christianity had found nothing worthy of condemnation. If, as many historians believe, Matthew, Luke, and The Acts of the Apostles were written during Domitian's reign, the emphasis on Christian loyalty found in these works may reflect a Christian response to new imperial measures against the faith. Cumulatively, therefore, the evidence suggests that the practice of treating the profession of Christianity as a capital offense dates to the reign of Domitian, but, as is true of so much of the history of early Christianity, there is simply insufficient evidence to assert this conclusion with certainty.

While Pliny's letter is the earliest account of a Roman trial of Christians outside of the New Testament, there are fairly numerous accounts of such trials from later in the second century. In these later accounts, the Roman officials, like Pliny, more or less uniformly asked the Christians to confirm or deny their faith before judgment was passed and granted pardon to each Christian who recanted and sacrificed to the Roman gods. It is likely that this procedure of inquiry and pardon became common practice precisely because of the exchange of letters between Pliny and Trajan, as we know that the Roman emperors maintained imperial archives of important policy letters and edicts for reference by subsequent emperors and provincial governors.[6]

---

6. Fergus Millar, *The Emperor in the Roman World* (Ithaca: Cornell University Press, 1992), 259–72.

The capital punishment inflicted on Christians who refused to worship the pagan gods or the Roman emperor was certainly good cause for Christians to strive to reverse this policy by convincing Rome of their loyalty. Christian polemical writings of the second century C.E. consistently asserted that Christians were loyal to Rome and the emperor, even if Christians would not worship Rome's gods or emperor. The Christian emphasis on this profession of loyalty is apparent in an early Christian letter, probably written within a decade or so of the letters between Pliny and Trajan, addressed to Christians living in the very same provinces of Bithynia and Pontus.

> 3.6 2 Peter 1:1; 2:12–14 (written late first or early second century C.E.[7])
> [1.1] Peter, an Apostle of Jesus Christ, to the exiles of the Dispersion in Pontus, Galatia, Cappadocia, Asia and Bithynia. . . .
> [2.12] Maintain good conduct towards the Gentiles, so that in case they speak against you as wrongdoers, they may see your good deeds and glorify God on the day of visitation. Be subject for the Lord's sake to every human institution, whether it be to the emperor as supreme, or to governors as sent by him to punish those who do wrong and to praise those who do right.

THE "CHRISTIAN PROBLEM" AFTER TRAJAN

The "Christian problem" continued after Trajan's death, with sporadic localized persecutions during the reigns of Hadrian, Antoninus Pius, and Marcus Aurelius. The emperors of the second century C.E. consistently followed Trajan's policy of not searching for the Christians and punishing them only if brought to trial, but there seem to have been many people willing to bring such charges.

> 3.7 *Letter To Diognetus* 5.11–17 (ca. 120s C.E.) This anonymous Christian work is sometimes attributed to Quadratus of Asia Minor.
> [The Christians] love all men, and by all men are persecuted. They are unknown, and still they are condemned; they are put to death, and yet they are brought to life. They are poor, and yet they make many rich; they are completely destitute, and yet they enjoy complete abundance. They are dishonored, and in their very dishonor are glorified; they are defamed, and are vindicated. They are reviled, and yet they bless; when they are affronted, they still pay due respect. When they do good, they are punished as evildoers; undergoing punishment, they rejoice because they are brought to life. They are treated by the Jews as foreigners and enemies, and are hunted down

---

7. Most historians believe that 2 Peter is pseudo-epigraphic and dates to at least a generation after Peter's death. Some historians accept the traditional Christian attribution of this letter to Peter himself and therefore date the letter no later than about 64 C.E. If this early dating is correct, then the letter would be further evidence that the Christians were unpopular among the masses from an early date.

by the Greeks; and all the time those who hate them find it impossible to justify their enmity.

Even if the official Roman policy was not to conduct active searches for Christians, Christians were always subject to being reported to the local Roman authorities by their neighbors. By the early second century C.E., most people undoubtedly understood that the charge of being a Christian meant serious trouble for the accused. People being what they are, it appears that at least some individuals were willing to accuse neighbors of being Christians in order to harass social, economic, or political rivals in much the same way as charges of witchcraft or communism have been used in more modern societies. Such conduct is certainly what is implied by an edict issued by the emperor Hadrian.

3.8 Rescript Of The Emperor Hadrian (Publius Aelius Hadrianus, Emperor 117–138 C.E.) as quoted by Eusebius in *Ecclesiastical History* 4.9.
To C. Minucius Fundanus [Proconsul of Asia, ca. 124/125 C.E.]
I received a letter written to me from his Excellency Serenius Granianus, your predecessor. I think that the matter ought not to remain without inquiry, to prevent men from being harassed or helping the rascality of informers. If then the provincials can make out a clear case on these lines against the Christians so as to plead it in open court, let them be influenced by this alone and not by opinions or mere outcries. For it is far more correct if anyone wishes to make an accusation for you to examine this point. If then anyone accuses them, and shows that they are acting illegally, decide the point according to the nature of the offense, but by Hercules, if any one brings the matter forward for the purpose of blackmail, investigate strenuously and be careful to inflict penalties adequate to the crime.

While the exact intent of Hadrian's letter has been the subject of some debate among historians, the simplest and most straight forward interpretation is to see it as a reaffirmation of Trajan's policy: the profession of Christianity was still a punishable crime, but like other crimes it had to be proven in open court in accordance with the applicable law. However, the letter also indicates that the accusation that a person was a Christian might be used for purposes of "blackmail," the Greek could also mean "slander" or "false accusation," and that Hadrian wanted any such abuse of the legal system strenuously punished.

Somewhat later in Hadrian's reign, during the period of approximately 132–135 C.E., the Jews of Palestine rose again in revolt against Rome in what is known as the Second Jewish War. The sources for the Second Jewish War are fragmentary, but it is clear that Rome brutally suppressed the rebellion. Before the final collapse of the rebellion it appears that the Jewish leaders took punitive measures against the Christians of Palestine, perhaps for religious reasons but perhaps also out of frustration and anger that the Christians generally refused to join Jews in fighting Rome.

3.9 Justin Martyr, *The First Apology* 31 (ca. 155 C.E.)

> ... [Jews] consider us their enemies and opponents, putting us to death
> or punishing us, as you do, whenever they can, as you can realize—
> for in the Jewish War recently past Bar-Cochba, the leader of the
> revolt of the Jews, ordered Christians only to be subjected to terrible
> punishments, unless they would deny Jesus the Christ and blas-
> pheme [him].

The sporadic persecutions and martyrdoms of Christians during the first
half of the second century C.E. did not go entirely unnoticed by the social and
political elite of the Roman Empire. By 110–130 C.E. Roman historians like
Tacitus and Suetonius were mentioning incidents between the Roman government and Christians, an indication of the growing awareness of the new faith.
At approximately the same time, a famous pagan philosopher made reference
to Christianity in such a way as to indicate that Christians were also earning a
reputation for steadfastness in the face of death.

3.10 Epictetus, *Discourses* 4.7.1–6[8] (published after death by his pupil
Arrian)

> If then a man whose will is not set on dying or living, but who is con-
> tent with what is given him, comes before the Tyrant, what prevents
> him from coming without fear? Nothing. Now suppose a man is of
> the same mind in regard to property as this man in regard to his
> body; suppose he feels the same about wife and children. Suppose, in
> a word, he is so distracted and desperate that he regards it as indif-
> ferent whether he has these things are not. . . . How can any tyrant,
> how can any guards or swords inspire fear in such a one? Yet if mad-
> ness can produce this attitude of mind, if even habit can produce it
> in the Galilaeans, can reason and demonstration teach no one that
> God has made all things in the world, and the world itself as a whole
> to have its own end without hinderance, but its individual parts to
> subserve the whole?

In response to the animosity of many local peoples and the official disapproval of Roman policy, a number of second-century Christians wrote literary
defenses of the Christian faith, known as "apologies." The apology was a long-
established classical literary form and today it is difficult to determine whether
such works were ever actually sent to the emperors in question, much less
whether any emperor bothered to read such a work. Yet, the circulation of these
apologies provided a means by which educated Christians could defend and
justify their faith to the literate, upper classes of the Roman Empire and thus

---

8. A second possible reference to Christians occurs at *Discourses* 2.9.16–22, but such a conclusion would require assuming that Epictetus has mistakenly referred to Jews when he meant
"Gallileans."

marked an important early step in the Christian effort to find acceptance for their faith within the larger society. The earliest complete apology to have survived was written by Justin, a Christian who lived in Rome.

3.11 Justin Martyr, *The First Apology* 1–5 (written ca. 155 C.E.)

[1] To the Emperor Titus Aelius Hadrianus Antoninus Pius Augustus Caesar, and to Verissimus his son [Marcus Aurelius], the Philosopher, and to Lucius [Verus] the Philosopher, son of Caesar by nature and of Augustus by adoption, a lover of culture, and to the Sacred Senate and the whole Roman people—on behalf of men of every nation who are unjustly hated and reviled, I, Justin, son of Priscus and grandson of Bacchius, of Flavia Neapolis in Syria Palestina, being myself one of them, have drawn up this plea and petition.

[2] Reason requires that those who are truly pious and philosophers should honor and cherish the truth alone, scorning merely to follow the opinions of the ancients, if they are worthless. Nor does sound reason only require that one should not follow those who do or teach what is unjust; the lover of truth ought to choose in every way, even at the cost of his own life, to speak and do what is right, though death should take him away. So do you, since you are called pious and philosophers and guardians of justice and lovers of culture, at least give us a hearing—and it will appear if you are really such. For in these pages we do not come before you with flattery, or as if making a speech to win your favor, but asking you to give judgment according to strict and exact inquiry—not moved by prejudice or respect for superstitious men, or by irrational impulse and long-established evil rumor, giving a vote which would really be against yourselves. For we are firmly convinced that we can suffer no evil unless we are proved to be evildoers or shown to be criminals. You can kill us, but cannot do us any real harm.

[3] But so that no one may think that this is an unreasonable and presumptuous utterance, we ask that the charges against us be investigated. If they are shown to be true, [let us] be punished as is proper. But if nobody has proofs against us, true reason does not allow [you] to wrong innocent men because of an evil rumor—or rather [to wrong] yourselves when you decide to pass sentence on the basis of passion rather than judgment....

[4] The mere ascription of a name means nothing, good or bad, except for the actions connected with the name. Indeed as far as the name charged against us goes, we are very gracious people. But we do not think it right to ask for a pardon because of the name if we are proved to be criminals—and on the other hand, if neither the appellation of the name nor our conduct shows us to be wrongdoers, you must face the problem whether in punishing unjustly men against

whom nothing is proved you will yourselves owe a penalty to justice. Neither reward nor punishment should follow from a name unless something admirable or evil can actually be shown about it. Among yourselves you do not penalize the accused before conviction; but with us you take the name as proof, although, as far as the name goes, you ought rather to punish our accusers. For we are accused of being Christians; and it is not right to hate graciousness. Again, if one of the accused denies the charge, saying he is not [a Christian], you dismiss him, as having no proof of misconduct against him; but if he confesses that he is one, you punish him because of his confession. You ought rather to investigate the life of the confessor and the renegade, so that it would appear from their actions what sort of person each is. . . .

[5] What can all this mean? You do not make judicial inquiries in our case, though we are bound neither to commit crimes nor to hold such godless ideas. Instead, you punish us injudicially without deliberation, driven by unreasoning passion and the whips of evil demons. The truth must be told. . . .

In almost the same year as Justin's *Apology*, another persecution of Christians took place in the province of Asia, modern southwestern Turkey. The following letter from the church of Smyrna in Asia described the martyrdom of their bishop Polycarp (ca. 156 C.E.) during the reign of the Emperor Antoninus Pius (138–161 C.E.) and gave vivid evidence of the extent of popular animosity towards the Christians.

3.12 The Martyrdom Of Polycarp (ca. 156 C.E.)

The church of God that sojourns at Smyrna to the church of God that sojourns at Philomelium, and to all those of the holy and Catholic Church who sojourn in every place: may mercy, peace, and love be multiplied from God the Father and our Lord Jesus Christ.

[1] We write you, brethren, the things concerning those who suffered martyrdom, especially the blessed Polycarp, who put an end to the persecution by sealing it, so to speak, through his own witness. For almost everything that led up to it happened in order that the Lord might show once again a martyrdom conformable to the gospel. For he waited to be betrayed, just as the Lord did, to the end that we also might be imitators of him, "not looking only to that which concerns ourselves, but also to that which concerns our neighbors." For it is a mark of true and steadfast love for one not only to desire to be saved oneself, but all the brethren also.

[2] Blessed and noble, indeed, are all the martyrdoms that have taken place according to God's will; for we ought to be very reverent in ascribing to God power over all things. For who would not admire their nobility and patient endurance and love of their Master? Some

of them, so torn by scourging that the anatomy of their flesh was visible as far as the inner veins and arteries, endured with such patience that even the bystanders took pity and wept; others achieved such heroism that not one of them uttered a cry or a groan, thus showing all of us that at the very hour of their tortures the most noble martyrs of Christ were no longer in the flesh, but rather that the Lord stood by them and conversed with them. And giving themselves over to the grace of Christ they despised the tortures of this world, purchasing for themselves in the space of one hour the life eternal. To them the fire of their inhuman tortures was cold; for they set before their eyes escape from the fire that is everlasting and never quenched, while with the eyes of their heart they gazed upon the good things reserved for those that endure patiently, "which things neither ear has heard nor eye has seen, nor has there entered into the heart of man." But they were shown to them by the Lord, for they were no longer men, but were already angels. Similarly, those condemned to the wild beasts endured fearful punishments, being made to lie on sharp shells and punished with other forms of various torments, in order that [the devil] might bring them, if possible, by means of the prolonged punishment, to a denial of their faith.

[3] Many, indeed, were the machinations of the devil against them. But, thanks be to God, he did not prevail against them all. For the most noble Germanicus encouraged their timidity through his own patient endurance—who also fought with the beasts in a distinguished way. For when the proconsul wishing to persuade him, bade him have pity on his youth, he forcibly dragged the wild beast toward himself, wishing to obtain more quickly a release from their wicked and lawless life. From this circumstance, all the crowd, marveling at the heroism of the God-loving and God-fearing race of the Christians, shouted: "Away with the atheists! Make search for Polycarp!"

[4] But a Phrygian, named Quintus, lately arrived from Phrygia, took fright when he saw the wild beasts. In fact, he was the one who had forced himself and some others to come forward voluntarily. The proconsul by much entreaty persuaded him to take the oath and to offer the sacrifice. For this reason, therefore, brethren, we do not praise those who come forward of their own accord, since the gospel does not teach us so to do.

[5] The most admirable Polycarp, when he first heard of it, was not perturbed, but desired to remain in the city. But the majority induced him to withdraw, so he retired to a farm not far from the city and there stayed with a few friends, doing nothing else night and day but pray for all men and for the churches through out the world, as was his constant habit. And while he was praying, it so happened, three days before his arrest, that he had a vision and saw his pillow blazing

with fire, and turning to those who were with him he said, "I must be burned alive."

⁶ And while those who were searching for him continued their quest, he moved to another farm, and forthwith those searching for him arrived. And when they did not find him, they seized two young slaves, one of whom confessed under torture. For it was really impossible to conceal him, since the very ones who betrayed him were of his own household. And the chief of the police, who chanced to have the same name as Herod, was zealous to bring him into the arena in order that he might fulfill his own appointed lot of being made a partaker with Christ; while those who betrayed him should suffer the punishment of Judas himself.

⁷ Taking, therefore, the young slave on Friday about supper time, the police, mounted and with their customary arms, set out as though "hasting after a robber." And late in the evening they came up with him and found him in bed in the upper room of a small cottage. Even so he could have escaped to another farm, but he did not wish to do so, saying, "God's will be done." Thus, when he heard of their arrival, he went downstairs and talked with them, while those who looked on marveled at his age and constancy, and at how there should be such zeal over the arrest of so old a man. Straightway he ordered food and drink, as much as they wished, to be set before them at that hour, and he asked them to give him an hour so that he might pray undisturbed. And when they consented, he stood and prayed—being so filled with the grace of God that for two hours he could not hold his peace, to the amazement of those who heard. And many repented that they had come to get such a devout old man.

⁸ When at last he had finished his prayer, in which he remembered all who had met with him at any time, both small and great, both those with and those without renown, and the whole Catholic Church through out the world, the hour of departure having come they mounted him on an ass and brought him into the city. It was a great Sabbath. And there the chief of the police, Herod, and his father, Nicetas, met him and transferred him to their carriage, and tried to persuade him, as they sat beside him, saying, "What harm is there to say 'Lord Caesar,' and to offer incense and all that sort of thing, and to save yourself?"

At first he did not answer them. But when they persisted, he said, "I am not going to do what you advise me."

Then when they failed to persuade him, they uttered dire threats and made him get out with such speed that in dismounting from the carriage he bruised his shin. But without turning around, as though nothing had happened, he proceeded swiftly, and was led into the arena, there being such a tumult in the arena that no one could be heard.

⁹ But as Polycarp was entering the arena, a voice from heaven came to him, saying, "Be strong, Polycarp, and play the man." No one saw the one speaking, but those of our people who were present heard the voice.

And when finally he was brought up, there was a great tumult on hearing that Polycarp had been arrested. Therefore, when he was brought before him, the proconsul asked him if he were Polycarp. And when he confessed that he was, he tried to persuade him to deny [the faith], saying, "Have respect to your age—and other things that customarily follow this, such as, "Swear by the fortune of Caesar; change your mind; say, 'Away with the atheists!'"

But Polycarp looked with earnest face at the whole crowd of lawless heathen in the arena, and motioned to them with his hand. Then, groaning and looking up to heaven, he said, "Away with the atheists!"

But the proconsul was insistent and said: "Take the oath, and I shall release you. Curse Christ."

Polycarp said: "Eighty-six years I have served him, and he never did me any wrong. How can I blaspheme my King who saved me?" ¹⁰ And upon his persisting still and saying, "Swear by the fortune of Caesar," he answered, "If you vainly suppose that I shall swear by the fortune of Caesar, as you say, and pretend that you do not know who I am, listen plainly: I am a Christian. But if you desire to learn the teaching of Christianity, appoint a day and give me a hearing."
The proconsul said, "Try to persuade the people."

But Polycarp said, "You, I should deem worthy of an account; for we have been taught to render honor, as is befitting, to rulers and authorities appointed by God so far as it does us no harm; but as for these, I do not consider them worthy that I should make defense to them." ¹¹ But the proconsul said: "I have wild beasts. I shall throw you to them, if you do not change your mind."

But he said: "Call them. For repentance from the better to the worse is not permitted us; but it is noble to change from what is evil to what is righteous."

And again [he said] to him, "I shall have you consumed with fire, if you despise the wild beasts, unless you change your mind."

But Polycarp said: "The fire you threaten burns but an hour and is quenched after a little; for you do not know the fire of the coming judgment and everlasting punishment that is laid up for the impious. But why do you delay? Come, do what you will." ¹² And when he had said these things and many more besides he was inspired with courage and joy, and his face was full of grace, so that not only did it not fall with dismay at the things said to him, but on the contrary, the proconsul was astonished, and sent his own herald into the midst of the arena to proclaim three times: "Polycarp has confessed himself to be a Christian."

When this was said by the herald, the entire crowd of heathen and Jews who lived in Smyrna shouted with uncontrollable anger and a great cry: "This one is the teacher of Asia, the father of the Christians, the destroyer of our gods, who teaches many not to sacrifice nor to worship."

Such things they shouted and asked the Asiarch Philip that he let loose a lion on Polycarp. But he said it was not possible for him to do so, since he had brought the wild-beast Sports to a close. Then they decided to shout with one accord that he burn Polycarp alive. For it was necessary that the vision which had appeared to him about his pillow should be filled, when he saw it burning while he was praying, and turning around had said prophetically to the faithful who were with him, "I must be burned alive."

[13] Then these things happened with such dispatch, quicker than can be told—the crowds in so great a hurry to gather wood and faggots from the workshops and the baths, the Jews being especially zealous, as usual, to assist with this. When the fire was ready, and he had divested himself of all his clothes and unfastened his belt, he tried to take off his shoes, though he was not heretofore in the habit of doing this because [each of] the faithful always vied with one another as to which of them would be first to touch his body. For he had always been honored, even before his martyrdom, for his holy life. Straightway then, they set about him the material prepared for the pyre. And when they were about to nail him also, he said: "Leave me as I am. For he who grants me to endure the fire will enable me also to remain on the pyre unmoved, without the security you desire from the nails."

[14] So they did not nail him, but tied him. And with his hands put behind him and tied, like a noble ram out of a great flock ready for sacrifice, a burnt offering ready and acceptable to God, he looked up to heaven and said: "Lord God Almighty, Father of thy beloved and blessed Servant Jesus Christ, through whom we have received full knowledge of thee, the God of angels and powers and all creation and of the whole race of the righteous who live in thy presence: I bless thee, because thou hast deemed me worthy of this day and hour, to take my part in the number of the martyrs, in the cup of thy Christ, for resurrection to eternal life of soul and body in the immortality of the Holy Spirit; among whom may I be received in thy presence this day as a rich and acceptable sacrifice, just as thou hast prepared and revealed beforehand and fulfilled, thou that art the true God without any falsehood. For this and for everything I praise thee, I bless thee, I glorify thee, through the eternal and heavenly High Priest, Jesus Christ, thy beloved Servant, through whom be glory to thee with him and Holy Spirit both now and unto the ages to come. Amen."

¹⁵ And when he had concluded the Amen and finished his prayer, the men attending to the fire lighted it. And when the flame flashed forth, we saw a miracle, we to whom it was given to see. And we are preserved in order to relate to the rest what happened. For the fire made the shape of a vaulted chamber, like a ship's sail filled by the wind, and made a wall around the body of the martyr. And he was in the midst, not as burning flesh, but as bread baking or as gold and silver refined in a furnace. And we perceived such a sweet aroma as the breath of incense or some other precious spice.

¹⁶ At length, when the lawless men saw that his body could not be consumed by the fire, they commanded an executioner to go to him and stab him with a dagger. And when he did this [a dove and*] a great quantity of blood came forth, so that the fire was quenched and the whole crowd marveled that there should be such a difference between the unbelievers and the elect. And certainly the most admirable Polycarp was one of these [elect], in whose times among us he showed himself an apostolic and prophetic teacher and bishop of the Catholic Church in Smyrna. Indeed, every utterance that came from his mouth was accomplished and will be accomplished.

*[*This phrase is probably a later insertion into the text.]*

¹⁷ But the jealous and malicious evil one, the adversary of the race of the righteous, seeing the greatness of his martyrdom and his blameless life from the beginning, and how he was crowned with the wreath of immortality and had borne away an incontestable reward, so contrived it that his corpse should not be taken away by us, although many desired to do this and to have fellowship with his holy flesh. He instigated Nicetas, the father of Herod and brother of Alce, to plead with the magistrate not to give up his body, "else," said he, "they will abandon the Crucified and begin worshiping this one." This was done at the instigation and insistence of the Jews, who also watched when we were going to take him from the fire, being ignorant that we can never forsake Christ, who suffered for the salvation of the whole world of those who are saved, the faultless for the sinners, nor can we ever worship any other. For we worship this One as Son of God, but we love the martyrs as disciples and imitators of the Lord, deservedly so, because of their unsurpassable devotion to their own King and Teacher. May it be also our lot to be their companions and fellow disciples!

¹⁸ The captain of the Jews, when he saw their contentiousness, set it [his body] in the midst and burned it, as was their custom. So we later took up his bones, more precious than costly stones and more valuable than gold, and laid them away in a suitable place. There the Lord will permit us, so far as possible, to gather together in joy and gladness to celebrate the day of his martyrdom as a birthday, in

memory of those athletes who have gone before, and to train and make ready those who are to come hereafter.

[19] Such are the things concerning the blessed Polycarp, who, martyred at Smyrna along with twelve others from Philadelphia, is alone remembered so much the more by everyone, that he is even spoken of by the heathen in every place. He was not only a noble teacher, but also a distinguished martyr, whose martyrdom all desire to imitate as one according to the gospel of Christ. By his patient endurance he overcame the wicked magistrate and so received the crown of immortality; and he rejoices with the apostles and all the righteous to glorify God the Father Almighty and to bless our Lord Jesus Christ, the Savior of our souls and Helmsman of our bodies and Shepherd of the Catholic Church throughout the world.

[20] You requested, indeed, that these things be related to you more fully, but for the present we have briefly reported them through our brother Marcion. When you have informed yourselves of these things, send this letter to the brethren elsewhere, in order that they too might glorify the Lord, who makes his choices from his own servants. To him who is able by his grace and bounty to bring us to his everlasting Kingdom, through his Servant, the only-begotten Jesus Christ, be glory, honor, might, majesty, throughout the ages. Greet all the saints. Those with us greet you and also Evarestus, who wrote this, with his whole household.

[21] The blessed Polycarp was martyred on the second day of the first part of the month Xanthicus, the seventh day before the kalends of March, a great Sabbath, at two o'clock P.M. He was arrested by Herod, when Philip of Tralles was high priest, and Statius Quadratus was proconsul, but in the everlasting reign of our Lord Jesus Christ. To him be glory, honor, majesty and the eternal throne, from generation to generation. Amen.

[22] We bid you farewell, brethren, as you live by the word of Jesus Christ according to the gospel, with whom be glory to God the Father and Holy Spirit, unto the salvation of his holy elect; just as the blessed Polycarp suffered martyrdom, in whose footsteps may it be our lot to be found in the Kingdom of Jesus Christ.

Colophon From The Main Manuscript Tradition

These things Gaius copied from the papers of Irenaeus, a disciple of Polycarp; he also lived with Irenaeus. And Isocrates, wrote it in Corinth from the copy of Gaius. Grace be with all.

I, Pionius, again wrote it from the aforementioned copy, having searched for it according to a revelation of the blessed Polycarp, who appeared to me, as I shall explain in the sequel. I gathered it together when it was almost worn out with age, in order that the Lord Jesus

Christ might bring me also with his elect unto his heavenly
Kingdom. To him be glory with the Father and Holy Spirit unto the
ages of ages. Amen.

Colophon From The Moscow Manuscript

These things Gaius copied from the papers of Irenaeus. He also lived
with Irenaeus, who had been a disciple of the holy Polycarp. For this
Irenaeus at the time of the martyrdom of Bishop Polycarp, was in
Rome and taught many; and many of his excellent and orthodox
writings are in circulation, in which he mentions Polycarp, for he was
taught by him. He ably refuted every heresy and handed down the
ecclesiastical and Catholic rule, as he had received it from the saint.
He says this also: that once when Marcion, after whom the
Marcionites are called, met the holy Polycarp and said, "Do you
know us, Polycarp?" he said to Marcion, "I know you; I know the
first-born of Satan." And this fact is also found in the writings of
Irenaeus, that on the day and at the hour when Polycarp was martyred in Smyrna, Irenaeus, being in the city of Rome, heard a voice
like a trumpet saying, "Polycarp has suffered martyrdom."

From these papers of Irenaeus, then, as was said above, Gaius
made a copy, and from Gaius's copy Isocrates made another in
Corinth. And I, Pionius, again from the copies of Isocrates wrote
according to the revelation of holy Polycarp, when I searched for it,
and gathered it together when it was almost worn out with age, in
order that the Lord Jesus Christ might bring me with his elect unto
his heavenly Kingdom. To whom be glory with the Father and the
Son and the Holy Spirit unto the ages of ages. Amen.

Polycarp may have been the victim of an unauthorized search by local officials, as embarrassment over an illegal seizure by the local town officials is one
possible explanation for the Proconsul Statius Quadratus's apparent pretense of
not knowing that Polycarp was brought before him as a Christian. In his
Ecclesiastical History Eusebius preserved an alleged rescript of the emperor
Antoninus Pius rebuking the local officials in Asia for their conduct in this affair.

3.13 Recript Of Antoninus Pius (161 C.E.) (qtd. by Eusebius *Ecclesiastical
History* 4.13.1–7)

The Emperor Caesar Marcus Aurelius Antoninus Augustus Armenicus,
Pontifex Maximus, Tribune for the fifteenth time, Consul for the third
time, to the Council of Asia, greeting. I know that the gods also take
care that such men should not escape notice, for they would be far
more likely to punish those who are unwilling to worship them than
you are. But you drive them into tumult, for you confirm them in the
opinion which they hold by accusing them as atheists, and they too
when so accused might well prefer apparent death rather than life for

the sake of their own God. Wherefore they are also conquerors because they sacrifice their lives rather than obey and do what you command. With regard to the earthquakes which have taken place and are still going on it is not out of place to remind you that when they happen you are depressed, and so set up a comparison between our position and theirs. They obtain increased confidence towards God, but you the whole of the time neglect the other gods and the worship of the immortal. But when Christians worship him you harry and persecute them to death. And many of the provincial governors wrote formerly on behalf of such men to our divine father, and he replied that they were not to be interfered with unless they appeared to be plotting against the Roman government. And to me also many reported about such men, and to them I too replied consistently with my father's opinion. But if anyone persist in taking action against any one of such persons, on the ground that he is so, let that one who is accused be released from the charge, even if it appear that he is such, but the accuser shall be liable to penalty. Published at Ephesus in the Council of Asia.

The greater weight of historical opinion is that this rescript is a later Christian forgery, but some historians have argued that it represents an authentic rescript altered by later Christians and that the local community leaders of Asia were indeed chastised for stirring up anti-Christian sentiment, presumably to calm the local population after the series of earthquakes mentioned in the letter, and for allowing official searches to be carried out for Christians, in contradiction of the policy established by Trajan.[9]

The Martyrdom of Polycarp stated that the populace of Smyrna was angered by the fact that the bishop Polycarp was "the destroyer of our gods, who teaches many not to sacrifice nor to worship." Such a charge was often summed up by the pagan accusation that Christians were "atheists." While a charge of atheism sounds peculiar to modern ears, pagans were truly shocked by the Christian denial of the divine powers that pagans perceived to be a constant part of everyday life. Moreover, the Christian refusal to acknowledge the old gods was also perceived as dangerous to the local communities, since the pagan gods were thought to punish with natural disasters and war those peoples who did not acknowledge their power. The popular perception that Christians were "destroyers of our gods," or worse, can be found in several popular literary works from this period.

3.14 Lucian, *Alexander the False Prophet* 25, 38 (ca. 180 C.E.) These events took place in the reign of Antoninus Pius (138–161 C.E.).

9. See, for example, Marta Sordi, *The Christians and the Roman Empire* (Norman: University of Oklahoma Press, 1994), 69–70.

[25] When at last many sensible men, recovering, as it were, from profound intoxication, combined against him [Alexander], especially all the followers of Epicurus, and when in the cities they began gradually to detect all the trickery and buncombe of the show, he issued a promulgation designed to scare them, saying that Pontus was full of atheists and Christians who had the hardihood to utter the vilest abuse of him; these he bade them drive away with stones if they wanted to have the god gracious. . . .

[38] He established a celebration of the mysteries, with torchlight ceremonies and priestly offices, which was to be held annually, for three days in succession, in perpetuity. On the first day, as at Athens, there was a proclamation, worded as follows: "If any atheist or Christian or Epicurean has come to spy upon the rites, let him be off, and let those who believe in the god perform the mysteries, under the blessing of Heaven." Then, at the very outset, there was an "expulsion," in which he took the lead, saying, "Out with the Christians," and the whole multitude chanted in response, "Out with the Epicureans!"

3.15 Apuleius, *Metamorphoses, or The Golden Ass* 9.14 (perhaps ca. 160 C.E.)

The baker who purchased me was otherwise a good and very modest man but his wife was the wickedest of all women and he suffered extreme miseries to his bed and his house so that I myself, by Hercules, often in secret felt pity for him. There was not one single vice which that woman lacked, but all crimes flowed together into her heart as into a filthy latrine; cruel, perverse, man-crazy, drunken, stubborn, obstinate, avaricious in petty theft, wasteful in sumptuous expenses, an enemy to faith and chastity, she also despised the gods and instead of a certain religion she claimed to worship a god whom she called "only." In his honor she practiced empty rites and ceremonies and she deceived all men and her miserable husband, drinking unmixed wine early in the morning and giving up her body to continual whoring.[10]

Even where Christians enjoyed widespread acceptance they always faced the risk of being brought up on charges by a single neighbor and thus always had to live with the threat of arrest and trial. This is perhaps what happened to Justin of Rome, who less than a decade after he wrote his *First Apology* to the emperor Antoninus Pius was arrested and executed for being a Christian.

10. While here the woman could be seen as either Jewish or Christian simply on the basis of her monotheism, the fact that she practiced "empty rites and ceremonies" and drank wine early in the morning (a possible reference to the Eucharist, recall Pliny the Younger's statement that the Christians met early in the morning for worship) leads many historians to believe that a Christian was meant. As discussed in Appendix B, the references to her sexual practices would also support such an interpretation.

3.16 The Martyrdom Of Justin (concerning events in 165 C.E.)

[1] In the time of the lawless partisans of idolatry, wicked decrees were passed against the godly Christians in town and country, to force them to offer libations to vain idols; and accordingly the holy men, having been apprehended, were brought before the prefect of Rome, Rusticus by name. And when they had been brought before his judgment-seat, Rusticus the prefect said to Justin, "Obey the gods at once, and submit to the kings." Justin said, "To obey the commandments of our Savior Jesus Christ is worthy neither of blame nor of condemnation." Rusticus the prefect said, "What kind of doctrines do you profess?" Justin said, "I have endeavored to learn all doctrines; but I have acquiesced at last in the true doctrines, those namely of the Christians, even though they do not please those who hold false opinions." Rusticus the prefect said, "Are those the doctrines that please you, you utterly wretched man?" Justin said, "Yes, since I adhere to them with right dogma." Rusticus the prefect said, "What is the dogma?" Justin said, "That according to which we worship the God of the Christians, whom we reckon to be one from the beginning, the maker and fashioner of the whole creation, visible and invisible; and the Lord Jesus Christ, the Son of God, who had also been preached beforehand by the prophets as about to be present with the race of men, the herald of salvation and teacher of good disciples. And I, being a man, think that what I can say is insignificant in comparison with His boundless divinity, acknowledging a certain prophetic power, since it was prophesied concerning Him of whom now I say that He is the Son of God. For I know that of old the prophets foretold His appearance among men."

[2] Rusticus the prefect said, "Where do you assemble?" Justin said, "Where each one chooses and can: for do you fancy that we all meet in the very same place? Not so; because the God of the Christians is not circumscribed by place; but being invisible, fills heaven and earth, and everywhere is worshiped and glorified by the faithful." Rusticus the prefect said, "Tell me where you assemble, or into what place do you collect your followers?" Justin said, "I live above one Martinus, at the Timiotinian Bath; and during the whole time (and I am now living in Rome for the second time) I am unaware of any other meeting than his. And if any one wished to come to me, I communicated to him the doctrines of truth." Rusticus said, "Are you not, then, a Christian?" Justin said, "Yes, I am a Christian."

[3] Then said the prefect Rusticus to Chariton, "Tell me further, Chariton, are you also a Christian?" Chariton said, "I am a Christian by the command of God." Rusticus the prefect asked the woman Charito, "What say you, Charito?" Charito said, "I am a Christian by the grace of God." Rusticus said to Euelpistus, "And what are you?"

Euelpistus, a servant of Caesar, answered, "I too am a Christian, having been freed by Christ; and by the grace of Christ I partake of the same hope." Rusticus the prefect said to Hierax, "And you, are you a Christian?" Hierax said, "Yes, I am a Christian, for I revere and worship the same God." Rusticus the prefect said, "Did Justin make you Christians?" Hierax said, "I was a Christian, and will be a Christian." And Paeon stood up and said, "I too am a Christian." Rusticus the prefect said, "Who taught you?" Paeon said, "From our parents we received this good confession." Euelpistus said, "I willingly heard the words of Justin. But from my parents also I learned to be a Christian." Rusticus the prefect said, "Where are your parents?" Euelpistus said, "In Cappadocia." Rusticus says to Hierax, "Where are your parents?" And he answered, and said, "Christ is our true father, and faith in Him is our mother; and my earthly parents died; and I, when I was driven from Iconium in Phrygia, came here." Rusticus the prefect said to Liberianus, "And what say you? Are you a Christian, and unwilling to worship [the gods]?" "Liberianus said, "I too am a Christian, for I worship and reverence the only true God."

[4] The prefect says to Justin, "Hearken, you who are called learned, and think that you know true doctrines; if you are scourged and beheaded, do you believe you will ascend into heaven?" Justin said, "I hope that, if I endure these things, I shall have His gifts. For I know that, to all who have thus lived, there abides the divine favor until the completion of the whole world." Rusticus the prefect said, "Do you suppose, then, that you will ascend into heaven to receive some recompense?" Justin said, "I do not suppose it, but I know and am fully persuaded of it." Rusticus the prefect said, "Let us, then, now come to the matter in hand, and which presses. Having come together, offer sacrifice with one accord to the gods." Justin said, "No right-thinking person falls away from piety to impiety." Rusticus the prefect said, "Unless ye obey, ye shall be mercilessly punished." Justin said, "Through prayer we can be saved on account of our Lord Jesus Christ, even when we have been punished, because this shall become to us salvation and confidence at the more fearful and universal judgment-seat of our Lord and Savior." Thus also said the other martyrs: "Do what you will, for we are Christians, and do not sacrifice to idols."

[5] Rusticus the prefect pronounced sentence, saying, "Let those who have refused to sacrifice to the gods and to yield to the command of the emperor be scourged, and led away to suffer the punishment of decapitation, according to the laws." The holy martyrs having glorified God, and having gone forth to the accustomed place, were beheaded, and perfected their testimony in the confession of the Savior. And some of the faithful having secretly removed their bodies,

laid them in a suitable place, the grace of our Lord Jesus Christ having
wrought along with them, to whom be glory for ever and ever. Amen.

In the decade after Justin's martyrdom the Graeco-Roman sources on
Christianity become more numerous and these sources indicate that the
Christians were attracting the attention of not just popular writers, but also of
philosophers, serious writers, and even an emperor. The greater interest displayed in Christianity was not necessarily a good sign for Christians, however,
as the same sources indicate that during the late 160s and 170s C.E. popular animosity and contempt for Christians was on the increase.

The following passage by the pagan Lucian describes the career of
Peregrinus Proteus, a well-known Cynic philosopher who had been a Christian
earlier in his life, even being imprisoned for the faith at one point. Peregrinus
died by burning himself alive at the completion of the Olympic games in 165
C.E., after having advertised the coming suicide for several years in advance.
Lucian, who witnessed the suicide, portrayed Peregrinus as a con-man trapped
by his own boasting into an unintended suicide, but other ancient writers were
more favorable in their evaluation of Peregrinus. In reading the following text,
note that Lucian's scornful comments about the nature of the Christian faith
and its followers also give evidence of the strong moral and social support the
Christian communities extended to their members.

3.17 Lucian, *On the Death of Peregrinus* 9–14, 16 (written shortly after
the death of Peregrinus in 165 C.E.)

⁹ This creation and masterpiece of nature, this Polyclitan canon, as
soon as he came of age, was taken in adultery in Armenia and got a
sound thrashing, but finally jumped down from the roof and made
his escape, with a radish stopping his vent. Then he corrupted a
handsome boy, and by paying three thousand drachmas to the boy's
parents, who were poor, bought himself off from being brought
before the governor of the province of Asia.

¹⁰ All this and the like of it I propose to pass over; for he was still
unshapened clay, and our "holy image" had not yet been consum-
mated for us. What he did to his father, however, is very well worth
hearing; but you all know it—you have heard how he strangled the
aged man, unable to tolerate his living beyond sixty years. Then,
when the affair had been noised abroad, he condemned himself to
exile and roamed about, going to one country after another.

¹¹ It was then that he learned the wondrous lore of the Christians, by
associating with their priests and scribes in Palestine. And—how else
could it be?—in a trice he made them all look like children; for he
was prophet, cult-leader, head of the synagogue, and everything, all
by himself. He interpreted and explained some of their books and
even composed many, and they revered him as a god, made use of
him as a lawgiver, and set him down as a protector, next after that

other, to be sure, whom they still worship, the man who was crucified in Palestine because he introduced this new cult into the world.
[12] Then at length Proteus was apprehended for this and thrown into
prison, which itself gave him no little reputation as an asset for his
future career and the charlatanism and notoriety-seeking that he was
enamored of. Well, when he had been imprisoned, the Christians,
regarding the incident as a calamity, left nothing undone in the effort
to rescue him. Then, as this was impossible, every other form of attention was shown him, not in any casual way but with assiduity; and
from the very break of day aged widows and orphan children could
be seen waiting near the prison, while their officials even slept inside
with him after bribing the guards. Then elaborate meals were brought
in, and sacred books of theirs were read aloud, and excellent
Peregrinus—for he still went by that name—was called by them "the
new Socrates."

[13] Indeed, people came even from the cities in Asia, sent by the
Christians at their common expense, to succor and defend and
encourage the hero. They show incredible speed whenever any such
public action is taken; for in no time they lavish their all. So it was
then in the case of Peregrinus; much money came to him from them
by reason of his imprisonment, and he procured not a little revenue
from it. The poor wretches have convinced themselves, first and
foremost, that they are going to be immortal and live for all time, in
consequence of which they despise death and even willingly give
themselves into custody, most of them. Furthermore, their first law-
giver persuaded them that they are all brothers of one another after
they have transgressed once for all by denying the Greek gods and by
worshipping that crucified sophist himself and living under his laws.
Therefore they despise all things indiscriminately and consider them
common property, receiving such doctrines traditionally without
any definite evidence. So if any charlatan and trickster, able to profit
by occasions, comes among them, he quickly acquires sudden wealth
by imposing upon simple folk.

[14] However, Peregrinus was freed by the then governor of Syria, a man
who was fond of philosophy. . . .

[16] He left home, then, for the second time, to roam about, possessing
an ample source of funds in the Christians, through whose ministra-
tions he lived in unalloyed prosperity. For a time he battened himself
thus; but then, after he had transgressed in some way even against
them—he was seen, I think, eating some of the food that is forbidden them—they no longer accepted him, and so, being at a loss, he
thought he must sing a palinode and demand his possessions back
from his city. Submitting a petition, he expected to recover them by
order of the Emperor. Then, as the city sent representatives to oppose

the claim, he achieved nothing, but was directed to abide by what he had once for all determined, under no compulsion from anyone.

Lucian's account of Peregrinus brings to mind the warnings to Palestinian Christians about false teachers contained in the early Christian church manual known as the *Didache*:

> Welcome every apostle on arriving, as if he were the Lord. But he must not stay beyond one day. In case of necessity, however, the next day too. If he stays three days, he is a false prophet. On departing, an apostle must not accept anything save sufficient food to carry him till his next lodging. If he asks for money, he is a false prophet. (*Didache* 11.4–6)

Lucian's depiction of the Christians as simple, poorly-educated people, who accepted teachings on faith rather reason, is consistent with the picture presented by the pagan author Celsus a decade later in his book *True Discourse* (Selection 3.22, below.). Another possible indication of the common perception of Christians as riff-raff and the like can be found in the writings of the pagan Aelius Aristides, who is usually thought to have been referring to Christians when he wrote of those "blasphemous people in Palestine."

3.18 Aelius Aristides (ca. 117–181 C.E.), "Speech on the Four" 2.394ff (mid-second century C.E.)

> Who on earth could tolerate these enemies [the Cynic philosophers] who lash out more solecism than words? . . . When they steal, they say that they "share." They call their envy "philosophy" and their mendacity "disdain of worldly goods." They frequent the doorways, talking more often to the doorkeepers than to the masters, making up for their lowly conditions by using impudence. They deceive like flatterers, handle insults like superior men, combining the two most opposite and repugnant vices: vileness and insolence. Their behavior is very similar to those blasphemous people in Palestine. They, too, manifest their impiety by the obvious signs that they do not recognize those who are above them, and they separated themselves from the Greeks and from everything good. They are incapable as far as they are concerned of contributing in any matter whatsoever toward any common good, but when it comes to undermining home life, bringing trouble and discord into families and claiming to be leaders of all things, they are the most skillful men.

The increasing tension between Christians and pagans during the reign of Marcus Aurelius is probably attributable at least in part to the circumstances of his reign, which was marked by difficult and lengthy wars on the frontiers and by the spread of plague throughout the Roman Empire. These were exactly the kinds of events that might cause pious pagans to believe that Rome suffered because the gods were offended by the Christians and their faith.

Marcus Aurelius spent much of his reign campaigning in wars against the tribes along the Danube River frontier and during these campaigns he kept a personal diary in which he himself made one reference to Christians.

3.19 Marcus Aurelius, *Meditations* 11.3 (ca. 170 C.E.)
What a soul that is which is ready, if at any moment it must be separated from the body, and ready either to be extinguished or dispersed or continue to exist; but so that this readiness comes from a man's own judgement, not from mere obstinacy, as with the Christians, but considerately and with dignity and in a way to persuade another, without tragic show.

Marcus Aurelius was a Stoic philosopher and while there were many points in common between Christian and Stoic ethics, his diary passage seems to reflect a Stoic's distaste for the emotional zeal and the fervor displayed by the Christians brought to trial before the Roman authorities. It is easy to believe that, as in the case of Pliny the Younger, such fervor and zeal might in itself antagonize the local officials and peoples, who in difficult times sought only to preserve peace and prosperity by honoring the traditional gods. Christians were aware of the increasing animosity shown by many local populations during Marcus Aurelius's reign and from this period we have two Christian apologies addressed to Marcus Aurelius, both protesting the treatment of the Christians. The first was written by Melito, the bishop of Sardis.

3.20 Melito Bishop of Sardis, *To Antoninus* (ca. 175 C.E.) quoted by Eusebius *Ecclesiastical History* 4.26.5–11
And in the book to the emperor [Marcus Aurelius] he [Melito] relates that in his time we were treated as follows: "It has never before happened as it is now that the race of the religious should be persecuted and driven about by new decrees throughout Asia. For shameless informers and lovers of other people's property have taken advantage of the decrees, and pillage us openly, harrying night and day those who have done nothing wrong." And after other points he says, "And if this is done as your command, let it be assumed that it is well done, for no righteous king would ever have an unrighteous policy, and we gladly bear the honor of such death. But we submit to you this single request, that you will first take cognizance yourself of the authors of such strife, and judge righteously whether they are worthy of death and punishment, or of acquittal and immunity. But, if it be not from you that there comes this counsel and this new decree (and it would be improper even against barbarian enemies), we beseech you all the more not to neglect us in this brigandage by a mob." He then continues as follows: "Our philosophy first grew up among the barbarians, but its full flower came among your nation in the great reign of your ancestor Augustus, and became an omen of

good to your empire, for from that time the power of the Romans became great and splendid. You are now his happy successor, and shall be so along with your son, if you protect the philosophy which grew up with the empire and began with Augustus. Your ancestors nourished it together with the other cults, and the greatest proof that our doctrine flourished for good along with the empire in its noble beginning is the fact that it met no evil in the reign of Augustus,[11] but on the contrary everything splendid and glorious according to the wishes of all men. The only emperors who were ever persuaded by malicious men to slander our teaching were Nero and Domitian, and from them arose the lie, and the unreasonable custom of falsely accusing Christians. But their ignorance was corrected by your pious fathers, who wrote many rebukes to many, whenever any dared to take new measures against Christians. Your grandfather Hadrian shows this in his letters to many, and especially to the proconsul Fundanus, the governor of Asia, and your father, while you were joined with him in the administration of the world, wrote to the cities that no new measures should be taken concerning us.[12] Among these are letters to the Larisians and to the Thessalonians and the Athenians and to all the Greeks. Since you hold the same opinion about them and, indeed, one which is far kinder and more philosophic, we are persuaded of your doing all which we beg of you.

The second apology, written about the same year as Melito's, was by an Athenian Christian who condemned the injustice of the Roman practice of punishing Christians without any investigation of how Christians actually lived their lives.

3.21 Athenagoras Of Athens (active second half of the second century C.E.), *Plea on Behalf of the Christians* 1–3 (ca. late 176 or early 177 C.E.)
To the Emperors Marcus Aurelius Antoninus and Lucius Aurelius Commodus, conquerors of Armenia and Sarmatia, and—what is more important—philosophers.
[1] In your Empire, Your Most Excellent Majesties, different peoples observe different laws and customs; and no one is hindered by law or fear of punishment from devotion to his ancestral ways, even if they are ridiculous. . . .
Accordingly, while everyone admires your mildness and gentleness and your peaceful and kindly attitude toward all, they enjoy

---

11. Melito was at best either ignorant or disingenuous in this assertion. Augustus died in 14 C.E., well before the ministry of Jesus or the foundation of the Christian church.

12. Melito, if quoted accurately by Eusebius, either overlooked or was unaware that a number of martyrdoms occurred during Antoninus Pius's reign, including Telesphorus, the bishop of Rome, and Polycarp, the bishop of Smyrna.

equal rights under the law. The cities, according to their rank, share in equal honor, and the whole Empire through your wisdom enjoys profound peace.

But you have not cared for us who are called Christians in this way. Although we do no wrong, but, as we shall show, are of all men most religiously and rightly disposed toward God and your Empire, you allow us to be harassed, plundered, and persecuted, the mob making war on us only because of our name. We venture, therefore, to state our case before you. From what we have to say you will gather that we suffer unjustly and contrary to all law and reason. Hence we ask you to devise some measures to prevent our being the victims of false accusers.

The injury we suffer from our persecutors does not concern our property or our civil rights or anything of less importance. For we hold these things in contempt, although they appear weighty to the crowd. We have learned not only not to return blow for blow, nor to sue those who plunder and rob us, but to those who smite us on one cheek to offer the other also, and to those who take away our coat to give our overcoat as well. But when we have given up our property, they plot against our bodies and souls, pouring upon us a multitude of accusations which have not the slightest foundation, but which are the stock in trade of gossips and the like.

² If, indeed, anyone can convict us of wrongdoing, be it trifling or more serious, we do not beg off punishment, but are prepared to pay the penalty however cruel and unpitying. But if the accusation goes no farther than a name—and it is clear that up to today the tales about us rest only on popular and uncritical rumor, and not a single Christian has been convicted of wrongdoing—it is your duty, illustrious, kind, and most learned Emperors, to relieve us of these calumnies by law. Thus, as the whole world, both individuals and cities, shares your kindness, we too may be grateful to you, rejoicing that we have ceased to be defamed.

It does not befit your sense of justice that others, accused of wrongdoing, are not punished before they have been convicted, while with us the mere name is of more weight than legal proof. Our judges, moreover, do not inquire if the accused has committed any wrong, but let loose against the name as if it were a crime. But no name in and of itself is good or bad. It is by reason of the wicked or good actions associated with names that they are bad or good. You know all that better than anyone, seeing you are versed in philosophy and thoroughly cultured.

That is why those who are tried before you, though arraigned on the most serious charges, take courage. For they know that you will examine their life and not be influenced by names if they mean nothing, or by accusations if they are false. Hence they receive a sentence of condemnation on a par with one of acquittal. We claim for ourselves, therefore, the same treatment as others. We should not be hated and punished because we are called Christians, for what has a name to do with our being criminals? Rather should we be tried on charges brought against us, and either acquitted on our disproving them or punished on our being convicted as wicked men, not because of a name (for no Christian is wicked unless he is a hypocrite), but because of a crime. . . .

I must at the outset of my defense beg you, illustrious Emperors, to hear me impartially. Do not prejudge the case through being influenced by popular and unfounded rumor, but apply your love of learning and of truth to our cause. Thus you will not be led astray through ignorance, and we, disproving the uncritical rumors of the crowd, shall cease to be persecuted.

³ Three charges are brought against us: atheism, Thyestean feasts, and Oedipean intercourse.* If these are true, spare no class; proceed against our crimes; destroy us utterly with our wives and children, if anyone lives like a beast. Beasts, indeed, do not attack their own kind. Nor for mere wantonness do they have intercourse, but by nature's law and only at the season of procreation. . . . You yourselves, moreover, are witness to the fact that we are guilty of none of these things, since it is only the confession of a name that you forbid. It remains for you, then, to examine our lives and teachings, our loyalty and obedience to you, to your house, and to the Empire. By doing so you will concede to us no more than you grant to our persecutors. And we shall triumph over them, giving up our very lives for the truth without any hesitation. . . .

*In Greek mythology, Thyestes in ignorance ate the flesh of his two sons and Oedipus in ignorance married his own mother. See the similar reference at Selection 3.29, below.

CELSUS'S CHALLENGE TO THE CHRISTIAN FAITH

By the mid to late 170s C.E., the tenets of Christianity were sufficiently well-known that a pagan writer named Celsus attempted to address directly the social and intellectual issues raised by Christian belief. Celsus's book *True Doctrine* is not extant, as it was ordered banned and burned by the Christian emperors of the fourth century C.E., but approximately 70 percent of the text of the book has survived in quotations found in rebuttals written by Christian authors. The most important of these rebuttals was by the great Christian scholar Origen, whose *Against Celsus* (ca. 240) refuted arguments raised in *True Doctrine*. The following selections from Celsus deal with his cultural and social criticisms of Christianity, and his intellectual criticism of Christian belief is dealt with in the next section concerning the pagan intellectual opposition to Christianity.

3.22 Celsus, *True Doctrine* (ca. 175–181 C.E.) Section citations are to Origen's *Against Celsus*.

¹·¹ The first point which Celsus brings forward, in his desire to throw discredit upon Christianity, is that the Christians entered into secret

associations with each other, contrary to law, saying that "of associations some are public, and that these are in accordance with the laws;
others, again, secret, and maintained in violation of the laws." And
his wish is to bring into dispute what are termed the "love feasts" of
the Christians. . .

As the military conqueror of the many peoples of the Mediterranean basin,
Rome was naturally concerned with the possibility of revolt and took active
measures to root out and suppress secret societies. As long as the Roman
authorities did not recognize Christianity as a permitted religion, the gatherings of Christians for worship constituted a punishable offense.

[1.6] And he [Celsus] next proceeds to bring a charge against the Savior
Himself, alleging that it was by means of sorcery that He [Jesus] was
able to accomplish the miracles which He performed. . . .

The practice of magic, good or bad, was a capital offense under Roman law and
thus Celsus's assertion that Jesus practiced sorcery was a very serious accusation.

[1.7] Moreover, since he [Celsus] frequently calls the Christian doctrine a
secret system (of belief), we must confute him on this point also, since
almost the entire world is better acquainted with what Christians preach
than with the favorite opinions of philosophers. For who is ignorant of
the statement that Jesus was born of a virgin, and that He was crucified,
and that His resurrection is an article of faith among many, and that a
general judgment is announced to come, in which the wicked are to be
punished according to their deserts, and the righteous to be duly
rewarded? And yet the mystery of the resurrection, not being understood, is made a subject of ridicule among unbelievers. In these circumstances, to speak of the Christian doctrine as a secret system, is altogether
absurd. But that there should be certain doctrines, not made known to
the multitude, which are (revealed) after the exoteric ones have been
taught, is not a peculiarity of Christianity alone, but also of philosophic
systems, in which certain truths are exoteric and others esoteric. . . .

[1.9] And he [Celsus] asserts that certain persons who do not wish either
to give or to receive a reason for what they believe, keep repeating
"Do not examine, but believe!" and, "Your faith will save you!" And he
alleges that such also say, "The wisdom of this life is bad, but that
foolishness a good thing." To which we have to answer, that if it were
possible for all to leave the business of life, and devote themselves to
philosophy, no other method ought to be adopted by any one, but
this alone. . . . But since the course alluded to is impossible, partly on
account of the necessities of life, partly on account of the weaknesses
of men, as only a very few individuals devote themselves earnestly to
study, what better method could be devised with a view of assisting
the multitude, than that which was delivered by Jesus to the heathen?

Celsus's accusation that Christians directed their missionary work at the young, the uneducated, and the impressionable seems to have stung Origen, who responded to the accusation in several places in *Against Celsus*. Nevertheless, even Origen was forced to admit that many Christians came from the lower orders of society and were able to understand little other than the most basic doctrinal instruction.

> [1.10] In the next place, since our opponents keep repeating these statements about faith, we must say that, considering faith a useful thing for the multitude, we admit that we teach those men to believe without reasons, who are unable to abandon all other employments, and give themselves to an examination of arguments. . . .
>
> [1.27] And although, among the multitude of converts to Christianity, the simple and ignorant necessarily outnumbered the more intelligent, as the former class always does the latter, yet Celsus, unwilling to take note of this, thinks that this philanthropic doctrine, which reaches to every soul under the sun, is vulgar, and on account of its vulgarity and its want of reasoning power, obtained a hold only over the ignorant. And yet he himself admits that it was not the simple alone who were led by the doctrine of Jesus to adopt His religion; for he acknowledges that there were amongst them some persons of moderate intelligence, and gentle disposition, and possessed of understanding, and capable of comprehending allegories. . . .
>
> [6.10] And there are some who are capable of receiving nothing more than an exhortation to believe, and to these we address that alone; while we approach others, again, as far as possible, in the way of demonstration, by means of question and answer.

In writing *True Doctrine*, Celsus used the common classical literary device of presenting his work as a conversation among individuals. One of these individuals was portrayed as a Jew and this figure was used to present some of Celsus's sharpest attacks on the Christian faith. Perhaps Celsus used a Jewish speaker for this purpose precisely to emphasize that Christians were but a splinter group of a far older faith and that there was open conflict between the two groups.

> [1.28] And since, in imitation of a rhetorician training a pupil, he introduces a Jew, who enters into a personal discussion with Jesus, and speaks in a very childish manner, altogether unworthy of the gray hairs of a philosopher, let me endeavor, to the best of my ability, to examine his statements, and show that he does not maintain, throughout the discussion, the consistency due to the character of a Jew. For he represents him disputing with Jesus, and confuting Him, as he thinks, on many points; and in the first place, he accuses Him of having "invented his birth from a virgin," and upbraids Him with being "born in a certain Jewish village, of a poor woman of the country, who gained her subsistence by spinning, and who was turned out of

doors by her husband, a carpenter by trade, because she was convicted of adultery; that after being driven away by her husband, and
wandering about for a time, she disgracefully gave birth to Jesus, an
illegitimate child, who having hired himself out as a servant in Egypt
on account of his poverty, and having there acquired some miraculous powers, on which the Egyptians greatly pride themselves,
returned to his own country, highly elated on account of them, and
by means of these proclaimed himself a God." Now, as I cannot allow
anything said by unbelievers to remain unexamined, but must investigate everything from the beginning, I give it as my opinion that all
these things worthily harmonize with the predictions that Jesus is the
Son of God. . . .

1.32 But let us now return to where the Jew is introduced, speaking of
the mother of Jesus, and saying that "when she was pregnant she was
turned out of doors by the carpenter to whom she had been
betrothed, as having been guilty of adultery, and that she bore a child
to a certain soldier named Panthera"; and let us see whether those
who have blindly concocted these fables about the adultery of the
Virgin with Panthera, and her rejection by the carpenter, did not
invent these stories to overturn His miraculous conception by the
Holy Ghost: for they could have falsified the history in a different
manner, on account of its extremely miraculous character, and not
have admitted, as it were against their will, that Jesus was born of no
ordinary human marriage. It was to be expected, indeed, that those
who would not believe the miraculous birth of Jesus would invent
some falsehood.

The story that Jesus was the bastard son of a Roman soldier named
Panthera[13] can be traced back to the mid-second century C.E. The story apparently stayed in circulation for several centuries, as it is mentioned in the works
of the fourth-century Christian bishop Epiphanius.[14] Christians accused Jews
of starting the story and perhaps Jews did help circulate the story to refute the
Christian accounts of Jesus' virgin birth.

2.4 The Jew, then, continues his address to converts from his own
nation thus: "Yesterday and the day before, when we visited with
punishment the man who deluded you, ye became apostates from
the law of your fathers;" showing by such statements (as we have just

---

13. Panthera ("Panther") was a common surname among Roman soldiers of the first and sec-
ond centuries C.E. See L. Patterson, "The Origin of the Name Panthera," *Journal of Theological
Studies* 19 (1917–18): 79–80. For a general discussion of the fairly extensive sources alleging
Jesus' illegitimate birth, see Raymond E. Brown, *The Birth of the Messiah* (New York: Doubleday
& Company, 1977), 534–42; and John P. Meier, *A Marginal Jew* (New York: Doubleday, 1991),
96, 222–30.

14. Epiphanius, *Panarion* 78.7.5. Epiphanius attempted to explain away the story by claiming
that "panther" was the surname of Joseph's father.

demonstrated) anything but an exact knowledge of the truth. But what he advances afterwards seems to have some force, when he says: "How is it that you take the beginning of your system from our worship, and when you have made some progress you treat it with disrespect, although you have no other foundation to show for your doctrines than our law?"

The Romans were a conservative people who gave much greater weight and respect to traditional religions than to new religions and this Roman trait undoubtedly encouraged the Christians to emphasize their faith's derivation from Judaism. Christianity's emphasis on its Jewish heritage puzzled many non-Christians because of the obvious animosity between Jews and Christians and the fact that Christians rejected so much of Jewish tradition, teaching, and belief.

> [2.55] The Jew continues his address to those of his countrymen who are converts, as follows: "Come now, let us grant to you that the prediction was actually uttered. Yet how many others are there who practice such juggling tricks, in order to deceive their simple hearers, and who make gain by their deception?—as was the case, they say, with Zamolxis in Scythia, the slave of Pythagoras; and with Pythagoras himself in Italy; and with Rhampsinitus in Egypt (the latter of whom, they say, played at dice with Demeter in Hades, and returned to the upper world with a golden napkin which he had received from her as a gift); and also with Orpheus among the Odrysians, and Protesilaus in Thessaly, and Hercules at Cape Taenarus, and Theseus. But the question is, whether any one who was really dead ever rose with a veritable body. Or do you imagine the statements of others not only to be myths, but to have the appearance of such, while you have discovered a becoming and credible termination to your drama in the voice from the cross, when he breathed his last, and in the earthquake and the darkness? That while alive he was of no assistance to himself, but that when dead he rose again, and showed the marks of his punishment, and how his hands were pierced with nails: who beheld this? A half-frantic woman, as you state, and some other one, perhaps, of those who were engaged in the same system of delusion, who had either dreamed so, owing to a peculiar state of mind, or under the influence of a wandering imagination had formed to himself an appearance according to his own wishes, which has been the case with numberless individuals; or, which is most probable, one who desired to impress others with this portent, and by such a falsehood to furnish an occasion to impostors like himself."

The society of the Roman Empire was marked by enormous disparities in wealth and social standing, with near insurmountable social and political barriers between the numerically very small social and political elite and the great masses of the Empire's populace. Celsus attacked Christian belief by arguing that only the lower classes were attracted to the faith, since that fact alone would be enough to discredit Christianity among the upper class. While Celsus almost certainly exaggerated the facts for polemical purposes, modern historians agree that during the first two centuries C.E. most Christians came from the working urban poor, rather than from the rich and powerful.[15]

> [3.49] This statement also is untrue, that it is "only foolish and low individuals, and persons devoid of perception, and slaves, and women, and children, of whom the teachers of the divine word wish to make converts...."
>
> [3.50] But let us see what those statements of his are which follow next in these words: "Nay, we see, indeed, that even those individuals, who in the market-places perform the most disgraceful tricks, and who gather crowds around them, would never approach an assembly of wise men, nor dare to exhibit their arts among them; but wherever they see young men, and a mob of slaves, and a gathering of unintelligent persons, thither they thrust themselves in, and show themselves off." Observe, now, how he slanders us in these words, comparing us to those who in the market-places perform the most disreputable tricks, and gather crowds around them!
>
> [3.52] Observe now with regard to the following statement of Celsus, "We see also those persons who in the market-places perform most disreputable tricks, and collect crowds around them," whether a manifest falsehood has not been uttered, and things compared which have no resemblance. He says that these individuals, to whom he compares us, "Who perform the most disreputable tricks in the market-places and collect crowds, would never approach an assembly of wise men, nor dare to show off their tricks before them; but wherever they see young men, and a mob of slaves, and a gathering of foolish people, thither do they thrust themselves in and make a display." Now, in speaking thus he does nothing else than simply load us with abuse, like the women upon the public streets, whose object is to slander one another; for we do everything in our power to secure that our meetings should be composed of wise men, and those things among us which are especially excellent and divine we then venture to bring forward publicly in our discussions when we have an abundance of intelligent hearers, while we conceal and pass by in silence the truths of deeper import when we see that our audience is composed of simpler minds, which need such instruction as is figuratively termed "milk."

15. Robin Lane Fox, *Pagans and Christians* (New York: Alfred A. Knopf, 1986), 301, 311–12; Ramsay MacMullen, *Christianizing the Roman Empire* (New Haven: Yale University Press, 1984), 37-39. For an opposing perspective, see Rodney Stark, *The Rise of Christianity* (Princeton: Princeton University Press, 1996), 29–47, and the sources cited therein.

3.55 He [Celsus] asserts, "We see, indeed, in private houses workers in wool and leather, and fullers, and persons of the most uninstructed and rustic character, not venturing to utter a word in the presence of their elders and wiser masters; but when they get hold of the children privately, and certain women as ignorant as themselves, they pour forth wonderful statements, to the effect that they ought not to give heed to their father and to their teachers, but should obey them; that the former are foolish and stupid, and neither know nor can perform anything that is really good, being preoccupied with empty trifles; that they alone know how men ought to live, and that, if the children obey them, they will both be happy themselves, and will make their home happy also. And while thus speaking, if they see one of the instructors of youth approaching, or one of the more intelligent class, or even the father himself, the more timid among them become afraid, while the more forward incite the children to throw off the yoke, whispering that in the presence of father and teachers they neither will nor can explain to them any good thing, seeing they turn away with aversion from the silliness and stupidity of such persons as being alto-gether corrupt, and far advanced in wickedness, and such as would inflict punishment upon them; but that if they wish (to avail them-selves of their aid), they must leave their father and their instructors, and go with the women and their playfellows to the women's apart-ments or to the leather shop, or to the fuller's shop, that they may attain to perfection; and by words like these they gain them over."

Some indication of the strength of the Roman preference for tradition can be seen in the fact that the concept which we would describe as "ancestral" the Romans described by the phrase *mos maiorum*, which literally means "the custom of the greater ones." Romans were especially conservative with respect to religious ceremony and quite literally believed that even an unintentional mistake or hesi-tation in performing the literal words and forms of the traditional ceremonies, much less an intentional change, rendered the ceremonies ineffective.[16] To aban-don even the forms of worship used by one's ancestors, much less the worship of the ancestral gods themselves, was a serious offense to the gods and risked bring-ing down divine wrath upon Roman society at large. For this reason the Romans, who as a whole intensely disliked the Jews, nevertheless respected Jewish religion for its great antiquity and tolerated its continued worship within the Empire, notwithstanding the several Jewish revolts of the first two centuries C.E. However, Christians were quite clearly a recent splinter group from the Jewish faith and thus could derive no benefit from this Roman toleration for ancient faiths.

5.35 The argument of Celsus appears to point by these illustrations to this conclusion: that it is "an obligation incumbent on all men to live

16. See, e.g., Pliny the Elder, *Natural History* 28.2(3).10–11.

according to their country's customs, in which case they will escape censure; whereas the Christians, who have abandoned their native usages, and who are not one nation like the Jews, are to be blamed for giving their adherence to the teaching of Jesus."

In his criticism of the Christian faith, Celsus also brought to bear scorn and sharp humor against the logic of Christian teachings. In the next passage, Celsus mocked the Christian effort to glorify the crucifixion of Jesus against the accusations of Jews quoting Deuteronomy 21:22–23: "And if a man has committed a crime punishable by death and he is put to death, and you hang him on a tree, his body shall not remain all night upon the tree, but you shall bury him the same day, for a hanged man is accursed by God; you shall not defile your land which the Lord your God gives you for an inheritance."[17]

> 6.34 And in all their writings (is mention made) of the tree of life, and a resurrection of the flesh by means of the "tree," because, I imagine, their teacher was nailed to a cross, and was a carpenter by craft; so that if he had chanced to have been cast from a precipice, or thrust into a pit, or suffocated by hanging, or had been a leather-cutter, or stone-cutter, or worker in iron, there would have been (invented) a precipice of life beyond the heavens, or a pit of resurrection, or a cord of immortality, or a blessed stone, or an iron of love, or a sacred leather! Now what old woman would not be ashamed to utter such things in a whisper, even when making stories to lull an infant to sleep?

Besides attacking Christianity for being but a recently devised faith, Celsus also sought to attack Christianity by demonstrating that its teachings were inconsistent with the Jewish faith from which Christianity claimed to be derived.

> 7.18 Celsus adds: "Will they not besides make this reflection? If the prophets of the God of the Jews foretold that he who should come into the world would be the Son of this same God, how could he command them through Moses to gather wealth, to extend their dominion, to fill the earth, to put their enemies of every age to the sword, and to destroy them utterly, which indeed he himself did—as Moses says— threatening them, moreover, that if they did not obey his commands, he would treat them as his avowed enemies; whilst, on the other hand, his Son, the man of Nazareth, promulgated laws quite opposed to these, declaring that no one can come to the Father who loves power, or riches, or glory; that men ought not to be more careful in providing food than the ravens; that they were to be less concerned about their

---

17 After execution of an individual, as a further disgrace the body would be impaled ("hung") upon a tree or wooden post for public display. See accounts of this at Joshua 8:29 and 10:26–27; 2 Samuel 4:12; see also, Acts 5:30 and 10:39. For the Talmudic tradition that Jesus was stoned and then hung up for display on the eve of Passover, see Selection 2.4 and R. Joseph Hoffman, *Jesus Outside the Gospels* (Buffalo: Prometheus, 1984), 48–50.

raiment than the lilies; that to him who has given them one blow, they should offer to receive another? Whether is it Moses or Jesus who teaches falsely? Did the Father, when he sent Jesus, forget the commands which he had given to Moses? Or did he change his mind, condemn his own laws, and send forth a messenger with counter instructions?"

[8.12] In what follows, some may imagine that he says something plausible against us. "If," says he, "these people worshiped one God alone, and no other, they would perhaps have some valid argument against the worship of others. But they pay excessive reverence to one who has but lately appeared among men, and they think it no offense against God if they worship also His servant."

In the last passage Celsus played upon the uncertainty among second-century Christians as to the exact relationship of God and Christ in what was supposed to be a monotheistic religion. The nature of the relationship among God, Jesus, and the Holy Spirit was a point of great debate and concern among Christians, and most of the Christian "heresies" of the third and fourth centuries C.E. were based on differing beliefs as to the nature of the relationship. The debate among Christians on this issue during the second century led to beginning of the development of the orthodox doctrine of the Trinity. About 180 C.E., Theophilus, the bishop of Antioch, wrote concerning the *triados* of God, His Word, and His Wisdom,[18] and about 212 C.E., Tertullian became the earliest extant Christian writer to use the word *trinitas* in discussing this relationship.[19] However, the Christian uncertainty about the exact nature of the relationship continued into the third century C.E., as reflected in Origen's response to Celsus's accusation: that Celsus is wrong because Christians "do not hold that the Son is mightier than the Father, but inferior" (*Contra Celsus* 8.15).

[8.41] "You", says he [Celsus], "mock and revile the statues of our gods; but if you reviled Bacchus or Hercules in person, you would not perhaps have done so with impunity. But those who crucified your god, when present among men, suffered nothing for it, either at the time or during the whole of their lives.

Early Christians often argued that the truth of their religion was evidenced by Christ's power over demons and pagan gods, and here Celsus threw this logic back at the Christians. Origen did not directly respond to Celsus's challenge at this point, but later on at *Contra Celsus* 8.41 Origen wrote, "We throw ridicule not upon lifeless statues, but upon those only who worship them," and further stated that the Jewish people were in fact most severely punished by God with the destruction of their Temple and nation in 70 C.E.

18. Theophilus, *Ad Autolycum* 2.15.
19. Tertullian, *Against Praxeas* 2.

PAGAN INTELLECTUAL ARGUMENTS AGAINST CHRISTIANITY

Celsus was one of the earliest pagan writers to address the implications of the new concepts of the divine and the natural order taught by Christians. Some of his strongest attacks were directed at Christian teachings concerning the nature of God and the relationship of man to the physical world. At approximately the same time that Celsus wrote *True Doctrine*, the Greek writer Galen (129–199 C.E.), a renowned doctor who for a time was the personal physician of the emperor Marcus Aurelius himself, addressed similar concerns about the Jewish conception of the divine. Together, these two pagan authors provide an intriguing picture of the ways in which the traditional pagan religion of the social elite differed from the concepts taught by Jews and Christians.

> 3.23 Galen The Physician, *On the Usefulness of the Parts of the Body* 11.14 (ca. 169–176 C.E.)
>
> It is precisely this point in which our own opinion and that of Plato and of the other Greeks who follow the right method in natural science differs from the position taken up by Moses. For the latter it seems enough to say that God simply willed the arrangement of matter and it was presently arranged in due order; for he believes everything to be possible with God, even should he wish to make a bull or a horse out of ashes. We, however, do not hold this; we say that certain things are impossible by nature and that God does not even attempt such things at all but that he chooses the best out of the possibilities of becoming. We say therefore that since it was better that the eyelashes should always be equal in length and number, it was not that he just willed and they were instantly there; for even if he should just will numberless times, they would never come into being in just this manner out of a soft skin; and in particular, it was altogether impossible for them to stand erect unless fixed on something hard. We thus say that God is the cause both of the choice of the best in the products of creation themselves and of the selection of the matter. For since it was required, first that the eyelashes should stand erect and secondly that they should be kept equal in length and number, he planted them firmly in a cartilaginous body. If he had planted them in a soft and fleshy substance he would have suffered a worse failure not only than Moses but also than a bad general who plants a wall or a camp in marshy ground.

> 3.24 Celsus, *True Doctrine* 4.2, 14; 5.14 (quoted by Origen in *Against Celsus*)
>
> [4.2] But that certain Christians and (all) Jews should maintain, the former that there has already descended, the latter that there will descend, upon the earth a certain God, or Son of a God, who will make the inhabitants of the earth righteous, is a most shameless assertion, and one the refutation of which does not need many words. . . .

[4.14] God is good, and beautiful, and blessed, and that in the best and most beautiful degree. But if he come down among men, he must undergo a change, and a change from good to evil, from virtue to vice, from happiness to misery, and from best to worst. Who, then, would make choice of such a change? It is the nature of a mortal, indeed, to undergo change and remolding, but of an immortal to remain the same and unaltered. God, then, could not admit of such a change. . . .

[5.14] It is folly on their part to suppose that when God, as if He were a cook, introduces the fire (which is to consume the world), all the rest of the human race will be burnt up, while they alone will remain, not only such of them as are then alive, but also those who are long since dead, which latter will arise from the earth clothed with the selfsame flesh (as during life); for such a hope is simply one which might be cherished by worms. For what sort of human soul is that which would still long for a body that had been subject to corruption? Whence, also, this opinion of yours is not shared by some of the Christians, and they pronounce it to be exceedingly vile, and loathsome, and impossible; for what kind of body is that which, after being completely corrupted, can return to its original nature, and to that selfsame first condition out of which it fell into dissolution? Being unable to return any answer, they betake themselves to a most absurd refuge, viz., that all things are possible to God. And yet God cannot do things that are disgraceful, nor does He wish to do things that are contrary to His nature; nor, if (in accordance with the wickedness of your own heart) you desired anything that was evil, would God accomplish it; nor must you believe at once that it will be done. For God does not rule the world in order to satisfy inordinate desires, or to allow disorder and confusion, but to govern a nature that is upright and just. For the soul, indeed, He might be able to provide an everlasting life; while dead bodies, on the contrary, are, as Heraclitus observes, more worthless than dung. God, however, neither can nor will declare, contrary to all reason, that the flesh, which is full of those things which it is not even honorable to mention, is to exist for ever. For He is the reason of all things that exist, and therefore can do nothing either contrary to reason or contrary to Himself.

These passages by Galen and Celsus reflect both the monotheistic tendencies of paganism in the second century C.E. and a sense of god as the creator of the material world. However, the god of Celsus and Galen was not omnipotent, as both Celsus and Galen saw the divine as being limited and circumscribed by the natural laws of creation itself. Moreover, Celsus thought that god had organized the material world as a unified whole which was good and perfect in itself and not intrinsically flawed or merely for the benefit of man, as Christians taught.

3.25 Celsus, *True Doctrine* 4.74–75, 99; 7.68 (ca. 175–181 C.E.) (quoted by Origen in *Against Celsus*)

4.74 He [Celsus] next, in many words, blames us for asserting that God made all things for the sake of man. Because from the history of animals, and from the sagacity manifested by them, he would show that all things came into existence not more for the sake of man than of the irrational animals.

4.75 In the next place, he [Celsus] adds "Although you may say that these things—plants and trees and herbs and thorns—grow for the use of men, why will you maintain that they grow for the use of men rather than for that of the most savage of irrational animals?" Let Celsus then say distinctly that the great diversity among the products of the earth is not the work of Providence, but that a certain fortuitous concurrence of atoms gave birth to qualities so diverse, and that it was owing to chance that so many kinds of plants and trees and herbs resemble one another, and that no disposing reason gave existence to them, and that they do not derive their origin from an understanding that is beyond all admiration. . . .

4.99 In addition to all that he has already said, Celsus subjoins the following: "All things, accordingly, were not made for man, any more than they were made for lions, or eagles, or dolphins, but that this world, as being God's work, might be perfect and entire in all respects. For this reason all things have been adjusted, not with reference to each other, but with regard to their bearing upon the whole. And God takes care of the whole, and (His) providence will never forsake it; and it does not become worse; nor does God after a time bring it back to Himself; nor is He angry on account of men any more than on account of apes or flies; nor does He threaten these beings, each one of which has received its appointed lot in its proper place. . . ."

7.68 Is it not true that all things are ordered according to God's will, and that His providence governs all things? Is not everything which happens in the universe, whether it be the work of God, of angels, of other demons, or of heroes, regulated by the law of the Most High God? Have these not had assigned them various departments of which they were severally deemed worthy?

Another aspect of Galen's and Celsus's criticism of Christianity was that its members accepted on faith matters that were properly the subject of rational investigation and reason.

3.26 Galen The Physician, *On the Pulse* 2.4; 3.3 (ca. 176–180 C.E.)

2.4 . . . .it would at any rate be much better to add to the statement about the eight qualities [of the blood's pulse], if not a cogent demonstration at least a reassuring and sufficient explanation, so that one should not at the very beginning, as if one had come into the school of Moses and Christ, hear talk of undemonstrated laws, and that where it is least appropriate.

[3.3] One might more easily teach novelties to the followers of Moses and Christ than to the physicians and philosophers who cling fast to their schools.

On the Prime Mover (date unknown) as quoted in *Life of Galen* by Ibn Abi Usaibi'a (1203–1270 C.E.), who quotes from Ibn al-Matran's lost Arabic translation of the lost Greek text.

If I had in mind people who taught their pupils in the same way as the followers of Moses and Christ teach theirs—for they order them to accept everything on faith—I should not have given you a definition.

In spite of Galen's disdain for the faith-based obstinacy of Christians, he admired other facets of Christian teachings.

3.27 Galen The Physician, *Summary of Plato's Republic* (written ca. 180 C.E.) as quoted by Abu'l Fida (died after 1329 C.E.) in his *Universal Chronicle* (This quotation has survived in the works of several Arabic writers. The phrases in [ ] indicate additional language appearing in these other works.)

Most people are unable to follow any demonstrative argument consecutively; hence they need parables, and benefit from them . . . just as now we see the people called Christians drawing their faith from parable [and miracles], and yet sometimes acting in the same way [as those who philosophize]. For their contempt of death, [and of its sequel,] is patent to us every day, and likewise their restraint in cohabitation. For they include not only men but also women who refrain from cohabiting all through their lives; and they also number individuals who, in self-discipline and self-control in matters of food and drink, and in their keen pursuit of justice, have attained a pitch not inferior to that of genuine philosophers.

The criticisms of Celsus and Galen against the faith-based teachings of the Christians were founded in an intellectual tradition of rational inquiry dating back to the Greek civilization of the fifth and sixth centuries B.C.E. However, this classical tradition of rational investigation was dying away by the late second century C.E., and after 250 C.E. it appears infrequently in the extant sources.[20] Some modern historians have attempted to account for this shift in perspective with explanations such as a "loss of confidence" in the ability of the individual to shape and control his destiny. They have characterized the period after 250 C.E. as marked by the growth of the worst sort of religious superstition

---

20. See the discussion of this issue by Ramsay MacMullen, *Christianity & Paganism in the Fourth to Eighth Centuries* (New Haven: Yale University Press, 1997), 74–102 and Peter Brown, *The Making of Late Antiquity* (Cambridge: Harvard University Press, 1978), 1–26.

and excess.[21] However, it is fairer to state that the Mediterranean world experienced a shift in the way the masses perceived and explained the relationship
between the worlds of spirit and everyday life. The newer view perceived less
distinct boundaries between the two worlds and allowed for much more frequent direct intervention in the affairs of everyday life by divine powers of
every sort. In many respects this "new" perspective was actually a resurfacing of
older forms of popular religious belief that had been covered over, but not
destroyed, by the rational tradition of the educated Graeco-Roman governing
elites. However, the resurfacing of these popular beliefs was shaped by the
developing monotheistic tendencies of the first, second, and third centuries C.E.,
as during this period both the educated and uneducated came to believe that
there was an ultimate divine power behind the world and that the traditional
gods and goddesses were either merely aspects of this great god or part of a hierarchy of lesser divinities beneath the ultimate divinity. This developing "pagan
monotheism" was easily accounted for by Christian teachings that described a
world created by and under the rule of the "great god," but which also acknowledged the existence of angels and demons of many different lower ranks and
powers. The shift in the religious beliefs of the masses toward a view of the
divine more compatible with the Christian perspective undoubtedly facilitated
the growth of the Christian faith in the third and fourth centuries C.E.

THE PERSECUTION OF CHRISTIANS IN THE LATE 170S C.E.

Celsus seems to have concluded his *True Doctrine* with a plea to the Christians
that they not hold themselves apart from the civil and social life of the larger
world around them.

> 3.28 Celsus, *True Doctrine* 8.73, 75 (written ca. 175–181 C.E.) qtd. by Origen
> in *Against Celsus.*
>
> [8.73] In the next place, Celsus urges us "to help the emperor with all our
> might, and to labor with him in the maintenance of justice, to fight
> for him; and if he requires it, to fight under him, or lead an army
> along with him.". . . We do indeed not fight under him, although he
> requires it; but we fight on his behalf, forming a special army—an
> army of piety—by offering our prayers to God. . . .
> [8.75] Celsus also urges us to "take office in the government of the country,
> if that is required for the maintenance of the laws and the support of
> religion". . . . And it is not for the purpose of escaping public duties

---

21. This observation is made by Peter Brown, *The Making of Late Antiquity* (Cambridge:
Harvard University Press, 1978), 10–11. Brown and other historians, while acknowledging the
decline in learning and "rational belief" during this period, argue that the more significant factor was the change in perceptions as to where divine power interacted with the human world.
Ibid. at 11–26. See also Ramsay MacMullen, *Christianity & Paganism in the Fourth to Eighth
Centuries* (New Haven: Yale University Press, 1997), 74–102, 153; Ramsay MacMullen, *Changes
in the Roman Empire* (Princeton: Princeton University Press, 1990), 114, 117–29.

that Christians decline public office, but that they may reserve themselves for a diviner and more necessary service in the Church of God-
for the salvation of man.

At the time Celsus wrote *True Doctrine*, the Roman Empire had suffered
plague and war for almost fifteen years. Accordingly, his plea that Christians
end their refusal either to participate in military service to defend the Roman
Empire or to take public office to help at home implicitly raises the question of
the social consequences to Christians arising from this refusal. The Christian
refusal to perform military service or public office is relatively easy to understand from the Christian perspective because the routines of both military and
public service were intimately interwoven with the symbols and worship of the
pagan gods. Much of public office and military service revolved around the frequent performance of religious rites and celebrations, which required an extensive administrative effort to supply and organize. According to Tertullian, many
second-century Christians thought it inconceivable in practice that a good
Christian could perform either military service or public office without compro-
mising his or her faith. These pagan religious ceremonies and festivals were also
the center of social life for both civilians and soldiers, so the refusal of Christians
to participate in these communal functions served to isolate Christians from
their neighbors and community. Under such circumstances, Christians earned a
reputation for being at best anti-social and at worst dangers to the community
because of their provocative attitudes toward the gods. During the years of war
and plague in the reign of Marcus Aurelius, segments of the pagan populace grew
increasingly hostile towards Christians because of the perceived threat to the
public safety and welfare. While no official persecution was instituted, the popular mistrust of the Christians led to severe, if localized, persecutions of Christian
communities, such as the persecution of the Christian communities in Vienna
(Vienne) and Lugdunum (Lyons) in Gaul (France) in 177 C.E.

> 3.29 The Epistle Of The Gallican Churches (quoted by Eusebius
> *Ecclesiastical History* 5.1.3–61)
> [3] The servants sojourning in Vienne and Lyons in Gaul to the brethren
> in Asia and Phrygia, who have the same faith and hope of redemp-
> tion as you. Peace, grace and glory from God the Father and Christ
> Jesus, our Lord. . . .
> [4] The greatness of the persecution here, and the terrible rage of the
> heathen against the saints, and the suffering of the blessed martyrs,
> are more than we can narrate accurately, nor can they be put down
> in writing. For with all his might the adversary attacked us, fore-
> shadowing his coming which is shortly to be, and tried everything,
> practicing his adherents and training them against the servants of
> God, so that we were not merely excluded from houses and baths and
> markets, but we were even forbidden to be seen at all in any place

whatever. But against them the grace of God did captain us; it rescued the weak, and marshaled against them steadfast pillars of men able by patience to draw to themselves all the attack of the enemy. They came together and endured every kind of abuse and punishment, they counted many things as few in their zeal for Christ, and did indeed prove that the sufferings of this present time are not worthy to be compared with the glory which shall be revealed to us.

[7] First, they endured nobly all that was heaped upon them by the mob; howls and stripes and dragging about, and rapine and imprisonment and stoning, and all things which are wont to happen at the hands of an infuriated populace against its supposed enemies and focs; then they were dragged into the marketplace by the tribune and by the chief authorities of the city, were indicted and confessed, and at last they were shut up until the coming of the governor. Then they were brought before the governor, and when he used all his cruelty against them, then intervened Vettius Epagathus, one of the brethren. . . . His character forbade him to endure the unreasonable judgment given against us, and, overcome with indignation, he asked to be heard himself in defense of the brethren to the effect that there was nothing atheistic or impious among us. He was howled down by all those around the judgement-seat, for he was a man of position, and the governor would not tolerate the just requests he had put forward but merely asked if he were a Christian himself. He then confessed in clear tones and was himself taken into the ranks of martyrs. He was called the "Comforter of Christians," but had the Comforter in himself, the spirit of Zacharias which he had shown by the fullness of his love when he chose to lay down even his own life for the defense of the brethren, for he was and is a true disciple of Christ, and he follows the Lamb wheresoever he goes.

[10] The rest were then divided and the first martyrs were obviously ready, and they fulfilled the confession of martyrdom with all readiness, but some others appeared not to be ready, and failed in training and in strength, unable to endure the strain of a great conflict, and about ten in number failed, as those born out of due time. They caused us great grief and immeasurable mourning, and hindered the zeal of the others who had not been arrested. Yet they, although suffering all the terrors, nevertheless remained with the martyrs and did not desert them. But at that point we were all greatly terrified by uncertainty as to their confession, not fearing the threatened punishment but looking towards the end and afraid lest some one should fall away. Yet day by day those who were worthy went on being arrested, completing their number, so as to collect from the two churches all the zealous and those through whom the life of the

locality was kept together. There were also arrested certain heathen slaves of our members, since the governor had publicly commanded that we should all be prosecuted, and these, by the snare of Satan, fearing the tortures which they saw the saints suffering, when the soldiers urged them, falsely accused us of Thyestean feasts and Oedipodean intercourse, and things which it is not right for us either to speak of or to think of or even to believe that such things could ever happen among men. When this rumor spread all men turned like beasts against us, so that even if any had formerly been lenient for friendship's sake they then became furious and raged against us, and there was fulfilled that which was spoken by our Lord, that "The time will come when whosoever killeth you will think that he doeth God service." Then at last the holy martyrs suffered tortures beyond all description, for Satan was striving to wring some blasphemy even from them. . . .

[20] Sanctus also himself endured nobly, beyond measure or human power, all the ill-treatment of men, for though the wicked hoped through persistence and the rigor of his tortures to wring from him something wrong, he resisted them with such constancy that he did not even tell his own name, or the race or the city whence he was, nor whether he was slave or free, but to all questions answered in Latin, "I am a Christian." This he said for name and city and race and for everything else, and the heathen heard no other sound from him. For this reason the governor and the torturers were very ambitious to subdue him. . . .

[25] Biblis, too, one of those who had denied, did the devil bring to torture (thinking that he had already swallowed her up and wishing to condemn her through blasphemy as well), to force her to say impious things about us, as though she were already broken and weak. But she recovered under torture, and, as it were, woke up out of deep sleep, being reminded through this transitory punishment of the eternal torments in hell, and contradicted the blasphemers, saying, "How would such men eat children, when they are not allowed to eat the blood even of irrational animals?" And after this she confessed herself a Christian and was added to the ranks of the martyrs. . . .

[32] Then a great dispensation of God was given, and the measureless mercy of Jesus was so manifested, as had rarely happened among the brethren, but is not beyond the skill of Christ. For those who at the first arrest had denied were imprisoned themselves and shared in the terrors, for this time not even their denial was any advantage to them; but those who confessed what they were were imprisoned as Christians, no other accusation being brought against them, the others however were held as murderers and foul persons and punished twice as much as the rest. . . .

[43] But Attalus was himself loudly called for by the crowd, for he was well known. He went in, a ready combatant, for his conscience was clear, and he had been nobly trained in Christian discipline, and had ever been a witness for truth among us. He was led round the amphitheater and a placard was carried before him on which was written in Latin, "This is Attalus, the Christian." The people were very bitter against him, but when the governor learnt that he was a Roman, he commanded him to be put back with the rest, who were in the jail, about whom he had written to the emperor and was waiting for his reply.

[45] But the intervening time was not idle or fruitless for them but through their endurance was manifested the immeasurable mercy of Christ, for through the living the dead were being quickened and martyrs gave grace to those who had denied. And there was great joy to the Virgin Mother who had miscarried with them as though dead, and was receiving them back alive. For through them the majority of those who had denied were again brought to birth and again conceived and quickened again, and learned to confess, and now alive and vigorous, made happy by God who wills not the death of the sinner, but is kind towards repentance, went to the judgement seat, in order that they might again be interrogated by the governor. For Caesar had written that they should be tortured to death, but that if any should recant they should be let go, and at the beginning of the local feast (and this is widely attended by the concourse of all the heathen to it) the governor led them to the judgement seat, making a show and spectacle of the blessed men to the mob. He accordingly examined them again, beheaded all who appeared to possess Roman citizenship, and sent the rest to the beasts. . . .

[58] . . . the governor and the people showed the like unrighteous hatred against us that the Scripture might be fulfilled, "Let him that is unlawful be unlawful still, and he that is righteous be righteous still." For those who had been strangled in the jail they threw to the dogs, and watched carefully night and day that none should be cared for by us. Then they threw out the remains left by the beasts and by the fire, torn and charred, and for many days watched with a military guard the heads of the rest, together with their trunks, all unburied. And some raged and gnashed their teeth at the remains, seeking some further vengeance from them, others laughed and jeered, glorifying their idols and ascribing to them the punishment of the Christians, and the gentler, who seemed to have a little sympathy, mocked greatly, saying, "Where is their god and what good to them was their worship, which they preferred beyond their lives?" Their conduct thus varied, but in our circle great grief obtained, because we could not bury the bodies

in the earth, for night did not avail us for this, nor did money persuade nor entreaty shame, but in every way they watched, as though they would make some great gain, that the bodies should not obtain burial. [62] . . . thus the bodies of the martyrs,[22] after having been exposed and insulted in every way for six days, and afterwards burned and turned to ashes, were swept by the wicked into the River Rhone which flows nearby, that not even a relic of them might still appear upon the earth. And this they did as though they could conquer God and take away their rebirth in order, as they said, "that they might not even have any hope of resurrection, through trusting in which they have brought in strange and new worship and despised terrors, going readily and with joy to death; now let us see if they will rise again, and if their God be able to help them and to take them out of our hands."

Because the letter mentions both that the persecution began before the governor's arrival and that there was an exchange of letters between the governor and the emperor while the Christians were being held, this persecution must have lasted for at least several months. The letter also indicates that the persecution began with the general populace rather than the imperial officials and that the populace was greatly distressed and offended that a respectable man of position like Vettius Epagathus could be a Christian. In spite of the obvious animosity of the local population towards Christians, Marcus Aurelius's response reaffirmed the official policy laid out in Trajan's letter to Pliny the Younger more than sixty years earlier and reversed the governor's order not to release those Christians who recanted.

The letter is also of great interest because of the explicit statements given for the populace's hatred of Christians. The first accusation was that the Christians participated in cannibalism and sexual misconduct ("Thyestean feasts and Oedipodean intercourse") and the second accusation was the "strange and new worship" involving the rejection of the old gods and the acceptance of new beliefs such as the physical resurrection of the dead. It is common-place for many modern writers to pass over the charges of cannibalism and sexual misconduct as though they were merely the "typical slanders" used by ancients against any unpopular group. But in fact there is much contemporary evidence preserved by Christians themselves to indicate that various fringe or "heretical" groups of Christians engaged in ritual prostitution and "free sex," and there are even accusations that some of these groups used aborted fetuses in the eucharistic services. (These Christian accounts of sexual misconduct and cannibalism are discussed in Appendix B.) Such conduct by a fringe Christian sect would have undoubtedly caused problems for the other Christian communities, and a

---

22. Forty-eight Christians are known to have been martyred at Lugdunum. W. H. C. Frend, *Martyrdom and Persecution in the Early Church* (Oxford: Basil Blackwell, 1965), 2–3 and the sources cited therein.

few years after the persecution in Lugdunum and Vienne, the new bishop for these towns, Irenaeus, identified and attacked these various heretical groups in his treatise, *Against Heresies.*

The persecution of Christians during the latter years of Marcus Aurelius's reign was not restricted to Gaul. Evidence exists for a persecution in North Africa that came to a climax shortly after Marcus Aurelius's death on March 17, 180 C.E.

3.30 *The Acts Of The Scillitan Martyrs* from a manuscript in the British Museum, concerning events on July 17, 180 C.E.

In the consulship of Praesens, then consul for the second time, and Claudian, on the 17th of July, Speratus, Nartzalus and Cittinus, Donata, Secunda, Vestia were brought to trial at Carthage in the council chamber. The proconsul Saturninus said to them: "You may merit the indulgence of our lord the emperor, if you return to a right mind."

Speratus said: "We have never done harm to any, we have never lent ourselves to wickedness; we have never spoken ill of any, but have given thanks when ill-treated, because we hold our own emperor in honor."

The proconsul Saturninus said: "We also are religious people, and our religion is simple, and we swear by the genius of our lord the emperor, and pray for his safety, as you also ought to do."

Speratus said: "If you will give me a quiet hearing, I will tell you the mystery of simplicity."

Saturninus said: "If you begin to speak evil of our sacred rites, I will give you no hearing; but swear rather by the genius of our lord the emperor."

Speratus said: "I do not recognize the empire of this world, but rather I serve that God, whom no man has seen nor can see. I have not stolen, but if I buy anything, I pay the tax, because I recognize my Lord, the King of kings and Emperor of all peoples."

The proconsul Saturninus said to the rest: "Cease to be of this persuasion."

Speratus said: "The persuasion that we should do murder, or bear false witness, that is evil."

The proconsul Saturninus said: "Have no part in this madness."

Cittinus said: "We have none other to fear save the Lord our God who is in heaven."

Donata said: "Give honor to Caesar as unto Caesar, but fear to God."

Vestia said: "I am a Christian."

Secunda said: "I wish to be none other than what I am."

The proconsul Saturninus said to Speratus: "Do you persist in remaining a Christian?"

Speratus said: "I am a Christian."

And all were of one mind with him.

The proconsul Saturninus said: "Do you desire any space for consideration?"

Speratus said: "When the right is so clear, there is nothing to consider."

The proconsul Saturninus said: "What have you in your case [satchel]?"

Speratus said: "The Books, and the letters of a just man, one Paul."

The proconsul Saturninus said: "Take a reprieve of thirty days and think it over."

Speratus again said: "I am a Christian." And all were of one mind with him.

The proconsul Saturninus read out the sentence from a tablet: "Whereas Speratus, Nartzalus, Cittinus, Donata, Vestia, Secunda, and the rest have confessed that they live in accordance with the religious rites of the Christians, and, when an opportunity was given them of returning to the usage of the Romans, persevered in their obstinacy, it is our pleasure that they should suffer by the sword."

Speratus said: "Thanks be to God!"

Nartazalus said: "Today we are martyrs in Heaven: thanks be to God!"

The proconsul Saturninus commanded that proclamation be made by the herald: "I have commanded that Speratus, Nartzalus, Cittinus, Veturius, Felix, Aquilinus, Laetantius, Januaria, Generosa, Vestia, Donata, Secunda be led forth to execution."

They all said: "Thanks be to God!"

And so all were crowned with martyrdom together, and reign with the Father and Son and Holy Spirit for ever and ever. Amen.

The Acts of the Scillitan Martyrs is a good example of the "acts of the martyrs" that were based on the official Roman trial records. Indeed, this particular *Acts* seems to have added little to the material found in the Roman trial record. A matter of interest with respect to this particular trial is the fact that the Christian writer Tertullian, who lived in Carthage in North Africa less than a generation later, wrote that the Roman governor Saturninus was "the first to draw the sword" on Christians in Africa.[23] If true, Tertullian's statement would indicate that prior to 180 C.E. either the local Roman authorities made no serious effort to find or persecute the Christians of North Africa or the number of North African Christians was too small to have come to the attention of the Roman governors.

Marcus Aurelius died campaigning on the northern frontier in 180 C.E., when he was seemingly upon the verge of a significant strategic victory in the wars to secure the Danubian River defenses. His son Commodus (180–192 C.E.) negotiated a quick peace with the Germanic tribes and returned to Rome to

---

23. Tertullan, *To Scapula* 3.

secure the throne. While historians argue whether Commodus squandered an opportunity to achieve a "lasting" solution to the problem of the frontier defense in this part of the Empire, the Roman Empire was generally at peace during his reign and Eusebius wrote that the persecutions of Christians that marked the late 170s C.E. wound down during Commodus's reign.

3.31 Eusebius of Caesarea, *Ecclesiastical History* 5.21.1 (ca. 311–323 C.E., concerning events after 180 C.E.)

And at the same time in the reign of Commodus [180–192 C.E.] our treatment was changed to a milder one, and by the grace of God peace came on the churches throughout the whole world.

In spite of Eusebius's statement, however, there is evidence that at least a few troubles continued during the early years of Commodus's reign.

3.32 Tertullian, *To Scapula* 5 (ca. 212 C.E.) The passage concerns events in 185 C.E.

When Arrius Antoninus was driving things hard in Asia, all the Christians of the province, in one united band, presented themselves before his judgment seat; on which, ordering a few to be led forth to execution, he said to the rest, "O miserable men, if you wish to die, you have cliffs or ropes."

The son of a Roman centurion, Tertullian (160–220 C.E.) was the Christian literary giant of his day and his writings ranged over a wide spectrum of Christian thought. A fierce foe of heretics and an unflinching defender of the faith, Tertullian strongly shaped the future direction of Western Christian thought. His writings also contain much valuable information concerning the social and legal status of Christianity during that period, such as the facts that the mere profession of Christianity was still a crime in his time and that many Christians still held themselves aloof from military service and public office.

3.33 Tertullian, *To the Peoples* 1.3 (197 C.E.)

No name of a crime stands against us, but only the crime of a name. Now this in very deed is neither more nor less than the entire odium which is felt against us. The name is the cause. . . . In order, therefore, that the issue may be withdrawn from the offensive name, we are compelled to deny it; then upon our denial we are acquitted, with an entire absolution for out past. . . . What crime, what offense, what fault is there in a name?

3.34 Tertullian, *On Idolatry* 17, 19 (ca. 200 C.E.)

[17] Hence arose, very lately, a dispute whether a servant of God should take the administration of any dignity or power, if he be able, whether by some special grace, or by adroitness, to keep himself intact from every species of idolatry. . . . And so let us grant that it is possible for any

one to succeed in moving, in whatsoever office, under the mere name of the office, neither sacrificing nor lending his authority to sacrifices; not farming out victims; not assigning to others the care of temples; not looking after their tributes; not giving spectacles at his own or the public charge, or presiding over the giving them; making proclamation or edict for no solemnity; not even taking oaths; moreover (what comes under the head of power), neither sitting in judgement on any's life or character, for you might bear with his judging about money; neither condemning nor forecondemning; binding no one, imprisoning or torturing no one—if it is credible that all this is possible. . . .

[19] In that last section, decision may seem to have been given likewise concerning military service, which is between dignity and power. But now inquiry is made about this point, whether a believer may turn himself unto military service, and whether the military may be admitted unto the faith, even the rank and file, or each inferior grade, to whom there is no necessity for taking part in sacrifices or capital punishments. There is no agreement between the divine and the human sacrament, the standard of Christ and the standard of the devil, the camp of light and the camp of darkness. One soul cannot be due to two masters—God and Caesar. . . . For albeit soldiers had come unto John, and received the formula of their rule; albeit, likewise, a centurion had believed; still the Lord afterward, in disarming Peter, unbelted every soldier.

Tertullian also indicates that the accusations that Christians engaged in cannibalism and sexual immorality persisted into his generation.

3.35 Tertullian, *Apology* 2.1 (197 C.E.)

But now, if it is really certain that we are of all men the most criminal, why do you yourselves treat us otherwise than those like us, the rest of the criminal class, when the same treatment belongs to the same fault? Whatever you charge against us, when you so charge others, they use their own eloquence, they hire the advocacy of others, to prove their innocence. There is freedom to answer, to cross-question, since in fact it is against the law for men to be condemned, undefended and unheard. But to Christians alone it is forbidden to say anything to clear their case, to defend Truth, to save the judge from being unjust. No! One thing is looked for, one alone, the one thing needful for popular hatred—the confession of the name! Not investigation of the charge! Yet, if you are trying any other criminal, it does not follow at once from his confessing to the name of murderer, or temple robber, or adulterer, or enemy of the state (to touch on our indictments!), that you are satisfied to pronounce sentence, unless you pursue all the consequent investigation, such as the character of the act, how often, where, how, when he did it, his accessories, his confederates. In our case nothing of the kind! Yet it ought just as much to be wrung out of us (whenever that false charge is made) how many murdered babies each of us has tasted, how many acts of incest he had done in the dark, what cooks were there—yes, and what dogs. Oh! The glory of that magistrate who had brought to light some Christian who had eaten up to date a hundred babies!

Tertullian's writings confirm that the common people continued to blame the Christian refusal to honor the gods as the cause of misfortune in the world, a belief that lay behind so much of the popular animosity toward the Christian faith.

3.36 Tertullian, *Apology* 40.2 (197 C.E.)
If the Tiber reaches the walls, if the Nile does not rise to the fields, if the sky does not move [i.e., no rain] or the earth does, if there is famine, if there is plague, the cry is at once, "The Christians to the lion." What, all of them to a single lion?

Beliefs such as this continued even after Christians came to control the government of the Roman Empire. In the early fifth century C.E., for example, St. Augustine quoted the common proverb, "*Pluvia defit, causa Chrisitiani sunt*"— "If the rains fail, the Christians are the cause."[24] Tertullian, however, roared his defiance at such accusations and the threats that accompanied them.

3.37 Tertullian, *Apology* 50.13 (197 C.E.)
But nothing whatever is accomplished by your cruelties, each more exquisite than the last. It is the bait that wins more men for our school. We multiply whenever we are mown down by you: the blood of Christians is seed.

From the end of the second century C.E. comes one of the most famous of Christian epitaphs, that of Marcellus Avircius, the bishop of Hieropolis in Phrygia, who died about 200 C.E. The text of the epitaph was preserved in a fourth-century C.E. work entitled "The Life of Avircius," but the tombstone itself, with the inscription partially intact, was found by archaeologists in 1883 and now resides in the Vatican Museum. The tombstone is one of the earliest known Christian inscriptions. Its use of oblique Christian imagery and the reference to "everyone who understands and agrees" seems to indicate that Marcellus was concerned that his tombstone might be desecrated, if his faith were known. Today, it is difficult to believe that the people of Hieropolis would not have known that Marcellus was a Christian bishop, but if this interpretation is correct, then the inscription is further evidence of the popular animosity toward Christians.

---

24. Augustine, *City of God* 2.3.

3.38 The Epitaph Of Marcellus Avircius (ca. 200 C.E.)

I, a citizen of the elect city, erected this tomb in my lifetime,
That I might have clearly there a place for my body;
My name is Avircius, a disciple of the pure Shepherd
who feeds the flocks of sheep on mountains and plains,
who has great all-seeing eyes;
He taught me [. . .] faithful scriptures.
To Rome he sent me to behold sovereignty
and to see a queen, golden robed and golden sandaled;
a people I saw there which has a splendid seal,
And I saw the plain of Syria and all the cities, and Nisibis,
crossing the Euphrates; but everywhere I met with brethren;
With Paul before me, I followed, and Faith everywhere led the way
and served food everywhere, the Fish from the spring—
immense, pure, which the pure Virgin caught
and gave to her friends to eat for ever,
with good wine, giving the cup with the loaf.
These things I Avircius ordered to be written thus in my presence.
I am truly seventy two years old.
Let him who understands these things, and everyone who is in
    agreement, pray for Avircius.
No one is to put anyone else into my tomb:
Otherwise he is to pay the Roman treasury 2,000 gold pieces
And my good native city of Hieropolis 1,000 gold pieces.

4 | STRUGGLE AND ACCOMMODATION: THE THIRD CENTURY C.E.

The Severian Dynasty (193–235 C.E.) established by Septimus Severus (193–211 C.E.) was largely successful in defending Rome's frontiers and maintaining peace within the Empire. The end of the Severian dynasty in 235 C.E., however, began a fifty-year period known as the "Years of the Barrack Emperors," during which the breakdown of the emperor's control over the legions and the absence of any system of orderly succession to the emperor's position led to more or less constant internal rebellion and the near collapse of the Roman Empire. During the period 235–284 C.E. at least twenty-five individuals were recognized in Rome as emperor and there were numerous other claimants for the throne. The emperor Gallienus (253–268 C.E.), for example, had to contend with at least eighteen other claimants to the throne during his reign. During the Years of the Barrack Emperors, rivals to the sitting emperor often managed to seize control of large sections of the Roman Empire and the Roman frontier defenses were repeatedly compromised, as the legions were diverted from their regular frontier garrison duties to the civil wars over the emperorship.

Unfortunately for Rome, this period of internal turmoil coincided with increasingly serious external threats. A new ruling dynasty in Persia sought to challenge Rome's eastern borders, and along the Danube and Rhine Rivers previously unknown tribes like the Saxons, Franks, Alamanni, Vandals, and Goths began to test Rome's defenses. By the middle part of the third century C.E., Persian and barbarian armies were breaking through Rome's frontier defenses with some regularity and on occasion penetrating deep into the interior provinces. Three events in the third quarter of the century demonstrated the depth of the Rome's crisis: in 251 C.E. Trajan Decius (249–251 C.E.) became the first Roman emperor to be killed in battle; in 260 C.E. Valerian (253–260 C.E.) became the first Roman emperor to be captured by an enemy of Rome; and in 271 C.E. the emperor Aurelian (270–275 C.E.) abandoned the province of Dacia, which lay north of the Danube River, as indefensible.

The Roman Empire seemed to be slipping towards a complete collapse when a series of soldier-emperors from Rome's Balkan provinces began to turn the tide. Of particular note, Aurelian (270–275 C.E.) recaptured the areas usurped by the Gallic Empire in the West and Palmyra in the East, and Probus (277–282 C.E.) did much to stabilize the Western Empire's frontiers with a series of victories against the Franks, Germans, and various bandit and rebel groups.

Rome's recovery was solidified during the reign of Diocletian (284–305 C.E.). In 286 C.E., in an effort to provide for closer supervision of both the frontiers and the legions, Diocletian appointed his trusted friend Maximian as co-emperor and together the two men set about reorganizing the legions, the frontier defenses, and the administrative bureaucracy and repairing the economic damage done by the half-century of civil wars and invasions. In 293 C.E., Diocletian appointed two "junior" emperors, each called a "Caesar," to aid the two senior emperors, each called an "Augustus," and divided the Empire into four administrative prefectures, each governed by one of the four rulers. Diocletian's "tetrarchy" allowed for closer supervision of the various parts of the Empire and recalled the succession scheme of the Five Good Emperors in that each Augustus was supposed to select a competent Caesar, rather than a mere kinsman, to hold partial power and ultimately succeed to the Augustus's position. The Caesars were given broad powers and exercised real discretion in their administrative areas, but by the force of his personality Diocletian was able to maintain both the appearance and substance of a unified system of rule among the four tetrarchs. By 298 C.E., the tetrarchs were largely successful in restoring both internal order and the frontier defenses, but at the cost of a huge increase in government expenditures for new fortifications, additional troops, and a much larger administrative bureaucracy.

About 301 C.E., Diocletian turned his attention to the rampant inflation and other economic problems the Roman Empire suffered as a legacy of the Barrack Emperors and his own expenditures. While his efforts to reorganize the currency and establish wage and price controls to control inflation were not entirely successful, by 305 C.E. Diocletian thought his work was largely accomplished and so he gave up his throne, becoming the first Roman emperor ever to retire voluntarily from office. Diocletian also pressured Maximian into retiring also at this time, but Maximian soon attempted to reclaim his position. While the Roman Empire was never again as strong as in the first and second centuries C.E., by his extraordinary effort Diocletian had succeeded in preserving the Roman Empire and establishing the basis upon which it would survive the fourth century C.E.

During the Years of the Barrack Emperors, the Senate of Rome lost essentially all of its remaining power and authority to the emperors. When first Carus (282–283 C.E.) and then Diocletian asserted that the legions alone could bestow the authority to rule the Empire, the senate lost even the token right to confirm the legal authority of a new emperor. As succession to the throne became openly dependent on sheer military might, without even the façade of legitimacy bestowed by the senate's confirmation of a new emperor, emperors increasingly sought to bolster their legitimacy by adopting the trappings of autocratic Eastern rulers and claiming a special relationship with the gods. While most of the third-century emperors respected the Roman tradition that emperors did not become divine until after death, their claims of a special relationship with the gods, their deification after death, and the increasingly eastern and autocratic style of imperial government did not bode well for relations with the Christians.

During the third century C.E., Christianity grew significantly stronger in a number of crucial ways. First, although Christians still formed only a small minority of the Empire's total population, the number of Christians grew at an extraordinary rate during the troubled times of the third century, especially when compared to the various pagan cults. By 300 C.E., Christians seem to have constituted about 8–10 percent of the Roman Empire's total population of 55 to 60 million people.[1] Second, the third century saw a significant strengthening of Christianity's organizational structure. During this period the bishops consolidated their essentially absolute power within the individual churches and increased their collective power by beginning to meet in regional synods to discuss and debate important issues of doctrine, discipline, and organization. It was also during the third century that the orthodox churches as a whole began to adopt a hierarchical structure that rather closely paralleled the geographic organization of the Roman Empire's provincial administrative structure. Third, over the course of the century the Christian churches as a whole managed to accumulate significant wealth as a result of the individual contributions of members and the corporate ownership of property. During the years of turmoil in the mid-third century C.E., the Christian churches seem to have been among the few, if not the only, institutions in the Roman Empire with both the resources and the will to minister to the social and economic needs of the urban masses.[2] As a result of all these factors, by the end of the third century C.E., Christianity was beginning to resemble a state within a state, with its own governing structures and significant financial resources.

The growth of numbers and the development of better lines of communication and authority created new problems for the Christian church, however. As the individual Christian communities came into more regular contact with one another, it soon became apparent that Christian belief had developed in an extraordinarily rich and diverse fashion during the years of persecution and relative isolation. The formulation and refinement of a common "orthodox" Christian theology would be the single most important issue facing Christians during the third and fourth centuries C.E., but the emotional intensity and divisiveness of the debate

---

1. Ramsay MacMullen, in *Christianizing the Roman Empire* (New Haven: Yale University Press, 1984), 85, estimates that there were perhaps 5 million Christians in 300 C.E., whereas Rodney Stark, in *The Rise Of Christianity* (Princeton: Princeton University Press, 1996), 7, estimates some 6.3 million Christians by 300 C.E. Robin Lane Fox, in *Pagans and Christians* (New York: Alfred A. Knopf, Inc., 1989), 592, favors a somewhat lower number, estimating that Christians may have formed only 4 or 5 percent of the population by 312 C.E.

2. See the discussion of the significance of these contributions, and particularly of the wealth contributed by women, by Robin Lane Fox at *Pagans and Christians* (New York: Alfred A. Knopf, Inc., 1989), 308–11 and by Peter Brown at "Church and Leadership," Philippe Aries and George Duby (eds.) *A History of Private Life: Vol. 1 From Pagan Rome to Byzantium*, ed. Paul Veyne, Arthur Goldhammer, trans. (Cambridge: Harvard University Press, 1987), 279–80.

over what constituted "orthodoxy" was in many ways a more serious threat to the future of the Christian church than Roman persecution.

CHRISTIANITY UNDER THE SEVERIAN DYNASTY

The third century C.E. began with a series of local persecutions of Christians during the reign of Septimus Severus (193–211 C.E.). Although the persecutions under Septimus Severus do not appear to have been either widespread or particularly severe, his reign was the occasion of one of the most famous of all Christian martyrdoms, that of Perpetua and Felicitas.

> 4.1 Scriptores Historiae Augustae, *Life of Septimus Severus* 16.8–9; 17.1–2 (ca. late fourth century C.E.)
>
> [In 202 C.E., Septimus Severus promoted] his elder son and appointed him consul as a colleague to himself; and without further delay, while still in Syria, the two entered upon their consulship. After this, having first raised his soldiers' pay, he turned his steps towards Alexandria, and while on his way thither he conferred numerous rights upon communities of Palestine. He forbade conversion to Judaism under heavy penalties and enacted a similar law in regard to the Christians. He then gave the Alexandrians the privilege of a local senate, for they were still without any public council.

> 4.2 Eusebius of Caesarea, *Ecclesiastical History* 6.1.1 (ca. 311–323 C.E.)
>
> Now when [Septimus] Severus also was stirring up persecution against the churches, in every place splendid martyrdoms of the champions of piety were accomplished. . . .

> 4.3 The Martyrdom of Perpetua and Felicitas. The following events took place in Carthage, Africa, in April of about 203 C.E.
>
> ¹ If instances of ancient faith which both testified to the grace of God and edified persons were written expressly for God's honor and humans' encouragement, why shouldn't recent events be similarly recorded for those same purposes? For these events will likewise become part of the past and vital to posterity, in spite of the fact that contemporary esteem for antiquity tends to minimize their value. And those who maintain that there is a single manifestation of the one Holy Spirit throughout the ages ought to consider that since a fullness of grace has been decreed for the last days of the world these recent events should be considered of greater value because of their proximity to those days. For "In the last days," says the Lord, "I shall diffuse my spirit over all humanity and their sons and daughters shall prophesy; the young shall see visions, and the old shall dream dreams."
>
> Just as we valued those prophecies so we acknowledge and reverence the new visions which were promised. And we consider the other powers of the Holy Spirit to be instruments of the Church to

which that same Spirit was sent to administer all gifts to all people, just as the Lord allotted. For this reason we deem it necessary to disseminate the written accounts for the glory of God, lest anyone with a weak or despairing faith might think that supernatural grace prevailed solely among the ancients who were honored either by their experience of martyrdom or visions. For God always fulfills what he promises, either as proof to non-believers or as an added grace to believers.

And so, brothers and dear ones, we share with you those things which we have heard and touched with our hands, so that those of you who were eyewitnesses of these deeds may be reminded of the glory of the Lord, and those of you now learning of it through this narration may associate yourselves with the holy martyrs and, through them, with the Lord Jesus Christ to whom there is glory and honor forever. Amen.

2 Arrested were some young catechumens: Revocatus and Felicitas (both servants), Saturninus, Secundulus, and Vibia Perpetua, a young married woman about twenty years old, of good family and upbringing. She had a father, mother, two brothers (one was a catechumen like herself), and an infant son at the breast. The following account of her martyrdom is her own, a record in her own words of her perceptions of the event:

3While I was still with the police authorities (she said) my father out of love for me tried to dissuade me from my resolution. "Father," I said, "do you see here, for example, this vase, or pitcher, or whatever it is?" "I see it," he said. "Can it be named anything else than what it really is?" I asked, and he said, "No." "So I also cannot be called anything else than what I am, a Christian." Enraged by my words my father came at me as though to tear out my eyes. He only annoyed me, but he left, overpowered by his diabolical arguments.

For a few days my father stayed away. I thanked the Lord and felt relieved because of my father's absence. At this time we were baptized and the Spirit instructed me not to request anything from the baptismal waters except endurance of physical suffering.

A few days later we were imprisoned. I was terrified because never before had I experienced such darkness. What a terrible day! Because of crowded conditions and rough treatment by the soldiers the heat was unbearable. My condition was aggravated by my anxiety for my baby. Then Tertius and Pomponius, those kind deacons who were taking care of our needs, paid for us to be moved for a few hours to a better part of the prison where we might refresh ourselves. Leaving the dungeon we all went about our own business. I nursed my child, who was already weak from hunger. In my anxiety for the infant I spoke to my mother about him, tried to console my brother, and asked that they care for my son. I suffered intensely because I sensed their agony on my account. These were the trials I had to endure for many days. Then I was granted the privilege of having my son remain with me in prison. Being relieved of my anxiety and concern for the infant, I immediately regained my strength. Suddenly the prison became my palace, and I loved being there rather than any other place. ⁴ Then my brother said to me, "Dear sister, you already have such a great reputation that you could ask for a vision indicating whether you will be condemned or freed." Since I knew that I could speak with the Lord, whose great favors I had already experienced, I confidently promised to do so. I said I would tell my brother about it the next day. Then I made my request and this is what I saw.

There was a bronze ladder of extraordinary height reaching up to heaven, but it was so narrow that only one person could ascend at a time. Every conceivable kind of iron weapon was attached to the sides of the ladder: swords, lances, hooks, and daggers. If anyone climbed up carelessly or without looking upwards, he/she would be mangled as the flesh adhered to the weapons. Crouching directly beneath the ladder was a monstrous dragon who threatened those climbing up and tried to frighten them from the ascent.

Saturus went up first. Because of his concern for us, he had given himself up voluntarily after we had been arrested. (He had been our source of strength but was not with us at the time of arrest.) When he reached the top of the ladder he turned to me and said, "Perpetua, I'm waiting for you, but be careful not to be bitten by the dragon." I told him that in the name of Jesus Christ the dragon could not harm me. At this the dragon slowly lowered its head as though afraid of me. Using its head as the first step, I began my ascent.

At the summit I saw an immense garden, in the center of which sat a tall, grey-haired man dressed like a shepherd, milking sheep. Standing around him were several thousand white-robed people. As he raised his head he noticed me and said, "Welcome, my child." Then he beckoned me to approach and gave me a small morsel of the cheese he was making. I accepted it with cupped hands and ate it. When all those surrounding us said, "Amen," I awoke, still tasting the sweet cheese. I immediately told my brother about the vision, and we both realized that we were to experience the sufferings of martyrdom. From then on we gave up having any hope in this world.

⁵ A few days later there was a rumor that our case was to be heard. My father, completely exhausted from his anxiety, came from the city to see me, with the intention of weakening my faith. "Daughter," he said, "have pity on my grey head. Have pity on your father if I have the honor to be called father by you, if with these hands I have brought you to the prime of your life, and if I have always favored you above your brothers, do not abandon me to the reproach of men.

Consider your brothers; consider your mother and your aunt; consider your son who cannot live without you. Give up your stubbornness before you destroy all of us. None of us will be able to speak freely if anything happens to you."

These were the things my father said out of love, kissing my hands and throwing himself at my feet. With tears he called me not daughter, but woman. I was very upset because of my father's condition. He was the only member of my family who would find no reason for joy in my suffering. I tried to comfort him saying, "Whatever God wants at this tribunal will happen, for remember that our power comes not from ourselves but from God." But utterly dejected, my father left me.
[6] One day as we were eating we were suddenly rushed off for a hearing. We arrived at the forum and the news spread quickly throughout the area near the forum, and a huge crowd gathered. We went up to the prisoners' platform. All the others confessed when they were questioned. When my turn came my father appeared with my son. Dragging me from the step, he begged: "Have pity on your son!"

Hilarion, the governor, who assumed power after the death of the proconsul Minucius Timinianus, said, "Have pity on your father's grey head; have pity on your infant son; offer sacrifice for the emperors' welfare." But I answered, "I will not." Hilarion asked, "Are you a Christian?" And I answered, "I am a Christian." And when my father persisted in his attempts to dissuade me, Hilarion ordered him thrown out, and he was beaten with a rod. My father's injury hurt me as much as if I myself had been beaten, and I grieved because of his pathetic old age. Then the sentence was passed; all of us were condemned to the beasts. We were overjoyed as we went back to the prison cell. Since I was still nursing my child who was ordinarily in the cell with me, I quickly sent the deacon Pomponius to my father's house to ask for the baby, but my father refused to give him up. Then God saw to it that my child no longer needed my nursing, nor were my breasts inflamed. After that I was no longer tortured by anxiety about my child or by pain in my breasts.
[7] A few days later while all of us were praying, in the middle of a prayer I suddenly called out the name "Dinocrates." I was astonished since I hadn't thought about him till then. When I recalled what had happened to him I was very disturbed and decided right then that I had not only the right, but the obligation, to pray for him. So I began to pray repeatedly and to make moaning sounds to the Lord in his behalf. During that same night I had this vision: I saw Dinocrates walking away from one of many very dark places. He seemed very hot and thirsty, his face grimy and colorless. The wound on his face was just as it had been when he died. This Dinocrates was my blood-brother who at the age of seven died very tragically from a cancerous

disease which so disfigured his face that his death was repulsive to everyone. It was for him that I now prayed. But neither of us could reach the other because of the great distance between. In the place where Dinocrates stood was a pool filled with water, and the rim of the pool was so high that it extended far above the boy's height. Dinocrates stood on his toes as if to drink the water but in spite of the fact that the pool was full, he could not drink because the rim was so high!

I realized that my brother was in trouble, but I was confident that I could help him with his problem. I prayed for him every day until we were transferred to the arena prison where we were to fight wild animals on the birthday of Geta Caesar. And I prayed day and night for him, moaning and weeping so that my petition would be granted.
[8] On the day that we were kept in chains, I had the following vision: I saw the same place as before, but Dinocrates was clean, well-dressed, looking refreshed. In place of the wound there was a scar, and the fountain which I had seen previously now had its rim lowered to the boy's waist. On the rim, over which water was flowing constantly, there was a golden bowl filled with water. Dinocrates walked up to it and began to drink; the bowl never emptied. And when he was no longer thirsty, he gladly went to play as children do. Then I awoke, knowing that he had been relieved of his suffering.
[9] A few days passed. Pudens, the official in charge of the prison (the official who had gradually come to admire us for our persistence), admitted many prisoners to our cell so that we might mutually encourage each other. As the day of the games drew near, my father, overwhelmed with grief, came again to see me. He began to pluck out his beard and throw it on the ground. Falling on his face before me, he cursed his old age, repeating such things as would move all creation. And I grieved because of his old age.
[10] The day before the battle in the arena, in a vision I saw Pomponius the deacon coming to the prison door and knocking very loudly. I went to open the gate for him. He was dressed in a loosely fitting white robe, wearing richly decorated sandals. He said to me, "Perpetua, come. We're waiting for you!" He took my hand and we began to walk over the extremely rocky and winding paths. When we finally arrived short of breath, at the arena, he led me to the center saying, "Don't be frightened! I'll be here to help you." He left me and I stared out over a huge crowd which watched me with apprehension. Because I knew that I had to fight with the beasts, I wondered why they hadn't yet been turned loose in the arena. Coming toward me was some type of Egyptian, horrible to look at, accompanied by fighters who were to help defeat me. Some handsome young men came forward to help and encourage me. I was stripped of my clothing, and suddenly I was a man. My assistants began to rub me with

oil as was the custom before a contest, while the Egyptian was on the opposite side rolling in the sand. Then a certain man appeared, so tall that he towered above the amphitheater. He wore a loose purple robe with two parallel stripes across the chest; his sandals were richly decorated with gold and silver. He carried a rod like that of an athletic trainer, and a green branch on which were golden apples. He motioned for silence and said, "If this Egyptian wins, he will kill her with the sword; but if she wins, she will receive this branch." Then he withdrew.

We both stepped forward and began to fight with our fists. My opponent kept trying to grab my feet but I repeatedly kicked his face with my heels. I felt myself being lifted up into the air and began to strike at him as one who was no longer earth-bound. But when I saw that we were wasting time, I put my two hands together, linked my fingers, and put his head between them. As he fell on his face I stepped on his head. Then the people began to shout and my assistants started singing victory songs. I walked up to the trainer and accepted the branch. He kissed me and said, "Peace be with you, my daughter." And I triumphantly headed towards the Sanavivarian Gate.[3] Then I woke up realizing that I would be contending not with wild animals but with the devil himself. I knew, however, that I would win. I have recorded the events which occurred up to the day before the final contest. Let anyone who wishes to record the events of the contest itself, do so.

[11] The saintly Saturus also related a vision which he had and it is recorded here in his own hand. Our suffering had ended (he said), and we were being carried toward the east by four angels whose hands never touched us. And we floated upward, not in a supine position, but as though we were climbing a gentle slope. As we left the earth's atmosphere we saw a brilliant light, and I said to Perpetua who was at my side, "This is what the Lord promised us. We have received his promise."

And while we were being carried along by those four angels we saw a large open space like a splendid garden landscaped with rose trees and every variety of flower. The trees were as tall as cypresses whose leaves rustled gently and incessantly. And there in that garden-sanctuary were four other angels, more dazzling than the rest. And when they saw us they showed us honor, saying to the other angels in admiration, "Here they are! They have arrived."

And those four angels who were carrying us began trembling in awe and set us down. And we walked through a violet-strewn field where we met Jocundus, Saturninus, and Artaxius who were burned alive in that same persecution, and Quintus, also a martyr, who had

---

3. The Porta Sanavivaria (Gate of Life) was the gate by which victorious gladiators would exit the arena. The defeated would be carried out through the Porta Libitinensis (Gate of Death).

died in prison. We were asking them where they had been, when the other angels said to us, "First, come this way. Go in and greet the Lord." [12] We went up to a place where the walls seemed constructed of light. At the entrance of the place stood four angels who put white robes on those who entered. We went in and heard a unified voice chanting endlessly, "Holy, holy, holy." We saw a white haired man sitting there who, in spite of his snowy white hair, had the features of a young man. His feet were not visible. On his right and left were four elderly gentlemen and behind them stood many more. As we entered we stood in amazement before the throne. Four angels supported us as we went up to kiss the aged man, and he gently stroked our faces with his hands. The other elderly men said to us, "Stand up." We rose and gave the kiss of peace. Then they told us to enjoy ourselves. I said to Perpetua, "You have your wish." She answered, "I thank God, for although I was happy on earth, I am much happier here right now." [13] Then we went out, and before the gates we saw Optatus the bishop on the right and Aspasius the priest and teacher on the left, both looking sad as they stood there separated from each other. They knelt before us saying, "Make peace between us, for you've gone away and left us this way." But we said to them, "Aren't you our spiritual father, and our teacher? Why are you kneeling before us?" We were deeply touched and we embraced them. And Perpetua began to speak to them in Greek and we invited them into the garden beneath a rose tree. While we were talking with them, the angels said to them, "Let them refresh themselves, and if you have any dissensions among you, forgive one another." This disturbed both of them and the angels said to Optatus, "Correct your people who flock to you as though returning from the games, fighting about the different teams." It seemed to us that they wanted to close the gates, and there we began to recognize many of our friends, among whom were martyrs. We were all sustained by an indescribable fragrance which completely satisfied us. Then in my joy, I awoke.

[14] The remarkable visions narrated above were those of the blessed martyrs Saturus and Perpetua, just as they put them in writing. As for Secundulus, while he was still in prison God gave him the grace of an earlier exit from this world, so that he could escape combat with the wild beasts. But his body, though not his soul, certainly felt the sword.

[15] As for Felicitas, she too was touched by God's grace in the following manner. She was pregnant when arrested, and was now in the eighth month. As the day of the contest approached she became very distressed that her martyrdom might be delayed, since the law forbade the execution of a pregnant woman. Then she would later have to shed her holy and innocent blood among common criminals. Her

friends in martyrdom were equally sad at the thought of abandoning such a good friend to travel alone on the same road to hope.

And so, two days before the contest, united in grief they prayed to the Lord. Immediately after the prayers her labor pains began. Because of the additional pain natural for an eighth-month delivery, she suffered greatly during the birth, and one of the prison guards taunted her; "If you're complaining now, what will you do when you'll be thrown to the wild beasts? You didn't think of them when you refused to sacrifice." She answered, "Now it is I who suffer, but then another shall be in me to bear the pain for me, since I am now suffering for Him." And she gave birth to a girl whom one of her sisters reared as her own daughter.

[16] Since the Holy Spirit has permitted, and by permitting has willed, that the events of the contest be recorded, we have no choice but to carry out the injunction (rather, the sacred trust) of Perpetua, in spite of the fact that it will be an inferior addition to the magnificent events already described. We are adding an instance of Perpetua's perseverance and lively spirit. At one time the prisoners were being treated with unusual severity by the commanding officer because certain deceitful men had intimated to him that the prisoners might escape by some magic spells. Perpetua openly challenged him: "Why don't you at least allow us to freshen up, the most noble of the condemned, since we belong to Caesar and are about to fight on his birthday? Or isn't it to your credit that we should appear in good condition on that day?" The officer grimaced and blushed, then ordered that they be treated more humanely and that her brothers and others be allowed to visit and dine with them. By this time the prison warden was himself a believer.

[17] On the day before the public games, as they were eating the last meal commonly called the free meal, they tried as much as possible to make it instead an *agape*. In the same spirit they were exhorting the people, warning them to remember the judgment of God, asking them to be witnesses to the prisoners' joy in suffering, and ridiculing the curiosity of the crowd. Saturus told them, "Won't tomorrow's view be enough for you? Why are you so eager to see something you hate? Friends today, enemies tomorrow! Take a good look so you'll recognize us on that day." Then they all left the prison amazed, and many of them began to believe.

[18] The day of their victory dawned, and with joyful countenances they marched from the prison to the arena as though on their way to heaven. If there was any trembling it was from joy, not fear. Perpetua followed with quick step as a true spouse of Christ, the darling of God, her brightly flashing eyes quelling the gaze of the crowd. Felicitas too, joyful because she had safely survived childbirth and

was now able to participate in the contest with the wild animals, passed from one shedding of blood to another; from midwife to gladiator, about to be purified after child-birth by a second baptism. As they were led through the gate they were ordered to put on different clothes; the men, those priests of Saturn, the women, those of the priestesses of Ceres. But that noble woman stubbornly resisted even to the end. She said, "We've come this far voluntarily in order to protect our rights, and we've pledged our lives not to recapitulate on any such matter as this. We made this agreement with you." Injustice bowed to justice and the guard conceded that they could enter the arena in their ordinary dress. Perpetua was singing victory psalms as if already crushing the head of the Egyptian. Revocatus, Saturninus, and Saturus were warning the spectators, and as they came within sight of Hilarion they informed him by nods and gestures: "You condemn us; God condemns you." This so infuriated the crowds that they demanded the scourging of these men in front of the line of gladiators. But the ones so punished rejoiced in that they had obtained yet another share in the Lord's suffering.

[19] Whoever said, "Ask and you shall receive," granted to these petitioners the particular death that each one chose. For whenever the martyrs were discussing among themselves their choice of death, Saturus used to say that he wished to be thrown in with all the animals so that he might wear a more glorious crown. Accordingly, at the outset of the show he was matched against a leopard but then called back; then he was mauled by a bear on the exhibition platform. Now Saturus detested nothing as much as a bear and he had already decided to die by one bite from the leopard. Consequently, when he was tied to a wild boar the professional gladiator who had tied the two together was pierced instead and died shortly after the games ended, while Saturus was merely dragged about. And when he was tied up on the bridge in front of the bear, the bear refused to come out of his den; and so a second time Saturus was called back unharmed.

[20] For the young women the devil had readied a mad cow, an animal not usually used at these games, but selected so that the women's sex would be matched with that of the animal. After being stripped and enmeshed in nets, the women were led into the arena. How horrified the people were as they saw that one was a young girl and the other, her breasts dripping with milk, had just recently given birth to a child. Consequently both were recalled and dressed in loosely fitting gowns.

Perpetua was tossed first and fell on her back. She sat up, and being more concerned with her sense of modesty than with her pain, covered her thighs with her gown which had been torn down one side. Then finding her hair-clip which had fallen out, she pinned back her loose hair thinking it not proper for a martyr to suffer with disheveled hair; it might seem that she was mourning in her hour of triumph. Then she stood up. Noticing that Felicitas was badly bruised, she went to her, reached out her hands and helped her to her feet. As they stood there the cruelty of the crowds seemed to be appeased and they were sent to the Sanavivarian Gate. There Perpetua was taken care of by a certain catechumen, Rusticus, who stayed near her. She seemed to be waking from a deep sleep (so completely had she been entranced and imbued with the Spirit). She began to look around her and to everyone's astonishment asked, "When are we going to be led out to that cow, or whatever it is?" She would not believe that it had already happened until she saw the various markings of the tossing on her body and clothing. Then calling for her brother she said to him and to the catechumen, "Remain strong in your faith and love one another. Do not let our excruciating suffering become a stumbling block for you."

[21] Meanwhile, at another gate Saturus was similarly encouraging the soldier, Pudens. "Up to the present," he said, "I have not been harmed by any of the animals, just as I foretold and predicted. So that you will now believe completely, watch as I go back to die from a single leopard bite." And so at the end of that contest, Saturus was bitten once by the leopard that had been set loose, and bled so profusely from that one wound that as he was coming back the crowd shouted in witness to his second baptism: "Salvation by being cleansed! Salvation by being cleansed! [*Salvum lotum*[4]]" And that man was truly saved who was cleansed in this way.

Then Saturus said to Pudens the soldier, "Goodbye, and remember my faith. Let these happenings be a source of strength for you, rather than a cause of anxiety." Then asking Pudens for a ring from his finger, he dipped it into the wound and returned it to Pudens as a legacy, a pledge and remembrance of his death. And as he collapsed he was thrown with the rest to that place reserved for the usual throat slitting. And when the crowd demanded that the prisoners be brought out into the open so that they might feast their eyes on death by the sword, they voluntarily arose and moved where the crowd wanted them. Before doing so they kissed each other so that their martyrdom would be completely perfected by the rite of the kiss of peace.

The others, without making any movement or sound, were killed by the sword. Saturus in particular, since he had been the first to climb the ladder and was to be Perpetua's encouragement, was the first to die. But Perpetua, in order to feel some of the pain, groaning as she was struck

---

4. *Salvum lotum* was a customary greeting of good omen when people met at the public baths. It can be translated as "Salvation/health by being washed/ cleansed." Here the crowd shouts it ironically at the Christian Saturus.

between the ribs, took the gladiator's trembling hand and guided it to her throat. Perhaps it was that so great a woman, feared as she was by the unclean spirit, could not have been slain had she not herself willed it.

O brave and fortunate martyrs, truly called and chosen to give honor to our Lord Jesus Christ! And anyone who is elaborating upon, or who reverences or worships that honor, should read these more recent examples, along with the ancient, as sources of encouragement for the Christian Community. In this way, there will be new examples of courage witnessing to the fact that even in our day the same Holy Spirit is still efficaciously present, along with the all powerful God the Father and Jesus Christ our Lord, to whom there will always be glory and endless power. Amen.

The arrest and martyrdom of Perpetua and her fellow catechumens seems to have occurred only a year or so after Septimus Severus's edict against conversion to Christianity and it has been suggested that the two events were related.[5] The Roman governor of Carthage at the time, Publius Aelius Hilarianus, is known from other sources to have been both an ambitious politician and a religious conservative, and he may have hoped to advance his career by arresting some Christians for public punishment at the upcoming games in honor of the birthday of Severus's younger son, Geta.[6] The arrest and trial of a few slaves and low-ranking individuals would presumably have made the point of Hilarianus's loyalty to the gods and the emperor without unduly disturbing the upper classes, but if this were the governor's plan it was greatly complicated by the arrest of Perpetua, the daughter of a well-to-do family. The reluctance of the governor to proceed to trial and punishment under such circumstances is perhaps evidenced by the fact that Perpetua and the other catechumens were initially held only under informal house arrest and were not actually transferred to a prison until after they were baptized. Baptism completed the catechumens' conversion to Christianity in violation of Septimus's edict and left the governor with no choice but to proceed with a formal trial of the group, regardless of their individual social status.

Various details about the catechumens presented in the martyrdom of Perpetua and Felicitas reflect many of the fundamental differences between Christians and the larger society of the period. In the patriarchal and hierarchical cultures of the ancient Mediterranean world, women were almost always defined in terms of their roles as the daughters, wives, and mothers of men, and yet Perpetua rejected each of these roles in turn for the new role of "Christian"

5. Joyce E. Salisbury, *Perpetua's Passion: The Death and Memory of a Young Roman Woman* (New York: Routledge, 1997), 81–83. This book is an excellent account of the story of Perpetua and her fellow martyrs as seen within the social and cultural context of the period. The discussion here follows Salisbury's interpretation.

6. Ibid.

and was allowed to assume a leadership role among the prisoners. Moreover, the group of Christians imprisoned with Perpetua reflected that the Christian communities of this period, in contrast to the rigid social and economic structures of the Roman Empire as a whole, were formed of slave and free, men and women, young and old, rich and poor. The account also reveals the extensive support a Christian could expect to receive from other Christians in a time of trouble. Such moral and physical support would have served as a powerful attraction to the urban masses that otherwise lived in what one historian has called the "dim, hopeless obscurity of plebian life."[7] In short, the revolutionary and egalitarian qualities of Christian communities like Perpetua's were in sharp contrast to the customs of the larger pagan societies. The same qualities also provide a benchmark for measuring the ways in which the later Christian church of the fourth and fifth centuries C.E. reverted to more traditional cultural values during the rapid growth of membership that followed Christianity's rise to political dominance in the Roman Empire.

The martyrdom of Perpetua and her friends occurred at games held in honor of the birthday of the Caesar Geta, who shortly afterward became co-emperor of the Roman Empire alongside his older brother Caracalla. A few years after the martyrdom of Perpetua, in 211 C.E., Geta was murdered by Caracalla, who became sole emperor (211–217 C.E.). The next year Caracalla extended Roman citizenship to most of the male inhabitants in the Empire.

4.4 *Constitutio Antoniniana* Giessen Papyrus No. 40 col. 1 (212 C.E.)

The Emperor Caesar Marcus Aurelius Severus Antoninus Augustus [Caracalla] declares: [. . .] I may show my gratitude to the immortal gods for preserving me in such [. . .] Therefore I consider that in this way I can [. . .] render proper service to their majesty [. . .] by bringing with me to the worship [?] of the gods all who enter into the number of my people. Accordingly, I grant Roman citizenship to all [aliens] throughout the world, with no one remaining outside the citizen bodies except the *dediticii*.* For it is proper that the multitude should not only help carry[?] all the burdens but should also now be included in my victory. This edict shall [. . .] the majesty of the Roman people [. . .]

The meaning here is uncertain; literally, the term means "people who surrendered [to the Romans]."

Modern historians have debated whether Caracalla's grant of citizenship to all free males was the final act in the longstanding Roman policy of gradually extending citizenship to the conquered peoples of its Empire, or was instead merely intended to divert attention from Caracalla's murder of Geta and many of Geta's followers. Shortly after the grant of citizenship, one contemporary Roman took an even more cynical view of Caracalla's motives.

---

7. Samuel Dill, *Roman Society From Nero to Marcus Aurelius* (London: MacMillan, 1911), 256.

4.5 Cassius Dio, *Roman History* 78.9.5 (ca. 214–226 C.E.)

This was the reason why he [Caracalla] made all the people in his empire Roman citizens; nominally he was honoring them, but his real purpose was to increase his revenues by this means, inasmuch as aliens did not have to pay most of these taxes.

Regardless of the motive for Caracalla's grant of citizenship, one effect of the grant was to make it more difficult for Christians to avoid those civic obligations of citizenship that were related to the worship and honor of the pagan gods and the emperor. Much of public office revolved around the financing, organizing, and holding of various public religious festivals, and most urban social life centered on these festivals. The Christian refusal to participate in these events only accentuated the distinctive differences between Christians and their neighbors at a time when Christianity was still seeking wider acceptance. At the same time, many, but not all, Christians sought to avoid military duty because a soldier's life in arms not only violated the moral teachings held by many Christians, but was deeply intertwined with pagan religious worship, pagan symbols, and the emperor's cult. As in the days of Marcus Aurelius, remaining separate from the social life of the larger community and avoiding governmental and military service in an age of increasing threat to the Roman Empire could only have served to make Christians unpopular among the more conservative elements of both the imperial administration and the general population.

While Christians were persecuted on a number of occasions during the years of the Severian dynasty, there was a Christian tradition that not all of the Severian emperors were opposed to Christian belief. Some support for this tradition may be found in pagan sources.

4.6 Scriptores Historiae Augustae, *Life of Severus Alexander* 29.1–3 (late fourth century C.E.)

Before I tell of his [Severus Alexander, Emperor 222–235 C.E.] wars and his campaigns and his victories, I will relate a few details of his private everyday life. His manner of living was as follows: First of all, if it were permissible, that is to say, if he had not lain with his wife, in the early morning hours he would worship in the sanctuary of his Lares, in which he kept statues of the deified emperors—of whom, however, only the best had been selected—and also of certain holy souls, among them Apollonius, and according to a contemporary writer, Christ, Abraham, Orpheus, and others of this same character and, besides, the portraits of his ancestors. If this act of worship were not possible, he would ride about, or fish, or walk, or hunt, according to the character of the place in which he was.

The Scriptores Historiae Augustae are among the most problematic and unreliable of the extant ancient sources, and many historians are reluctant to place too much emphasis on the statement that Severus kept a statue of Christ in his private sanctuary.[8] Even if true, the account would seem to indicate only that Christ was but one of the many gods that Severus Alexander worshipped, and not that Severus was a Christian himself. However, the religious syncretism indicated by the account does reflect the fact that during the second and third centuries C.E. many pagans were beginning to adopt a form of monotheistic belief, which saw the various divinities as but different aspects or servants of one "great god." This belief could be easily accommodated within the Christian system of a great God overseeing a creation filled with a hierarchy of angels and demons of various sorts. The growing coincidence between pagan and Christian religious views as to the divine order of universe was a positive factor in Christianity's rapid growth during the third century C.E.

THE EARLY YEARS OF THE BARRACK EMPERORS

The death of Severus Alexander in 235 C.E. marked the end of the Severian dynasty and the beginning of a half century of turmoil and near anarchy in the Roman Empire. If any of the later Severian emperors had in fact shown either an interest in Christian belief or a tolerance for its followers, such interest or tolerance was not found in the next regime.

> 4.7 Eusebius of Caesarea, *Ecclesiastical History* 6.28.1 (ca. 311–323 C.E.)
> But to resume. When [Severus] Alexander the Emperor of the Romans [222–235 C.E.] had brought his principate to an end after thirteen years, he was succeeded by Maximin Caesar [Maximinus I Thrax, 235–238 C.E.] He, through ill-will towards the house of Alexander, since it consisted for the most part of believers, raised a persecution, ordering the leaders of the Church alone to be put to death, as being responsible for the teaching of the Gospel.

Maximinus Thrax was soon dead and with his death the persecution came to an end. After the relatively brief reign of Gordian III (238–244 C.E.), there then came an emperor who was thought by later Christians to have been a Christian himself.

> 4.8 Eusebius of Caesarea, *Ecclesiastical History* 6.34 (ca. 311–323 C.E.)
> When after six whole years Gordian [Gordian III, 238–244 C.E.] brought his government of the Romans to an end, Philip [244–249 C.E.] along with his son Philip succeeded to the principate. It is recorded that he, being a Christian, wished on the day of the last paschal vigil to share along with the multitude the prayers at the church, but was not permitted to enter by him who was then presiding, until he confessed and numbered himself among those who were reckoned to be in sin and were occupying the place of penitence; for that otherwise, had he

---

8. Scholarly attitudes towards the Scriptores Historiae Augustae are summarized at "Historia Augusta," by John F. Matthews, *The Oxford Classical Dictionary* (Oxford: Oxford University Press, 1996), 713.

not done so, he would never have been received by [the president] on account of the many charges made concerning him. And it is said that he obeyed readily, displaying by his actions how genuine and pious was his disposition toward the fear of God.

There is only fragmentary evidence to support Eusebius's statement that Philip was a Christian and this belief may have developed as a result of the contrast between the toleration of Christians during his reign and the persecution under his successor, Trajan Decius (249–251 C.E.).[9] However, the mid-third century C.E. is a poorly documented period in the history of the Roman Empire and it is possible that Philip in fact did either tolerate and/or have some ties to the Christian faith.

The fact that Christians might believe that a Roman emperor was himself a Christian raises the questions of just how rapidly Christianity was spreading within the Roman Empire during this period and into what levels of the Empire's society. A passage written by Origen seems to indicate that, whatever their numbers, by the 240s C.E. the Christians were beginning to make inroads among the Empire's social elite.

> 4.9 Origen, *Against Celsus* 3.9 (ca. late 240s C.E.)
> But since he [Celsus] is manifestly guilty of falsehood in the statements which follow, let us examine his assertion when he says, "If all men wished to become Christians, the latter would not desire such a result." Now that the above statement is false is clear from this, that Christians do not neglect, as far as in them lies, to take measures to disseminate their doctrine throughout the whole world. Some of them, accordingly, have made it their business to itinerate not only through cities, but even villages and country houses, that they might make converts to God. And no one would maintain that they did this for the sake of gain, when sometimes they would not accept even necessary sustenance; or if at any time they were pressed by a necessity of this sort, were contented with the mere supply of their wants, although many were willing to share (their abundance) with them, and to bestow help upon them far above their need. At the present day, indeed, when, owing to the multitude of Christian believers, not only rich men, but persons of rank, and delicate and high-born ladies, receive the teachers of Christianity, some perhaps will dare to say that it is for the sake of a little glory that certain individuals assume the office of Christian instructors.

Claims such as Origen's concerning the great numbers and/or social prominence of Christians in the society of the Roman Empire must be treated with care. While Christian authors routinely emphasized the numbers and/or social standing of Christians, there is little if any support for such claims in the pagan

---

9. Robin Lane Fox, *Pagans and Christians* (New York: Alfred A. Knopf, 1986), 452–54; Robert M. Grant, *Augustus to Constantine* (New York: Barnes & Noble, 1970), 167–70.

sources or the archaeological evidence.[10] The extant literary and archaeological sources, for example, indicate that while there were Christians in the Roman legions and the imperial household during the 250s C.E., there were no more than one or two Christian senators in the entire Empire[11] and that Christianity had made very little headway among the rural populace.[12] The majority of Christians at this time seem to have belonged to the free urban poor. The absolute number of Christians at any time during the third century, or any other century in antiquity, is difficult to estimate because statistics are essentially non-existent. We do, however, possess one statistic concerning the size of the Christian community in the city of Rome in 251 C.E.

> 4.10 Eusebius of Caesarea, *Ecclesiastical History* 6.43.11–12 (ca. 311–323 C.E.)
>
> This vindicator [Novatus], then, of the Gospel did not know that there should be one bishop in a catholic church, in which he was not ignorant (for how could he be?) that there are forty-six presbyters, seven deacons, seven sub-deacons, forty-two acolytes, fifty-two exorcists, readers, and door-keepers, above fifteen hundred widows and persons in distress, all of whom are supported by the grace and loving kindness of the Master. But not even did this great multitude, so necessary in the Church, that number who by God's providence were rich and multiplying, nor an immense and countless laity, turn him from such a desperate failure and recall him to the Church.

On the basis of these numbers, Edward Gibbons estimated that there were perhaps 50,000 Christians in Rome and that Christians totaled about 5 percent of the empire's population.[13] Robin Lane Fox has argued that both estimates are too high, reasoning that women and children formed a disproportionate number of the Christian population and that the church at Rome was one of the largest in the Empire.[14] Fox thus estimates that around 250 C.E. Christians, as a "guess," constituted only about 2 percent of the Empire's population.[15] This estimate is very close to Rodney Stark's estimate that Christians constituted about 1.9 percent of the Empire's population by 250 C.E.[16]

Because ancient Christian authors typically claimed high numbers for the Christian faith, historians consider the following passages by Origen to be significant

---

10. The evidence is summarized by Robin Lane Fox, *Pagans and Christians* (New York: Alfred A. Knopf, Inc., 1989), 268–82. See also, Rodney Stark, *The Risk of Christianity* (San Francisco: HarperSanFrancisco, 1997), 5.

11. Fox, *Pagans and Christians*, 311–12.

12. Ibid.

13. Edward Gibbons, *The Decline and Fall of the Roman Empire*, chapter 15.

14. Fox, *Pagans and Christians*, 268–69.

15. Ibid., 317. Fox's estimate is in line with that of Robert M. Grant, who estimated that in 200 C.E. there were about 7,000 Christians in Rome, out of a total population of about 700,000. Robert M. Grant, *Early Christianity and Society: Seven Studies* (New York: Harper & Row, 1977), 6.

16. Rodney Stark, *The Rise of Christianity* (Princeton: Princeton University Press, 1996), 7.

for the candid admission that only a few Christians, "easily numbered," had been martyrs for their faith up to his day and that Christians formed only a small part of the population in the late 240s C.E.

> 4.11 Origen, *Against Celsus* 3.8; 8.69 (ca. late 240s C.E.)
>
> [3.8] For in order to remind others, that by seeing a few engaged in a struggle for their religion, they also might be better fitted to despise death, some, on special occasions, and these individuals who can be easily numbered, have endured death for the sake of Christianity. . . . [8.69] As the question stated is, "What would happen if the Romans were persuaded to adopt the principals of the Christians, to despise the duties paid to the recognized gods and to men, and to worship the Most High?" this is my answer to the question. We say that "if two" of us "shall agree on earth as touching anything that they shall ask, it shall be done for them of the Father" of the just, "which is in heaven"; for God rejoices in the agreement of rational beings, and turns away from discord. . . And what are we to expect, if not only a very few agree, as at present, but the whole of the Empire of Rome?

In further support of a low estimate for the total number of Christians at this time, we should note that Eusebius wrote both that Origen was responsible for converting "a large number" of people to Christianity during his forty or fifty years of teaching and that seven of Origen's students and converts died as martyrs during the persecutions of the third century (*Ecclesiastical History* 6.3.13–4.1). Seven martyrs out of "a large number" of converts would not seem to convey the sense of praise intended by Eusebius, if "a large number" of people had the same meaning to Eusebius as it does to the modern reader.

THE PERSECUTION OF TRAJAN DECIUS

While Origen proclaimed the spread of Christian belief in *Against Celsus*, his book also indicated rising tensions between Christians and pagans during the 240s C.E.

> 4.12 Origen, *Against Celsus* 3.15 (ca. late 240s C.E.)
>
> But again, that it is not the fear of external enemies which strengthens our union, is plain from the fact that this cause, by God's will, has already, for a considerable time, ceased to exist. And it is probable that the secure existence, so far as regards the world, enjoyed by believers at present, will come to an end, since those who calumniate Christianity in every way are again attributing the present frequency of rebellion to the multitude of believers, and to their not being persecuted by the authorities as in old times. For we have learned from the Gospel neither to relax our efforts in days of peace, and to give ourselves up to repose, nor, when the world makes war upon us, to become cowards, and apostatize from the love of the God of all things which is in Jesus Christ.

The "secure existence" did end with a series of persecutions during the late 240s and 250s C.E. The first persecution was during the reign of Trajan Decius (249–251 C.E.), but it is difficult to determine the immediate cause of the persecution.

> 4.13 Eusebius of Caesarea, *Ecclesiastical History* 6.39.1 (ca. 311–323 C.E.)
> But to resume. When Philip had reigned for seven years he was succeeded by [Trajan] Decius. He, on account of his enmity towards Philip, raised a persecution against the churches, in which Fabian was perfected by martyrdom at Rome, and was succeeded in the episcopate by Cornelius.

The text of Trajan Decius's edict of December of 249 C.E. has not survived, but we have some indication of its contents from other sources. The edict seems to have commanded all Roman citizens to sacrifice to the gods for the safety of the emperor and the Empire. It appears that the edict expressly exempted Jews from the obligation to sacrifice but did not mention Christians at all, and so some historians believe the edict was in fact aimed against Christians. The edict may, however, have had another purpose. Just two years earlier, in 248 C.E. during the reign of Philip, the Roman Empire had celebrated the one-thousandth anniversary of the founding of the city of Rome. The Romans themselves were uncertain as to the exact year of Rome's founding, however, and Trajan Decius, who had overthrown Philip, may simply have intended to take advantage of the uncertainty to repeat the celebration for his own political benefit.

Trajan Decius's order that all citizens were to sacrifice to the gods is reflected in some of the more interesting archaeological discoveries from this period, a number of certificates of sacrifice issued to various individuals. The following certificate was discovered at Fayoum, Egypt in 1893 C.E.

> 4.14 A Certificate Of Sacrifice (June 26, 250 C.E.)
> To The Commissioners for Sacrifices in the Village of Alexander's Island, from Aurelius Diogenes, Son of Satabus, of the Village of Alexander's Island, Aged 72; Scar on Right Eyebrow.
> 	I have always sacrificed to the gods, and now in your presence, in accordance with the terms of the edict, I have done sacrifice and poured libations and tasted the sacrifices, and I request you to certify to this effect. Farewell
> 				Presented By Me, Aurelius Diogenes
> 	I Certify That I Witnessed His Sacrifice, Aurelius Syrus.
> Dated this first year of the Emperor Caesar Gaius Messius Quintus Trajanus Decius, Pius, Felix, Augustus, the second of Epiph. (June 26, 250 C.E.)

Approximately forty-two of these certificates of sacrifice have been found in Egypt, all apparently prepared by the same hand. Because of the administrative

nightmare that would have resulted from any attempt to issue certificates to all
the inhabitants of the Roman Empire, these certificates were probably issued
only in instances in which particular individuals were suspected of Christian
belief or disloyalty to the emperor.

Regardless of whether or not the edict of 249 C.E. was directed against the
Christians, the edict certainly led to persecution of the Christian populace as
local officials sought to enforce the order for universal sacrifice. Dionysius,
bishop of Alexandria, indicates that while a persecution had started in his community even prior to the edict, it was the edict that shocked his congregation
and led many, particularly the "more eminent persons" and those in "public
positions," promptly to turn apostate.

> 4.15 Dionysius, *Letter to Fabius, Bishop of Antioch* (ca. 250 C.E.) as quoted
> by Eusebius in *Ecclesiastical History* 6.41.1, 8–13
>> [1] It was not with the imperial edict that the persecution began
>> amongst us, but it preceded it by a whole year. . . .
>> [8] And this state of things continued at its height for a long time. But
>> strife and civil war came upon wretched men and turned on them-
>> selves the fury of which we had been the object; and for a brief space
>> we breathed again, since they had no time to indulge their anger
>> against us.
>> [9] Straightway, however, the news was spread abroad of the change
>> from that rule that had been more kindly to us, and great was the fear
>> of threatened punishment that hung over us. And, what is more, the
>> edict arrived, and it was almost like that which was predicted by our
>> Lord, well nigh the most terrible of all, so as, if possible, to cause to
>> stumble even the elect. Howsoever that be, all cowered with fear. And
>> of many of the more eminent persons, some came forward immedi-
>> ately through fear, others in public positions were compelled to do so
>> by their business, and others were dragged by those around them.
>> Called by name they approached the impure and unholy sacrifices,
>> some pale and trembling, as if they were not for sacrificing but rather
>> to be themselves the sacrifices and victims to the idols, so that the
>> large crowd that stood around heaped mockery upon them, and it
>> was evident that they were by nature cowards in everything, cowards
>> both to die and to sacrifice. But others ran eagerly towards the altars,
>> affirming by their forwardness that they had not been Christians
>> even formerly; concerning whom the Lord very truly predicted that
>> they shall hardly be saved. Of the rest, some followed one or other of
>> these, others fled; some were captured, and of these some went as far
>> as bonds and imprisonment, and certain, when they had been shut
>> up for many days, then forswore themselves even before coming into
>> court, while others, who remained firm for a certain time under tor-
>> tures, subsequently gave in.

Many common Christians resented the wide-spread apostasy among the clergy and the more socially prominent Christians and that led to a serious problem when the persecution ended with Decius's death in 251 C.E. Divisions arose within many churches over whether the lapsed Christians should be readmitted at all and especially whether the lapsed clergy, even if readmitted, should be allowed to resume their positions and conduct the Eucharist and other sacred rites. The orthodox churches as a whole opted for the full readmission of all the lapsed who repented and did penance. This forgiveness included lapsed clergy, as the orthodox churches reasoned that the sanctity of the Eucharist and the other rites of the faith were not dependent upon the worth of the individual conducting the service. However, a significant minority of the clergy and lay members strongly resisted the readmission of the lapsed. In this and later persecutions, dioceses split apart over this issue as congregations divided into separate churches with rival clergy. The controversy was not ultimately resolved until the late fourth and early fifth centuries C.E., when the Christian emperors were able to use the legal and military resources of the central government to compel the dissolution of the dissident churches.

Persecutions like that under Trajan Decius created other serious problems for the clergy. Those clerics who sought to evade arrest for the purpose of directing the resistance of their congregations from hiding found their moral authority compromised when other Christians confessed their faith and went to prison to await exile or martyrdom. A related problem arose from the fact that these "confessors" were widely seen by Christians as having entered into a new relationship with God, which gave the confessors special powers on earth while they awaited martyrdom, including the authority to forgive the sins of others. For many lapsed Christians, seeking the forgiveness of a confessor who was soon to die was much easier than seeking the forgiveness of a priest or bishop who intended to survive the persecution and resume his position afterwards, and so the easy manner in which many confessors granted forgiveness for sins struck at the heart of the clergy's ability to maintain discipline over their congregations.

The clergy was also confronted by the problem of the immoral conduct of some confessors while they awaited death. Christians firmly believed that martyrdom for Christ washed away all sins and guaranteed entry into heaven. A letter by Cyprian, bishop of Carthage, indicates that at least a few confessors used this "guarantee" to indulge in the worst of conduct while they awaited punishment.

4.16. Cyprian, *The Unity of the Church* 20–21 (April, 251 C.E.)
[20] Nor let any one marvel, beloved brethren, that even some of the confessors advance to these lengths, and thence also that some others sin thus wickedly, thus grievously. For neither does confession make a man free from the snares of the devil, nor does it defend a man who is still placed in the world, with a perpetual security from temptations, and dangers, and onsets, and attacks of the world; otherwise

we should never see in confessors those subsequent frauds, and for-
nications, and adulteries, which now with groans and sorrow we
witness in some. Whosoever that confessor is, he is not greater, or
better, or dearer to God than Solomon, who, although so long as he
walked in God's ways, retained that grace which he had received from
the Lord, yet after he forsook the Lord's way he lost also the Lord's
grace. And therefore it is written, "Hold fast that which thou hast, lest
another take thy crown." But assuredly the Lord would not threaten
that the crown of righteousness might be taken away, were it not
that, when righteousness departs, the crown must also depart.

[21] Confession is the beginning of glory, not the full desert of the
crown; nor does it perfect our praise, but it initiates our dignity; and
since it is written, "He that endureth to the end, the same shall be
saved," whatever has been before the end is a step by which we ascend
to the summit of salvation, not a terminus wherein the full result of
the ascent is already gained. He is a confessor; but after confession his
peril is greater, because the adversary is more provoked. He is a confessor; for this cause he ought the more to stand on the side of the
Lord's Gospel, since he has by the Gospel attained glory from the
Lord. For the Lord says, "To whom much is given, of him much shall
be required; and to whom more dignity is ascribed, of him more service
is exacted." Let no one perish by the example of a confessor; let no one
learn injustice, let no one learn arrogance, let no one learn treachery,
from the manners of a confessor. . . .

In any persecuted community there are individuals willing to abandon their
allegiance to the governmental authorities responsible for the persecution.
During the mid-third century C.E. then, not all Christians were horrified by the
thought that the Roman Empire might collapse as a result of civil war or barbarian invasion. The following text indicates that at least some Christians in
Cappadocia, a province located within modern Turkey, aided and participated
in the Gothic invasion of the province in 254–255 C.E. After the invaders moved
on, the local Christian bishops were forced to take steps to punish those
Christians who had either helped the invaders or taken advantage of the resulting disorder to loot their neighbors' properties or make slaves of others.

4.17 Gregory Thaumaturgus, *Canonical Epistle*, Canons 5–10 (ca. 255
C.E.)

Canon 5: But others deceive themselves by fancying that they can
retain the property of others which they may have found as an equivalent for their own property which they have lost. In this way verily,
just as the Boradi and Goths brought the havoc of war on them, they
make themselves Boradi and Goths to others. Accordingly we have
sent to you our brother and comrade in old age, Euphrosynus, with
this view, that he may deal with you in accordance with our model

here, and teach you against whom you ought to admit accusations, and whom you ought to exclude from your prayers.

Canon 6: Moreover, it has been reported to us that a thing has happened in your country which is surely incredible, and which, if done at all, is altogether the work of unbelievers, and impious men, and men who know not the very name of the Lord; to wit, that some have gone to such a pitch of cruelty and inhumanity, as to be detaining by force certain captives who have made their escape. Dispatch ye commissioners into the country, lest the thunderbolts of heaven fall all too surely upon those who perpetrate such deeds.

Canon 7: Now, as regards those who have been enrolled among the barbarians, and have accompanied them in their eruption in a state of captivity, and who, forgetting that they were from Pontus, and Christians, have become such thorough barbarians, as even to put those of their own race to death by the gibbet or strangulation, and to show their roads or houses to the barbarians, who else would have been ignorant of them, it is necessary for you to debar such persons even from being auditors in the public congregations, until some common decision about them is come to by the saints assembled in council, and by the Holy Spirit antecedently to them.

Canon 8: Now those who have been so audacious as to invade the houses of others, if they have once been put on their trial and convicted, ought not to be deemed fit even to be hearers in the public congregation. But if they have declared themselves and made restitution, they should be placed in the rank of the repentant.

Canon 9: Now, those who have found in the open field or in their own houses anything left behind them by the barbarians, if they have once been put on their trial and convicted, ought to fall under the same class of the repentant. But if they have declared themselves and made restitution, they ought to be deemed fit for the privilege of prayer.

Canon 10: And they who keep the commandment ought to keep it without any sordid covetousness, demanding neither recompense, nor reward, nor fee, nor anything else that bears the name of acknowledgment.

At almost the same time that Bishop Gregory was concerned with the penance to be rendered by his fallen Christians, another persecution began in 257 C.E. under the Emperor Valerian (253–260 C.E.).

4.18 Dionysius Bishop of Alexandria, *Letter to Hermammon* (257 C.E.) quoted in Eusebius *Ecclesiastical History* 7.10.1–4.

. . . .and Valerian [Emperor 253–260 C.E.] along with his son Gallienus succeeded to the government. Once more we may learn from his letter to Hermammon the description that Dionysius gives of him also;

in which he gives an account of the following kind: "And to John also it is likewise revealed: 'and there was given to him,' says he, 'a mouth speaking great things and blasphemy, and there was given to him authority and forty and two months.' One may wonder at both of these things under Valerian, and of them note especially the nature of his previous conduct, how mild and friendly he was to the men of God. For not a single one of the emperors before him was so kindly and favorably disposed towards them, not even those who were said to have been openly Christians, as he manifestly was, when he received them at the beginning in the most intimate and friendly manner; indeed all his house had been filled with godly persons, and was a church of God. But the master and ruler of the synagogue of the Egyptian magicians persuaded him to get rid of them, bidding him slay and pursue the pure and holy men, as being rivals and hinderers of his abominable and disgusting incantations (for indeed they are and were capable by their presence and sight, and by merely breathing on them and uttering words, of scattering the designs of the baneful demons). And he advised him to perform unhallowed rites, and abominable juggleries and ill-omened sacrifices, such as cutting the throats of wretched boys and sacrificing children of hapless parents and opening up the entrails of new-born babes, and cutting up and mincing the handiwork of God, as if all this would bring them divine favor."

The difficult position of a bishop during a period of persecution was demonstrated by the fate of Bishop Cyprian of Carthage. During the persecution of Trajan Decius, Cyprian had gone into hiding and by letters directed his congregation's resistance to the persecution. Cyprian was severely criticized by some members of the congregation for hiding instead of confessing the faith, and the criticism apparently weighed heavily upon him during the following years. At the start of Valerian's persecution, Cyprian again went into hiding to direct his congregation.

4.19 Cyprian, *Epistle* 81 (ca. 257 C.E.)
Cyprian to his brother Successus, greeting.
[1] The reason why I could not write to you immediately, dearest brother, was that all the clergy, being placed in the very heat of the contest, were unable in any way to depart hence, all of them being prepared in accordance with the devotion of their mind for divine and heavenly glory. But know that those have come whom I had sent to the City for this purpose, that they might find out and bring back to us the truth, in whatever manner it had been decreed respecting us. For many various and uncertain things are current in men's opinions. But the truth concerning them is as follows, that Valerian had sent a

rescript to the Senate,[17] to the effect that bishops and presbyters and deacons should immediately be punished; but that senators, and men of importance, and Roman knights, should lose their dignity, and moreover be deprived of their property; and if, when their means were taken away, they should persist in being Christians, then they should also lose their heads; but that matrons should be deprived of their property, and sent into banishment. Moreover, people of Caesar's household, whoever of them had either confessed before, or should now confess, should have their property confiscated, and should be sent in chains by assignment to Caesar's estates. The Emperor Valerian also added to this address a copy of the letters which he sent to the presidents of the provinces concerning us; which letters we are daily hoping will come, waiting according to the strength of our faith for the endurance of suffering, and expecting from the help and mercy of the Lord the crown of eternal life. But know that Xistus was martyred in the cemetery on the eighth day of the Ides of August, and with him four deacons. Moreover, the prefects in the City are daily urging on this persecution; so that, if any are presented to them, they are martyred, and their property claimed by the treasury.

[2] I beg that these things may be made known by your means to the rest of our colleagues, that everywhere, by their exhortation, the brotherhood may be strengthened and prepared for the spiritual conflict, that every one of us may think less of death than of immortality; and, dedicated to the Lord, with full faith and entire courage, may rejoice rather than fear in this confession, wherein they know that the soldiers of God and Christ are not slain, but crowned. I bid you, dearest brother, ever heartily farewell in the Lord.

Valerian's persecution was the earliest known attempt by the Roman government to attack Christianity as an institution rather than merely as a collection of individuals; the Roman officials closed the churches and persecuted the clergy as leaders of the faith, rather than merely as Christians. Moreover, as Cyprian's letter indicates, the persecution also seems to have been the first official instance of refusing to pardon in full those Christians who recanted. Thus, Valerian's persecution reflected a growing recognition that Christianity was becoming a potentially serious political and social threat to the Roman government and the emperor's authority.

The edicts of Valerian were widely evaded by Christians through bribery and the cooperation of local officials, many of whom refused to enforce the edicts. Cyprian himself was able to hide from the authorities during the first wave of persecution. However, Cyprian, who was familiar with the yearly circuit that the

---

17. Cyprian's letter concerns the second anti-Christian rescript of Valerian.

Roman governor traveled through the province of Africa, was merely waiting until the governor came to Carthage before surrendering, in order that his martyrdom might occur before his own congregation.

4.20 Cyprian, *Epistle* 82 (257 C.E.)

Cyprian to the presbyters and deacons, and all the people, greeting.

[1] When it had been told to us, dearest brethren, that the jailers had been sent to bring me to Utica, and I had been persuaded by the counsel of those dearest to me to withdraw for a time from my gardens, as a just reason was afforded I consented. For the reason that it is fit for a bishop, in that city in which he presides over the Church of the Lord, there to confess the Lord, and that the whole people should be glorified by the confession of their prelate in their presence. For whatever, in that moment of confession, the confessor-bishop speaks, he speaks in the mouth of all, by inspiration of God. But the honor of our Church, glorious as it is, will be mutilated if I, a bishop placed over another church, receiving my sentence or my confession at Utica, should go thence as a martyr to the Lord, when indeed, both for my own sake and yours, I pray with continual supplications, and with all my desires entreat, that I may confess among you, and there suffer, and thence depart to the Lord even as I ought. Therefore here in a hidden retreat I await the arrival of the proconsul returning to Carthage, that I may hear from him what the emperors have commanded upon the subject of Christian laymen and bishops, and may say what the Lord will wish to be said at that hour.

[2] But do you, dearest brethren, according to the discipline which you have ever received from me out of the Lord's commands, and according to what you have so very often learnt from my discourse, keep peace and tranquillity; nor let any of you stir up any tumult for the brethren, or voluntarily offer himself to the Gentiles. For when apprehended and delivered up, he ought to speak, inasmuch as the Lord abiding in us speaks in that hour, who willed that we should rather confess than profess. But for the rest, what it is fitting that we should observe before the proconsul passes sentence on me for the confession of the name of God, we will with the instruction of the Lord arrange in common. May our Lord make you, dearest brethren, to remain safe in His Church, and condescend to keep you. So be it through His mercy.

After Cyprian surrendered to the Roman authorities, he was brought to trial before the governor.

4.21 Acts Of Cyprian (Corpus Scriptorum Eccleiasticorum Latinorum III.3, pp. 110–114)

[1] When the Emperor Valerian was consul for the fourth, and Gallienus for the third time, on 30 August [257 C.E.], at Carthage, Paternus, the proconsul, in his council-chamber thus spoke to Cyprian, bishop:

Paternus: The most sacred Emperors Valerian and Gallienus have honored me with letters, wherein they enjoin that all those who do not observe the religion of Rome, shall make profession of their return to Roman rites; I have made accordingly inquiry as to how you call yourself; what answer do you make to me?

Cyprian: I am a Christian, and bishop; I know no other gods beside the one and true God, who made heaven and earth, the sea, and all things therein; this God we Christians serve, to him we pray day and night, for ourselves, for all mankind, for the health of the Emperors themselves.

Paternus: Do you persist in this purpose?

Cyprian: That good purpose, which knows God, cannot be changed.

Paternus: You can then, obeying the mandate of the Emperors, go into exile to the city of Curubis.

Cyprian: I go.

Paternus: The letters, wherewith I have been honored by the emperors, speak of presbyters as well as of bishops; I would know of you, therefore, who be they, who are presbyters in this city?

Cyprian: By an excellent and beneficial provision of your laws you have forbidden any to be informers; therefore they cannot be discovered and denounced by me; but they will be found in their own cities.

Paternus: I am today making inquiry here.

Cyprian: Our rules forbid any man to offer himself for punishment, and your ordinances discourage the same; they may not therefore offer themselves, but they will be discovered by your inquiries.

Paternus: They shall be discovered by me. They [the emperors] further ordain that no meetings be held in any place, and that the Christians shall not enter their cemeteries; if any transgress this wholesome ordinance, he shall suffer death.

Cyprian: Do as you have been instructed.

[2] Then Paternus the proconsul bade them lead away the bishop Cyprian into exile. During his long absence in exile on this account Aspasius Paternus was succeeded by Galerius Maximus who bade the bishop Cyprian be recalled from exile, and brought before him. Cyprian, the holy martyr, chosen of God, returned from Curubis, to which he had been exiled by order of Aspasius Paternus, then proconsul, and by official orders abode in his own gardens. There he was in daily expectation that he should be visited as had been shown him. While he remained there, suddenly on 13 September, in the consulship of Tuscus and Bassus [258 C.E.], there came to him two chief officials; one the chief equerry on the proconsular staff of Galerius, the other marshal of the guard on the same staff; they placed him between them in a chariot, and carried him to the villa of Sextus,

whither Galerius Maximus had retired for the recovery of his health. By order of the proconsul he was reserved for hearing on another day; so the blessed Cyprian withdrew under guard and was privately lodged in the house of the chief equerry of the staff of the most honorable Galerius Maximus, proconsul, in Saturn Street, between the temples of Venus and of Salus. Thither flocked the whole multitude of the brethren; when holy Cyprian knew this, he bade that the girls should be kept in, seeing they all continued in the open street before the gate of the officer's house.

[3] So on the next day, 14 September, a great crowd was collected early at the villa of Sextus, as the proconsul commanded. And the same day Cyprian was brought before him as he sat for judgment in the court called Sauciolum.

Galerius Maximus: Are you Thascius Cyprianus?

Cyprian: I am.

Galerius Maximus: The most sacred emperors have commanded you to conform to the Roman rites.

Cyprian: I refuse.

Galerius Maximus: Take heed for yourself.

Cyprian: Do as you are bid; in so clear a case I may not take heed.

[4] Galerius, after briefly conferring with his judicial council, with much reluctance pronounced the following sentence: "You have long lived an irreligious life, and have drawn together a number of men bound by an unlawful association, and professed yourself an open enemy to the gods and the religion of Rome; and the pious, most sacred and august Emperors, Valerian and Gallienus, and the most noble Caesar Valerian, have endeavored in vain to bring you back to conformity with their religious observances; whereas, therefore you have been apprehended as principal and ringleader in these infamous crimes, you shall be made an example to those whom you have wickedly associated with you; the authority of law shall be ratified in your blood." He then read the sentence of the court from a written tablet: "It is the sentence of this court that Thascius Cyprianus be executed with the sword."

Cyprian: Thanks be to God.

[5] After this sentence the crowd of brethren cried: "Let us also be beheaded with him." Hence arose an uproar among the brethren, and a great crowd accompanied him. So Cyprian was led forth on to the land of Sextus, and there he divested himself of his mantle, and kneeled upon the ground, and bowed in prayer to the Lord. And when he had divested himself of his mantle and handed it to the deacons, he stood clad in his linen garment, and prepared to await the executioner.

When the executioner arrived Cyprian charged his friends that they should give to the executioner twenty-five golden pieces. Napkins

and handkerchiefs were strewn before him by the brethren. Thereafter
blessed Cyprian bound his eyes with his own hand, but as he could
not fasten the ends of the handkerchief for himself, the presbyter
Julian and Julian the subdeacon fastened them for him.

So the blessed Cyprian suffered, and his body was laid out hard by
to content the curiosity of the heathen. Thence it was removed by night,
and, accompanied by tapers and torches, was conducted with prayers in
great triumph to the burial-ground of Macrobius Candidianus the
procurator, which lies on the Mappalian way near the fishponds. A
few days later Galerius Maximus the proconsul died.

The most blessed martyr Cyprian suffered on the fourteenth day
of September [258 C.E.] under the Emperors Valerian and Gallienus,
but in the reign of our Lord Jesus Christ, to whom is honor and glory
for ever and ever. Amen

Cyprian, while not of the senatorial order, was from the upper levels of
provincial society and he was treated with due deference by the Roman authorities after his arrest. Not all bishops were so fortunate and on many occasions
the Roman authorities moved much more decisively to try and punish the
Christian bishops, as Bishop Fructuosus of Tarragona, Spain learned in 259
C.E., the year after Cyprian's martyrdom.

4.22 The Acts Of Fructuosus 1.1, 2.1–9.
1 It was on the Lord's day, 16 January, in the year that Aemilianus and
Bassus were consuls [259 C.E.], that Bishop Fructuosus and his deacons Augurius and Eulogius were arrested. . . .
2 The next day in prison he [Fructuosus] baptized our brother
Rogatianus. After spending six days in jail they were brought out for
a hearing on Friday, January 21.

The governor Aemilianus said, "Bring in the bishop Fructuosus,
Augurius, and Eulogius." A court official said, "They are present."

The governor Aemilianus said to Fructuosus, "Were you aware of
the emperors' orders?"

Fructuosus said, "I do not know their orders. I am a Christian."

The governor Aemilianus said, "They have ordered you to worship the gods."

Fructuosus said, "I worship the one God who has made heaven
and earth, the sea, and all that is in them."

The governor Aemilianus said, "Do you know that the gods exist?"

"No, I do not," said Fructuosus.

Aemilianus said, "You will know later."

Fructuosus looked up to the Lord and began to pray within himself. The governor Aemilianus said, "These are obeyed, these are
feared, and these are adored; if the gods are not worshipped, then the
images of the emperors are not adored."

The governor Aemilianus said to Augurius, "Do not listen to the words of Fructuosus."

Augurius said, "I worship God almighty."

The governor Aemilianus said to Eugolius, "Do you not also worship Fructuosus?"

"No," said Eugolius, "I do not worship Fructuosus, but I worship the one whom he worships."

Aemilianus the governor said to Fructuosus, "You are a bishop?"

"Yes, I am," said Fructuosus.

"You were," said Aemilianus. And he sentenced them to be burnt alive. . .

In 260 C.E., while campaigning in the East against the Persians, Valerian was treacherously seized by the Persians at a peace conference and he remained a prisoner of the Persians for the rest of his life. With Valerian's capture the persecution of Christians quickly wound down, as Valerian's son, the emperor Gallienus (253–268 C.E.), offered a formal peace to the church later that same year.

4.23 Epistle of the Emperor Gallienus To The Christian Bishops (ca. 260 C.E.) quoted in Eusebius *Ecclesiastical History* 7.13

The Emperor Caesar Publius Licinius Gallienus Pius Felix Augustus to Dionysius and Pinnas and Demetrius and the other bishops. I have given my order that the benefit of my bounty should be published throughout all the world, to the intent that they [the pagans] should depart from the places of worship, and therefore you also may use the ordinance contained in my Rescript, so that none may molest you. And this thing which it is within your power to accomplish has long since been conceded by me; and therefore Aurelius Quirinius, who is in charge of administration, will observe the ordinance given by me.

The text of Gallienus's rescript itself has been lost, but we know from other sources that the rescript restored church property, reopened Christian cemeteries, and granted freedom of worship to Christians.[18] Gallienus's letter was particularly significant for being addressed to the bishops of the Christian church, as it in effect constituted an imperial recognition of the church's hierarchy. The increasing acceptance of Christianity evidenced by Galleinus's edict was reflected in events a little more than a decade later when an Eastern synod of Christian bishops made an extraordinary appeal to the emperor Aurelian (270–275 C.E.) for help in enforcing the synod's decision against a fellow bishop.

4.24 Eusebius of Caesarea, *Ecclesiastical History* 7.28.4–29.2, 30.18–22 (ca. 311–323 C.E.)

[28.4] Gallienus [253–268 C.E.] having held the principate for fifteen entire years, Claudius [268–270 C.E.] was established as his successor. When he

---

18. Eusebius, *Ecclesiastical History* 7.13.1

had completed his second year, he gave over the government to Aurelian.

[29.1] In Aurelian's day a final synod of an exceedingly large number of bishops was assembled, and the leader of the heresy at Antioch [Paul, the bishop of Antioch], being unmasked and now clearly condemned by the heterodoxy by all, was excommunicated from the Catholic Church under heaven. . . .

[30.18] When Paul, then, had fallen from the episcopate as well as from his orthodoxy in the faith, Domnus, as has been said, succeeded to the ministry of the church at Antioch. But as Paul refused on any account to give up possession of the church building, the emperor Aurelian, on being petitioned, gave an extremely just decision regarding the matter, ordering the assignment of the building to those with whom the bishops of the doctrine in Italy and Rome should communicate in writing. Thus, then, was the aforesaid man driven with the utmost indignity from the church by the ruler of this world. Such indeed was the disposition of Aurelian towards us at that time. But as his reign advanced, he changed his mind with regard to us, and was now being moved by certain counsels to stir up persecution against us; and there was great talk about this on all sides. But as he was just on the point of so doing, and was putting, one might almost say, his signature to the decrees against us, the divine Justice visited him, and pinioned his arms, so to speak, to prevent his undertaking.

It was an extraordinary sign of the Roman Empire's growing acceptance of Christianity that the bishops of a religion whose followers were once executed for "the name alone" could appeal to the Roman emperor for assistance in enforcing their synod's decision over an internal church matter. However, Aurelian's reported vacillation concerning a policy of toleration toward the Christians was paralleled by the general population's unresolved attitudes toward the Christians. The disapproval of Christianity still found in certain quarters was reflected in a number of pagan oracles from this period recorded by St. Augustine, who quoted the oracles from *Philosophy From Oracles* by the late third-century pagan philosopher Porphyry.

4.25 Oracles by the Prophets of Apollo and Hecate (third century C.E.) qtd. in St. Augustine *City of God* 19.23 (413–426 C.E.)

To one who inquired what god he should propitiate in order to recall his wife from Christianity, Apollo replied in the following verses. . . . "You will probably find it easier to write lasting characters on the water, or lightly fly like a bird through the air, than to restore right feeling in your impious wife once she has polluted herself. Let her remain as she pleases in her foolish deception, and sing false laments to her dead God, who was condemned by right-minded judges, and perished ignominiously by a violent death."

And to those who ask why he was condemned to die, the oracle of the goddess [Hecate] replied, "The body, indeed, is always exposed to torments, but the souls of the pious abide in heaven. And the soul you inquire about has been the fatal cause of error to other souls which were not fated to receive the gifts of the gods, and to have the knowledge of immortal Jove. Such souls are therefore hated by the gods; for they who were fated not to receive the gifts of the gods, and not to know God, were fated to be involved in error by means of him you speak of. He himself, however, was good, and heaven has been opened to him as to other good men. You are not, then, to speak evil of him, but to pity the folly of men: and through him men's danger is imminent."

PORPHYRY'S ATTACK ON CHRISTIANITY

In the last quarter of the third century C.E., the intellectual and historical foundations of the Christian religion were strongly attacked by the pagan philosopher Porphyry, a follower of the neo-Platonic school of Plotinus. Porphyry, who had attended lectures by Origen and studied the Jewish scriptures and the Christian Gospels, was familiar with the tenets of Christianity but he found the faith philosophically unsatisfying and a threat to traditional culture. Porphyry wrote two significant works against the Christian faith, *Against the Christians* and *Prophecy From Oracles*. The force of Porphyry's challenge in these two books may be judged by the fact that during the fourth and fifth centuries C.E. Christians intentionally sought out and burned these books. Even one hundred and fifty years after Porphyry's death, Christian emperors were still issuing edicts ordering the destruction of his writings.[19] As a result, the texts of these two works are today preserved only in quotations found in the writings of his Christian opponents.[20]

Porphyry used his skills in textual criticism and historical method to attack both Christian interpretations of the Old Testament and the reliability of the Gospels. He also argued that the apostles misinterpreted Jesus' teachings and as a result the apostles had mistakenly worshiped Jesus rather than the true God. Finally, Porphyry claimed that the authors of the Gospels were ignorant of the Old Testament, inexperienced in historical investigation, and perhaps even intentionally fraudulent in their writings.[21]

---

19. Porphyry's writings were first ordered destroyed by Constantine the Great in a letter dating to ca. 333 C.E. (Socrates, *Ecclesiastical History* 1.9.30–31). In 448 C.E., an edict to similar effect was issued by the Emperors Theodosius II and Valentinian III. (*Justinian's Code* 1.1.3.1)

20. A number of historians have argued that, in addition to the direct quotations found in various Christian writers, Porphyry's arguments in *Against the Christians* were the basis of the pagan speaker's arguments in the Christian Macarius Magnes's *Apocritus*. See the discussion of this issue in R. Joseph Hoffman, *Porphyry's Against the Christians: The Literary Remains* (Amherst: Prometheus Books, 1994), 21–23.

21. Jerome, *Epistle* 57:9, reports the claim of falsification. See also, Macarius Magnes, *Apocritus* 2.12–15. The Apostle's ignorance of the Old Testament was supposedly demonstrated by the mistaken attributions to Old Testament passages found in the various Gospels. See, for example, the misattributions at Mark 1:2 and Matthew 13:35.

Porphyry's *Against the Christians* (ca. mid-270s C.E.), dealt with both the Old and the New Testaments, but with the exception of two passages concerning the proper dating of Moses, all of the extant fragments pertain to the Book of Daniel.[22] The Christians of this period believed that the Book of Daniel was written during the sixth century B.C.E., but Porphyry argued that an analysis of Daniel's text indicated that it was actually written during the time of Antiochus Ephinanes, 175-164 B.C.E., a date which is accepted by essentially all modern historians.

4.26 Jerome, *Commentary on Daniel*: Prologue (ca. 407 C.E.)
Porphyry wrote his twelfth book [of Against the Christians] against the prophecy of Daniel, denying that it was composed by the person to whom it is ascribed in its title, but rather by some individual who was living in Judaea at the time of Antiochus who was surnamed Ephiphanes. He furthermore alleged that Daniel did not foretell the future so much as he related the past, and lastly that whatever he spoke of up to the time of Antiochus contained authentic history, whereas anything he may have conjectured beyond that point was false, inasmuch as he would not have foreknown the future.

By demonstrating that Daniel was primarily a history written after the fact rather than a prophecy of future events, Porphyry attacked the prophetic value Christians placed on Daniel with respect to the coming of Christ. Later Christians responded vigorously to Porphyry's attack on Daniel, as Eusebius wrote three books defending the traditional view of Daniel, Apollinarius one book, and Jerome a commentary.

Porphyry's second book, *Philosophy From Oracles*, appears to have consisted of three books on the nature, forms, and worship of gods, daemons, and heroes. Porphyry (234–305 C.E.) apparently compared Jesus unfavorably to humans like Heracles and Pythagoras, who according to pagan belief were "heroes" elevated to divinity after death because of their great wisdom and deeds.

4.27 Porphyry, *Philosophy from Oracles* (late third century C.E.)
fragment, quoted in St. Augustine *City of God* 19.23
... he [Porphyry] says, "What we are going to say will certainly take some by surprise. For the gods have declared that Christ was very pious, and has become immortal, and that they cherish his memory; that the Christians, however, are polluted, contaminated, and involved in error. And many other such things," he says, "do the gods say against the Christians."
fragment, quoted in St. Augustine, *City of God* 19.23
"There are", he [Porphyry] says, "in a certain place very small earthly spirits, subject to the power of evil demons. The wise men of the

22. The following discussion is derived from Robert L. Wilken, *The Christians as the Romans Saw Them* (New Haven: Yale University Press, 1984), 137–43.

Hebrews, among whom was this Jesus, as you have heard from the
oracles of Apollo, cited above, turned religious persons from these
very wicked demons and minor spirits, and taught them rather to
worship the celestial gods, and especially to adore God the Father."
"This," he said, "the gods enjoin; and we have already shown how
they admonish the soul to turn to God, and command it to worship
Him. But the ignorant and the ungodly, who are not destined to
receive favors from the gods, nor to know the immortal Jupiter, not
listening to the gods and their messages, have turned away from all
gods, and have not only refused to hate, but have venerated the prohibited demons. Professing to worship God, they refuse to do those
things by which alone God is worshipped. For God, indeed, being the
Father of all, is in need of nothing; but for us it is good to adore Him
by means of justice, chastity, and other virtues, and thus to make life
itself a prayer to Him, by inquiring into and imitating His nature."
"For inquiry," he says, "purifies and imitation deifies us, by moving
us nearer to Him."

fragment, qtd. in St. Augustine, *Epistle* 102.2

Which of two kinds of resurrection corresponds to that which is
promised to us? Is it that of Christ, or that of Lazarus? They say, "If
the former, how can this correspond with the resurrection of those
who have been born by ordinary generations, seeing that He was not
thus born? If, on the other hand, the resurrection of Lazarus is said
to correspond to ours, here also there seems to be a discrepancy, since
the resurrection of Lazarus was accomplished in the case of a body
not yet dissolved, but the same body in which he was known by the
name of Lazarus; whereas ours is to be rescued after many centuries
from the mass in which it has ceased to be distinguishable from other
things. Again, if our state after the resurrection is one of blessedness,
in which the body shall be exempt from every kind of wound, and
from the pain of hunger, what is meant by the statement that Christ
took food, and showed his wounds after His resurrection? For if He
did it to convince the doubting, when the wounds were not real, He
practiced on them a deception; whereas, if He showed them what was
real, it follows that wounds received by the body shall remain in the
state which is to ensue after resurrection."

fragment, qtd. in St. Augustine, *Epistle* 102.8

"If Christ," they say, "declares himself to be the way of salvation, the
grace and the truth, and affirms that in him alone, and only to souls
believing in Him, is the way of return to God, what has become of
men who lived in the many centuries before Christ came?. . . .What,
then, has become of such an innumerable multitude of souls, who
were in no way blameworthy, seeing that He in whom alone saving
faith can be exercised had not yet favored men with His advent?. . . ."

"Why then," he asks, "did he who is called the Savior withhold himself for so many centuries of the world?"

fragment 63[23]

Why, when brought before the high priest or the governor did not
Christ utter a single word worthy of a wise man, of a divine man? He
could, however, have instructed his judge and those present to work
towards improving themselves. He allowed himself to be struck with
a reed, to be spat in the face and crowned with thorns. Would that he
had done like Apollonius, who after having spoken out boldly to the
Emperor Domitian, disappeared (suddenly) from the imperial court
and some hours later showed himself completely openly at
Dicaearchia, today Puteoli? Even if he had to suffer at God's command, and was obliged to accept the punishment, yet at least he
should not have endured the sufferings without some bold discourse,
some vigorous and wise words addressed to Pilate his judge, instead
of letting himself be insulted like some petty street-thief.

Notwithstanding Porphyry's attacks on the apostles, Jesus, and Christianity,
there were Christians who held a grudging respect for his skill and intellect and felt
obligated to explain why a philosopher of his stature rejected the Christian faith.

4.28 St. Augustine, *The City of God* 10.24, 32 (413–426 C.E.)

[24] It was therefore truly said that man is cleansed only by a Principle,
although the Platonists erred in speaking in the plural of principles.
But Porphyry, being under the dominion of these envious powers,
whose influence he was at once ashamed of and afraid to throw off,
refused to recognize that Christ is the Principle by whose incarnation we are purified. Indeed he despised Him, because of the flesh
itself which He assumed, that He might offer a sacrifice for our
purification—a great mystery, unintelligible to Porphyry's pride, which
that true and benignant Redeemer brought low by His humility, mani-
festing Himself to mortals by the mortality which He assumed, and
which the malignant and deceitful mediators are proud of wanting,
promising, as the boon of immortals, a deceptive assistance to
wretched men. . . .

[32] Porphyry, a man of no mediocre abilities, does not question that
such a way exists; for he believes that Divine Providence could not
have left men destitute of this universal way of delivering the soul.
For he does not say that this way does not exist, but that this great
boon and assistance has not yet been discovered, and has not come
to his knowledge. And no wonder; for Porphyry lived in an age when

---

23. Adolf von Harnack, "Porphyrius gegen die Christen, 15 Buchen, Zeugnisse, Fragmente
und Referate" as quoted in J. Stevenson (revised W. H. C. Frend), *A New Eusebius* (London:
SPCK, 1987), 270.

this universal way of the soul's deliverance—in other words, the Christian religion—was exposed to the persecutions of idolaters and demon-worshippers, and earthly rulers, that the number of martyrs or witnesses for the truth might be completed and consecrated, and that by them proof might be given that we must endure all bodily sufferings in the cause of the holy faith, and for the commendation of the truth. Porphyry, being a witness of these persecutions, concluded that this way was destined to a speedy extinction, and that it, therefore, was not the universal way of the soul's deliverance, and did not see that the very thing that thus moved him, and deterred him from becoming a Christian, contributed to the confirmation and more effectual commendation of our religion.

Porphyry's writings against the Christians may have been more than a mere intellectual challenge as there is some slight evidence to indicate that Porphyry was engaged by Diocletian or some other of the tetrarchs to prepare further materials intended to discredit the Christian faith prior to the initiation of another persecution in the early 300s C.E.[24] This persecution, known as the "Great Persecution" of Christianity began in 303 C.E.

24. See Porphyry's *Epistle to Marcella*, 4; R. Joseph Hoffman, *Porphyry's Against the Christians: The Literary Remains* (Amherst: Prometheus Books, 1994), 164; and Robin Lane Fox, *Pagans and Christians* (New York: Alfred A. Knopf, 1986), 593–94; 671–72.

5 | THE CROSS TRIUMPHANT: THE FOURTH CENTURY C.E.

T he fourth century C.E. was a time of fundamental change for the Roman
Empire. When the century began, the tetrarchy founded by Diocletian
appeared to be successful in its efforts to preserve both Rome's empire and its
traditional social order. The authority of the central government was more
firmly established and the frontiers more securely defended than had been the
case for several generations. Yet, the apparent stability of the Roman Empire in
300 C.E. only hid a number of significant administrative, economic, and social
problems that would come to the fore during the course of the fourth and fifth
centuries C.E. The Roman Empire was clearly weaker at the end of the fourth
century C.E. than at the century's beginning and the western half of the Empire
would collapse during the first two generations of the fifth century C.E. Of even
more fundamental significance for the future of Western Europe, however, was
the fact that during the fourth century C.E. Christianity came to dominate the
Roman Empire's government and society.

The most significant administrative problem facing the Roman emperors at
the start of the fourth century C.E. was the sheer cost of defending and governing the Empire. The Roman army grew significantly during the troubled years
of the third century C.E., perhaps doubling in size.[1] Over the same period the
governmental bureaucracy grew even more rapidly, as the emperors sought to
exert closer control and supervision over the provinces and the army in order
to both collect the necessary tax revenues and defend against potential
usurpers. It is estimated that whereas at the start of the third century C.E. the
Roman emperors employed only about 300 to 350 full-time individuals in
administering the Empire, by 300 C.E. this number had grown to some 30,000
or 35,000 people.[2] The expense of this vastly increased administrative and military structure was an enormous burden on the peoples of the Empire, and the
burden only grew more oppressive over the course of the fourth century C.E. as
the demands of the government and the military continued to grow in response

---

1. A. H. M. Jones, *Constantine and the Conversion of Europe* (Toronto: University of Toronto
Press, 1978), 29–30.

2. Ramsay MacMullen, *Corruption and the Decline of Rome* (New Haven: Yale University
Press, 1988), 144 and note 66; Ramsay MacMullen, *Christianity & Paganism in the Fourth to
Eighth Centuries* (New Haven: Yale University Press, 1997), 83.

to increasingly frequent and more severe conflicts with bandit groups, barbarians, and the Persian Empire.

Rome's efforts to collect the taxes necessary to pay for defense and administration exacerbated the already deep social and economic divisions within the Roman Empire. Ramsay MacMullen has written that the tendency of socio-economic development during the five centuries of the Roman Empire can be summarized by the statement that "fewer have more," and this trend accelerated during the fourth and fifth centuries.[3] The rich and powerful within the Empire sought to escape Rome's increasing demands for taxes and services by using their wealth and social and political influence to bribe or intimidate the local officials responsible for enforcing these obligations and by withdrawing from the cities, which were the key to Rome's administrative structure, to self-sustaining country estates. As a result, the tax burden fell disproportionately on the lower economic orders. Marginal agriculturists like small farmers and herders were particularly hard hit by the increasing tax burdens and more frequent warfare, and many historians believe that the Roman Empire's population slowly shrank during the fourth and fifth centuries C.E. as large segments of the rural population were simply unable to sustain their families on what remained after barbarian incursions and government taxes.[4]

Another part of the Empire's society hard hit by the tax burden was the decurion order, a relatively prosperous group from which the great majority of local government officials were drawn.[5] Under Roman law, these local governing officials were personally liable for shortfalls in tax collections and so the decurions had every incentive to take any measures necessary to ensure that the taxes were collected, however much misery this might mean for the masses. By the late third and early fourth centuries C.E., it is clear that many decurions were unable to meet Rome's demands for taxes and were being pushed into economic ruin. Many decurions attempted to flee the responsibilities of municipal service, but the emperors responded to the flight by making the positions hereditary. The increasing impoverishment and demoralization of the decurions weakened both the loyalty and the effectiveness of the local governments, which were the backbone of Rome's administrative system.

At the same time that Roman rule was being undermined by administrative, military, and social problems, the emperors were also faced with the increasingly

---

3. Ramsay MacMullen, *Roman Social Relations: 50 B.C. to A.D. 284* (New Haven: Yale University Press, 1974), 38.

4. See, e.g., A. E. R. Boak, *Manpower Shortage and the Fall of the Roman Empire in the West* (Ann Arbor: University of Michigan Press, 1955), 22–54; Michael Grant, *The Fall of the Roman Empire* (New York: Collier, 1990), 58; A.H.M. Jones, *The Later Roman Empire, 284–602* (Baltimore: John Hopkins University Press, 1964), Vol. II, 1043–1045. Other historians believe that the evidence is not conclusive on this point. See, e.g., Tim G. Porkin, *Demography and Roman Society* (Baltimore: John Hopkins University Press, 1992), 59–66.

5. Ramsay MacMullen, *Corruption and the Decline of Rome* (New Haven: Yale University Press, 1988), 44–48.

urgent problem of how to deal with the Christians. By the start of the fourth century C.E., approximately 8 to 10 percent of the Empire's population was Christian and this body formed, for most practical purposes, a state within a state. During the third century C.E., the Christian churches gradually adopted an administrative structure that geographically paralleled the Roman administrative system and the bishops began to meet more or less regularly in regional councils called synods to formulate policy on important questions of doctrine and discipline. As perpetual corporate bodies, many of the individual churches accumulated significant wealth, and the revenues available from these properties and the donations of individual Christians gave the church as a whole a financial strength available to few other institutions of the period. While there is no evidence to suggest that Christians as a body were disloyal either to Rome or the emperors, the emperors were aware that this increasingly numerous and wealthy religion taught both that the Christian God was a higher authority than the emperor and that many fundamental aspects of the traditional pagan society and religion were immoral institutions that should be abolished. Moreover, there were pagans who believed that the Empire's near collapse during the troubled years of the third century C.E. was the result of the gods' disapproval of the new faith and thus Rome's future survival depended on uniting the Empire's population against the Christians and in support of the traditional customs and religion. The tension between Christianity and the Roman government would have to be resolved, if a unified Empire were to face its enemies.

Diocletian himself was apparently reluctant to move against the Christian faith, but he ultimately accepted the arguments of the Caesar Galerius that the restoration and preservation of the traditional Roman order required the suppression of the Christians. That Diocletian and his fellow tetrarchs could take action against the Christians at the start of the fourth century C.E. was the direct result of their earlier success in dealing with usurpers and foreign invaders. With the security and administration of the Empire seemingly well in hand, the emperors could afford to turn their collective attention to the Christian problem. Thus it was that in 303 C.E. the "Great Persecution" of Christians began.

The Great Persecution was the most serious and sustained of all Roman persecutions of Christianity, but with the hindsight of a modern perspective the persecution appears to have had relatively little chance of success. Christianity was too well-established within the Empire's population to be easily rooted out, and the repressive measures adopted by the tetrarchs were based on a misunderstanding of the Christian movement. Apparently believing, with a typical upper-class Roman perspective, that the Christian churches were more or less similar in nature to the traditional pagan cults and had to be centered around the leadership of a small but socially elite hierarchy, Diocletian's first directives were aimed at "decapitating" the faith by arresting the bishops, destroying the formal places of worship, and burning the sacred texts. Only later would measures be directed against the broader membership of the church and then the persecution was greatly hindered by the unwieldy nature of the imperial bureaucracy. The tetrarchs found it difficult to enforce wide-spread compliance with the measures directed against the Christians because many local officials only half-heartedly carried out their instructions. This lack of zeal among the local officials may lie in the fact that by this time the Christians were a known quantity: people who, even if they were prone to a rather embarrassingly strident monotheism, were nonetheless respectable in their personal and ethical conduct and performed many works of charity. Moreover, Christians were now found at every level of society, including the imperial bureaucracy and the households of the tetrarchs themselves. (See, e.g., Selection 5.1) The reluctance to persecute the Christians extended even to the tetrarchs themselves, for while Galerius and Maximian vigorously pursued the persecution in their provinces, in the West the Caesar Constantius carried out only the orders to destroy buildings and books and took no steps to arrest or punish the clergy or their congregations. While the Great Persecution was ever after remembered by Christians as the period of the greatest threat to the faith, the true extent of the threat is demonstrated by the fact that during the eight years of the Great Persecution, only about 2,000 to 5,000 of the approximately 5 million Christians died as martyrs.[6]

THE STRUGGLE FOR POLITICAL POWER IN THE EARLY FOURTH CENTURY

In 305 C.E., only two years after the Great Persecution began, Diocletian and his co-Augustus Maximian retired from office in the first test of the plan of succession Diocletian had devised for the tetrarchy. The lack of any institutionalized process for succession to power had always been the most significant weakness of Rome's imperial system, as evidenced most dramatically by the turmoil of the third century C.E., so there must have been a general sigh of relief within the Empire when the Caesars Constantius and Galerius peacefully stepped up to the positions of co-Augusti and appointed Severus and Maximinus Daia as the new Caesars.

However, this relief was short-lived because the new tetrarchs quickly fell into conflict among themselves. In 306 C.E., the Western Augustus Constantius died in Britain and his army acclaimed his son Constantine as the new Western Augustus, ignoring the claims of Severus, the Western Caesar. Galerius, the Eastern Augustus, refused to accept Constantine's acclamation and raised Severus to the rank of Western Augustus, but ultimately Galerius was forced to appoint Constantine as a Caesar to avoid a possible civil war. Shortly thereafter, Maximian's son Maxentius proclaimed himself *princeps* in Italy in hopes of also being named a Caesar. When Severus led an army toward Italy to put down Maxentius, Maximian left retirement to support his son and publicly reclaimed his old title of Augustus. Severus's army deserted him upon hearing this news

---

6. See Ramsay MacMullen, *Changes in the Roman Empire* (Princeton: Princeton University Press, 1990), 157 and the sources cited therein at footnote 3. See also footnotes 17 and 18 of this chapter and the accompanying text.

and Severus was put to death by Maximian in 307 C.E. Maxentius then declared himself Augustus of the Western Empire.

In 307 C.E., Galerius prepared to move his army against Maxentius and Maximian. Maxentius and Maximian responded to the threat by forming an alliance with Constantine, in which Maximian gave his daughter to Constantine in marriage and proclaimed Constantine a co-Augusti. In the face of this new alliance and the uncertain loyalty of his troops, Galerius abandoned his planned attack against Italy and instead called upon Diocletian to leave retirement and reclaim the throne. Diocletian refused to resume the emperor-ship, but he did agree to meet with Maximian and Galerius in an effort to mediate the dispute. At a conference in 308 C.E., Maximian agreed to abandon his support for his son Maxentius and go back into retirement, while Licinius, a supporter of Galerius, was made Caesar. Constantine and Maximinus Daia demanded that they be made Augusti, but instead they were merely offered the title "Sons of Augustus," which they rejected. The conference thus produced only a short respite in the political conflict and by 310 C.E. five different indi-viduals were claiming the title of Augustus.

In 311 C.E. Galerius died and Licinius succeeded to the position of Eastern Augustus. The other Augusti continued to maneuver for advantage. Constantine now formed an alliance with Licinius and moved against Maxentius, invading Italy in 312 C.E. There, immediately prior to a battle with Maxentius's army near the Milvian Bridge over the Tiber River, Constantine ordered his troops to mark their shields with a Christian monogram, in a public appeal to the God of the Christians for support and victory. Constantine won the battle and the Senate of Rome proclaimed him a senior Augustus.

Early in 313 C.E., Constantine and Licinius met at Milan and issued a proclamation granting Christians the license to worship their religion without restriction. Later that same year Licinius defeated and killed Maximin Daia. Thus, in 313 C.E. Constantine and Licinius emerged as sole co-Augusti and Christianity became a legal religion in the Roman Empire.

THE GREAT PERSECUTION

The sources for the Great Persecution are fairly numerous and many of these sources were written by people living at the time. However, many ancient writers attributed the causation of great historical events to the decisions and whims of individuals and so the modern historian must exercise some care in separat-ing the underlying facts from the interpretations presented in the sources. This tendency to attribute historical causation to the acts of individuals is evident in the following account by the Christian Lactantius (245–323 C.E.) of the events that led up to the Great Persecution.

> 5.1 Lactantius, *On the Deaths of the Persecutors* 10–12 (ca. 317–318 C.E.)
> [10] Diocletian, as being of a timorous disposition, was a searcher into futurity, and during his abode in the East he began to slay victims,

that from their livers he might obtain a prognostic of events; and
while he sacrificed, some attendants of his, who were Christians,
stood by, and they put the immortal sign on their foreheads. At this
the demons were chased away, and the holy rites interrupted. The
soothsayers trembled, unable to investigate the wonted marks on the
entrails of the victims. They frequently repeated the sacrifices, as if
the former had been unpropitious; but the victims, slain from time
to time, afforded no tokens for divination. At length Tages, the chief
of the soothsayers, either from guess or from his own observation,
said, "There are profane persons here, who obstruct the rites." Then
Diocletian, in furious passion, ordered not only all who were assisting at the holy ceremonies, but also all who resided within the palace,
to sacrifice, and, in case of their refusal, to be scourged. And further,
by letters to the commanding officers, he enjoined that all soldiers
should be forced to the like impiety, under pain of being dismissed
the service. Thus far his rage proceeded; but at that season he did
nothing more against the law and religion of God. After an interval
of some time he went to winter in Bithynia; and presently Galerius
Caesar came thither, inflamed with furious resentment, and purpos-
ing to excite the inconsiderate old man to carry on that persecution
which he had begun against the Christians. I have learned that the
cause of his fury was as follows.

[11] The mother of Galerius, a woman exceedingly superstitious, was a
votary of the gods of the mountains. Being of such a character, she
made sacrifices almost every day, and she feasted her servants on the
meat offered to idols; but the Christians of her family would not partake of those entertainments; and while she feasted with the Gentiles,
they continued in fasting and prayer. On this account she conceived
ill-will against the Christians, and by woman-like complaints instigated her son, no less superstitious than herself, to destroy them. So,
during the whole winter, Diocletian and Galerius held councils
together, at which no one else assisted; and it was the universal opinion that their conferences respected the most momentous affairs of
the empire. The old man long opposed the fury of Galerius, and
showed how pernicious it would be to raise disturbances throughout
the world and to shed so much blood; that the Christians were wont
with eagerness to meet death; and that it would be enough for him
to exclude persons of that religion from the court and the army. Yet
he could not restrain the madness of that obstinate man. He
resolved, therefore, to take the opinion of his friends. Now this was
a circumstance in the bad disposition of Diocletian, that whenever
he determined to do good, he did it without advice, that the praise
might be all his own; but whenever he determined to do ill, which he
was sensible would be blamed, he called in many advisers, that his

own fault might be imputed to other men; and therefore a few civil magistrates, and a few military commanders, were admitted to give their counsel; and the question was put to them according to priority of rank. Some, through personal ill-will toward the Christians, were of the opinion that they ought to be cut off, as enemies of the gods and adversaries of the reestablished religious ceremonies. Others thought differently, but, having understood the will of Galerius, they, either from dread of displeasing or from a desire of gratifying him, concurred in the opinion given against the Christians. Yet not even then could the emperor be prevailed upon to yield his assent. He determined above all to consult his gods; and to that end he dispatched a soothsayer to inquire of Apollo at Miletus, whose answer was such as might be expected from an enemy of the divine religion. So Diocletian was drawn over from his purpose. But although he could struggle no longer against his friends, and against Caesar and Apollo, yet still he attempted to observe such moderation as to command the business to be carried through without bloodshed; whereas Galerius would have had all persons burnt alive who refused to sacrifice.

[12] A fit and auspicious day was sought out for the accomplishment of this undertaking; and the festival of the God Terminus, celebrated on the sevens of the kalends of March, was chosen, in preference to all others, to terminate, as it were, the Christian religion. "That day, the harbinger of death, arose, First cause of ill, and long enduring woes"; of woes which befell not only the Christians, but the whole earth. When that day dawned, in the eighth consulship of Diocletian and seventh of Maximian, suddenly, while it was yet hardly light, the prefect, together with chief commanders, tribunes, and officers of the treasury, came to the church in Nicomedia, and the gates having been forced open, they searched everywhere for an image of the Divinity. The books of the Holy Scriptures were found, and they were committed to the flames; the utensils and furniture of the church were abandoned to pillage: all was rapine, confusion, tumult. That church, situated on rising ground, was within view of the palace; and Diocletian and Galerius stood, as if on a watch-tower, disputing long whether it ought to be set on fire. The sentiment of Diocletian prevailed, who dreaded lest, so great a fire being once kindled, some part of the city might be burnt; for there were many and large buildings that surrounded the church. Then the Praetorian Guards came in battle array, with axes and other iron instruments, and having been let loose everywhere, they in a few hours leveled that very lofty edifice with the ground.

The fact that the Christian church occupied high ground within sight of the imperial palace is evidence that Christians and Christianity had become a more or less accepted part of the Empire's society in the years since the persecutions of the 250s C.E. While perceptive Christians had recognized the growing tension that preceded Diocletian's decision to move against the faith, something of the sheer shock of persecution after so many years of relative acceptance can be seen in the account of another contemporary Christian writer, Eusebius of Caesarea.

5.2 Eusebius of Caesarea, *Ecclesiastical History* 8.1.1–3, 1.7–8, 2.1, 2.4–3.1, 4.2–4, 6.8–10, 16.1 (ca. 311–323 C.E.)

[1.1–3] It is beyond our powers to describe in a worthy manner the measure and nature of that honor as well as freedom which was accorded by all men, both Greeks and barbarians, before the persecution in our day, to that word of piety toward the God of the universe which had been proclaimed through Christ to the world. Yet proofs might be forthcoming in the favors granted by the rulers to our people; to whom they would even entrust the government of the provinces, freeing them from agony of mind as regards sacrificing, because of the great friendliness that they used to entertain for their doctrine. Why need one speak of those in the imperial palaces and of the supreme rulers, who allowed the members of their households—wives, children, and servants—to practice openly to their face the divine word and conduct, and—one might say—permitted them even to boast of the freedom accorded to the faith? . . .

[1.7–8] But when, as the result of greater freedom, a change to pride and sloth came over our affairs, we fell to envy and fierce railing against one another, warring upon ourselves, so to speak, as occasion offered, with weapons and spears formed of words; and rulers attacked rulers and laity formed factions against laity, while unspeakable hypocrisy and pretense pursued their evil course to the furthest end: until the divine judgment with a sparing hand, as is its wont (for the assemblies were still crowded), quietly and moderately began to exercise its oversight, the persecution commencing with the brethren in the army. But when in our blindness we took not the least care to secure the goodwill and propitious favor of the Deity, but, like some kind of atheists, imagined that our affairs escaped all heed and oversight, we went on adding one wickedness to another; and those accounted our pastors, casting aside the sanctions of the fear of God, were inflamed with mutual contentions, and did nothing else but add to the strifes and the threats, the jealousy, enmity and hatred that they used one to another, claiming with all vehemence the objects of their ambition as if they were a despot's spoils; then indeed, then according to the word spoken by Jeremiah, the Lord hath darkened the daughter of Zion in his anger, and hath cast down from heaven the glory of Israel. . .

[2.1] All things in truth were fulfilled in our day, when we saw with our very own eyes the houses of prayer cast down to their foundations from top to bottom, and the inspired and sacred Scriptures committed to the flames in the midst of the market places, and the pastors of the churches, some shamefully hiding themselves here and there, while others were ignominiously captured and made a mockery by their enemies. . . .

2.4–5 It was the nineteenth year of the reign of Diocletian, and the month Dystrus, or March, as the Romans would call it, in which, as the festival of the Savior's Passion was coming on, an imperial letter was everywhere promulgated, ordering the razing of the churches to the ground and the destruction by fire of the Scriptures, and proclaiming that those who held high positions would lose all civil rights, while those in the households, if they persisted in their profession of Christianity, would be deprived of their liberty. Such was the first document against us. But not long afterwards we were further visited with other letters, and in them the order was given that the presidents of the churches should all, in every place, be first committed to prison, and then afterwards compelled by every kind of device to sacrifice.

3.1 Then indeed, then very many rulers of the churches contended with a stout heart under terrible torments, and displayed spectacles of mighty conflicts; while countless others, whose souls cowardice had numbed beforehand, readily proved weak at the first assault. . . .

4.2–4 For when he who had received the authority was just now awakening, as it were, from profound torpor, though he was in a secret and hidden manner already making attempts against the churches during the time that came after Decius and Valerian, and did not get himself in readiness for war against us all at once, but as yet made an attempt only upon those in the camps (for in this way he thought that the rest also could easily be taken, if first of all he were to get the better in the conflict with these): then one could see great numbers of those in the army most gladly embracing civil life, so that they might not prove renegades in their piety toward the Creator of the universe. For when the supreme commander [Veturius], whoever he was, was just making his first attempt at persecuting the soldiers—separating into classes and thoroughly sifting out those serving in the camps, giving them a choice whether they would obey and enjoy the rank they held, or else be deprived of it, if they continued to disobey the commandment—a great many soldiers of Christ's kingdom, without hesitation, unquestionably preferred to confess Him than retain the seeming glory and prosperity that they possessed. And already in rare cases one or two of these were receiving not only loss of honor but even death in exchange for their godly steadfastness, for as yet the instigator of the plot was working with a certain moderation and daring to proceed into blood only in some instances; fearing, presumably, the multitude of believers, and hesitating to plunge into the war against us all at once. . . . [7]

[6.8–10] Such were the things that were done in Nicomedia at the beginning of the persecution. But not long afterwards, when some in the district known as Melitene, and again on the other hand when others in Syria, had attempted to take possession of the Empire, an imperial command went forth that the presidents of the churches everywhere should be thrown into prison and bonds. And the spectacle of what followed surpasses all description; for in every place a countless number were shut up, and everywhere the prisons, that long ago had been prepared for murderers and grave robbers, were then filled with bishops and presbyters and deacons, readers and exorcists, so that there was no longer any room left there for those condemned for wrongdoing. Moreover, the first letter was followed by others, wherein the order had been given that those in prison should be allowed to go in liberty if they sacrificed, but if they refused, should be mutilated by countless tortures. . . .

[16.1] Such was the state of affairs that continued throughout the whole persecution; which came completely to an end, by the grace of God, in the tenth year [313 C.E.], though indeed it began to abate after the eighth year.

In contrast to Lactantius's emphasis on the malice of individuals, Eusebius explained the persecution with a perspective derived from the Old Testament: God allowed the persecution as punishment for the sins of Christians and their failure to properly honor God. In particular, Eusebius blamed the persecution on the doctrinal divisions within Christianity. While Diocletian and the tetrarchs certainly initiated the persecution for other reasons, the Great Persecution did expose deep and bitter theological divisions among the various Christian communities. In Carthage, for example, one sect of Christians posted armed guards outside a Roman prison in an effort to prevent the imprisoned members of a different Christian sect from receiving food and drink from friends and relatives.[8] The strain of persecution caused conflict even among Christians holding the same theological beliefs and these divisions continued into the reigns of the later Christian emperors.

5.3 Epiphanius, *Panarion* 68.1.1, 4, 8; 2.1–3; 3.1–4

[1.1] There exists a Melitian party in Egypt deriving from one Melitius, a bishop in the Thebaid, who was of the Catholic church and the orthodox faith, for his faith varied at no time from that of the holy Catholic church. . . .

---

7. Note that Eusebius's text provides the interesting detail that the persecution actually began with the removal of Christians serving in the military.

8. *Acta Saturnini* 17.

[1.4] He caused a schism, although he did not alter his faith. He was arrested during the persecution [of Diocletian] together with St. Peter, the bishop and martyr, and the other martyrs. . . .

[1.8] All of these, then, were arrested and put in prison to await martyrdom, and there they remained locked up for a long time. Others before them who had been handed over had been martyred, received the prize of victory and fallen asleep, but they as the leaders and as of higher station were being reserved for later.

[2.1–3] Now some had indeed been martyred, but others had lapsed from martyrdom and performed the unlawful act of idolatry; they had performed sacrifices under compulsion, and so having lapsed, sacrificed and transgressed, they approached the confessors and martyrs in order to obtain mercy through repentance. Some were soldiers, whereas others were clerics of various degree, presbyters and deacons and others. This caused a great commotion and disturbance among the martyrs, with some saying that those who had once lapsed, denied the faith, and not persevered in courage and in the contest ought not to be granted a chance to repent. . . . Those who spoke in this way were Melitius, Peleus and most of the other martyrs and confessors with them. . . .

[3.1–4] But the most holy Peter, who was a kindly man and as it were the father of all, begged and beseeched them. . . . Peter's words were on the side of mercy and kindness, and those of Melitius and his party on that of truth and zeal. This was the origin of the schism: the religious face which each side could put on its argument, with some saying one thing and others something else. For when Archbishop Peter saw that those with Melitius, carried away by an excess of divine zeal, were resisting his kindly counsel, he hung a curtain in the middle of the prison, stretching out a garment which was a kind of cloak and announcing [through] a deacon: Those who are of my mind come to me and those of Melitius' mind are with Melitius. And so they were divided; the majority of bishops, monks and presbyters, and the other orders were with Melitius, while a very few, some bishops and a few others, [were] with Archbishop Peter. From then one group prayed by itself and the other by itself, and each likewise performed the other sacred functions by itself.

As noted earlier, Diocletian and the tetrarchs initially aimed their first edicts at the Christian clergy and scriptures. A description of the means by which local officials carried out these edicts has survived in an account of events in the town of Cirta, Africa on May 19, 303 C.E.

5.4 Gesta Apud Zenophilum (*Corpus Scriptorum Ecclesiasticorum Latinorum* 26, pp. 186–188.)

In the eighth and seventh consulships of Diocletian and Maximian,

19th May [303 C.E.], from the records of Munatius Felix, high priest of the province for life, mayor (*curator*) of the colony of Cirta. Arrived at the house where the Christians used to meet, the Mayor said to Paul the bishop: "Bring out the writings of the law and anything else you have here, according to the order, so that you may obey the command."

The Bishop: "The readers have the Scriptures, but we will give what we have here."

The Mayor: "Point out the readers or send for them."

The Bishop: "You all know them."

The Mayor: "We do not know them."

The Bishop: "The municipal office knows them, that is, the clerks Edusius and Junius."

The Mayor: "Leaving over the matter of the readers, whom the office will point out, produce what you have."

Then follows an inventory of the church plate and other property, including large stores of male and female clothes and shoes, produced in the presence of the clergy, who include three priests, two deacons, and four subdeacons, all named, and a number of "diggers."

The Mayor: "Bring out what you have."

Silvanus and Carosus (two of the subdeacons): "We have thrown out everything that was here."

The Mayor: "Your answer is entered on the record."

After some empty cupboards had been found in the library, Silvanus then produced a silver box and a silver lamp, which he said he had found behind a barrel.

Victor (the mayor's clerk): "You would have been a dead man if you hadn't found them."

The Mayor: "Look more carefully, in case there is anything left here."

Silvanus: "There is nothing left. We have thrown everything out."

And when the dining-room was opened, there were found there four bins and six barrels.

The Mayor: "Bring out the Scriptures that you have so that we can obey the orders and command of the emperors."

Catullinus (another subdeacon) produced one very large volume.

The Mayor: "Why have you given one volume only? Produce the scriptures that you have."

Marcuclius and Catullinus (two subdeacons): "We haven't any more, because we are subdeacons; the readers have the books."

The Mayor: "Show me the readers."

Marcuclius and Catullinus: "We don't know where they live."

The Mayor: "If you don't know where they live, tell me their names."

Marcuclius and Catullinus: "We are not traitors:[9] here we are, order us to be killed."

The Mayor: "Put them under arrest."

They apparently weakened so far as to reveal one other reader, for the Mayor now moved on to the house of Eugenius, who produced four books.

The Mayor now turned on the other two subdeacons, Silvanus and Carosus:

The Mayor: "Show me the other readers."

Silvanus and Carosus: "The bishop has already said that Edusius and Junius the clerks know them all: they will show you the way to their houses."

Edusius and Junius: "We will show them, sir."

The Mayor went on to visit the six remaining readers. Four produced their books without demur. One declared that he had none, and the Mayor was content with entering his statement on the record. The last was out, but his wife produced his books; the Mayor had the house searched by the public slave to make sure that none had been overlooked. This task over, he addressed the subdeacons:

The Mayor: "If there has been any omission, the responsibility is yours."

As the persecution continued into 304 C.E. without any apparent prospect of a quick suppression of the Christians, the tetrarchs instituted measures against the broader membership of the church.

5.5 Eusebius, *On the Martyrs of Palestine*, 3.1 (ca. 314 C.E.)

Such was the course of action in the first year, when the presidents of the Church were alone menaced by the persecution. But when the second year came around [April of 304 C.E.] and, further, the war against us increased in intensity (Urban being at that time governor of the province), imperial edicts then visited us for the first time, in which by a general ordinance the command was given that in the several cities all the people in a body should sacrifice and offer libations to the idols.

While many officials did not zealously act to carry out the measures directed against Christians, there were of course individuals and local officials

---

9. The modern word "traitor" comes from the Latin *traditores*: "one who gives over [the Scripture]." The relative effectiveness of the measures against the Christian Scriptures can be seen in one interesting statistic: of the approximately 5,500 extant Greek manuscript witnesses to the text of the New Testament which date prior to the age of the printing press, only about 88 manuscript fragments (and no complete New Testament) are dated prior to 300 C.E.; Bruce M. Metzger, *The Text of the New Testament,* 3rd ed. (New York: Oxford University Press, 1992), 262; Robin Lane Fox, *The Unauthorized Version: Truth and Fiction in the Bible* (New York: Alfred A. Knopf, 1993), 139.

who supported the persecution of the Christians. Some no doubt acted from a real sense of repugnance at the Christian violation of traditional belief and custom. Others, however, merely sought to curry political favor, as seems to have been the case with a number of town councils that erected monuments and wrote petitions to the tetrarchs in support of the persecution.

5.6 Eusebius, *Ecclesiastical History*, 9.6.4–7.1 (ca. 311–323 C.E.) The events date to ca. 310 C.E.

> So mightily, indeed, did that hater of the good, Maximin [Maximinus Daia], contrive against us in a short space, that this persecution which he had stirred up seemed to us much more severe than the former one. In fact, in the midst of the cities—a thing that had never happened before—petitions presented against us by cities, and rescripts containing imperial ordinances in reply, were set up, engraved on brazen tablets; while the children in the schools had every day on their lips the names of Jesus and Pilate and the Memoirs[10] forged to insult us.

5.7 A Petition Against The Christians (OGIS No. 569) Discovered in 1892 C.E. in Aruf, Turkey (Arykanda, Lycia), this inscription dates to 311/312 C.E.

> To the masters of every nation and people, the Emperors and Caesars Galerius Valerius Maximinus and Valerius Licinianus Licnius, from the nation of the Lycians and Pamphylians, a petition and supplication. Since the gods your kinsmen have demonstrated to all their love of mankind, oh most divine kings, who are concerned with worship of them on behalf of the eternal security of yourselves, we considered it would be well to take refuge with your eternal majesty and make petition that the Christians, long suffering from madness, should at length be made to cease and not give offense by some ill-omened new cult to the worship due to the gods.

5.8 The Response of Maximinus to Petition, quoted in Eusebius, *Ecclesiastical History* 9.7.11–12

> ... And let as many as have been wholly rescued from that blind folly and error and returned to a right and goodly frame of mind rejoice indeed the more, as if they were delivered from an unexpected hurricane or severe illness and were reaping life's sweet enjoyment for the future. But if they persist in their accursed folly, let them be separated and driven far away from your city and neighborhood, even as you requested; that so, in accordance with your praiseworthy zeal in this respect, your city may be separated from all pollution and impiety, and, following its natural desire, may respond with due reverence to the worship of the immortal gods. ...

---

10. "Memoirs of Pontius Pilate" were forged and used as anti-Christian propaganda. See Eusebius, *Ecclesiastical History* 1.9.3–4 and 9.5.1.

In the end, Christianity survived the persecution. Diocletian, apparently recognizing that the persecution would not succeed, proceeded with his plans to retire in 305 C.E. Galerius, the prime instigator of the persecution, was not so fortunate.

5.9 Lactantius, *On the Deaths of the Persecutors* 33 (ca. 317–318 C.E.)
And now, when Galerius was in the eighteenth year of his reign, God struck him with an incurable plague. A malignant ulcer formed itself low down in his secret parts, and spread by degrees. The physicians attempted to eradicate it, and healed up the place affected. But the sore, after having been skinned over, broke out again; a vein burst, and the blood flowed in such quantity as to endanger his life. The blood, however, was stopped, although with difficulty. The physicians had to undertake their operations anew, and at length they cauterized the wound. In consequence of some slight motion of his body, Galerius received a hurt, and the blood streamed more abundantly than before. He grew emaciated, pallid, and feeble, and the bleeding then stanched. The ulcer began to be insensible to the remedies applied, and a gangrene seized all the neighboring parts. It diffused itself the wider the more the corrupted flesh was cut away, and everything employed as the means of cure served but to aggravate the disease. "The masters of the healing art withdrew." Then famous physicians were brought in from all quarters; but no human means had any success. Apollo and Aesculapius were besought importunately for remedies: Apollo did prescribe, and the distemper augmented. Already approaching to its deadly crisis, it had occupied the lower regions of his body: his bowels came out, and his whole seat putrefied. The luckless physicians, although without hope of overcoming the malady, ceased not to apply fomentations and administer medicines. The humors having been repelled, the distemper attacked his intestines, and worms were generated in his body. The stench was so foul as to pervade not only the palace, but even the whole city; and no wonder, for by that time the passages from his bladder and bowels, having been devoured by the worms, became indiscriminate, and his body, with intolerable anguish, was dissolved into one mass of corruption.

In 311 C.E., shortly before his horrible death, Galerius issued an edict that rescinded all of the previous anti-Christian measures, in an apparent act of desperation to obtain the favor of the Christian God who had proved so strong.

5.10 The Edict of Galerius as quoted by Lactantius in *On the Deaths of the Persecutors* 34 (ca. 317–318 C.E.)
Amongst our other regulations for the permanent advantage of the commonweal, we have hitherto studied to reduce all things to a conformity with the ancient laws and public discipline of the Romans. It

has been our aim in an especial manner, that the Christians also, who
had abandoned the religion of their forefathers, should return to
right opinions. For such willfulness and folly had, we know not how,
taken possession of them, that instead of observing those ancient
institutions, which possibly their own forefathers had established,
they, through caprice, made laws to themselves, and drew together
into different societies many men of widely different persuasions.
After the publication of our edict, ordaining the Christians to betake
themselves to the observance of the ancient institutions, many of
them were subdued through the fear of danger, and moreover many
of them were exposed to jeopardy; nevertheless, because great numbers still persist in their opinions, and because we have perceived that
at present they neither pay reverence and due adoration to the gods,
nor yet worship their own God, therefore we, from our wonted
clemency in bestowing pardon on all, have judged it fit to extend our
indulgence to those men, and to permit them again to be Christians,
and to establish the places of their religious assemblies; yet so as that
they offend not against good order. By another mandate* we purpose
to signify unto magistrates how they ought herein to demean themselves. Wherefore it will be the duty of the Christians, in consequence
of this our toleration, to pray to their God for our welfare, and for that
of the public, and for their own; that the commonweal may continue
safe in every quarter, and that they themselves may live securely in
their habitations.

Galerius seems to have died before the second mandate was ever issued.

CONSTANTINE AND HIS VISION OF THE CROSS

If 311 C.E. marked the end of the Great Persecution, the next year marked another
momentous step in Christianity's history. Constantine's vision of the Cross before
the Battle of the Milvian Bridge in 312 C.E. and his conversion to Christianity is
one of the best known of all ancient Christian stories, yet for historians it is one of
the most difficult historical events to understand or explain because of the
silences, inconsistencies, and ambiguities found in the extant accounts of these
events. The two most direct and extensive accounts of Constantine's vision, for
example, differ in many material points. Collectively, however, the sources clearly
indicate that between 310 C.E. and 315 C.E. Constantine's contemporaries saw a
marked change in his religious beliefs and orientation.

In 310 C.E., Constantine does not seem to have been perceived to be a
Christian by his contemporaries. The evidence for this belief lies mainly in a
panegyric delivered that year to Constantine in the city of Trier, shortly after his
victory over Maximian.

5.11 Panegyric to Constantine *Panegyrici Latini* 6.21.3–.22.1 (310 C.E.)
21.3 Fortune herself so ordered this matter that the happy outcome of
your affairs prompted you to convey to the immortal gods what you

had vowed at the very spot where you had turned aside toward the most beautiful temple in the whole world, or rather to the deity made manifest, as you saw. For you saw, I believe, O Constantine, your Apollo, accompanied by Victory, offering you laurel wreaths, each of which carries a portent of thirty years. For this is the number of human ages which are owed to you without fail—beyond the old age of a Nestor. And—now why do I say, "I believe"?—You saw, and recognized yourself in the likeness of him to whom the divine songs of the bards had prophesied that rule over the whole world was due. And this I think has now happened, since you are, O Emperor, like he, youthful, joyful, a bringer of health and very handsome. Rightly, therefore, have you honored those most venerable shrines with such great treasures that they do not miss their old ones, any longer. Now may all the temples be seen to beckon you to them, and particularly our Apollo, whose boiling waters punish perjuries—which ought to be especially hateful to you.

[22.1] Immortal gods, when will you grant that day on which this most manifestly present god, with peace reigning everywhere, may visit those groves of Apollo as well, both sacred shrines and steaming mouths of springs.

The author of this panegyric, which was apparently delivered in a public speech before Constantine and his court, openly declared that not only had the gods Apollo and Victory appeared in a vision to Constantine when he stopped to make sacrifice at the temple of Apollo Grannus, but that Apollo had extended his patronage and protection to Constantine. It is difficult to believe that the speaker would have made such public statements to Constantine himself, if at the time there were the slightest indication that Constantine had adopted the Christian faith. Less than two years later, however, Constantine had a vision from the Christian divinity, not Apollo, as he prepared for battle against Maxentius. This vision has been preserved in two separate Christian accounts.

5.12 Lactantius, *On the Deaths of the Persecutors* 44 (ca. 317–318 C.E.)

Civil warfare had already been stirred up between them [Maxentius and Constantine]. And although Maxentius kept himself at Rome, because he had received a warning that he would perish if he went outside the gates of the city, war was being waged, however, by capable leaders. Maxentius had the greater strength, because he had received his father's army from Severus and he had recently drawn out one of his own from the Moors and the Gaetulians.

The struggle went on, and the Maxentian forces were gaining until after Constantine, with strengthened courage and prepared for both outcomes, moved all his troops closer to the city and settled at the region of the Milvian Bridge. The day was approaching on which Maxentius had taken command, that is, the sixth day before the

November Kalends, and the fifth anniversary celebration was being ended. Constantine was directed in a dream to mark the celestial sign of God on his shields and thus to engage in battle. He did as he was ordered. He inscribed the name of Christ on the shields, using the initial letter X, crossed by the letter I with its top portion bent. Armed with this sign, the army took the sword. It proceeded against the enemy without any commander and crossed the bridge. The lines clashed on equal fronts; the battle raged on both sides with the greatest violence: "Flight was unheard of for the one and the other."

There was a sedition in the city, and the leader was charged with being a deserter of the public safety, and when he was seen—for he was holding a circus in honor of his anniversary—the people with one accord suddenly shouted that Constantine could not be conquered. Upset by this shout, he left, and, calling certain senators, ordered them to consult the Sibylline Books. In them, it was discovered that on that day the enemy of the Romans was to perish. He was led on to hope of victory by this oracle, and set out and came to the line of battle.

The bridge was cut down behind him. When he was seen, the fighting grew more intense, and the hand of God was over the battle line. The Maxentian line was routed, and he himself turned to flee and hastened toward the bridge which had been demolished. Overwhelmed by the rush of those fleeing, he was drowned in the Tiber.

When this most bitter of wars was over and Constantine was received as emperor with the great rejoicing of the Senate and the Roman people, he learned of the perfidy of Maximin; he seized letters and came upon the statues and images. The Senate decreed to Constantine, by reason of his virtue, the title of first name. . . . [i.e., the Senior Augustus].

5.13 Eusebius of Caesarea, *Life of Constantine* 1.27–32 (ca. 338 C.E.)

[27] Being convinced, however, that he [Constantine] needed some more powerful aid than his military forces could afford him, on account of the wicked and magical enchantments which were so diligently practiced by the tyrant, he sought Divine assistance, deeming the possession of arms and a numerous soldiery of secondary importance, but believing the co-operating power of Deity invincible and not to be shaken. He considered, therefore, on what God he might rely for protection and assistance. While engaged in this enquiry, the thought occurred to him that, of the many emperors who had preceded him, those who had rested their hopes in a multitude of gods, and served them with sacrifices and offerings, had in the first place been deceived by flattering predictions, and oracles which promised them all prosperity, and at last had met with an unhappy end, while not

one of their gods had stood by to warn them of the impending wrath of heaven; while one alone who had pursued an entirely opposite course, who had condemned their error, and honored the one Supreme God during his whole life, had found him to be the Savior and Protector of his empire, and the Giver of every good thing. Reflecting on this, and well weighing the fact that they who had trusted in many gods had also fallen by manifold forms of death, without leaving behind them either family or offspring, stock, name, or memorial among men: while the God of his father had given to him, on the other hand, manifestations of his power and very many tokens: and considering farther that those who had already taken arms against the tyrant, and had marched to the battlefield under the protection of a multitude of gods, had met with a dishonorable end (for one of them had shamefully retreated from the contest without a blow, and the other, being slain in the midst of his own troops, became, as it were, the mere sport of death); reviewing, I say, all these considerations, he judged it to be folly indeed to join in the idle worship of those who were no gods, and after such convincing evidence, to err from the truth; and therefore felt it incumbent on him to honor his father's God alone.

[28]Accordingly he called on him with earnest prayer and supplications that he would reveal to him who he was, and stretch forth his right hand to help him in his present difficulties. And while he was thus praying with fervent entreaty, a most marvelous sign appeared to him from heaven, the account of which it might have been hard to believe had it been related by any other person. But since the victorious emperor himself long afterwards declared it to the writer of this history, when he was honored with his acquaintance and society, and confirmed his statement by an oath, who could hesitate to accredit the relation, especially since the testimony of after-time has established its truth? He said that about noon, when the day was already beginning to decline, he saw with his own eyes the trophy of a cross of light in the heavens, above the sun, and bearing the inscription, CONQUER BY THIS. At this sight he himself was struck with amazement, and his whole army also, which followed him on this expedition, and witnessed the miracle.

[29] He said, moreover, that he doubted within himself what the import of this apparition could be. And while he continued to ponder and reason on its meaning, night suddenly came on; then in his sleep the Christ of God appeared to him with the same sign which he had seen in the heavens, and commanded him to make a likeness of that sign which he had seen in the heavens, and to use it as a safeguard in all engagements with his enemies.

[30] At dawn of day he arose, and communicated the marvel to his friends: and then, calling together the workers in gold and precious stones, he sat in the midst of them, and described to them the figure of the sign he had seen, bidding them represent it in gold and precious stones. And this representation I myself have had an opportunity of seeing.

[31] Now it was made in the following manner. A long spear, overlaid with gold, formed the figure of the cross by means of a transverse bar laid over it. On the top of the whole was fixed a wreath of gold and precious stones; and within this, the symbol of the Savior's name, two letters indicating the name of Christ by means of its initial characters, the letter P being intersected by X in its center: and these letters the emperor was in the habit of wearing on his helmet at a later period. From the cross-bar of the spear was suspended a cloth, a royal piece, covered with a profuse embroidery of most brilliant precious stones; and which, being also richly interlaced with gold, presented an indescribable degree of beauty to the beholder. This banner was of a square form, and the upright staff, whose lower section was of great length, bore a golden half-length portrait of the pious emperor and his children on its upper part, beneath the trophy of the cross, and immediately above the embroidered banner. The emperor constantly made use of this sign of salvation as a safeguard against every adverse and hostile power, and commanded that others similar to it should be carried at the head of all his armies.

[32] These things were done shortly afterwards. But at the time above specified, being struck with amazement at the extraordinary vision, and resolving to worship no other God save Him who had appeared to him, he sent for those who were acquainted with the mysteries of His doctrines, and inquired who that God was, and what was intended by the sign of the vision he had seen. They affirmed that He was God, the only begotten Son of the one and only God: that the sign which had appeared was the symbol of immortality, and the trophy of that victory over death which He had gained in time past when sojourning on earth. They taught him also the causes of His advent, and explained to him the true account of His incarnation. Thus he was instructed in these matters, and was impressed with wonder at the divine manifestation which had been presented to his sight. Comparing, therefore, the heavenly vision with the interpretation given, he found his judgment confirmed; and, in the persuasion that the knowledge of these things had been imparted to him by Divine teaching, he determined thenceforth to devote himself to the reading of the Inspired writings. Moreover, he made the priests of God his counselors, and deemed it incumbent on him to honor the God who had appeared to him with all devotion. And after this,

being fortified by well-grounded hopes in Him, he hastened to quench the threatening fire of tyranny.

There are obviously significant differences in these two accounts of Constantine's vision. Lactantius claims that Constantine had his vision in a dream the night before the battle, whereas Eusebius wrote that Constantine saw the vision in the sky during broad daylight, with the entire army as witness.[11] Further, Lactantius makes no reference to the "Conquer by this" inscription cited by Eusebius. Even the description of the symbol itself differs markedly.[12] It is difficult to determine which of the two accounts should be given the greater weight, since both writers apparently received their accounts directly from Constantine himself. Lactantius was the personal tutor of the young Constantine, a relationship that, in Roman society, carried great emotional attachment and personal loyalty, and he had kept in touch with Constantine during these events. Eusebius, a Christian bishop, came to know Constantine in the 320s C.E., and expressly stated that his account had come on oath from Constantine himself.

While there may be no general consensus among modern historians as to which account is more reliable, Lactantius's account should probably be given somewhat greater weight than Eusebius's account.[13] Lactantius's account was written less than eight years after the event, whereas Eusebius's account was written about twenty-eight years after the fact and may merely recount an "official" version created after the fact to meet political exigencies. Furthermore, unless one wishes to argue that Lactantius was simply confused, there is no logical explanation for Lactantius's description of the peculiar monogram used by Constantine other than it is what Constantine described to him. The superimposed chi-rho symbol described by Eusebius, however, was the common abbreviation for "chrestos" (the Greek for "good") and was used by the literate classes to mark favorite passages in the margins of manuscripts. Some historians have suggested that the chi-rho symbol used on labarum described by Eusebius was adopted by Constantine years after the battle as part of his efforts to convert the

---

11. Eusebius's description of Constantine's vision is consistent with a celestial phenomenon known as a "solar halo." It is caused by the fall of ice crystals across the rays of the sun and may appear as either a ring or rings of light around the sun or as a cross of light centered on the sun. Modern photographs of solar halos are reproduced in *Sky and Telescope* 54 (1977–78), 185ff. At the time of publication, photographs of solar halos are also available on the internet at http://www.meteoros.de/ee39ee61/ee46_b.htm.

12. Indeed, the variances between the two accounts are so great that the historian Robert M. Grant has suggested that the two accounts actually refer to two different events. Robert M. Grant, *Augustus to Constantine: The Emergence of Christianity in the Roman World* (New York: Barnes & Noble, 1970), 235.

13. See, e.g., Robin Lane Fox, *Pagans and Christians* (New York: Alfred A. Knopf, 1989), 613–17. Historians leaning toward the Eusebian account include Timothy D. Barnes, *Constantine and Eusebius* (Cambridge: Harvard University Press, 1981), 43 and notes; and A. H. M. Jones, *Constantine and the Conversion of Europe* (Toronto: University of Toronto Press, 1978), 84–85.

Roman Empire to the Christian faith, arguing that the chi-rho was already a familiar symbol among pagans and carried favorable cultural connotations, two advantages not found with Lactantius's device.[14] This theory would seem to bolstered by Eusebius's admission that Constantine did not at the time recognize the heavenly sign as being a Christian symbol and that it was only later during a dream that Constantine had a second vision and learned that the symbol had a Christian meaning. However, even this story of a dream may also be an after-the-fact political creation of Constantine: while Christians received visions from their God, the pagan gods visited their followers in dreams and thus Constantine may have been attempting to present a justification for his conversion couched in a form known and recognized by pagans.

There are two contemporary pagan sources that indicate that shortly after the Battle of the Milvian Bridge people were aware that Constantine was claiming to have entered into a relationship with a new divinity. The first of these sources is a panegyric delivered to Constantine in 313 C.E., and the second is the inscription placed on a triumphal arch erected by order of the Senate in Rome in 315 C.E. to commemorate Constantine's victory at the Milvian Bridge.

5.14 Panegyric to Constantine *Panegyrici Latini* 12.2.1–5, 4.1, 13.1–2, 26.1 (313 C.E.)

[2.1] And first I shall take up a topic which I believe no one up to now has ventured upon, to speak of your resolution in making the expedition before I praise the victory. Since the fear of an adverse omen has been put aside and the stumbling block removed, I shall avail myself of the freedom of our love for you, a love in which we wavered then among fears and prayers for the State. Could you have had so much foresight, Emperor, that you were the first to embark upon a war which had been stirred up with such vast resources, so much greed, so extensive a contagion of crimes, so complete a despair of pardon, when all your associates in imperial power were inactive and hesitating! What god, what majesty so immediate encouraged you, when almost all of your comrades and commanders were not only silently muttering but even openly fearful, to perceive on your own, against the counsels of men, against the warnings of soothsayers, that the time had come to liberate the City? You must share some secret with that divine mind, Constantine, which had delegated care of us to lesser gods and deigns to reveal itself to you alone. . . .

[4.1] Since you contemplated, you knew, you saw all these things, Emperor, and neither your nature nor your inherited sobriety allowed you to be foolhardy, tell us, I beg you, what you had as counsel if not a divine power? . . .

---

14. Robin Lane Fox, *Pagans and Christians* (New York: Alfred A. Knopf, 1986), 616–17; Alan Wardman, *Religion and Statecraft Among the Romans* (London: Granada, 1982), 137.

[13.1] Therefore the functions of all weapons serve your authority to different effect, Emperor. For you swords conquer, for you they preserve; when you fight they strike, when you forgive they protect. As that god, creator and master of the world, sends messages now sad, now glad, with his same thunderbolt, so the same shafts under your divine power distinguish between your enemies or petitioners by destruction or preservation. . . .

[26.1] For this reason, you, supreme creator of things, whose names you wished to be as many as the tongues of the nations (for what you yourself wish to be called we cannot know), whether you are some kind of force and divine mind spread over the whole world and mingled with all the elements and move of your own accord without the influence of any outside force acting upon you, or whether you are some power above all heaven which look down upon this work of yours from a higher pinnacle of Nature: you, I say, we beg and beseech to preserve this prince for all ages.

5.15 The Inscription on the Arch of Constantine (CIL vi.1139)
To the Emperor Caesar Flavius Constantine, Maximus, Pius, Felix, Augustus, the Roman Senate and People dedicated this arch, decorated with his victories, because, by the prompting of the Divinity, by the greatness of his mind, he with his army, at one moment by a just victory avenged the State both on the tyrant and all his party. To the liberator of the city. To the establisher of peace.

Neither the panegyric nor inscription on the Arch of Constantine refers to Constantine's purported vision prior to the Battle of the Milvian Bridge, although the Arch's inscription does make vague reference to "the prompting" of Constantine's "Divinity." There are no Christian symbols on the Arch of Constantine and the Arch's sculpted figures depict Constantine and his soldiers with normal legionary shield devices, being supported in battle by the traditional pagan deities. Likewise, the panegyrist attributed various divine qualities to Constantine in the traditional manner, although he never referred to any pagan god by name. The vague references of both the panegyric and the inscription to Constantine's unnamed patron deity would seem to be best understood as the politic response of the pagan political elite toward the still rather disreputable Christian faith of the new emperor.[15] What is clear, however, is that "Without a doubt, something has happened or has been acknowledged at last. Word has gotten around that the gods' names are no longer welcome, although their existence need not be denied: they are the lesser deities who care for lesser men."[16]

---

15. For an excellent discussion of these issues, see Robin Lane Fox, *Pagans and Christians* (New York: Alfred A. Knopf, 1986), 618–21.

16. C. E. V. Nixon and Barbara Saylor Rodgers, *In Praise of Later Roman Emperors: The Panegyrici Latini* (Berkeley: University of California Press, 1994), 293.

Like the question of Constantine's vision, the nature and depth of Constantine's subsequent commitment to Christianity is a hotly disputed issue among historians. In large part the dispute reflects the difficulty of separating Constantine's personal religious beliefs from his political acts as a Christian emperor in a pagan political environment. We find, for example, that for years after his conversion the coins issued by Constantine displayed the traditional pagan themes, with a particular emphasis on depictions of the pagan god known as the "Invincible Sun," and that Constantine continued to hold the traditional pagan offices of an emperor, such as the chief pagan priest (*pontifex maximus*) of the Roman Empire. Yet, looking at his career as a whole, there is little reason to doubt that after his conversion Constantine always considered himself a devout Christian, if admittedly with only a limited understanding of Christianity's tenets, and that within the political constraints of his time he acted whenever possible to advance the interests of the Christian church. The nature of his support for Christianity became clearer during the years after Constantine's ascension, especially once he won sole rule of the Empire.

CONSTANTINE AND LICINIUS

After Constantine achieved sole power in the Western Empire, he urged the Eastern Augustus Licinius to reaffirm Galerius's revocation of the anti-Christian legislation of the Great Persecution. In response, in 314 C.E., Licinius and Constantine issued a joint proclamation which reaffirmed that Christianity was a lawful religion of the Roman Empire.

5.16 The Edict of Milan issued 314 C.E., qtd. in Lactantius *On the Death of the Persecutors* 48 (ca. 317–318 C.E.)

When I, Constantine Augustus, and I also, Licinius Augustus, had met together under happy circumstances at Milan, and were giving consideration to all matters which pertained to the public good and security, we decided that these things, among others, which we saw would be for the advantage of many men, should be ordained first of all, namely, by which means reverence of the divinity was held. We believed that we should give both to Christians and to all men the freedom to follow religion, whichever one each one chose, so that whatever sort of divinity there is in heavenly regions may be gracious and propitious to us and to all who live under our government. And, therefore, we have determined that this purpose should be undertaken with sound and most upright reason, that we think the opportunity should be denied to no one whatsoever who has given his attention to the observance of the Christians or to that religion which he feels to be most suited to himself, so that the highest deity, whose religion we foster with free minds may be able to show to us in all affairs his customary favor and benevolence. Wherefore, it was fitting that your devotedness know that this was our pleasure, that all those conditions with reference to the Christians, which were contained in our former letters and sent to your office, now being completely removed, everything which seemed severe and opposed to our clemency may be annulled; and now all who have the wish to observe the religion of the Christians may hasten to do so without any worry or molestation. We believed that these things should be most fully made known to your Solicitude, so that you might know that we had given to those same Christians free and untrammeled opportunity to practice their religion. Since you see that this has been granted by us to these same Christians, your devotedness understands also that to others as well the freedom and full liberty has been granted, in accordance with the peace of our times, to exercise free choice in worshiping as each one has seen fit. This has been done by us so that nothing may seem to be taken away from anyone's honor or from any religion whatsoever. And in addition we have decreed that this should be decided concerning the Christians. If those same places, in which they had been formerly accustomed to assemble, and about which in the letters formerly sent to your devotedness a different order had been given; if some are seen to have purchased them before this, either from the treasury or from some other person, they shall restore the same to the Christians without money payment or any seeking of a price, all frustration and ambiguity being put away. Those who have received them as a gift shall likewise restore them to these same Christians as quickly as possible. Also, if those who have bought these places or those who have received them as a gift seek anything of our benevolence, let them apply to the vicar so that provision may be made for them through our clemency. All these things are to be taken care of for the body of the Christians by your direction and without delay. And since those same Christians are known to have possessed not only those places in which they were accustomed to assemble, but also others which belonged not to individual men but to the corporate society, that is, their churches, you will order that all these, according to the law which we have stated above, should be restored to these same Christians, that is, to their society and congregation, without any hesitation or quarrel, the above-mentioned reasonableness being preserved, that those who restore them without price shall, as we said, look for indemnity from our bounty. In all these provisions for the benefit of the aforementioned body of Christians, you will apply your most efficacious concern, so that our command may be very quickly fulfilled, and that in this also provision may be made through our bounty for the public peace. To this extent it will happen, therefore, that the divine favor toward us, as has been stated above, which we have experienced in such great matters, will continue through all time, that our successive acts will prosper with public blessings. And that the formula of our graciousness and of this sanction may reach the attention of all, it will be expected that this be written and proclaimed by you and that you publish it and bring it to the knowledge of all, so that it may not be possible that this provision of our generosity be hidden from anyone.

As a lawfully recognized religion, Christians had formal legal protection for their worship. The recognition of the Christian faith did not, however, resolve all the problems created by Roman persecution. The most common response of the average Christian when actually confronted by the civil authorities during the Great Persecution had been, as in the earlier persecutions, apostasy. This response was true for Christians at all levels of the church, including the clergy. Very few Christians chose martyrdom for their faith. Henri Gregoire estimates that during the Great Persecution a maximum of 2,000–3,000 Christians died as martyrs,[17] while W. H. C. Frend estimates the number at 3,000 to 3,500.[18] Such low totals were also typical of the earlier persecutions: Ramsay MacMullen estimates that "roughly one one-hundredth of one per cent" of Christians died as martyrs during the period ca. 250–311 C.E.[19] After the persecution ended, however, the great majority of these apostates repented and sought readmission. The church was thus faced with the problem of setting the conditions under which the apostates would be readmitted. This issue led to a significant split in many churches, particularly in North Africa where a sect known as the Donatists insisted that lapsed clergy could no longer perform valid church ceremonies such as the Eucharist or the installation of bishops. Although the Donatist movement survived into the fifth century C.E., the church as a whole adopted a liberal policy of readmission for both lay and clergy. The conditions of such forgiveness were reflected in the canons adopted by various regional church councils, such as that of Ancyra in the province of Galatia in Asia Minor.

5.17 Canons of the Council of Ancyra (314 C.E.)

Canon 1: With regard to those presbyters who have offered sacrifices and afterwards returned to the conflict, not with hypocrisy, but in sincerity, it has seemed good that they may retain the honor of their chair; provided they had not used management, arrangement, or persuasion, so as to appear to be subjected to the torture, when it was applied only in seeming and pretense. Nevertheless it is not lawful for them to make the oblation, nor to preach, nor in short to perform any act of sacerdotal function.

---

17. Henri Gregoire, *Les Persecutions dans l'empire romain* (1964), 166, 181 f., as cited by Ramsay MacMullen in *Changes in the Roman Empire* (Princeton: Princeton University Press, 1990), 156.

18. W. H. C. Frend, *Martyrdom and Persecution in the Early Church* (Oxford: Blackwell, 1965), 537.

19. Ramsay MacMullen *Changes In the Roman Empire* (Princeton: Princeton University Press, 1990), 156.

Canon 2: It is likewise decreed that deacons who have sacrificed and afterwards resumed the conflict, shall enjoy their other honors, but shall abstain from every sacred ministry, neither bringing forth the bread and the cup, nor making proclamations. Nevertheless, if any of the bishops shall observe in them distress of mind and meek humiliation, it shall be lawful to the bishops to grant more indulgence, or to take away [what has been granted].

Canon 3: Those who have fled and been apprehended, or have been betrayed by their servants; or those who have been otherwise despoiled of their goods, or have endured tortures, or have been imprisoned and abused, declaring themselves to be Christians; or who have been forced to receive something which their persecutors violently thrust into their hands, or meat [offered to idols], continually professing that they were Christians; and who, by their whole apparel, and demeanor, and humility of life, always give evidence of grief at what has happened; these persons, inasmuch as they are free from sin, are not to be repelled from the communion; and if, through an extreme strictness or ignorance of some things, they have been repelled, let them forthwith be re-admitted. This shall hold good alike of clergy and laity. It has also been considered whether laymen who have fallen under the same compulsion may be admitted to orders, and we have decreed that, since they have in no respect been guilty, they may be ordained; provided their past course of life be found to have been upright.

Canon 4: Concerning those who have been forced to sacrifice, and who, in addition, have partaken of feasts in honor of the idols; as many as were hauled away, but afterwards went up with a cheerful countenance, and wore their costliest apparel, and partook with indifference of the feast provided; it is decreed that all such be hearers for one year, and prostrators for three years, and that they communicate in prayers only for two years, and then return to full communion.

Canon 5: As many, however, as went up in mourning attire and sat down and ate, weeping throughout the whole entertainment, if they have fulfilled the three years as prostrators, let them be received without oblation; and if they did not eat, let them be prostrators two years, and in the third year let them communicate without oblation, so that in the fourth year they may be received into full communion. But the bishops have the right, after considering the character of their conversion, either to deal with them more leniently, or to extend the time. But, first of all, let their life before and since be thoroughly examined, and let the indulgence be determined accordingly.

Canon 6: Concerning those who have yielded merely upon threat of penalties and of the confiscation of their goods, or of banishment, and have sacrificed, and who till this present time have not repented nor been converted, but who now, at the time of this synod, have approached with a purpose of conversion, it is decreed that they be received as hearers till the Great Day, and that after the Great Day they be prostrators for three years, and for two years more communicate without oblation, and then come to full communion, so as to complete the period of six full years. And if any have been admitted to penance before this synod, let the beginning of the six years be reckoned to them from that time. Nevertheless, if there should be any danger or prospect of death whether from disease or any other cause, let them be received, but under limitation.

The process of working out the conditions of readmission continued for more than a decade after the end of the Great Persecution. Even the Council of Nicaea in 325 C.E., which is best known among modern Christians for the formulation of the Nicene Creed, had to deal with the issue of lapsed Christians.

LICINIUS AND CONSTANTINE

Licinius was a pagan and so it was perhaps inevitable that Constantine's public association with the Christian faith meant that the respective religions of the two co-Augusti would become a focal point in any political contest between the two for sole rule of the Roman Empire. When Licinius came to realize that Constantine wanted sole rule, and not merely a partition of the Empire between the two men, he attempted to foment revolt against Constantine and gradually initiated more restrictive measures against the Christians in his provinces, probably out of concern that the Christians would support Constantine in any civil war. In the meantime, Constantine granted ever greater privileges to the Christians in his portion of the Empire. In 317 C.E., Licinius began a more active persecution of the Christians in his territories.

> 5.18 Eusebius of Caesarea, *Ecclesiastical History* 10.8.10, 14–15, 17 (ca. 317–323 C.E.)
>
> [10] First, he [Licinius] drove away every Christian from his palace; thus by his own act depriving himself, wretched man, of the prayers to God on his behalf, which after the custom of their fathers they are taught to make for all men. Then he gave orders that the soldiers in cities were to be singled out and deprived of honorable rank, unless they chose to sacrifice to the demons. . . .
>
> [14] . . . . in the final stage of his madness he proceeded against the bishops. . . . and the most highly respected of these, by the contrivance of the governors, he put to death. And the manner in which they were murdered was strange and hitherto unheard of.
>
> [15] For instance, the things that were done at Amasea and the other cities of Pontus outdid every excess of cruelty. There some of the churches of God were again thrown down from the top to the bottom; others

they shut up, so that none of the accustomed worshippers might assemble or pay to God the service due him. . . .

[17] And in truth the sycophants among the governors, persuaded that they were doing what pleased the impious man, plied some of the bishops with penalties suitable for malefactors, and those who had done no wrong were led away and punished, wihtout a pretext, like murderers.

In 323 C.E., Constantine and his army pursued barbarians raiders into Licinius's provinces without permission and this incident was the excuse for the final break between the two men. The following year Constantine defeated Licinius in a series of battles and, after Licinius surrendered, executed Licinius, thereby becoming the sole emperor of the Roman Empire.

CONSTANTINE'S SUPPORT OF THE CHRISTIAN CHURCH

At the time Constantine adopted Christianity, Christians were still a small minority within the Roman Empire, numbering only between 2 1/2 million and 5 million people out of the some 50 to 60 million inhabitants of the Roman Empire.[20] However, the numbers and power of the church grew rapidly under Constantine and his sons, who used the apparatus and resources of the central government to advance Christianity and to strike at paganism. Massive government subsidies were given to Christian churches, while state funds for pagan worship were cut off, pagan temple assets were seized, and pagan worship was restricted by law. While pagans continued to participate in government, Christian belief gradually became a significant factor for advancement and position in the higher levels of civil administration.[21] Finally, Constantine and his Christian successors directed state-sanctioned violence against the opponents of the orthodox Christian churches. During Constantine's reign the prophets of the major sanctuaries of Apollo and other pagan gods were tortured to obtain "confessions" that the oracles had engaged in fraudulent prophecy.[22] Violence was also used against "heretical Christians," for after the Council of Nicaea defined "orthodoxy" Constantine excluded Christian "heretics" from the legal rights and protections accorded "orthodox" Christians. As Christianity became more firmly established under Constantine's sons and the later Christian emperors, the violence became more endemic as bishops directed bands of monks, soldiers, and urban Christian mobs against pagans, Jews, heretics, and even individual rivals within the church, while the emperors issued ever more severe decrees against heretics and pagans.

---

20. Robin Lane Fox, *Pagans and Christians* (New York: Alfred A. Knopf, 1989), 592; Ramsay MacMullen, *Christianizing the Roman Empire* (New Haven: Yale University Press, 1984), 85–86.

21. See, e.g., the discussion in A. H. M. Jones, *Constantine and the Conversion of Europe* (Toronto: University of Toronto Press, 1978), 179–80. This is not to imply that pagans did not continue to hold high positions within the government, particularly in law and the military, but as time went on religion became a significant factor for personal advancement.

22. Fox, *Pagans and Christians*, 671–72.

Among the earliest measures that Constantine undertook in favor of the Christian church was to make the Roman Empire's revenues available for use by the bishops in support of the faith.

5.19 A Rescript of Constantine I (written the winter of 312–313 C.E.) quoted in Eusebius, *Ecclesiastical History* 10.6.1–5

Constantine Augustus to Caecilian, bishop of Carthage. For as much as it has been our pleasure in all provinces, namely the African, the Numidian and the Mauretanian, that somewhat be contributed for expenses to certain specified members of the lawful and most holy Catholic religion, I have dispatched a letter to Ursus, the most distinguished finance minister of Africa, and have notified him that he be careful to pay over to thy Firmness three thousand folles. Do you therefore, when you shall secure delivery of the aforesaid sum of money, give orders that this money be distributed among all of the above mentioned persons in accordance with the schedule sent you by Hosius. But if, after all, you shall find that there is anything lacking for the fulfillment of this my purpose in respect of them all, you should ask without doubting whatsoever you find to be necessary from Heraclides, our procurator fiscal. For indeed when he was here I gave him orders that if thy Firmness should ask any money from him, he should be careful to pay it over without scruple. And since I have learnt that certain persons of unstable mind are desirous of turning aside the laity of the most holy and Catholic Church by some vile method of seduction, know that I have given such commands to Anulinus, the proconsul, and moreover to Patricius, the Vicar of the Prefects, when they were here, that they should give due attention in all other matters and especially in this, and not suffer such occurrence to be overlooked; therefore if you observe any such men continuing in this madness, do not thou hesitate to go to the above-mentioned judges and bring this matter before them so that (as I commanded when they were here) they may turn these people from their error. May the divinity of the great God preserve you for many years.

Another of Constantine's measures exempted Christian clerics from the onerous compulsory public services imposed by law on the decurions.

5.20 Theodosian Code 16.2.2 (Oct. 21, 319 C.E.)

The same Augustus [Constantine] to Octavianus, Governor of Lucania and Bruttium. Those who devote the services of religion to divine worship, that is, those who are called clerics, shall be exempt from all compulsory public services whatever, lest through the sacrilegious malice of certain persons, they should be called away from divine services.

As one might anticipate, access to state revenues and exemption from the economic burdens of municipal office were a powerful incentive for pagans of means and position to convert to Christianity, at least in name, and for all Christians, newly converted or not, to seek clerical office. It is therefore not surprising that in response to Constantine's grants the politically powerful used their wealth and influence to claim the positions of the Christian clerics.

> 5.21 Theodosian Code 16.2.3 (July 18, 329? C.E.)
> The same Augustus [Constantine] to Bassus, Praetorian Prefect. A constitution was issued* which directs that thenceforth no decurion or descendant of a decurion or even any person provided with adequate resources and suitable to undertake compulsory services shall take refuge in the name and the service of the clergy, but that in the place of deceased clerics thereafter only those persons shall be chosen as substitutes who have slender fortunes and who are not bound to such compulsory municipal services. But we have learned that those persons also are being disturbed who became associated with the clergy before the promulgation of the aforesaid law. We command, therefore, that the latter shall be freed from all annoyance, and that the former, who in evasion of public duties have taken refuge in the number of the clergy after the issuance of the law, shall be completely separated from that body, shall be restored to their orders and to the municipal councils, and shall perform their municipal duties.
> *This constitution is not extant.*

The extent to which Constantine attempted to assert Christian dominance in all spheres of life is reflected in his effort to reform the calendar by replacing the traditional Roman system with the seven-day week of the Jewish and Christian tradition, although with his customary political caution Constantine framed the edict in terms of honoring the pagan god Sol Invictus.

> 5.22 Justinian's Code 3.12.3 (March 7, 321 C.E.)
> Constantine to Elpidius. All judges, city-people and craftsmen shall rest on the venerable day of the Sun. But countrymen may without hindrance attend to agriculture, since it often happens that this is the most suitable day for sowing grain or planting vines, so that the opportunity afforded by divine providence may not be lost, for the right season is of short duration.

With this edict Constantine began the process by which the Mediterranean world would eventually adopt the Judeo-Christian week of seven days. Christians were less successful in substituting numbers for the names of the pagan gods given to the days of the week, and today the names of the week days in almost all European languages are derived from various pagan deities.

Constantine also supported the orthodox Christian faith by directing the coercive power of the Roman state against pagans. Constantine's use of force proved effective and later Christian historians of the fifth century recorded with satisfaction how the pagan majority had been cowed by the threat of violence.

5.23 Sozomen (active in the early fifth century), *Ecclesiastical History* 2.5 (ca. 440 C.E.) The events date to 331 C.E.

> As many nations and cities throughout the whole realm of his sub-jects retained a feeling of fear and veneration toward their vain idols, which led them to disregard the doctrines of the Christians, and to have a care for their ancient customs, and the manners and feasts of their fathers, it appeared necessary to the Emperor [Constantine] to teach the governors to suppress their superstitious rites of worship. He thought that this would be easily accomplished if he could get them to despise their temples and the images contained therein. To carry this project into execution he did not require military aid; for Christian men belonging to the palace went from city to city bearing imperial letters. The people were induced to remain passive from the fear that, if they resisted these edicts, they, their children, and their wives, would be exposed to evil. The vergers and the priests, being unsupported by the multitude, brought out their most precious treasures, and the idols called "Heaven Sent", and through these servitors, the gifts were drawn forth from the shrines and the hidden recesses in the temples. The spots previously inaccessible, and known only to the priests, were made accessible to all who desired to enter. Such of the images as were constructed of precious material, and whatever else was valuable, were purified by fire, and became public property. The brazen images which were skillfully wrought were car-ried to the city, named after the Emperor, and placed there as objects of embellishment, where they may still be seen in public places, as in the streets, the hippodrome, and the palaces. . . .
>
> The efforts of the Emperor succeeded to the utmost of his antic-ipations; for on beholding the objects of their former reverence and fear boldly cast down and stuffed with straw and hay, the people were led to despise what they had previously venerated, and to blame the erroneous opinion of their ancestors. Others, envious at the honor in which Christians were held by the emperor, deemed it necessary to imitate the acts of the ruler; others devoted themselves to an exami-nation of Christianity, and by means of signs, of dreams, or of con-ferences with bishops and monks, were convinced that it was better to become Christians. From this period, nations and citizens sponta-neously renounced their former opinion. . . .

Ramsay MacMullen has commented, "The fear inspired in his subjects, needing no armed force in supplement, is easily understood. The empire had never had on the throne a man given to such bloodthirsty violence as

Constantine."[23] Constantine's seizure of the pagan temple treasuries proved so lucrative that he was able to use the wealth to reinstitute a regular gold coinage within the Roman Empire, something that had not been possible during much of the third century C.E.

CONSTANTINE AND THE COUNCIL OF NICAEA

Constantine appears to have believed that Christianity could be made to serve as a source of unity and strength for Rome's empire by establishing a strong common bond among its many peoples. Such a purpose would explain why after his conversion Constantine was so troubled by the ferocious doctrinal disputes of the early fourth-century C.E. Christian church. The most significant of these doctrinal disputes was the conflict between orthodox Christians and Arian Christians concerning the relationship between Christ and God. Arians believed that Christ was inferior to God, while the orthodox proclaimed that God and Christ were co-equals. Constantine urged Christians to unite behind a single doctrine of faith.

> 5.24 Constantine's Letter to Arius (written 324 C.E.) qtd. in Eusebius *Life of Constantine* 2.64–65, 68.
>
> [64] Victor Constantinus, Maximus Augustus, to Alexander and Arius: I call that God to witness, as well I may, who is the helper of my endeavors, and the Preserver of all men, that I had a twofold reason for undertaking that duty which I have now performed.
>
> [65] My design then was, first, to bring the diverse judgments formed by all nations respecting the Deity to a condition, as it were, of settled uniformity; and, secondly, to restore to health the system of the world, then suffering under the malignant power of a grievous distemper. Keeping these objects in view, I sought to accomplish the one by the secret eye of thought, while the other I tried to rectify by the power of military authority. For I was aware that, if I should succeed in establishing, according to my hopes, a common harmony of sentiment among all the servants of God, the general course of affairs would also experience a change correspondent to the pious desires of them all.
>
> [68] . . . .having made a careful enquiry into the origin and foundation of these differences, I find the cause to be of a truly insignificant character, and quite unworthy of such fierce contention. Feeling myself, therefore, compelled to address you in this letter, and to appeal at the same time to your unanimity and sagacity, I call on Divine Providence to assist me in the task, while I interrupt your dissension in the character of a minister of peace. And with reason: for

---

23. Ramsay MacMullen, *Christianizing the Roman Empire* (New Haven: Yale University Press, 1984), 50.

if I might expect, with the help of a higher Power, to be able without difficulty, by a judicious appeal to the pious feelings of those who heard me, to recall them to a better spirit, even though the occasion of the disagreement were a greater one, how can I refrain from promising myself a far easier and more speedy adjustment of this difference, when the cause which hinders general harmony of sentiment is intrinsically trifling and of little moment?

The letter demonstrates Constantine's utter ignorance concerning the significance of the dispute between the Arian and orthodox positions, as he wrote that he considered the point of dispute "truly insignificant" and "intrinsically trifling and of little moment." Arius and his supporters were not willing to abandon their position, even for the emperor. Alarmed by such defiance and disunity within the church, Constantine called for a great council of Christian bishops to meet at Nicaea in 325 C.E. for the purpose of resolving the dispute. Of the approximately three hundred bishops who attended Constantine's conference, the overwhelming majority were from the Greek-speaking provinces of the Empire, as the Latin-speaking bishops of the western provinces generally took little interest in philosophical debates of this nature.

The opening ceremonies of the Council of Nicaea demonstrated the depth of the animosity among the competing factions, as the council had barely begun before the bishops began presenting petitions to Constantine for support in suppressing their rivals.

5.25 Socrates, *Ecclesiastical History* 1.8 (ca. 440 C.E.)
On the following day all the bishops were assembled together in one place; the emperor [Constantine] arrived soon after, and on his entrance stood in their midst, and would not take his place until the bishops by bowing intimated their desire that he should be seated— such was the respect and reverence which the emperor entertained for these men. When a silence suitable to the occasion had been observed, the emperor from his seat began to address them words of exhortation to harmony and unity, and entreated each to lay aside all private pique. For several of them had brought accusations against one another, and many had even presented petitions to the emperor the day before. But he, directing their attention to the matter before them, and on account of which they were assembled, ordered these petitions to be burnt, merely observing that "Christ enjoins him who is anxious to obtain forgiveness, to forgive his brother." When therefore he had strongly insisted on the maintenance of harmony and peace, he sanctioned again their purpose of more closely investigating the questions at issue.

Eusebius of Caesarea was one of the bishops who attended the Council of Nicaea and the following passage sets forth his eyewitness account of the proceedings.

5.26 Eusebius, *Life of Constantine* 1.6, 8, 10–14 (ca. 338 C.E.)

⁶ Then as if to bring a divine array against this enemy, he [Constantine] convoked a general council, and invited the speedy attendance of bishops from all quarters, in letters expressive of the honorable estimation in which he held them. Nor was this merely the issuing of a bare command but the emperor's good will contributed much to its being carried into effect: for he allowed some the use of the public means of conveyance, while he afforded to others an ample supply of horses for their transport. The place, too, selected for the synod, the city Nicaea in Bithynia (named from "Victory"), was appropriate to the occasion. As soon then as the imperial injunction was generally made known, all with the utmost willingness hastened thither, as though they would outstrip one another in a race; for they were impelled by the anticipation of a happy result to the conference, by the hope of enjoying present peace, and the desire of beholding something new and strange in the person of so admirable an emperor. . . . ⁸ But that assembly was less, in that not all who composed it were ministers of God; but in the present company, the number of bishops exceeded two hundred and fifty, while that of the presbyters and deacons in their train, and the crowd of acolytes and other attendants was altogether beyond computation. . . . ¹⁰ Now when the appointed day arrived on which the council met for the final solution of the questions in dispute, each member was present for this in the central building of the palace, which appeared to exceed the rest in magnitude. On each side of the interior of this were many seats disposed in order, which were occupied by those who had been invited to attend, according to their rank. As soon, then, as the whole assembly had seated themselves with becoming orderliness, a general silence prevailed, in expectation of the emperor's arrival. And first of all, three of his immediate family entered in succession, then others also preceded his approach, not of the soldiers or guards who usually accompanied him, but only friends in the faith. And now, all rising at the signal which indicated the emperor's entrance, at last he himself proceeded through the midst of the assembly, like some heavenly messenger of God, clothed in raiment which glittered as it were with rays of light, reflecting the glowing radiance of a purple robe, and adorned with the brilliant splendor of gold and precious stones. Such was the external appearance of his person; and with regard to his mind, it was evident that he was distinguished by piety and godly fear. This was indicated by his downcast eyes, the blush on his countenance, and his gait. For the rest of his personal excellencies, he surpassed all present in height of stature and beauty of form, as well as in majestic dignity of mien, and invincible strength and vigor. All these graces, united to a suavity of manner, and a serenity becoming

his imperial station, declared the excellence of his mental qualities to be above all praise. As soon as he had advanced to the upper end of the seats, at first he remained standing, and when a low chair of wrought gold had been set for him, he waited until the bishops had beckoned to him, and then sat down, and after him the whole assembly did the same.

[11] The bishop who occupied the chief place in the right division of the assembly then rose, and, addressing the emperor, delivered a concise speech, in a strain of thanksgiving to Almighty God on his behalf. When he had resumed his seat, silence ensued, and all regarded the emperor with fixed attention; on which he looked serenely round on the assembly with a cheerful aspect, and, having collected his thoughts, in a calm and gentle tone gave utterance to the following words.

[12] "It was once my chief desire, dearest friends, to enjoy the spectacle of your united presence; and now that this desire is fulfilled, I feel myself bound to render thanks to God the universal King, because, in addition to all his other benefits, he has granted me a blessing higher than all the rest, in permitting me to see you not only all assembled together, but all united in a common harmony of sentiment. I pray therefore that no malignant adversary may henceforth interfere to mar our happy state; I pray that, now the impious hostility of the tyrants has been forever removed by the power of God our Savior, that spirit who delights in evil may devise no other means for exposing the divine law to blasphemous calumny; for, in my judgment, intestine strife within the Church of God, is far more evil and dangerous than any kind of war or conflict; and these our differences appear to me more grievous than any outward trouble. Accordingly, when, by the will and with the co-operation of God, I had been victorious over my enemies, I thought that nothing more remained but to render thanks to him, and sympathize in the joy of those whom he had restored to freedom through my instrumentality; as soon as I heard that intelligence which I had least expected to receive, I mean the news of your dissension, I judged it to be of no secondary importance, but with the earnest desire that a remedy for this evil also might be found through my means, I immediately sent to require your presence. And now I rejoice in beholding your assembly; but I feel that my desires will be most completely fulfilled when I can see you all united in one judgment, and that common spirit of peace and concord prevailing amongst you all, which it becomes you, as consecrated to the service of God, to commend to others. Delay not, then, dear friends: delay not, ye ministers of God, and faithful servants of him who is our common Lord and Savior: begin from this moment to discard the causes of that disunion which has existed among you, and remove the perplexities of controversy by embracing the principles of peace. For

by such conduct you will at the same time be acting in a manner most pleasing to the supreme God, and you will confer an exceeding favor on me who am your fellow-servant."

[13] As soon as the emperor had spoken these words in the Latin tongue, which another interpreted, he gave permission to those who presided in the council to deliver their opinions. On this some began to accuse their neighbors, who defended themselves, and recriminated in their turn. In this manner numberless assertions were put forth by each party, and a violent controversy arose at the very commencement. Notwithstanding this, the emperor gave patient audience to all alike, and received every proposition with steadfast attention, and by occasionally assisting the argument of each party in turn, he gradually disposed even the most vehement disputants to a reconciliation. At the same time, by the affability of his address to all, and his use of the Greek language, with which he was not altogether unacquainted, he appeared in a truly attractive and amiable light, persuading some, convincing others by his reasonings, praising those who spoke well, and urging all to unity of sentiment, until at last he succeeded in bringing them to one mind and judgment respecting every disputed question.

[14] The result was that they were not only united as concerning the faith, but that the time for the celebration of the salutary feast of Easter was agreed on by all. Those points also which were sanctioned by the resolution of the whole body were committed to writing, and received the signature of each several member. Then the emperor, believing that he had thus obtained a second victory over the adversary of the Church, proceeded to solemnize a triumphal festival in honor of God.

By force of his personality and power as the first Christian emperor, Constantine pressured the bishops into an agreement over the resolution of the Arian controversy. The form of the agreement was memorialized by the words of the Nicene Creed, which was a modified form of the creed used by Eusebius's own church in Caesarea. Those bishops who refused to sign the Nicene Creed were sentenced to criminal exile by Constantine, a fact that helps explain the near unanimity of the bishops in favor of the creed. A number of bishops, like Eusebius himself, signed the Nicene Creed rather than face exile and then afterwards attempted to disavow their ratification of the creed.

5.27 The Creed of the Council of Nicaea (325 C.E.)
We believe in one God the Father All-sovereign, maker of all things visible and invisible; and in one Lord Jesus Christ, the Son of God, begotten of the Father, only-begotten, that is, of the substance [literally, from the inmost being] of the Father, God of God, Light of Light, true God of true God, begotten not made, of one substance with the Father, through whom all things were made, things in heaven and

things on earth; who for us men and for our salvation came down and was made flesh, and became man, suffered, and rose on the third day, ascended into the Heavens, is coming to judge living and dead. And in the Holy Spirit. And those that say, "There was when he was not," and, "Before he was begotten he was not," and that, "He came into being from what is not," or those that allege that the Son of God is "of another substance or essence" or "created" or "changeable" or "alterable," these the Catholic and Apostolic church anathematizes.

The adoption of the Nicene Creed, while of great significance for the future direction of the church, did not immediately resolve the doctrinal conflict over the nature of Christ. Very few of the bishops at the Council of Nicaea were from the Western provinces of the Roman Empire and because the Nicene Creed was written in Greek, which was no longer widely spoken in the Western provinces, it remained generally unknown among the Western churches for another generation or more. The issues addressed by the Nicene Creed were revisited by the Council of Constantinople in 381 C.E., which ratified a modified form of the Nicene Creed, and by the Council of Chalcedon in 450 C.E., which ratified the modified form of the Nicene Creed adopted by the Council of Constantinople. The "Nicene Creed" used by modern Christians is the modified version of the Creed of Nicaea adopted by the Council of Constantinople and ratified by the Council of Chalcedon.[24]

There was one immediate result of the adoption of the creed by the Council of Nicaea. By adopting a statement of "orthodox Christian belief," the bishops who prevailed at Nicaea drew a line in the sand with respect to all other forms of Christian belief. Christians who refused to adopt the orthodoxy defined at Nicaea would eventually be required to pay for their "heretical" beliefs in blood: more Christians died at the hands of Christians during the seventy-five years following the Council of Nicaea than had died as martyrs under the almost three hundred years of Roman persecution.[25]

In addition to the adoption of the Nicene Creed, the Council of Nicaea also addressed a number of other issues that divided the churches. These issues included the more or less perennial question of how to deal with apostates (in this case, those who lapsed during the persecutions of Licinius), the proper manner of dealing with the new converts who were claiming the positions of the bishops, the punishment for bishops who used their position to lend church funds at interest, and whether people were to stand or kneel when praying to God.

5.28 Canons of the Council of Nicaea (325 C.E.)

Canon 2. Forasmuch as, either from necessity, or through the urgency of individuals, many things have been done contrary to the Ecclesiastical

---

24. The evolution of the language of the Nicene Creed is set forth in Appendix D.

25. Ramsay MacMullen, *Christianity & Paganism in the Fourth to Eighth Centuries* (New Haven: Yale University Press, 1997), 14, and footnote 44. See also, Ramsay MacMullen, *Changes in the Roman Empire* (Princeton: Princeton University Press, 1990), 156, 267.

canon, so that men just converted from heathenism to the faith, and who have been instructed but a little while, are straightway brought to the spiritual layer, and as soon as they have been baptized, are advanced to the episcopate or the presbyterate, it has seemed right to us that for the time to come no such thing shall be done. For to the catechumen himself there is need of time and of a longer trial after baptism. For the apostolical saying is clear, "Not a novice; lest, being lifted up with pride, he fall into condemnation and the snare of the devil." But if, as time goes on, any sensual sin should be found out about the person, and he should be convicted by two or three witnesses, let him cease from the clerical office. And who so shall transgress these [enactments] will imperil his own clerical position, as a person who presumes to disobey the great Synod.

Canon 11: Concerning those who have fallen without compulsion, without the spoiling of their property, without danger or the like, as happened during the tyranny of Licinius, the Synod declares that, though they have deserved no clemency, they shall be dealt with mercifully. As many as were communicants, if they heartily repent, shall pass three years among the hearers; for seven years they shall be prostrators; and for two years they shall communicate with the people in prayers, but without oblation.[26]

Canon 12: As many as were called by grace, and displayed the first zeal, having cast aside their military girdles, but afterwards returned, like dogs, to their own vomit, (so that some spent money and by means of gifts regained their military stations); let these, after they have passed the space of three years as hearers, be for ten years prostrators. But in all these cases it is necessary to examine well into their purpose and what their repentance appears to be like. For as many as give evidence of their conversions by deeds, and not pretense, with fear, and tears, and perseverance, and good works, when they have fulfilled their appointed time as hearers, may properly communicate in prayers; and after that the bishop may determine yet more favorably concerning them. But those who take [the matter] with indifference, and who think the form of [not] entering the Church is sufficient for their conversion, must fulfill the whole time.

Canon 14: Concerning catechumens who have lapsed, the holy and great Synod has decreed that, after they have passed three years only as hearers, they shall pray with the catechumens.

Canon 17. Forasmuch as many enrolled among the Clergy, following covetousness and lust of gain, have forgotten the divine Scripture,

---

26. "Hearers" were those who stood just outside the door of the church; the "prostrators" stood within the body of the church behind the reading desk and went out with the catechumen; "without oblation" means the party may participate in the service, but may not offer or communicate with the faithful.

which says, "He hath not given his money upon usury," and in lending money ask the hundredth of the sum [as monthly interest], the
holy and great Synod thinks it just that if after this decree any one
be found to receive usury, whether he accomplish it by secret trans-
action or otherwise, as by demanding the whole and one half, or by
using any other contrivance whatever for filthy lucre's sake, he shall
be deposed from the clergy and his name stricken from the list.
Canon 20. Forasmuch as there are certain persons who kneel on the
Lord's Day and in the days of Pentecost, therefore, to the intent that
all things may be uniformly observed everywhere (in every parish), it
seems good to the holy Synod that prayer be made to God standing.

CONSTANTINE AND THE AFTERMATH OF THE COUNCIL OF NICAEA

Shortly after the Council of Nicaea completed its work, Constantine invited the
bishops to a banquet at an imperial palace to celebrate the newly established
unity of the church.

5.29 Eusebius of Caesarea, *Life of Constantine* 3.15 (ca. 338 C.E.)
About this time he completed the twentieth year of his reign. On this
occasion public festivals were celebrated by the people of the
provinces generally, but the emperor himself invited and feasted with
those ministers of God whom he had reconciled, and thus offered as
it were through them a suitable sacrifice to God. Not one of the bishops was wanting at the imperial banquet, the circumstances of which
were splendid beyond description. Detachments of the body-guard
and other troops surrounded the entrance of the palace with drawn
swords, and through the midst of these the men of God proceeded
without fear into the innermost of the imperial apartments, in which
some were the emperor's own companions at table, while others
reclined on couches arranged on either side. One might have thought
that a picture of Christ's kingdom was thus shadowed forth, and a
dream rather than reality.

Eusebius's implicit comparison of Constantine and the bishops to Christ
and the apostles at the Last Supper speaks to one of the perennial issues that has
confronted the Christian faith down through the centuries since Constantine:
was the Christian emperor or the Christian church to be supreme on earth?
Constantine practiced what is now known as the doctrine of Caesaropapism:
"the secular sovereign is by the grace of God supreme governor of the Church
within his dominions and is as such divinely authorized to dictate the religious
belief of his subjects."[27] In Constantine's case, this "grace of God" and heavenly

27. A. H. M. Jones, *Constantine and the Conversion of Europe* (Toronto: University of Toronto
Press, 1978), 205.

patronage was said to be conclusively demonstrated in his victories on the field of battle, and the same argument would be made by generations of subsequent emperors and kings. While Constantine certainly held the upper hand over the bishops during his lifetime, this issue would arise repeatedly during the fourth and fifth centuries C.E., as exemplified by the conflict between the bishop Ambrose and the emperor Theodosius, and would survive the collapse of the Roman Empire, as demonstrated by the conflicts between church and state in Western Europe during the Middle Ages and Renaissance and between the emperors and the church in the Byzantine Empire.

Constantine clearly believed that he had the right to direct the beliefs of his subjects and following his success at the Council of Nicaea, he quickly turned his attention to uprooting Christian heterodoxy, using the power of his government against both flesh and ideas.

> 5.30 Theodosian Code 16.5.1 (Sept. 1, 326 C.E.)
> Emperor Constantine Augustus to Dracilianus. The privileges that have been granted in consideration of religion must benefit only the adherents of the Catholic faith. It is our will, moreover, that heretics and schismatics shall not only be alien from these privileges, but shall also be bound and subjected to various compulsory public services.

> 5.31 Rescript of Constantine I (issued late 332 or early 333 C.E.) qtd. in Socrates *Ecclesiastical History* 1.9
> Victor Constantine Maximus Augustus, to the bishops and people. Since Arius has imitated wicked and impious persons, it is just that he should undergo the like ignominy. Wherefore as Porphyry, that enemy of piety, for having composed licentious treatises against religion, found a suitable recompense, and such as thenceforth branded him with infamy, overwhelming him with deserved reproach, his impious writings also having been destroyed; so now it seems fit both that Arius and such as hold his sentiments should be denominated Porphyrians, that they may take their appellation from those whose conduct they have imitated. And in addition to this, if any treatise composed by Arius should be discovered, let it be consigned to the flames, in order that not only his depraved doctrine may be suppressed, but also that no memorial of him may be by any means left. This therefore I decree, that if any one shall be detected in concealing a book compiled by Arius, and shall not instantly bring it forward and burn it, the penalty for this offense shall be death; for immediately after conviction the criminal shall suffer capital punishment. May God preserve you!

Constantine's example of striking at pagan and heretical belief by banning and burning their writings would be repeated by later Christian emperors, and the emperor Justinian (527–565 C.E.) would enact laws that provided for cutting off the hands of scribes who copied banned works.[28]

Constantine, notwithstanding the evident favor and patronage of the Christian God, was but mortal and eventually death came for him also, in 337 C.E. Like many Christians of the day, Constantine believed in but a single baptism for the forgiveness of sins and so he waited until his death bed to be baptized. His caution on such a point was most understandable in light of the terrible bloodshed that occurred during his rule. In one of the great ironies of history, Constantine asked Eusebius of Nicomedia, Arius's chief defender at Nicaea, to perform the ceremony, and so Constantine was baptized a Christian by a bishop who favored the faith condemned by Constantine's own Council of Nicaea. As a further great irony, Constantine—like any pagan Roman emperor—had anticipated that he would be deserving of deification upon his death and accordingly had erected a great statute of himself as the Sun-God on a tall column in the center of his new Christian capitol of Constantinople. For the rest of the fourth century C.E., this statute was a center of the religious cult worship of Constantine and Constantine would be consistently referred to as "deified" in edicts by his sons and later Christian emperors.[29] One can only imagine the thoughts of the Christian bishops as they walked past his column and observed the cult worship.

THE SONS OF CONSTANTINE

In preparing for his death, Constantine sought to divide the rule of the Roman Empire among his three sons and two nephews. Immediately upon Constantine's death, however, his three sons led the army in a "palace massacre," murdering Constantine's brothers, brothers-in-law, and older nephews. The three sons then divided the Empire amongst themselves, with Constantine II taking the Western provinces, Constantius the Eastern provinces, and Constans, the youngest, being assigned the governance of the central provinces of Africa, Italy and Illyricum under the supervision of Constantine II.

The fact that an Arian bishop was present at the time of Constantine's death was not merely an ironic coincidence; Constantine's three sons were themselves supporters of the Arian faith and after Constantine's death they strove to reverse the condemnation of Arianism by the Council of Nicaea. The following passage describes a contemporary pagan historian's bemused reaction to the confusion that resulted from the efforts of Constantius II (joint emperor from 337–350 C.E., sole emperor from 350–361 C.E.) to support the Arian doctrine.

---

28. W. S. Thurman, "How Justinian I Sought to Handle the Problem of Religious Dissent," *Greek Orthodox Theological Review* 13 (1968), 15–40; see also Theodosian Code 16.5.66 (burning of Nestorian books) and Justinian's Code 1.13.3, 1.5.58, and 1.5.16.3

29. Ramsay MacMullen, *Christianity & Paganism in the Fourth to Eighth Centuries* (New Haven: Yale University Press, 1997), 34–35.

5.32 Ammianus Marcellinus, *History* 21.16.18 (ca. 390 C.E.)
> The plain and simple religion of the Christians was bedeviled by Constantius with old wives' fancies. Instead of trying to settle matters he raised complicated issues which led to much dissension, and as this spread more widely he fed it with verbal argument. Public transport hurried throngs of bishops hither and thither to attend what they call synods, and by his attempts to impose conformity Constantius only succeeded in hamstringing the post service.

Constantine's sons fought one another as well as pagans and heretics. Constans was not content with ruling under his brother's supervision and in 340 C.E. he invaded Italy to assert the right to rule in his own name. The brothers fought at Aquileia, where Constantine II was killed in battle. Constans assumed rule over the Western provinces of the Empire and Constantius, who had been involved in continuous warfare with the Persians since 338 C.E., accepted Constans as co-emperor. Constans energetically defended the frontiers of the West, but he was unpopular with both the soldiers and the civilian populace and in 350 C.E. he was overthrown and killed by the usurper Magnentius. Taking advantage of a brief respite in the wars with Persia, Constantius moved his army westward against Magnentius and defeated him in a series of battles in 351 and 352 C.E.

During the course of the campaign against Magnentius, Constantius appointed as Caesar an older cousin named Gallus, who had been spared in the massacres after Constantine's death. Gallus proved to be unsuitable and Constantius had him executed in 354 C.E. In 355 C.E., realizing the need for a loyal colleague, Constantius appointed Julian, another cousin spared from execution at the time of Constantine's death, Caesar over Gaul and Britain.

JULIAN THE APOSTATE

Julian (332–363 C.E.) was the son of a half-brother of Constantine and had survived the palace massacre after Constantine's death because he was only five years of age at the time, although his father and seven other relatives were among those murdered. Although spared death by Constantine's sons, Julian was promptly sent to a remote fortress in Asia Minor and there he grew up in seclusion. Julian was given a Christian education, but he also received training in the classics, rhetoric, and philosophy, and during his youth he became a secret convert to paganism.

Julian was without military experience when Constantius made him Caesar, but in 357 C.E. Julian won a major battle against invading Germans and over the next two years conducted a successful campaign to restore the Rhine River defenses. In 359 C.E. the Persians again declared war on the Romans and invaded the Eastern provinces governed by Constantius. As Constantius prepared to move against Persia, he ordered Julian to send many of his best troops to join Constantius's army. This order seems not to have reflected military necessity but rather Constantius's growing fear of the increasingly popular Julian. In 361 C.E. Julian's soldiers refused to march east and instead proclaimed Julian Augustus. Constantius refused to accept the acclamation of Julian and in 361 C.E. both men led armies toward Constantinople to resolve the dispute by battle. Constantius, however, fell sick on the march west and prior to dying named Julian his successor. Thus, Julian became sole emperor in 361 C.E.

It was not until Julian became sole emperor that he openly declared his apostasy from Christianity. Thereafter, Julian took strong measures to revive paganism and put an end to the special privileges granted Christians by Constantine and his sons.

> 5.33 Ammianus Marcellinus, *History* 21.2.4–5; 22.5.1–4; (ca. 390 C.E.)
>
> 21.2.4-5 To frustrate any opposition and win universal good will he [Julian] pretended to adhere to the Christian religion, from which he had secretly apostatized long before. A few only were in his confidence, and knew that his heart was set on divination and augury and all the other practices followed by worshippers of the old gods. To conceal this for the time being he went to church on the holy day which the Christians celebrate in January and call Epiphany, and departed after joining in their customary worship. . . .
>
> 22.5.1-4 Although Julian from his earliest boyhood had nursed an inclination toward the worship of the pagan gods, which gradually grew into an ardent passion as he grew older, fear of the consequences had kept him from practicing its rites except in the greatest possible secrecy. Now, however, that this fear was removed and he saw that the time had come when he could do as he liked, he revealed what was in his heart and directed in plain unvarnished terms that the temples should be opened, sacrifices brought to their altars, and the worship of the old gods restored. To make this ordinance more effective he summoned to the palace the Christian bishops, who were far from being of one mind, together with their flocks, who were no less divided by schism, and warned them in polite terms to lay aside their differences and allow every man to practice his belief boldly without hindrance. His motive in insisting on this was that he knew that tolerance would intensify their divisions and that henceforth he would no longer have to fear a unanimous public opinion. Experience had taught him that no wild beasts are such dangerous enemies to man as Christians are to one another.

Julian understood that paganism could not be restored by mere imperial edicts and so he undertook to reorganize and revitalize the pagan religions. In particular, Julian seems to have recognized that paganism needed to adopt a moral and ethical system comparable to that of Christianity, if it were to ultimately succeed against the Christians.

5.34 Julian the Apostate, *Epistle 22* (362 C.E.–June?)

To Arcasius, High Priest of Galatia: The Hellenic religion does not yet prosper as I desire, and it is the fault of those who profess it; for the worship of the gods is on a splendid and magnificent scale, surpassing every prayer and every hope. May Adrasteia pardon my words, for indeed no one, a little while ago, would have ventured even to pray for a change of such a sort or so complete within so short a time. Why, then, do we think that this is enough, why do we not observe that it is their benevolence to strangers, their care for the graves of the dead and the pretended holiness of their lives that have done most to increase atheism. I believe that we ought really and truly to practice every one of these virtues. And it is not enough for you alone to practice them, but so must all the priests in Galatia, without exception. Either shame or persuade them into righteousness or else remove them from their priestly office, if they do not, together with their wives, children and servants, attend the worship of the gods but allow their servants or sons or wives to show impiety toward the gods and honor atheism more than piety. In the second place, admonish them that no priest may enter a theatre or drink in a tavern or control any craft or trade that is base and not respectable. Honor those who obey you, but those who disobey, expel from office. In every city establish frequent hostels in order that strangers may profit by our benevolence; I do not mean for our own people only, but for others also who are in need of money. I have but now made a plan by which you may be well provided for this; for I have given directions that 30,000 modii of corn shall be assigned every year for the whole of Galatia, and 60,000 pints of wine. I order that one-fifth of this be used for the poor who serve the priests, and the remainder be distributed by us to strangers and beggars. For it is disgraceful that, when no Jew ever has to beg, and the impious Galilaeans support not only their own poor but ours as well, all men see that our people lack aid from us. Teach those of the Hellenic faith to contribute to public service of this sort, and the Hellenic villages to offer their first fruits to the gods; and accustom those who love the Hellenic religion to these good works by teaching them that this was our practice of old. At any rate Homer makes Eumaeus say: "Stranger, it is not lawful for me, not even though a baser man than you should come, to dishonor a stranger. For from Zeus come all strangers and beggars. And a gift, though small, is precious." Then let us not, by allowing others to outdo us in good works, disgrace by such remissness, or rather, utterly abandon, the reverence due to the gods. If I hear that you are carrying out these orders I shall be filled with joy.

As for the government officials, do not interview them often at their homes, but write to them frequently. And when they enter the city no priest must go to meet them, but only meet them within the vestibule when they visit the temples of the gods. Let no soldier march before them into the temple, but any who will may follow them; for the moment that one of them passes over the threshold of the sacred precinct he becomes a private citizen. For you yourself, as you are aware, have authority over what is within, since this is the bidding of the divine ordinance. Those who obey it are in very truth god-fearing, while those who oppose it with arrogance are vainglori-ous and empty-headed.

I am ready to assist Pessinus if her people succeed in winning the favor of the Mother of the Gods. But, if they neglect her, they are not only not free from blame, but, not to speak harshly, let them beware of reaping my enmity also. "For it is not lawful for me to cherish or to pity men who are the enemies of the immortal gods." Therefore persuade them, if they claim my patronage, that the whole commu-nity must become suppliants of the Mother of the Gods.

In addition to his efforts to reorganize pagan religious worship, Julian also sought to reestablish among the Empire's ruling classes the social and political values founded upon the classical pagan literary tradition. The core education taught to the children of the upper classes consisted of rhetoric and literature for private rhetoricians in academies and schools, and this education was a pre-requisite for advancement in government service. Julian apparently hoped that by exposing children to a pagan-dominated tradition, young children and adults might be encouraged to return to paganism as he had done, and so he issued legislation to the effect that only pagan teachers could legally teach the core education. Modern historians have noted that much of Christianity's suc-cess was based on being spread vertically between generations, from elder to youth, rather than horizontally among people of similar age or social standing, and Julian may have recognized from his own childhood experience the signifi-cant influence that pagan tutors might have on the young, as the bond between tutor and student was especially strong and close in Roman culture.[30] The reestablishment of pagan dominance in the education system also held out the possibility that the increasing Christianization of the Empire's civil adminis-tration might be reversed.

5.35 Julian the Apostate, *Epistle 36* (June 17, 362 C.E.)

I hold that a proper education results, not in laboriously acquired symmetry of phrases and language, but in a healthy condition of mind, I mean a mind that has understanding and true opinions about things good and evil, honorable and base. Therefore, when a man thinks one thing and teaches his pupils another, in my opinion he fails to educate exactly in proportion as he fails to be an honest

---

30. Robin Lane Fox, *Pagans and Christians* (New York: Alfred A. Knopf, 1986), 312.

man. And if the divergence between a man's convictions and his
utterances is merely in trivial matters, that can be tolerated some-
how, though it is wrong. But if in matters of the greatest importance
a man has certain opinions and teaches the contrary, what is that but
the conduct of hucksters, and not honest but thoroughly dissolute
men in that they praise most highly the things that they believe to be
most worthless, thus cheating and enticing by their praises those to
whom they desire to transfer their worthless wares. Now all who profess to teach anything whatever ought to be men of upright character, and ought not to harbor in their souls opinions irreconcilable
with what they publicly profess; and, above all, I believe it is necessary that those who associate with the young and teach them rhetoric should be of that upright character; for they expound the writings
of the ancients, whether they be rhetoricians or grammarians, and
still more if they are sophists. For these claim to teach, in addition to
other things, not only the use of words, but morals also, and they
assert that political philosophy is their peculiar field. Let us leave
aside, for the moment, the question whether this is true or not. But
while I applaud them for aspiring to such high pretensions, I should
applaud them still more if they did not utter falsehoods and convict
themselves of thinking one thing and teaching their pupils another.
What! Was it not the gods who revealed all their learning to Homer,
Hesiod, Demosthenes, Herodotus, Thucydides, Isocrates and Lysias?
Did not these men think that they were consecrated, some to
Hermes, others to the Muses? I think it is absurd that men who
expound the works of these writers should dishonor the gods whom
they used to honor. Yet, though I think this absurd, I do not say that
they ought to change their opinions and then instruct the young. But
I give them this choice: either not to teach what they do not think
admirable, or, if they wish to teach, let them first really persuade their
pupils that neither Homer nor Hesiod nor any of these writers whom
they expound and have declared to be guilty of impiety, folly and
error in regard to the gods, is such as they declare. For since they
make a livelihood and receive pay from the works of those writers,
they thereby confess that they are most shamefully greedy of gain,
and that, for the sake of a few drachmae, they would put up with anything. It is true that, until now, there were many excuses for not
attending the temples, and the terror that threatened on all sides
absolved men for concealing the truest beliefs about the gods. But
since the gods have granted us liberty, it seems to me absurd that
men should teach what they do not believe to be sound. But if they
believe that those whose interpreters they are and for whom they sit,
so to speak, in the seat of the prophets, were wise men, let them be
the first to emulate their piety toward the gods. If, however, they

think that those writers were in error with respect to the most honored gods, then let them betake themselves to the churches of the Galilaeans to expound Matthew and Luke, since you Galilaeans are obeying them when you ordain that men shall refrain from temple-worship. For my part, I wish that your ears and our tongues might be "born anew," as you would say, as regards these things in which may I ever have part, and all who think and act as is pleasing to me.

For religious and secular teachers let there be a general ordinance to this effect: Any youth who wishes to attend the schools is not excluded; nor indeed would it be reasonable to shut out from the best way boys who are still too ignorant to know which way to turn, and to overawe them into being led against their will to the beliefs of their ancestors. Though indeed it might be proper to cure these, even against their will, as one cures the insane, except that we concede indulgence to all for this sort of disease. For we ought, I think, to teach, but not punish, the demented.

Christians were horrified by Julian's edict and they vilified him for this measure long after his death. Julian's measure was not a success, however, and even pagan supporters of Julian thought that he had gone too far with this legislation.

5.36 Ammianus Marcellinus, *History* 22.10.6 (ca. 390 C.E.)
But he [Julian] was guilty of one harsh act which should be buried in lasting oblivion; he banned adherents of Christianity from practicing as teachers of rhetoric or literature.

Julian attempted to fight Christian belief on an intellectual and cultural basis without resort to physical violence, even though he had first-hand experience of the terrible coercion the Christian emperors and clergy had used against pagans and heretics. His rejection of this sort of physical violence appears in a number of his letters.

5.37 Julian the Apostate
Epistle 37 (362 C.E.)
To Atarbius: I affirm by the gods that I do not wish the Galilaeans to be either put to death or unjustly beaten, or to suffer any other injury; but nevertheless I do assert absolutely that the god-fearing must be preferred to them. For through the folly of the Galilaeans almost everything has been overturned, whereas through the grace of the gods are we all preserved. Wherefore we ought to honor the gods and the god-fearing, both men and cities.
Epistle 40 (late 362 or early 363 C.E.)
To Hecebolius: I have behaved to all the Galilaeans with such kindness and benevolence that none of them has suffered violence anywhere or been dragged into a temple or threatened into anything else

of the sort against his own will. But the followers of the Arian church, in the insolence bred by their wealth, have attacked the followers of Valentine* and have committed in Edessa such rash acts as could never occur in a well-ordered city. Therefore, since by their most admirable law they are bidden to sell all they have and give to the poor so they may attain more easily to the kingdom of the skies, in order to aid those persons in that effort, I have ordered that all their funds, namely, that belong to the church of the people of Edessa, are to be taken over that they may be given to the soldiers, and that its property be confiscated to my private purse. This is in order that poverty may teach them to behave properly and that they may not be deprived of that heavenly kingdom for which they still hope. And I publicly command you citizens of Edessa to abstain from all feuds and rivalries, else will you provoke even my benevolence against yourselves, and being sentenced to the sword and to exile and to fire pay the penalty for disturbing the good order of the commonwealth.

*Valentine was the founder of a Gnostic sect in the second century.

Epistle 41 (August 1, 362 C.E.)

To the citizens of Bostra: I thought that the leaders of the Galilaeans would be more grateful to me than to my predecessor in the administration of the Empire. For in his reign it happened to the majority of them to be sent into exile, prosecuted, and cast into prison, and moreover, many whole communities of those who are called "heretics" were actually butchered, as at Samosata and Cyzicus, in Paphlagonia, Bithynia, and Galatia, and among many other tribes also villages were sacked and completely devastated; whereas, during my reign, the contrary has happened. For those who had been exiled have had their exile remitted, and those whose property was confiscated have, by a law of mine received permission to recover all their possessions. Yet they have reached such a pitch of raving madness and folly that they are exasperated because they are not allowed to behave like tyrants or to persist in the conduct in which they at one time indulged against one another, and afterwards carried on toward us who revered the gods. They therefore leave no stone unturned, and have the audacity to incite the populace to disorder and revolt, whereby they both act with impiety toward the gods and disobey my edicts, humane though these are. At least I do not allow a single one of them to be dragged against his will to worship at the altars; nay, I proclaim in so many words that, if any man of his own free will choose to take part in our lustral rites and libations, he ought first of all to offer sacrifices of purification and supplicate the gods that avert evil. So far am I from ever having wished or intended that anyone of those sacrilegious men should partake in the sacrifices that we most revere, until he has purified his soul by supplications to the gods, and his body by the purifications that are customary.

It is, at any rate, evident that the populace who have been led into error by those who are called "clerics," are in revolt because this license has been taken from them. For those who have till now behaved like tyrants are not content that they are not punished for their former crimes, but, longing for the power they had before, because they are no longer allowed to sit as judges and draw up wills and appropriate the inheritances of other men and assign everything to themselves, they pull every string of disorder, and, as the proverb says, lead fire through a pipe to fire, and dare to add even greater crimes to their former wickedness by leading on the populace to disunion. Therefore I have decided to proclaim to all communities of citizens, by means of this edict, and to make known to all, that they must not join in the feuds of the clerics or be induced by them to take stones in their hands or disobey those in authority; but they may hold meetings for as long as they please and may offer on their own behalf the prayers to which they are accustomed; that, on the other hand, if the clerics try to induce them to take sides on their behalf in quarrels, they must no longer consent to do so, if they would escape punishment.

I have been led to make this proclamation to the city of Bostra in particular, because their bishop Titus and the clerics, in the reports that they have issued, have made accusations against their own adherents, giving the impression that, when the populace were on the point of breaking the peace, they themselves admonished them not to cause sedition. Indeed, I have subjoined to this my decree the very words which he dared to write in his report: "Although the Christians are a match for the Hellenes in numbers, they are restrained by our admonition that no one disturb the peace in any place." For these are the very words of the bishop about you. You see how he says that your good behavior was not of your own choice, since, as he at any rate alleged, you were restrained against your will by his admonitions! Therefore, of your own free will, seize your accuser and expel him from the city,[31] but do you, the populace, live in agreement with one another, and let no man be quarrelsome or act unjustly. Neither let those of you who have strayed from the truth outrage those who worship the gods duly and justly, according to the beliefs that have been handed down to us from time immemorial;

---

31. Julian's counsel was apparently not followed, since Socrates, *Ecclesiastical History* 3.25, states that Titus was bishop of Bostra under the Emperor Jovian in 363 C.E.

nor let those of you who worship the gods outrage or plunder the houses of those who have strayed rather from ignorance than of set purpose. It is by reason that we ought to persuade and instruct men, not by blows, or insults, or bodily violence. Wherefore, again and often I admonish those who are zealous for the true religion not to injure the communities of the Galilaeans or attack or insult them. Nay, we ought to pity rather than hate men who in matters of the greatest importance are in such evil case. (For in very truth the greatest of all blessings is reverence for the gods, as, on the other hand, irreverence is the greatest of all evils. It follows that those who have turned aside from the gods to corpses and relics pay this as their penalty.) Since we suffer in sympathy with those who are afflicted by disease, but rejoice with those who are being released and set free by the aid of the gods. Given at Antioch on the First of August.

Because Julian had been raised and trained in the Christian faith, in contrast to many pagan opponents of Christianity, he was familiar with its teachings and tenets. Julian attempted to use his knowledge to attack the weak points of Christian belief on both an historical and an intellectual basis by writing a book entitled *Against the Galilaeans*. This book was banned by Christian emperors after his death but, as with the writings of Celsus and Porphyry, portions of Julian's book have survived in fragmentary quotations preserved in rebuttals written by his Christian opponents.

5.38 Julian the Apostate, *Against the Galilaeans* 39 A, 39 B, 41 E and 42 A (362–363 C.E.)

It is, I think, expedient to set forth to all mankind the reasons by which I was convinced that the fabrication of the Galilaeans is a fiction of men composed by wickedness. Though it has in it nothing divine, by making full use of that part of the soul which loves fable and is childish and foolish, it has induced men to believe that the monstrous tale is truth. Now since I intend to treat of all their first dogmas, as they call them, I wish to say in the first place that if my readers desire to try to refute me they must proceed as if they were in a court of law and not drag in irrelevant matter, or, as the saying is, bring counter-charges until they have defended their own views. For thus it will be better and clearer if, when they wish to censure any views of mine, they undertake that as a separate task, but when they are defending themselves against my censure, they bring no counter-charges.

Against the Galilaeans 209 D, 213 A, 213 B, 213 C

But I know not whence I was as it were inspired to utter these remarks. However, to return to the point at which I digressed, when I asked, "Why were you so ungrateful to our gods as to desert them for the Jews?" Was it because the gods granted the sovereign power to

Rome, permitting the Jews to be free for a short time only, and then forever to be enslaved and aliens?... Even Jesus, who was proclaimed among you, was one of Caesar's subjects. And if you do not believe me I will prove it a little later, or rather let me simply assert it now. However, you admit that with his father and mother he registered his name in the governorship of Cyrenius. But when he became man what benefits did he confer on his own kinsfolk? Nay, the Galilaeans answer, they refused to hearken unto Jesus. What? How was it then that this hardhearted and stubborn-necked people hearkened unto Moses; but Jesus, who commanded the spirits and walked on the sea, and drove out demons, and as you yourselves assert made the heavens and the earth—for no one of his disciples ventured to say this concerning him, save only John, and he did not say it clearly or distinctly; still let us at any rate admit that he said it—could not this Jesus change the dispositions of his own friends and kinsfolk to the end that he might save them?

Against the Galilaeans 253 D, 253 E, 261 E

And the words "The scepter shall not depart from Judah, nor a leader from his loins," were most certainly not said of the son of Mary, but of the royal house of David, which, you observe, came to an end with King Zedekiah. And certainly the Scripture can be interpreted in two ways when it says "until there comes what is reserved for him"; but you have wrongly interpreted it, "until he comes for whom it is reserved." But it is very clear that not one of these sayings relates to Jesus; for he is not even from Judah. How could he be when according to you he was not born of Joseph but of the Holy Spirit? For though in your genealogies you trace Joseph back to Judah, you could not invent even this plausibly. For Matthew and Luke are refuted by the fact that they disagree concerning his genealogy. However, as I intend to examine closely into the truth of this matter in my Second Book, I leave it till then.*

> *That portion of Julian's book has been lost and so we
> do not know what further arguments Julian made.

Against the Galilaeans 319 E, 320 B, 320 C

But do you point out to me where there is any statement by Moses of what was later on rashly uttered by Paul, I mean that "Christ is the end of the law." Where does God announce to the Hebrews a second law besides that which was established? Nowhere does it occur, not even a revision of the established law. For listen again to the words of Moses: "Ye shall not add unto the word which I command you, neither shall ye diminish aught from it. Keep the commandments of the Lord your God which I command you this day." And "Cursed be every man who does not abide by them all." But you have thought it a slight thing to diminish and to add to the things which were written

in the law; and to transgress it completely you have thought to be in every way more manly and more high-spirited, because you do not look to the truth but to that which will persuade all men.
Against the Galilaeans 327 A, 327 B

But you are so misguided that you have not even remained faithful to the teachings that were handed down to you by the apostles. And these also have been altered, so as to be worse and more impious, by those who came after. At any rate neither Paul nor Matthew nor Luke nor Mark ventured to call Jesus God. But the worthy John, since he perceived that a great number of people in many of the towns of Greece and Italy had already been infected by this disease, and because he heard, I suppose, that even the tombs of Peter and Paul were being worshipped—secretly, it is true, but still he did hear this—he, I say, was the first to venture to call Jesus God.

5.39 Cyril of Alexandria, *Patrologia graeca* 76.508c (ca. 420 C.E.)
Even those who are strong in faith were troubled because they thought he [Julian] knew the Holy Scriptures. He heaped up many testimonies from them in the Scripture's own words, although he did not understand what they meant. . . . [Many pagans] reproach Christians up and down. They cast his writings against us and assert that they are incomparably skillful and none of our teachers is capable of rebutting or refuting his ideas.

During the second year of his reign, Julian had the idea of revitalizing Judaism as means of combating the Christian faith. On his way east to fight the Persians, Julian wrote a letter to the Jews of Jerusalem, promising to help rebuild the Temple once he returned from the campaign.

5.40 Julian the Apostate, *Rescript to the Jews* (Epistle 51) (late 362 or early 363 C.E.)
To the community of the Jews: In times past, by far the most burdensome thing in the yoke of your slavery has been the fact that you were subjected to unauthorized ordinances and had to contribute an untold amount of money to the accounts of the treasury. Of this I used to see many instances with my own eyes, and I have learned of more, by finding the records which are preserved against you. Moreover, when a tax was about to be levied on you again I prevented it, and compelled the impiety of such obloquy to cease here; and I threw into the fire the records against you that were stored in my desks; so that it is no longer possible for anyone to aim at you such a reproach of impiety. My brother Constantius of honored memory was not so much responsible for these wrongs of yours as were the men who used to frequent his table, barbarians in mind, godless in soul. These I seized with my own hands and put them to

death by thrusting them into the pit, that not even any memory of their destruction might still linger amongst us. And since I wish that you should prosper yet more, I have admonished my brother Iulus, your most venerable patriarch, that the levy which is said to exist among you should be prohibited, and that no one is any longer to have the power to oppress the masses of your people by such exactions; so that everywhere, during my reign, you may have security of mind, and in the enjoyment of peace may offer more fervid prayers for my reign to the Most High God, the Creator, who has deigned to crown me with his own immaculate right hand. For it is natural that men who are distracted by any anxiety should be hampered in spirit, and should not have so much confidence in raising their hands to pray; but that those who are in all respects free from care should rejoice with their whole hearts and offer their suppliant prayers on behalf of my imperial office to Mighty God, even to him who is able to direct my reign to the noblest ends, according to my purpose. This you ought to do, in order that, when I have successfully concluded the war with Persia, I may rebuild by my own efforts the sacred city of Jerusalem, which for so many years you have longed to see inhabited, and may bring settlers there, and, together with you, may glorify the Most High God therein.

Christians were enraged by Julian's proposal to rebuild the Temple, as a living Jewish faith struck at the Christian teaching that Jesus had established a new covenant between God and mankind that supplanted the prior covenant between God and the Jews. While work on the rebuilding of the Temple was actually begun, the work stopped with Julian's death in 363 C.E. during a skirmish with Persian troops. Christians rejoiced over Julian's death and some even claimed that it was a Christian Roman soldier who had thrown the javelin that killed Julian, in just punishment for his apostasy.[32]

Julian's legacy in Christian memory is clear from the fact that he was ever after known as the Apostate. Most historians believe it doubtful that Julian could have reversed the tide running in favor of the Christian faith even if his reign had been longer, as by his day Christianity had penetrated deeply into the ruling classes of the Roman Empire and there was little meaningful competition from the moribund pagan faiths, in spite of pockets of strong support for paganism among the upper classes like the still prestigious, but politically powerless, Roman Senate. Perhaps a fitting legacy for Julian's quest, then, is the last known response ever given by the oracle of Apollo at Delphi, which was said to have been delivered to a question from Julian himself.

---

32. The pagan historian Ammianus Marcellinus, who was one of the Roman officers at the skirmish where Julian received his mortal wound, wrote that no one knew who had thrown the javelin. *History* 25.3.

5.41 The Last Oracle of Apollo at Delphi as quoted in *Vita S. Artemii* 35.
Tell the Emperor, the marvelously built sanctuary has fallen to earth;
Phoebus [Apollo] no longer has a hut,
Nor prophetic laurel leaves,
Nor flowing fountain,
And the waters which speak have withdrawn.

THE CHRISTIAN CONSOLIDATION OF DOMINANCE IN THE ROMAN EMPIRE

When Julian died in Persia in 363 C.E., the Roman army chose a Christian general named Jovian as the new emperor (363–364 C.E.). Jovian annulled the anti-Christian legislation of Julian, but he also proclaimed freedom of worship for all faiths. Jovian died after a reign of only eight months, however, and was succeeded by another Christian general, Valentinian I (364–375 C.E.). Valentinian appointed his brother Valens (364–378 C.E.) as co-emperor and then a few years later, in 367 C.E., appointed his own eight-year-old son Gratian (367–383 C.E.) as a third co-emperor.

While both Valentinian and Valens were Christians, they took different positions with respect to toleration of other forms of belief. Valentinian was an orthodox Christian, but he followed a policy of general religious toleration in the Western Empire. Valens, an Arian, actively supported Arianism against the orthodox church in the Eastern Empire, but he was generally tolerant of paganism. When Gratian began to rule he at first proclaimed religious toleration, but soon adopted measures to suppress both pagan and heretical belief.

Because Christianity had suffered little real harm during the short reign of Julian the Apostate, it would be an exaggeration to speak of a restoration of Christianity under Julian's Christian successors. The great power and influence of the Christian Church during and immediately after Julian's reign was reflected in the great wealth and prestige of its urban bishops. The temptations of such wealth and power would sometimes lead to violent competition among priests for the bishop's position.

5.42 Ammianus Marcellinus, *History* 27.3.12–13 (ca. 390 C.E.)
[12] But he [Viventius, prefect of Rome] too had to endure an alarming outbreak of violence by the turbulent populace [in 366 C.E.], which arose as follows. Damasus and Ursinus, whose passionate ambition to seize the episcopal throne passed all bounds, were involved in the most bitter conflict of interest, and the adherents of both did not stop short of wounds and death. Viventius, unable to end or abate the strife, was compelled by superior force to withdraw to the suburbs. The efforts of his partisans secured the victory for Damasus. It is certain that in the basilica of Sicininus, where the Christians assemble for worship, 137 corpses were found on a single day, and it was only with difficulty that the long-continued fury of the people was later brought under control.

[13] Considering the ostentatious luxury of life in the city it is only natural that those who are ambitious of enjoying it should engage in the most strenuous competition to attain their goal. Once they have reached it they are assured of rich gifts from ladies of quality; they can ride in carriages, dress splendidly, and outdo kings in the lavishness of their table. They might be truly happy if they would pay no regard to the greatness of the city, which they make a cloak for their vices, and follow the example of some provincial bishops, whose extreme frugality in food and drink, simple attire, and downcast eyes demonstrate to the supreme god and his true worshippers the purity and modesty of their lives. But enough of this digression; let me now return to my narrative.

During the reigns of Valentinian, Valens, and Gratian, the special privileges of the Christian churches were reaffirmed and new measures were promulgated against pagan worship.

5.43 Theodosian Code
16.2.21 (May 17, 371 C.E.)
> The same Augustuses [Gratian, Valens and Valentinian] to Ampelius, Prefect of the City: Those persons who have continuously served the Church shall be exempt from service in the municipal councils, provided, however, that it shall be established that they have devoted themselves to the cult of Our law before the beginning of Our reign. All others who have joined the ecclesiastics after this time shall be recalled.

16.2.24 (March 5, 377 C.E.)
> The Emperors Gratian, Valens and Valentinian to Cataphronius: We direct that priests, deacons, subdeacons, exorcists, lectors, doorkeepers, and likewise all persons who are of the first rank in the Church shall be exempt from the compulsory public services that are incumbent on persons.

16.5.4 (April 22, 376 or 378 C.E.)
> Emperors Valen, Gratian and Valentinian Augustuses to Hesperius Praetorian Prefect: Previously, in behalf of the religion of Catholic sanctity, in order that the illicit practice of heretical assembly should cease, We commanded that all places should be confiscated in which their altars were located under the false guise of religion, whether such assemblies were held in town or in the country outside the churches where Our peace prevails. If such forbidden practices should occur, either through the connivance of the judges or through the dishonesty of the profane, the same destruction shall ensue in either case.

When Valentinian I died in 375 C.E., Gratian was only seventeen years old. Gratian's advisors quickly made Gratian's younger brother Valentinian II, a mere four years old, co-Augustus, with control over the province of Illyricum.

Just three years later, in 378 C.E., Gratian's uncle and co-Augustus Valens died in battle against the Visigoths at the catastrophic Roman defeat at the Battle of Adrianople. In response to the suddenly deteriorated military situation, Gratian appointed an experienced general named Theodosius first commander of the Roman cavalry forces and then co-Augustus (379–395 C.E.) for the Eastern Empire. Theodosius was unable to drive the Visigoths out of the Empire, but by 382 C.E. he was able to negotiate an alliance with the Visigoths whereby the Visigoths agreed to help defend Rome's lower Danube River frontier against other barbarian tribes. The alliance did not give the emperors a chance to reorganize the Empire's defenses, however, as the very next year Gratian was overthrown by Magnus Maximus, the Roman commander of the forces in Britain. Magnus Maximus was able to seize control of Britain, Gaul, and Spain, but Valentinian II and his advisors were able to retain control of Italy and Illyricum. Theodosius, preoccupied with affairs in the Eastern provinces, was unable to move against Maximus, but Theodosius did name his own son Arcadius to be a co-Augustus.

The Wavering Century

Historians sometimes refer to the fourth century C.E. as the "wavering century" because the sources indicate that much of the Roman Empire's population was uncertain about committing to the Christian faith.[33] Not only were many pagans reluctant to adopt Christianity, but significant numbers of Christians flirted with conversion to Judaism or even a return to the various pagan forms of worship, particularly during the last quarter of the century. The apostasy of Christians was of great concern to the Christian emperors, who attempted to stop such defections by the imposition of serious legal penalties for apostasy.

5.44 Theodosian Code

16.7.1 (May 2, 381 C.E.)

> Emperors Gratian, Valentinian, and Theodosius Augustuses to Eutropius, Praetorian Prefect: Those Christians who have become pagans shall be deprived of the power and the right to make testaments, and every testament of such decedent, if there is a testament, shall be rescinded by the annulment of its foundation.

16.7.2 (May 20, 383 C.E.)

> The same Augustuses [Gratian, Valentinian, and Theodosius] to Postumianus, Praetorian Prefect: If Christians and those confirmed in the faith have turned to pagan rites and cults, We deny them all power to make a testament in favor of any person whatsoever, so that they shall be outside the Roman law. But if any persons are Christians and catechumens only and should neglect the venerable

---

33. Pierre Chuvin, *A Chronicle of the Last Pagans* (Cambridge: Harvard University Press, 1990), 4.

religion and go over to the altars and temples, and if they have children or brothers german,* that is, their own heirs or statutory ones, such Christians shall be deprived of the right to make a testament according to their own discretion in favor of any other persons whatsoever. The same general rule shall be observed with respect to their persons in taking property under a will, so that they may not vindicate for themselves any rights at all in taking inheritances under testaments, except for their own successions and statutory ones which could come to them from the goods of their parents or brothers german, even by the disposition of a last will duly executed, if the occasion should arise. They must unquestionably be excluded from all power not only to make testaments but also to enjoy them under any right of acquiring an inheritance.

*"having the same parents"

16.7.3 (May 21, 383 C.E.)

The same Augustuses [Gratian, Valentinian, and Theodosius] to Hypatius, Praetorian Prefect: By denying them the liberty to make testaments, We avenge the criminal act of Christians who turn to altars and temples. The disgraceful acts of those persons who have disdained the dignity of the Christian religion and name and have polluted themselves with Jewish contagions shall be punished also. . . .

These measures apparently did not resolve the problem because even more stringent statutes were promulgated just a few years later, during the period of 388–391 C.E. It is difficult to determine why the threat of apostasy became such an issue during this period, in part because we have so few personal accounts from the fourth century C.E. as to why people adopted Christianity in the first place. The best known first-person accounts of conversion from the fourth century are found in the writings of St. Augustine and the Christian historian Sozomen, who briefly described the circumstances surrounding the conversion of his grandfather and a close family friend about a generation before the ordinances of the 380s C.E.

5.45 Sozomen, *Ecclesiastical History* 5.15 (ca. 440 C.E.) These events date to the 350s C.E.

My grandfather was of pagan parentage; and, with his own family and that of Alaphion, had been the first to embrace Christianity in Bethelia [ca. 350 C.E.], a populous town near Gaza, in which there are temples highly reverenced by the people of the country, on account of their antiquity and structural excellence. . . . It is said that the above-mentioned families were converted through the instrumentality of the monk Hilarion. Alaphion, it appears, was possessed of a devil; and neither the pagans nor the Jews could, by any incantations and enchantments, deliver him from this affliction; but Hilarion, by simply calling on the name of Christ, expelled the demon, and Alaphion, with his whole family, immediately embraced Christianity.

5.46 Augustine of Hippo, *The Confessions of St. Augustine* 8.12.28–29 (ca. 397–400 C.E.) The events date to 386 C.E.

[28] But when a profound reflection had, from the secret depths of my soul, drawn together and heaped up all my misery before the sight of my heart, there arose a mighty storm, accompanied by as mighty a shower of tears. Which, that I might pour forth fully, with its natural expressions, I stole away from Alypius; for it suggested itself to me that solitude was fitter for the business of weeping. So I retired to such a distance that even his presence could not be oppressive to me. Thus was it with me at that time, and he perceived it; for something, I believe, I had spoken, wherein the sound of my voice appeared choked with weeping, and in that state had I risen up. He then remained where we had been sitting, most completely astonished. I flung myself down, how, I know not, under a certain fig-tree, giving free course to my tears, and the streams of mine eyes gushed out, an acceptable sacrifice unto Thee. And, not indeed in these words, yet to this effect, spake I much unto Thee: "But Thou, O Lord, how long?" "How long, Lord? Wilt Thou be angry for ever? Oh, remember not against us former iniquities"; for I felt that I was enthralled by them. I sent up these sorrowful cries: "how long, how long? Tomorrow, and tomorrow? Why not now? Why is there not this hour an end to my uncleanness?"

[29] I was saying these things and weeping in the most bitter contrition of my heart, when, lo, I heard the voice as of a boy or girl, I know not which, coming from a neighboring house, chanting, and oft repeating, "Take up and read; take up and read." Immediately my countenance was changed, and I began most earnestly to consider whether it was usual for children in any kind of game to sing such words; nor could I remember ever to have heard the like. So, restraining the torrent of my tears, I rose up, interpreting it no other way than as a command to me from Heaven to open the book, and to read the first chapter I should light upon. For I had heard of Antony, that, accidentally coming in whilst the gospel was being read, he received the admonition as if what was read were addressed to him, "Go and sell that thou hast, and give to the poor, and thou shalt have treasure in heaven; and come and follow me." And by such oracle was he forthwith converted unto Thee. So quickly I returned to the place where Alypius was sitting; for there had I put down the volume of the apostles, when I rose thence. I grasped, opened, and in silence read that paragraph on which my eyes first fell: "Not in rioting and drunkenness, not in chambering and wantonness, not in strife and envying; but put ye on the Lord Jesus Christ, and make not provision for the

flesh, to fulfill the lusts thereof." No further would I read, nor did I need; for instantly, as the sentence ended, by a light, as it were, of security infused into my heart, all the gloom of doubt vanished away.

Mass conversions to Christianity are better documented than personal conversions. In any account of a mass conversion to Christianity it is difficult to isolate the depth and nature of the personal commitment of the individuals involved, but many texts from the fourth and fifth centuries C.E. indicate that non-religious factors such as the opportunity for social advancement, the benefits of submitting to a strong patron, and protection against governmental oppression played at least as important a role as personal religious conviction.

5.47 Theodoret, *A History of the Monks of Syria* 17.1–4 (ca. 440 C.E.)

¹ Nor would it be pious to pass over the memory of the wondrous Abraham. . .

² [He] repaired to the Lebanon [ca. 400 C.E.?], where, he had heard, a large village was engulfed in the darkness of impiety. Hiding his monastic character under the mask of a trader, he with his companions brought along sacks as if coming to buy nuts—for this was the main produce of the village. Renting a house, for which he paid the owners a small sum in advance, he kept quiet for three or four days. Then, little by little, he began in a soft voice to perform the divine liturgy. When they heard the singing of psalms, the public crier called out to summon everyone together. Men, children and women assembled; they walled up the doors from outside, and heaping up a great pile of earth poured it down from the roof above. But when they saw them being suffocated and buried, and willing to do or say nothing apart from addressing prayer to God, they ceased from their frenzy, at the suggestion of their elders. Then opening the doors and pulling them out from the mass of earth, they told them to depart immediately.

³ At this very moment, however, collectors arrived to compel them to pay their taxes; some they bound, others they maltreated. But the man of God, oblivious of what had happened to them, and imitating the Master who when nailed to the cross showed concern for those who had done it, begged these collectors to carry out their work leniently. When they demanded guarantors, he voluntarily accepted the call, and promised to pay them a hundred gold pieces in a few days. Those who had performed so terrible a deed were overwhelmed with admiration at the man's benevolence; begging forgiveness for their outrage, they invited him to become their patron—for the village did not have a master; they themselves were both cultivators and masters. He went to the city (it was Emesa) and finding some of his friends negotiated a loan for the hundred gold pieces; then returning to the village he fulfilled his promise on the appointed day.

⁴ On observing his zeal, they addressed their invitation to him still more zealously. When he promised his consent if they undertook to build a church, they begged him to start operations at once. . . . After spending three years with them and guiding them well toward the things of God, he got another of his companions appointed in his place and went back to his monastic dwelling.

Theodoret has also preserved an eyewitness account of what has been described as the largest mass pagan conversion to Christianity to have survived in the ancient sources. The events date to the period of 425–440 C.E., in a place about 40 miles east of Antioch in Syria.

5.48 Theodoret, *A History of the Monks of Syria* 26.12–14, 22–23, 26 (ca. 440 C.E.)

¹² Since the visitors were beyond counting and they all tried to touch him [the Christian monk Symeon Stylites] and reap some blessing from his garments of skins, while he at first thought the excess of honor absurd and later could not abide the wearisomeness of it, he devised the standing on a pillar, ordering the cutting of a pillar first of six cubits, then of twelve, afterwards of twenty-two and now of thirty-six—for he yearns to fly up to heaven and to be separated from this life on earth. . . .

¹³ . . . .for the Ishmaelites [Bedouins], who were enslaved in their many tens of thousands to the darkness of impiety had been illuminated by his [Symeon's] standing upon the pillar. . . . The Ishmaelites, arriving in companies, 200 or 300 at the same time, sometimes even a thousand, disown with shouts their ancestral imposture; and smashing in front of this great luminary the idols they had venerated and renouncing the orgies of Aphrodite—it was this demon whose worship they had adopted originally—they receive the benefit of the divine mysteries, accepting laws from this sacred tongue and bidding farewell to their ancestral customs, as they disown the eating of wild asses and camels.

¹⁴ I myself was an eyewitness of this, and I have heard them disowning their ancestral impiety and assenting to the teaching of the Gospel. And I once underwent great danger: he [Symeon] told them to come up and receive from me the priestly blessing, saying they would reap the greatest profit therefrom. But they rushed up in a somewhat barbarous manner, and some pulled at me from in front, some from behind, others from the side, while those further back trod on the others and stretched out their hands, and some pulled at my beard and others grabbed at my clothing. I would have been suffocated by their too ardent approach, if he had not used a shout to disperse them. . . .

[22] Night and day he [Symeon] is standing within view of all; for having removed the doors and demolished a sizeable part of the enclosing wall, he is exposed to all as a new and extraordinary spectacle—now standing for a long time, and now bending down repeatedly and offering worship to God. Many of those standing by count the number of these acts of worship. Once one of those with me counted one thousand two hundred and forty-four of them, before slackening and giving up count. In bending down he always makes his forehead touch his toes—for his stomach's receiving food once a week, and little of it, enables his back to bend easily.

[23] As a result of his standing, it is said that a malignant ulcer has developed in his left foot, and that a great deal of puss oozes from it continually. Nevertheless, none of these afflictions has overcome his philosophy, but he bears them all nobly. . . .

[26] He can be seen judging and delivering verdicts that are right and just. These and similar activities he performs after the ninth hour—for the whole night and day until the ninth hour he spends praying. But after the ninth hour he first offers divine instruction to those present, and then, after receiving each man's request and working some cures, he resolves the strife of those in dispute. At sunset he begins his converse from then on with God.

The influence of the "holy man" in the spread of Christianity has been emphasized by modern historians.[34] In the cultural dynamics of the typical agricultural village, a "holy man" such as Symeon was an outsider who by his distinctiveness was seen to be in communion with the divine and who therefore could be trusted to arbitrate fairly the disputes of daily village life. The holy man also served as an intermediary and intercessor with a Divine power perceived by the humble peasant or villager as too exalted and mighty to be approached directly.

Mass conversions such as those described above by Theodoret obviously did not involve any meaningful understanding of Christian belief per se, but like Theodoret most fourth-century C.E. Christians who observed such incidents were content with the convert's belief, even if the belief lacked the understanding so important to moderns. Such was perhaps only to be expected in an age when learning and education of all sorts was in steep decline, and a person like Symeon was considered a "philosopher" on the basis of his fervent faith rather than any formal knowledge or training. For the great masses of the Roman world of late antiquity, religion was sufficient if during life it brought some modicum of protection from the terrible travails of life as a member of the

---

34. See, e.g., Peter Brown's *Society and the Holy in Late Antiquity* (Berkeley: University of California Press, 1982), 103–65 and *The Making of Late Antiquity* (Cambridge: Harvard University Press, 1978), 81–101; Averil Cameron, *The Mediterranean World in Late Antiquity* (London: Routledge, 1993), 71–75.

lower classes and carried a promise of a better existence after death. If conversion to Christianity brought some respite from the oppression and brutality of the common person's day-to-day existence in the late Roman world, then there would always be people willing to convert for such reason alone.

SYMMACHUS AND AMBROSE

During the political turmoil of the early 380s C.E., pagan members of the Roman Senate attempted to reverse one of the anti-pagan measures adopted by the Christian emperors. In approximately 30 B.C.E., Caesar Augustus erected an altar to Victory in the house of the Roman Senate and this altar continued in use in the senate house until the Christian emperor Gratian ordered it removed in 382 C.E. During his life, Gratian rejected a number of senatorial petitions for the restoration of the altar, but in 384 C.E., the year after Gratian's death, the Roman Senate again petitioned the new emperor Valentinian II (375–392 C.E.) for the restoration of the altar. The senate's petition was presented by Quintus Aurelius Symmachus (340–402 C.E.), the most distinguished pagan member of the senate. Although for the most part written in the flowery rhetorical style which then dominated Roman public speech, portions of Symmachus's plea for religious toleration carry a simple eloquence and great emotional weight even today.

> 5.49 Symmachus, *Dispatches to the Emperor* (Relatio 3, 384 C.E.)
> [1] As soon as the most honorable Senate, always devoted to you, knew that crimes were made amenable to law, and that the reputation of late times was being purified by pious princes, it, following the example of a more favorable time, gave utterance to its long suppressed grief, and bade me be once again the delegate to utter its complaints. But through wicked men audience was refused me by the divine Emperor, otherwise justice would not have been wanting, my lords and emperors, of great renown, Valentinian, Theodosius, and Arcadius, victorious and triumphant, ever august.
> [2] In the exercise, therefore, of a twofold office, as your Prefect I attend to public business, and as delegate I recommend to your notice the charge laid on me by the citizens. Here is no disagreement of wills, for men have now ceased to believe that they excel in courtly zeal, if they disagree. To be loved, to be reverenced, to be esteemed is more than imperial sway. Who could endure that private disagreement should injure the state? Rightly does the Senate censure those who have preferred their own power to the reputation of the prince.
> [3] But it is our task to watch on behalf of your Graces. For to what is it more suitable that we defend the institutions of our ancestors, and the rights and destiny of our country, than to the glory of these times, which is all the greater when you understand that you may not do anything contrary to the custom of your ancestors? We demand then the restoration of that condition of religious affairs which was so long advantageous to the state. . . .

[8] . . . .The divine Mind has distributed different guardians and different cults to different cities. As souls are separately given to infants as they are born, so to peoples the genius of their destiny. Here comes in the proof from advantage, which most of all vouches to man for the gods. For, since our reason is wholly clouded, whence does the knowledge of the gods more rightly come to us, than from the memory and evidence of prosperity? Now if a long period gives authority to religious customs, we ought to keep faith with so many centuries, and to follow our ancestors, as they happily followed theirs.

[9] Let us now suppose that Rome is present and addresses you in these words: "Excellent princes, fathers of your country, respect my years to which pious rites have brought me. Let me use the ancestral ceremonies, for I do not repent of them. Let me live after my own fashion, for I am free. This worship subdued the world to my laws, these sacred rites repelled Hannibal from the walls, and the Senones from the capitol. Have I been reserved for this, that in my old age I should be blamed? I will consider what it is thought should be set in order, but tardy and discreditable is the reformation of old age."

[10] We ask, then, for peace for the gods of our fathers and of our country. It is just that all worship should be considered as one. We look on the same stars, the sky is common, the same world surrounds us. What difference does it make by what pains each seeks the truth? We cannot attain to so great a secret by one road. . . .

[17] May the unseen guardians of all sects be favorable to your Graces, and may they especially, who in old time assisted your ancestors, defend you and be worshipped by us. We ask for that state of religious matters which preserved the empire for the divine parent of your Highnesses, and furnished that blessed prince with lawful heirs. That venerable father beholds from the starry height the tears of the priests, and considers himself censured by the violation of that custom which he willingly observed.

[18] Amend also for your divine brother that which he did by the counsel of others, cover over the deed which he knew not to be displeasing to the Senate. For it is allowed that legation was denied access to him, lest public opinion should reach him. It is for the credit of former times, that you should not hesitate to abolish that which is proved not to have been the doing of the prince.

At the time of Symmachus's appeal, the emperor Valentinian II was only thirteen years old. Ambrose, the bishop of Milan, then the imperial capital of the Western Empire, heard of Symmachus's petition and immediately sought to oppose it, fearful that the young emperor might be swayed to grant the request. Ambrose was himself a former high ranking Roman official who, while still a

Christian catechumen, had been raised to the bishopric of Milan in 374 C.E. by proclamation of the Christian congregation. Ambrose's installation as bishop within eight days of being baptized says much about the ways in which the Christian church had changed during the course of the fourth century C.E.

5.50 Paulinus of Florence, *Life of Ambrose* 5–9 (ca. 422 C.E.)

[5] He [Ambrose] received a liberal education and then left Rome to practice as a barrister in the court of the Praetorian Prefect. So magnificently did he plead his cases that he was chosen by his Excellency Probus, then Praetorian Prefect, to be a member of his judicial council. He was next given consular rank as Governor of the Provinces of Liguria and Aemilia and so came to Milan.

[6] During this period Auxentius died [in 374 C.E.]; he was a bishop of the Arian sect, who had kept possession of the Church at Milan since Dionysius, Confessor of the faith, of blessed memory, had been sent into exile. Seeing that the people were threatening to riot over the choice of a new bishop, and being responsible for quelling riots, Ambrose proceeded to the cathedral, in case the city populace should be roused to dangerous courses. While he was addressing those assembled there, a child's voice (it is said) suddenly cried out: "Ambrose for Bishop!" Hearing these words, the whole crowd changed its cry and began clamoring in unison: "Ambrose for Bishop!" So it came about that, where before there had been the most violent dissension, with Arians and Catholics each wanting the other party to be defeated and a bishop of their own consecrated, suddenly they agreed on this man with a miraculous and incredible unanimity.

[7] Realizing this, Ambrose left the church and had his dais got ready for him (being about to become a bishop he naturally mounted to a higher place). Then, contrary to his usual practice, he ordered some people to be put to the torture. But even while he was doing this, the crowd kept clamoring for him saying: "Your sin be upon us." But the cry of this crowd was not like that of the Jewish crowd, who by their words shed Our Lord's blood, when they said: "His blood be upon us." These people, knowing him to be only a catechumen, were assuring him, with the voice of faith, of the forgiveness of all his sins by the grace of baptism. Really disturbed by now, and back at home, he proposed to dedicate himself to philosophical meditation. . . .

Failing to obtain leave to do this, he had some of the common women of the town brought openly into his house, for the sole purpose of inducing the people to change their minds at the sight of them. But they only shouted more insistently than ever: "Your sin be upon us."

[8] When he saw that nothing brought him nearer his purpose, he took to flight, leaving the city in the middle of the night. . . . And when the

people found Ambrose they kept him under guard, while a message was sent to the most gracious Emperor, at that time Valentinian[35]. . . . [9] While the outcome of the message was being awaited, Ambrose again resorted to flight and stayed secretly for a time on the estate of a certain gentleman of rank named Leontius. But when the answer to the message came, Leontius handed him over to the authorities. For the Vicarius had been ordered to press on with the completion of the business and, as he wished to carry out those instructions, he had issued a proclamation warning everybody that if they had any regard for themselves or their possessions they had better hand the man over. So he was handed over and brought back to Milan and then he recognized that it was God's will for him and that he could not continue to resist. He insisted, however, that he must be baptized by a Catholic bishop, for he was most carefully on his guard against the Arian heresy. After his baptism he passed through (it is said) all the grades of the Church's ministry and was consecrated bishop on the eighth day amid universal goodwill and rejoicing.

Ambrose was a friend of Symmachus, but it was clear to Ambrose where his duty lay as bishop. Ambrose wrote two letters to Valentinian II asking that the senate's petition be denied. The first letter seems to have been written when Ambrose first learned of the petition, even before actually obtaining a copy of it.

5.51 St. Ambrose, *Epistle 81* (384 C.E.)

[1] Ambrose, Bishop, to the most blessed Prince and most Christian Emperor Valentinian: As all men who live under the Roman sway engage in military service under you, the Emperors and Princes of the world, so too do you yourselves owe service to Almighty God and our holy faith. For salvation is not sure unless everyone worship in truth the true God, that is the God of the Christians, under Whose sway are all things; for He alone is the true God, Who is to be worshiped from the bottom of the heart; for "the gods of the heathen," as Scripture says, "are devils."

[2] Now everyone is a soldier of this true God, and he who receives and worships Him in his inmost spirit, does not bring to His service dissimulation, or pretense, but earnest faith and devotion. And if, in fine, he does not attain to this, at least he ought not to give any countenance to the worship of idols and to profane ceremonies. For no one deceives God, to whom all things, even the hidden things of the heart, are manifest.

[3] Since, then, most Christian Emperor, there is due from you to the true God both faith and zeal, care and devotion for the faith, I wonder

---

35. The emperor's approval was not ordinarily required, but this was a special case because Ambrose was a high-ranking imperial official and Milan was the capital of the Western Empire.

how the hope has risen up to some, that you would feel it a duty to restore by your command altars to the gods of the heathen, and furnish the funds requisite for profane sacrifices; for whatsoever has long been claimed by either the imperial or the city treasury you will seem to give rather from your own funds, than to be restoring what is theirs. [4] And they are complaining of their losses, who never spared our blood, who destroyed the very buildings of the churches. And they petition you to grant them privileges, who by the last Julian law denied us the common right of speaking and teaching, and those privileges whereby Christians also have often been deceived; for by those privileges they endeavored to ensnare some, partly through inadvertence, partly in order to escape the burden of public requirements; and, because all are not found to be brave, even under Christian princes, many have lapsed.

[5] Had these things not been abolished I could prove that they ought to be done away by your authority; but since they have been forbidden and prohibited by many princes throughout nearly the whole world, and were abolished at Rome by Gratian of august memory, the brother of your Clemency, in consideration of the true faith, and rendered void by a rescript; do not, I pray you, either pluck up what has been established in accordance with the faith, nor rescind your brother's precepts. In civil matters if he established anything, no one thinks that it ought to be treated lightly, while a precept about religion is trodden under foot.

[6] Let no one take advantage of your youth; if he be a heathen who demands this, it is not right that he should bind your mind with the bonds of his own superstition; but by his zeal he ought to teach and admonish you how to be zealous for the true faith, since he defends vain things with all the passion of truth. I myself advise you to defer to the merits of illustrious men, but undoubtedly God must be preferred to all. . . .

[12] And so, remembering the legation lately entrusted to me, I call again upon your faith. I call upon your own feelings not to determine to answer according to this petition of the heathen, nor to attach to an answer of such a sort the sacrilege of your subscription. Refer to the father of your Piety, the Emperor Theodosius, whom you have been wont to consult in almost all matters of greater importance. Nothing is greater than religion, nothing more exalted than faith.

[13] If it were a civil cause the right of reply would be reserved for the opposing party; it is a religious cause, and I the bishop make a claim. Let a copy of the memorial which has been sent be given me, that I may answer more fully, and then let your Clemency's father be consulted on the whole subject, and vouchsafe an answer. Certainly if anything else is decreed, we bishops cannot contentedly suffer it and

take no notice; you indeed may come to the church, but will find either no priest there, or one who will resist you.

[14] What will you answer a priest who says to you, "The church does not seek your gifts, because you have adorned the heathen temples with gifts. The Altar of Christ rejects your gifts, because you have made an altar for idols, for the voice is yours, the hand is yours, the subscription is yours, the deed is yours. The Lord Jesus refuses and rejects your service, because you have served idols, for He said to you: "Ye cannot serve two masters." . . .

[16] What will you answer your father also? who with greater grief will address you, saying, "You judged very ill of me, my son, when you supposed that I could have connived at the heathen. No one ever told me that there was an altar in the Roman Senate House, I never believed such wickedness as that the heathen sacrificed in the common assembly of Christians and heathen, that is to say that the Gentiles should insult the Christians who were present, and that Christians should be compelled against their will to be present at the sacrifices. Many and various crimes were committed whilst I was Emperor. I punished such as were detected; if any one then escaped notice, ought one to say that I approved of that of which no one informed me? You have judged very ill of me, if a foreign superstition and not my own faith preserved the empire."

[17] Wherefore, O Emperor, since you see that if you decree anything of that kind, injury will be done, first to God, and then to your father and brother, I implore you to do that which you know will be profitable to your salvation before God.

Valentinian II denied the senate's petition to restore the Altar of Victory. Notwithstanding his victory, however, Ambrose wrote a second letter not long after the emperor's decision that more directly addressed the points raised in Symmachus's petition.

5.52 St. Ambrose, *Epistle 82* (Autumn, 384 C.E.)

Ambrose, bishop, to the most blessed prince and most clement Emperor Valentinian Augustus:

[1] The illustrious prefect of the city, Symmachus, has made an appeal to your Clemency that the altar which was removed from the Senate House in the city of Rome be restored to its place. You, O Emperor, still young in age, a new recruit without experience, but a veteran in faith, did not approve the appeal of the pagans. The very moment I learned this I presented a request in which, although I stated what seemed necessary to suggest, I asked that I be given a copy of the appeal.

[2] Not doubtful, therefore, regarding your faith, but foreseeing the care that is necessary, and being confident of a kindly consideration, I am answering the demands of the appeal with this discourse, making this

one request that you will not expect eloquence of speech but the force of facts. For, as holy Scripture teaches, the tongue of the wise and studious man is golden, decked with glittering words and shining with the gleam of eloquence, as though some rich hue, capturing the eyes of the mind by the comeliness of its appearance, dazzling in its beauty. But this gold, if you examine it carefully, though outwardly precious, within is a base metal. Ponder well, I beg you, and examine the sect of the pagans. They sound weighty and grand; they support what is incapable of being true; they talk of God, but they adore a statue.

[3] The distinguished prefect of the city has brought forth in his appeal three points which he considers of weight; namely, that (according to him) Rome is asking again for her ancient rites, that the priests and Vestal virgins should be given their stipends, and since these stipends have been refused to the priests there has been general famine.

[4] According to the first proposal, as he says, Rome is shedding tears with sad and mournful complaints, asking again for her ancient ceremonies. The sacred objects, he says, drove Hannibal from the city and the Senones from the Capitol. But at the same time as the power of the sacred objects is proclaimed, their weakness is betrayed. Hannibal reviled the sacred objects of the Romans for a long time, and while the gods warred against themselves the conqueror reached the city's walls. Why did they allow themselves to be besieged when the weapons of their gods did battle for them?

[5] Why should I make mention of the Senones, whom, when they penetrated the innermost recesses of the Capitol, the Roman forces could not have withstood had not a goose (with its frightened cackling) betrayed them. See what sort of protectors guard the Roman temples. Where was Jupiter at that time? Was he making a statement through a goose?

[6] Why do I refuse to admit that their sacred objects warred in behalf of the Romans? Hannibal, too, worshiped the same gods. Let them choose whichever they wish. If these sacred objects conquered in the Romans, then they were overcome in the Carthaginians. If they triumphed in the Carthaginians, they certainly did not help the Romans.

[7] Let us have no more grudging complaint from the people of Rome. Rome has authorized no such complaints. She addresses them with the words: "Why do you stain me each day with the useless blood of the harmless herd? Trophies of victory depend not on entrails of sheep but on the strength of warriors. I subdued the world by other skills. Camillus was a soldier of mine who slew those who had captured the Tarpeian rock and brought back the standards which had been taken from the Capitol. Valor laid low those whom religion had not reached. What shall I say of Attilius, who bestowed the service of

his death? Africanus found his triumphs not amid the altars of the
Capitol but among the ranks of Hannibal. Why do you give me these
examples of ancient heroes? I despise the ceremonies of the Neroes.
Why mention emperors of two months' duration? And the downfall
of kings coupled with their rising? Or is it something new, perhaps,
for the barbarians to have overrun their territory? In those wretched
and strange cases when an emperor was held captive, and then a
world held captive under an emperor, was it the Christians who
revealed the fact that the ceremonies which promised victory were
falsified? Was there then no altar of Victory? I lament my downfall.
My old age is accompanied by shame over that disgraceful bloodshed. But I am not ashamed to be converted in my old age along with
the whole world. Surely it is true that no age is too late to learn. Let
that old age feel shame which cannot rectify itself. It is not the old age
of years which is entitled to praise, but that of character. There is no
disgrace in going on to better things. This alone I had in common
with the barbarians, that I did not know God before. Your sacrifice
consists in the rite of being sprinkled with the blood of beasts. Why
do you look for God's words in dead animals? Come and learn of the
heavenly warfare which goes on on earth. We live here, but we war
there. Let God Himself, who established the mystery of heaven, teach
me about it, not man who does not know himself. Whom more than
God shall I believe concerning God? How can I believe you who
admit that you do not know what you worship?"

[8] So great a secret, it is said, cannot be reached by one road. We
[Christians] know on God's word what you do not know. And what
you know by conjecture we have discovered from the very wisdom
and truth of God. Your ways do not agree with ours. You ask peace
for your gods from the emperors; we beg peace for our emperors
from Christ. You adore the works of your hands; we consider it
wrong to think that anything which can be made is God. God does
not wish to be worshiped in stones. Even your philosophers have
ridiculed these ideas.

[9] But if you say that Christ is not God because you do not believe that
He died (for you do not realize that that was a death of the body not
of the divinity, which has brought it about that no believer will die),
why is this so senseless to you who worship with insult and dispar-
age with honor, thinking that your god is a piece of wood? O worship
most insulting! You do not believe that Christ could have died. O
honorable stubbornness!

[10] But, says he, the ancient altars should be restored to the images, the
ornaments to the shrines. Let these demands be made by one who
shares their superstition. A Christian emperor knows how to honor
the altar of Christ alone. Why do they force pious hands and faithful

lips to do service to their sacrilege? Let the voice of our emperor utter the name of Christ and call on Him only whom he is conscious of, "for the heart of the king is in the hand of God." Has any heathen emperor raised an altar to Christ? While they demand the restoration of all things which used to be, they show by their own example what great reverence Christian emperors should give to the religion which they follow, since the heathens offered everything to their superstitions. ...
[22] The last and most important point remains, O Emperors, whether you ought to reinstate those helps which have profited you, for our opponent says: "Let them defend you and be worshiped by us!" This, most faithful Princes, is what we cannot tolerate, that they taunt us saying that they supplicate their gods in your name and without your command commit a great sacrilege. For they interpret your suppression of feelings as consent. Let them have their guardians to themselves; let these, if they can, protect their devotees. For, if they cannot help those who worship them, how can they help you who do not worship them? ...
[39] I have answered those who provoked me as though I had not been provoked, for my object was to refute the appeal, not to expose superstition. But let their very appeal, O Emperor, make you more cautious. After saying that of former princes, the earlier ones practiced the cult of their fathers, and the later ones did not abolish them, it was claimed in addition that if the religious practice of older princes did not set a pattern, the act of overlooking them on the part of the later ones did. This showed plainly what you owe to your faith, that you should not follow the pattern of heathen rites, and to your affection, that you should not set aside the decrees of your brother. If in their own behalf only they have praised the permission of those princes who, although they were Christians, did not abolish the heathen decrees, how much more ought you to defer to your brotherly affection, so that you who must overlook some things, even though you do not approve them, should not abrogate your brother's decrees; you should maintain what you judge to be in agreement with your own faith and the bond of brotherhood.

As pagan belief came under increasingly severe pressure in the 380s C.E., another pagan orator Libanius (314–353 C.E.) boldly spoke out against Christian repression, arguing that in the end the coercive tactics of the Christians were self-defeating.

5.53 Libanius, *Oration 30* 26–29 (386 C.E.)

But they [Christians who destroyed pagan shrines] alone of all were judges of the charges they brought, and, having judged, themselves played the part of executioner. To what end? For the worshippers of the gods thenceforth to be barred from their own rites and be converted

> to theirs? But this is utter nonsense. Who doesn't know that, as a result of their very sufferings, people have come to admire more than ever their previous condition, just as in physical desire the lover has only to be barred from the act and he does it all the more and becomes more ardent toward the object of his affections. If such conversions of mind could be effected simply by the destruction of the temples, they would have been long ago destroyed by your decree, for you would long since have been glad to see this conversion. But you knew that you could not, and so you never laid a finger on these shrines. These people [the Christians], even if they looked forward to such a result, ought to have advanced toward it in step with you, and should have let the emperor share in their ambition. It would have been better, surely, to succeed in their objective by staying on the right side of the law rather than by abusing it.
>
> And if they tell you that some other people have been converted by such measures and now share their religious beliefs, do not overlook the fact that they speak of conversions apparent, not real. Their converts have not really been changed—they only say they have. This does not mean that they have exchanged one faith for another—only that this crew [the Christians] have had the wool pulled over their eyes. They go to their ceremonies, join their crowds, go everywhere these do, but when they adopt an attitude of prayer they either invoke no god at all or else they invoke the gods. It is no proper invocation from such a place, but it is an invocation for all that. In plays, the actor who takes the part of a tyrant is not a tyrant, but just the same as he was before putting on the mask; so here, everyone keeps himself unchanged, but he lets them think he has been changed. Now what advantage have they won when adherence to their doctrine is a matter of words and the reality is absent? Persuasion is required in such matters, not constraint. If a person fails in persuasion, fails and employs constraint, nothing has been accomplished, though he thinks it has. It is said that in their very own rules it does not appear, but that persuasion meets with approval and compulsion is deplored. Then why these frantic attacks on the temples, if you cannot persuade and must needs resort to force? In this way you would obviously be breaking your own rules.

Libanius, a pagan professor of rhetoric in Antioch, was not punished for his words, but neither did he succeed in stopping the Christian use of physical coercion against pagan worship.

Ambrose and Theodosius I

In 388 C.E., Magnus Maximus attempted to invade Italy while Valentinian II was campaigning in Pannonia. In response, Theodosius led an army into Italy, where he defeated and executed Maximus that same year. Theodosius took up residence in the imperial capital of Milan while his generals moved to reoccupy Maximus's provinces of Gaul, Spain, and Britain. It was at this time, while he was attempting to consolidate his authority over the Western provinces recently held by Maximus, that Theodosius came into conflict with Ambrose.

The conflict between Ambrose and Theodosius arose not over theological doctrine but out of the long-simmering dispute concerning the proper spheres of action for the civil and the religious authorities. Constantine had attempted to use Christianity to provide a religious unity that would strengthen and serve the political position of the emperor. After Constantine's death, a succession of Christian emperors had meddled in the doctrinal affairs of the church for both private religious and political purposes. The issue of whether the church or the emperor was to be supreme came to a head in 388 and 390 C.E., when Ambrose twice confronted Theodosius over the emperor's exercise of civil authority. Ambrose's familiarity with the wielding and uses of secular political power would serve him well in the conflict with the emperor .

The first dispute between Ambrose and Theodosius arose out of an incident in Callinicum, a Roman garrison town on the frontier with the Persian Empire. In 388 C.E., a Christian mob acting under the direction of the local bishop attacked and burned several heretical Christian churches and a Jewish synagogue. Theodosius was apparently concerned with the security implications of offending the inhabitants of an important frontier garrison town and so he ordered the synagogue rebuilt at the bishop's expense and the ringleaders of the mob punished. Ambrose intervened in an effort to overturn the emperor's order.

5.54 Paulinus of Florence, *Life of Ambrose* 22 (ca. 422 C.E.)

It was after Maximus had been put to death, when the Emperor Theodosius was at Milan and Bishop Ambrose at Aquileia, that the Christians in a certain military stronghold in the East burnt down the Jewish synagogue and the sacred grove of the Valentinians, because the Jews and the Valentinians had insulted some Christian monks (for the Valentinian sect worships thirty gods). The Count of the East sent a report of this to the Emperor, who on receipt of it ordered the synagogue to be rebuilt by the bishop of the place and the monks to be punished. But when the purport of this order had come to the ears of that revered man, Bishop Ambrose, as he could not hurry off himself at the moment, he sent the Emperor a letter in which he represented to him that his decree should be withdrawn and that he himself should be granted an audience. He added that, if he were not a fit person to receive a hearing from the Emperor, he would not be a fit person to receive a hearing from the Lord on his behalf or to have prayers and petitions entrusted to him by the Emperor. He was even ready to face death over this issue rather than disguise his thoughts, if that was going to make an apostate of the Emperor, who had issued an order so unjust to the Church.

5.55 Ambrose, *Epistle 40, to the Emperor Theodosius I* (December of 388 C.E.)
I am continually beset with almost unending cares, O most blessed emperor, but never have I felt such anxiety as now, for I see that I must be careful not to have ascribed to me anything resembling an act of sacrilege. I beg you, therefore, give ear with patience to what I say. For, if I am not worthy of a hearing from you, I am not worthy of offering sacrifice to you, I to whom you have entrusted the offering of your vows and prayers. Will you yourself not hear one whom you wish heard when he prays in your behalf? . . .

It was reported by a count of military affairs in the East that a synagogue [at Callinicum] was burned, and this at the instigation of a bishop. You gave the order for those who were involved to be punished and the synagogue rebuilt at the bishop's expense. My charge is not that you should have waited for the bishop's testimony; for bishops quell disturbances and are eager for peace unless they deeply feel some wrong against God or insult to the church. But suppose that this particular bishop was over impetuous in burning the synagogue, and too timid at the judgement seat; are you not afraid, Emperor, that he may comply with your pronouncement and do you not fear he may become an apostate?

Are you not afraid of what will perhaps ensue, his resisting the count in so many words? Then he [the count] will have to make him either an apostate or a martyr. . . .

Let no one call the bishop to task for performing his duty: that is the request I make of your Clemency. And although I have not read that the edict was revoked, let us consider it revoked. What if other more timid persons should, through fear of death, offer to repair the synagogue at their expense, or the count, finding this previously determined, should order it to be rebuilt from the funds of Christians? Will you, O Emperor, have the count an apostate, and entrust to him the insignia of victory, or give the labarum, which is sanctified by Christ's name, to one who will rebuild a synagogue which knows not Christ? Order the labarum carried into the synagogue and let us see if they do not resist.

Shall a place be provided out of the spoils of the Church for the disbelief of the Jews, and shall this patrimony, given to Christians by the favor of Christ, be transferred to the treasuries of unbelievers? We read that, of old, temples were reared for idols from the plunder taken from the Cimbrians and from the spoils of the enemy. The Jews will write on the front of their synagogue the inscription: "The Temple of Impiety, erected from the spoils of the Christians."

Is your motive a point of discipline, O Emperor? Which is of more importance: a demonstration of discipline or the cause of religion? The maintenance of civil law should be secondary to religion. . . .

There is really no adequate cause for all this commotion, people being punished so severely for the burning of a building, and much less so, since a synagogue has been burned, an abode of unbelief, a house of impiety, a shelter of madness under the damnation of God Himself. . . . God forbids us to make intercession for those that you think should be vindicated. . . .

If I were pleading according to the law of the nations, I would mention how many of the Church's basilicas the Jews burned in the time of Julian. . . .

The churches' basilicas were burned by the Jews and nothing was restored, nothing was demanded in return, nothing was required. Moreover, what could a synagogue in a distant town contain, when everything there is not much, is of no value, is of no account. In fine, what could those scheming Jews have lost in this act of plunder? These are but the devices of Jews wishing to bring false charges, so that by reason of their complaints an extraordinary military inquiry may be demanded and soldiers sent who will perhaps say what was said here some time before your accession, O Emperor: "How will Christ be able to help us who are sent to avenge Jews? They lost their own army, they wish to destroy ours."

Furthermore, into what false charges will they not break forth, when they even falsely accused Christ with their false witnesses. Into what false charges will men not break forth when they were liars even in matters divine? . . .

And although they refuse to be bound by the laws of Rome, thinking them outrageous, they now wish to be avenged, so to speak, by Roman laws. Where were those laws when they set fire to the domes of the sacred basilicas? If Julian did not avenge the Church, because he was an apostate, will you, O Emperor, avenge the harm done the synagogue, because you are a Christian? . . .

How important it is for you, O Emperor, not to feel bound to investigate or punish a matter which no one up to now has investigated or punished! It is a serious matter to jeopardize your faith in behalf of the Jews! When Gideon had slain the sacred calf, the heathens said, "Let the gods themselves avenge the injury done to them." Whose task is it to avenge the synagogue? Christ whom they slew, whom they denied? Or will God the Father avenge those who did not accept the Father, since they did not accept the Son? . . .

Now, O Emperor, I beg you not to hear me with contempt, for I fear for you and myself, as says the holy man: "Wherefore was I born to see the ruin of my people," that I should commit an offense against God?

> Indeed, I have done what I could do honorably, that you might hear me
> in the palace rather than make it necessary to hear me in the Church.

In response to Ambrose's threat to condemn the emperor from the pulpit
over the restoration of the synagogue, Theodosius offered to use imperial funds
rather than church funds to rebuild the synagogue. Ambrose refused this compromise and demanded complete amnesty for the Christians involved. When
Theodosius hesitated, Ambrose delivered a church sermon against any compromise on this issue and thereafter refused to perform the Eucharist at any
worship service attended by Theodosius. Theodosius, who was in the midst of
consolidating his political control over Maximus's former territories, could not
afford an open break with the most important bishop of the Western Empire
and so he gave in to Ambrose's demands. Ambrose himself described the scene
of the emperor's capitulation.

5.56 Ambrose, *Epistle 41, to His Sister Marcella* (late 388 C.E.)
> You condescended to write me saying that your Holiness was still anx-
> ious because I had written that I was anxious. I am surprised that you
> did not receive my letter in which I wrote that peace had flowed back
> upon me. For, when the report came that the synagogue of the Jews
> and an assembly place of the Valentinians had been burned at the
> instigation of a bishop, the order was made, while I was at Aquilia, for
> the bishop to rebuild the synagogue, and the monks who had burned
> the Valentinians's building to be punished. Thus, when I accom-
> plished nothing by frequent attempts, I wrote and sent a letter to the
> emperor, and when he came to church I delivered this sermon. . . .
>
> When I came down from the pulpit, he [the emperor Theodosius]
> said to me: "You spoke about me." I answered: "I preached what is
> intended to benefit you." Then he said: "I really made too harsh a
> decision about the bishop's repairing the synagogue. The monks do
> many outrageous things." Then Timosius, general of the cavalry and
> infantry, began being abusive about the monks. I answered him: "I am
> dealing with the emperor, as is fitting, for I know that he hears the
> Lord; but one must deal otherwise with you, for you speak so rudely."
>
> Then, when I had stood for some time, I said to the emperor: "Let
> me confidently sacrifice in your behalf; set my mind at rest." When
> he continued sitting and nodding, and made no promise openly, and
> I remained standing, he said he would correct the edict. I immedi-
> ately went on to say that he should end the whole investigation, so
> that the count would not harm the Christians in any way on the pre-
> text of an investigation. He promised. I said to him: "I am acting on
> your promise," and I repeated: "I am acting on your promise." "Go
> ahead," he said, "on my promise." So I went to the altar, but I would
> not have done so if he had not fully promised. Indeed, so great was
> the grace of the Offering that I myself felt the favor had been very

pleasing to our God, and that we were in the presence of God. Thus, all was done as I wished.

Although Ambrose was victorious in his first confrontation with Theodosius, from a modern perspective Ambrose's religious bigotry and intoleration make him seem to support the worse cause in the Callinicum incident. A scant two years later, however, Ambrose acted in a more favorable light when he held Theodosius accountable for ordering the massacre of thousands of civilians in the town of Thessalonica, Greece.

5.57 Sozomen, *Ecclesiastical History* 7.25 (ca. 440 C.E., concerning events in 390 C.E.)

> After the death of Eugenius, the emperor went to Milan, and repaired toward the church to pray within its walls. When he drew near the gates of the edifice, he was met by Ambrose, the bishop of the city, who took hold of him by his purple robe, and said to him, in the presence of the multitude, "Stand back! a man defiled by sin, and with hands imbrued in blood unjustly shed, is not worthy, without repentance, to enter within these sacred precincts, or partake of the holy mysteries." The emperor, struck with admiration at the boldness of the bishop, began to reflect on his own conduct, and, with much contrition, retraced his steps. The occasion of the sin was as follows. When Buthericus was general of the troops in Illyria, a charioteer saw him shamefully exposed at a tavern, and attempted an outrage; he was apprehended and put in custody. Some time after, some magnificent races were to be held at the hippodrome, and the populace of Thessalonica demanded the release of the prisoner, considering him necessary to the celebration of the contest. As their request was not attended to, they rose up in sedition and finally slew Buthericus. On hearing of this deed, the wrath of the emperor was excited immediately, and he commanded that a certain number of the citizens should be put to death. The city was filled with the blood of many unjustly shed; for strangers, who had but just arrived there on their journey to other lands, were sacrificed with the others. There were many cases of suffering well worthy of commiseration, of which the following is an instance. A merchant offered himself to be slain as a substitute for his two sons who had both been selected as victims, and promised the soldiers to give them all the gold he possessed, on condition of their effecting the exchange. They could not but compassionate his misfortune, and consented to take him as a substitute for one of his sons, but declared that they did not dare to let off both the young men, as that would render the appointed number of the slain incomplete. The father gazed on his sons, groaning and weeping; he could not save either from death, but he continued hesitating until they had been put to death, being overcome by an equal love for

each. I have also been informed, that a faithful slave voluntarily offered to die instead of his master, who was being led to the place of execution. It appears that it was for these and other acts of cruelty that Ambrose rebuked the emperor, forbade him to enter the church, and excommunicated him. Theodosius publicly confessed his sin in the church, and during the time set apart for penance, refrained from wearing his imperial ornaments, according to the usage of mourners. He also enacted a law prohibiting the officers entrusted with the execution of the imperial mandates, from inflicting the punishment of death till thirty days after the mandate had been issued, in order that the wrath of the emperor might have time to be appeased, and that room might be made for the exercise of mercy and repentance. . . .

5.58 Theodoret, *Ecclesiastical History* 5.17 (ca. 440 C.E., concerning events in 390 C.E.)

Thessalonica is a large and very populous city, belonging to Macedonia, but the capital of Thessaly and Achaia, as well as of many other provinces which are governed by the prefect of Illyricum. Here arose a great sedition, and several of the magistrates were stoned and violently treated. The emperor was fired with anger when he heard the news, and unable to endure the rush of his passion, did not even check its onset by the curb of reason, but allowed his rage to be the minister of his vengeance. When the imperial passion had received its authority, as though itself an independent prince, it broke the bonds and yoke of reason, unsheathed swords of injustice right and left without distinction, and slew innocent and guilty together. No trial preceded the sentence. No condemnation was passed on the perpetrators of the crimes. Multitudes were mowed down like ears of corn in harvest-tide. It is said that seven thousand perished. News of this lamentable calamity reached Ambrose. The emperor on his arrival at Milan wished according to custom to enter the church. Ambrosius met him outside the outer porch and forbade him to step over the sacred threshold. "You seem, sir, not to know," said he, "the magnitude of the bloody deed that has been done. Your rage has subsided, but your reason has not yet recognized the character of the deed. Peradventure your Imperial power prevents your recognizing the sin, and power stands in the light of reason. We must however know how our nature passes away and is subject to death; we must know the ancestral dust from which we sprang, and to which we are swiftly returning. We must not because we are dazzled by the sheen of the purple fail to see the weakness of the body that it robes. You are a sovereign, Sir, of men of like nature with your own, and who are in truth your fellow slaves; for there is one Lord and Sovereign of mankind, Creator of the Universe. With what eyes then will you look

on the temple of our common Lord—with what feet will you tread
that holy threshold, how will you stretch forth your hands still dripping with the blood of unjust slaughter? How in such hands will you
receive the all holy Body of the Lord? How will you who in your rage
unrighteously poured forth so much blood lift to your lips the precious Blood? Be gone. Attempt not to add another crime to that
which you have committed. Submit to the restriction to which the
God the Lord of all agrees that you be sentenced. He will be your
physician, He will give you health." Educated as he had been in the
sacred oracles, Theodosius knew clearly what belonged to priests and
what to emperors. He therefore bowed to the rebuke of Ambrose,
and retired sighing and weeping to the palace. After a considerable
time, when eight months had passed away, the festival of our Savior's
birth came round and the emperor sat in his palace shedding a storm
of tears. . . .

5.59 Ambrose, *Epistle 51* (390 C.E.)
   To the most august Emperor Theodosius, Ambrose, bishop
      Sweet to me is the recollection of your friendship in the past, and
I recall the favor of benefits which you have bestowed with supreme
favor upon others at my frequent requests. Hence, you may infer that
I could not have avoided meeting you through any feeling of ingrati-
tude, for I had always heretofore ardently desired your coming. I
shall briefly set forth the reason for acting as I did. . . .
      Should I keep silence? Then would my conscience be bound, my
voice snatched from me—most wretched of all conditions. And
where would be the significance of the saying that if a bishop declare
not to the wicked, the wicked shall die in his iniquity, and the bishop
shall be guilty of punishment because he has not warned the wicked?
      Understand this, august Emperor! I cannot deny that you are
zealous for the faith; I do not disvow that you have a fear of God—
but you have a natural vehemence which you quickly change to pity
when one endeavors to soothe it. When one stirs it up, you so excite
it that you can hardly check it. If only no one would enkindle it, if no
one would arouse it! This I gladly commend to you: Restrain yourself, and conquer by love of duty your natural impetuosity.
      This vehemence I have preferred to commend privately to your
own considerations rather than to rouse it publicly perchance by any
action of mine. I preferred to fail somewhat in my duty rather than
in submission, that others should look for priestly authority in me
instead of your failing to find reverence in me, who am most devoted.
The result would be that, though you restrained your vehemence,
your ability to get counsel might be unimpaired. I proffered the
excuse of bodily illness, truly severe, and only to be eased by men

being milder. Yet I would have preferred to die rather than not await your arrival in two or three days. But that was not what I did.

The affair which took place in the city of Thessalonica and with no precedent within memory, that which I could not prevent from taking place, which I had declared would be most atrocious when I entered pleas against it so many times, and which you yourself, by revoking it too late, manifestly considered to have been very serious, this when done I could not extenuate. It was first heard of when the synod had met on the arrival of Gallican bishops. No one failed to lament, no one took it lightly. Your being in fellowship with Ambrose was not an excuse for your deed; blame for what had been done would have been heaped upon me even more had no one said there must needs be a reconciliation with our God.

Are you ashamed, O Emperor, to do what King David the Prophet did, the forefather of the family of Christ according to the flesh? He was told that a rich man who had many flocks had seized and killed a poor man's one ram on the arrival of a guest, and recognizing that he himself was being condemned in this tale, for he had himself done so, he said: "I have sinned against the Lord." Do not be impatient, O Emperor, if it is said to you: "You have done what was declared to King David by the Prophet." For if you listen carefully to this and say: "I have sinned against the Lord," if you repeat the words of the royal Prophet: "Come, let us adore and fall down before him, and weep before our Lord who made us," it will be said also to you: "Since you repent, the Lord forgives you your sin and you shall not die." . . .

These things I have written not to disconcert you but that the examples of kings may stir you to remove this sin from your kingdom, for you will remove it by humbling your soul before God. You are a man, you have met temptation—conquer it. Sin is not removed except by tears and penance. No angel or archangel can remove it; it is God Himself who alone can say: "I am with you;" if we have sinned, He does not forgive us unless we do penance.

I urge, I ask, I beg, I warn, for my grief is that you, who were a model of unheard of piety, who had reached the apex of clemency, who would not allow the guilty to be in peril, are not now mourning that so many guiltless have perished. Although you waged battles most successfully, and were praiseworthy also in other respects, the apex of your deeds was always your piety. The Devil envied you this, your most outstanding possession. Conquer him while you still have the means of doing so. Do not add another sin to your sin nor follow a course of action which has injured many followers.

I among all other men, a debtor to your Piety, to whom I cannot be ungrateful, this piety which I discover in many emperors and match in only one, I, I say, have no charge of arrogance against you, but I do have one of fear. I dare not offer the Holy Sacrifice if you intend to be present. Can that which is not allowable, after the blood of one man is shed, be allowable when many persons' blood was shed? I think not.

Lastly, I am writing with my own hand what you alone may read. Thus, may the Lord free me from all anxieties, for I have learned very definitely what I may not do, not from man nor through man. In my anxiety, on the very night that I was preparing to set forth you appeared [in my dreams] to have come to the church and I was not allowed to offer the Holy Sacrifice. I say nothing of the other things I could have avoided, but bore for love of you, as I believe. May the Lord make all things pass tranquilly. Our God admonishes us in many ways, by heavenly signs, by the warnings of the Prophets, and He wills that we understand even by the visions of sinners. So we will ask Him to remove these disturbances, to preserve peace for you who are rulers, that the faith and peace of the Church continue, for it avails much if her emperors be pious Christians. . . .

I love, I cherish, I attend you with prayers. If you trust me, follow me; if, I say, you trust me, acknowledge what I say; if you do not trust me, pardon what I do in esteeming God more than you. May you, the most blessed and eminent Emperor Augustus, together with your holy offspring, enjoy perpetual peace.

5.60 Paulinus of Florence, *Life of Ambrose* 24 (ca. 422 C.E.)
When the Bishop [Ambrose] learnt what had happened, he refused the Emperor admission to the cathedral, nor would he pronounce him fit to sit in the congregation or to receive the Sacraments until he had done public penance. When the Emperor remonstrated that David had committed adultery and murder, both together, his immediate reply was, "As you imitated him in his transgressions, imitate him in his amendment." The Emperor took these words so much to heart that he did not shrink even from public penance; and the effect of his making amends was to give the Bishop a second victory.

Ambrose's victories in his two confrontations with Theodosius held great significance for the future direction of Western civilization. In the struggle between the church and Caesaropapism, Ambrose's triumph over Theodosius, the last emperor to rule over a unified Roman Empire, helped tip the balance at least temporarily in favor of the church. In Western Europe, the political advantage gained by the church was solidified by the collapse of the Western Roman Empire over the next two generations and the absence of any strong civil governments in Western Europe for several centuries thereafter. In the eastern part of the Empire, however, where the Roman Empire evolved into the Byzantine Empire and survived for another thousand years, the emperors were generally able to assert a great deal of control over the church and the Greek

Orthodox Church was forced to engage in a much longer and ultimately less successful effort to assert its independence of the secular authorities.

THEODOSIUS I AND THE SUPRESSION OF PAGANISM

While Ambrose and Theodosius engaged in two tense confrontations over the issue of the supremacy between church and state in the secular world, Theodosius's zeal for the orthodox faith was never in question and his reign was one of utmost severity against heretics and pagans. The use of state-sanctioned violence against paganism was typified by Theodosius's appointment of Maternus Cynegius as praetorian prefect of the East for 384–388 C.E., with the express mission of finding and destroying all pagan temples in which sacrifices were still conducted. Shortly after the incident at Callinicum, Theodosius issued a new series of edicts against paganism, heresy, and apostasy.

> 5.61 Theodosian Code 16.4.2 (June 16, 388 C.E.)
>
> Emperors Valentinian, Theodosius and Arcadius to Eusignius, Praetorian Prefect: There shall be no opportunity for any man to go out to the public and to argue about religion or to discuss it or to give any counsel. If any person hereafter, with flagrant and damnable audacity, should suppose that he may contravene any law of this kind or if he should dare to persist in his action of ruinous obstinacy, he shall be restrained with a due penalty and proper punishment.

> 16.10.10 (Feb. 24, 391 C.E.)
>
> The same Augustuses [Emperors Valentinian, Theodosius and Arcadius] to Albinus, Praetorian Prefect: No person shall pollute himself with sacrificial animals; no person shall slaughter an innocent victim; no person shall approach the shrines, shall wander through the temples, or revere the images formed by mortal labor, lest he become guilty by divine and human laws. . . .

> 16.7.4 (May 11, 391 C.E.)
>
> Emperors Valentinian, Theodosius and Arcadius to Flavianus, Praetorian Prefect: If any persons should betray the holy faith and should profane holy baptism, they shall be segregated from the community of all men, shall be disqualified from giving testimony, and, as We have previously ordained, they shall not have testamentary capacity; they shall inherit from no person, and by no person shall they be designated as heirs. We should also have ordered them to be expelled and removed to a distance if it had not appeared to be a greater punishment to dwell among men and to lack the approval of men. But never shall they return to their former status; the disgracefulness of their conduct shall not be expiated by penitence nor concealed by the shadow of any carefully devised defense or protection, since fiction and fabrication cannot protect those persons who have

polluted the faith which they had vowed to God, who have betrayed the divine mystery and have gone over to profane doctrines. Help is extended to those persons who have slipped and to those who go astray, but those who are lost, that is, those who profane holy baptism, shall not be aided by any expiation through penitence, which customarily avails in other crimes.

16.5.20 (May 19, 391 C.E.)
Copy of a Sacred Imperial Letter. We order that the polluted contagions of the heretics shall be expelled from the cities and driven forth from the villages. No opportunity shall be available to them for any gathering, so that in no place may a sacrilegious cohort of such men be collected. No conventicles, either public or hidden, shall be granted to the perversity of such persons as retreats for their false doctrines.

As Christian officials and bishops moved across the provinces to enforce the imperial edicts, they encountered scattered resistance from local pagan populations who wished to preserve their traditional worship. One of the most famous instances of armed pagan resistance occurred in the town of Apamea, Syria, in 391 or 392 C.E. At first, the new Christian bishop was successful in his efforts to destroy the local pagan temples.

5.62 Theodoret, *Ecclesiastical History* 5.21
The first of the bishops to put the edict [of Theodosius I] in force and destroy the shrines in the city committed to his care was Marcellus, trusting rather in God than in the hands of a multitude. The occurrence is remarkable, and I shall proceed to narrate it. On the death of John, bishop of Apamea, whom I have already mentioned, the divine Marcellus, fervent in spirit, according to the apostolic law, was appointed in his stead. Now there had arrived at Apamea the prefect of the East with two tribunes and their troops. Fear of the troops kept the people quiet. An attempt was made to destroy the vast and magnificent shrine of Jupiter, but the building was so firm and solid that to break up its closely compacted stones seemed beyond the power of man; for they were huge and well and truly laid, and moreover clamped fast with iron and lead. When the divine Marcellus saw that the prefect was afraid to begin the attack, he sent him on to the rest of the towns; while he himself prayed to God to aid him in the work of destruction. Next morning there came uninvited to the bishop a man who was no builder, or mason, or artificer of any kind, but only a laborer who carried stones, and timber on his back. "Give me," said he, "two workmen's pay; and I promise you I will easily destroy the temple." The holy bishop did as he was asked, and the following was the fellow's contrivance. Round the four sides of the temple went a portico united to it, and on which its

upper story rested. The columns were of great bulk, commensurate with the temple, each being sixteen cubits in circumference. The quality of the stone was exceptionally hard, and offering great resistance to the masons' tools. In each of these the man made an opening all round, propping up the superstructure with olive timber before he went on to another. After he had hollowed out three of the columns, he set fire to the timbers. But a black demon appeared and would not suffer the wood to be consumed, as it naturally would be, by the fire, and stayed the force of the flame. After the attempt had been made several times, and the plan was proved ineffectual, news of the failure was brought to the bishop, who was taking his noontide sleep. Marcellus forthwith hurried to the church, ordered water to be poured into a pail, and placed the water upon the divine altar. Then, bending his head to the ground, he besought the loving Lord in no way to give in to the usurped power of the demon, but to lay bare its weakness and exhibit His own strength, lest unbelievers should henceforth find excuse for greater wrong. With these and other like words he made the sign of the cross over the water, and ordered Equitius, one of his deacons, who was armed with faith and enthusiasm, to take the water and sprinkle it in faith, and then apply the flame. His orders were obeyed, and the demon, unable to endure the approach of the water, fled. Then the fire, affected by its foe the water as though it had been oil, caught the wood, and consumed it in an instant. When their support had vanished the columns themselves fell down, and dragged the other twelve with them. The side of the temple which was connected with the columns was dragged down by the violence of their fall, and carried away with them. The crash, which was tremendous, was heard throughout the town, and all ran to see the sight. No sooner did the multitude hear of the flight of the hostile demon than they broke out into a hymn of praise to God.

Bishop Marcellus was not so fortunate in his effort to destroy another temple in the outskirts of Apamea, when "fear of the troops" did not keep the people quiet.

5.63 Sozomen, *Ecclesiastical History* 7.15 (ca. 440 C.E.)

There were still pagans in many cities, who contended zealously in behalf of their temples; as for instance, the inhabitants of Petraea and of Areopolis, in Arabia; of Raphi and Gaza, in Palestine; of Heriopolis in Phoenicia; and of Apamea, on the river Axius, in Syria. I have been informed that the inhabitants of the last named city often armed men of Galilee and the peasants of Lebanon in defense of their temples; and that at last, they even carried their audacity to such a height, as to slay a bishop named Marcellus. This bishop had commanded the demolition of all the temples in the city and villages, under the

supposition that it would not be easy otherwise for them to be converted from their former religion. Having heard that there was a very
spacious temple at Aulon, a district of Apamea, he repaired there
with a body of soldiers and gladiators. He stationed himself at a distance from the scene of conflict, beyond the reach of the arrows; for
he was afflicted with the gout, and was unable to fight, to pursue, or
to flee. While the soldiers and gladiators were engaged in the assault
against the temple, some pagans, discovering that he was alone, hastened to the place where he was separated from the combat; they
arose suddenly and seized him, and burnt him alive. The perpetrators of this deed were not then known, but, in the course of time,
they were detected, and the sons of Marcellus determined upon
avenging his death. The council of the province, however, prohibited
them from executing this design, and declared that it was not just
that the relatives or friends of Marcellus should seek to avenge his
death, when they should rather return thanks to God for having
accounted him worthy to die in such a cause.

The provincial council's ironic response to the sons of Marcellus was typical of the resentment toward Christian religious oppression found in many
parts of the Roman Empire.

In 392 C.E., the same year as Marcellus's death, a revolt broke out against
Theodosius in the Western provinces of the Empire. The armies led by Eugenius,
a nominal Christian, and his allies are the last known Roman forces to have
contended for the emperor's throne under pagan banners.

5.64 Sozomen, *Ecclesiastical History* 7.22, 24 (ca. 440 C.E., concerning
events in 392 C.E.)

²² While Theodosius was thus occupied in the wise and peaceful government of his subjects in the East, and in the service of God, intelligence was brought that Valentinian had been strangled. Some say
that he was put to death by the eunuchs of the bedchamber, at the
solicitation of Arbogastes, a military chief, and of certain courtiers, who
were displeased because the young prince had begun to walk in the
footsteps of his father, concerning the government, and contrary to the
opinions approved by them. Others assert, however, that Valentinian
committed the fatal deed with his own hands, because he found himself impeded in attempting deeds which are not lawful in one of his
years; and on this account he did not deem it worth while to live; for
although an emperor, he was not allowed to do what he wished. It is
said that the boy was noble in person, and excellent in royal manners;
and that, had he lived to the age of manhood, he would have shown
himself worthy of holding the reins of empire, and would have surpassed his father in magnanimity and justice. But though endowed
with these promising qualities, he died in the manner above related.

A certain man named Eugenius, who was by no means sincere in his professions of Christianity, aspired to sovereignty, and assumed the symbols of imperial power. He was hoping to succeed in the attempt safely; for he was led by the predictions of individuals who professed to foresee the future, by the examination of the entrails and livers of animals and the course of the stars. Men of the highest rank among the Romans were addicted to these superstitions. Flavian, then a praetorian prefect, a learned man, and one who appeared to have an aptitude for politics, was noted for being conversant with every means of foretelling the future. He persuaded Eugenius to take up arms by assuring him that he was destined for the throne, that his warlike undertakings would be crowned with victory, and that the Christian religion would be abolished. Deceived by these flattering representations, Eugenius raised an army and took possession of the gates into Italy, as the Romans call the Julian Alps, an elevated and precipitous range of mountains; these he seized beforehand and forti-fied, for they had but one path in the narrows, and were shut in on each side by precipices and the loftiest mountains. Theodosius was perplexed as to whether he ought to await the issue of the war, or whether it would be better in the first place to attack Eugenius; and in this dilemma, he determined to consult John, a monk of Thebais, who, as I have before stated, was celebrated for his knowledge of the future. He therefore sent Eutropius, a eunuch of the palace, and of tried fidelity, to Egypt, with orders to bring John, if possible, to court; but, in case of his refusal, to learn what ought to be done. When he came to John, the monk could not be persuaded to go to the emperor, but he sent word by Eutropius that the war would termi-nate in favor of Theodosius, and that the tyrant would be slain; but that, after the victory, Theodosius himself would die in Italy. The truth of both of these predictions was confirmed by events. . . .

[24] When he had completed his preparations for war, Theodosius declared his younger son Honorius emperor, and leaving him to reign at Constantinople conjointly with Arcadius, who had previ-ously been appointed emperor, he departed from the East to the West at the head of his troops. His army consisted not only of Roman sol-diers, but of bands of barbarians from the banks of the Ister. It is said that when he left Constantinople, he came to the seventh milestone, and went to pray to God in the church which he had erected in honor of John the Baptist; and in his name prayed that success might attend the Roman arms, and besought the Baptist himself to aid him. After offering up these prayers he proceeded toward Italy, crossed the Alps, and took the first guard-posts. On descending from the heights of these mountains, he perceived a plain before him covered with infantry and cavalry, and became at the same time aware that some

of the enemy's troops were lying in ambush behind him, among the recesses of the mountains. The advance guard of his army attacked the infantry stationed in the plain, and a desperate and very doubtful conflict ensued. Further, when the army surrounded him, he considered that he had come into the power of men, and could not be saved even by those who would desire to do so, since those who had been posted in his rear were seizing the heights; he fell prone upon the earth, and prayed with tears, and God instantly answered him; for the officers of the troops stationed in ambush on the height sent to offer him their services as his allies, provided that he would assign them honorable posts in his army. As he had neither paper nor ink within reach, he took up some tablets, and wrote on them the high and befitting appointments he would confer upon them, provided that they would fulfill their promise to him. Under these conditions they advanced to the emperor. The issue did not yet incline to either side, but the battle was still evenly balanced in the plain, when a tremendous wind descended into the face of the enemy. It was such a one as we have never before recorded, and broke up the ranks of the enemies. The arrows and darts which were sent against the Romans, as if projected by the opposing ranks, were turned upon the bodies of those who had cast them; and their shields were wrenched from their hands, and whirled against them with filth and dust. Standing thus exposed, in a defenseless condition, to the weapons of the Romans, many of them perished, while the few who attempted to effect an escape were soon captured. Eugenius threw himself at the feet of the emperor, and implored him to spare his life; but while in the act of offering up these entreaties, a soldier struck off his head. Arbogastes fled after the battle, and fell by his own hands. It is said that while the battle was being fought, a demoniac presented himself in the temple of God which is in the Hebdomos, where the emperor had engaged in prayer on starting out, and insulted John the Baptist, taunting him with having his head cut off, and shouted the following words: "You conquer me, and lay snares for my army." The persons who happened to be on the spot, and who were waiting impatiently to learn some news of the war, were amazed, and wrote an account of it on the day that it occurred, and afterwards ascertained that it was the same day as that on which the battle had been fought. Such is the history of these transactions.

5.65 Socrates, *Ecclesiastical History* 5.25 (ca. 440 C.E., concerning events in 392 C.E.)

There was in the Western regions a grammarian named Eugenius, who after having for some time taught the Latin language, left his school, and was appointed to service at the palace, being constituted chief secretary to the emperor. Possessing a considerable degree of eloquence, and being on that account treated with greater distinction than others, he was unable to bear his good fortune with moderation. For associating with himself Arbogastes, a native of Galatia Minor, who then had the command of a division of the army, a man harsh in manner and very bloodthirsty, he determined to usurp the sovereignty. These two therefore agreed to murder the Emperor Valentinian, having corrupted the eunuchs of the imperial bed-chamber. These, on receiving tempting promises of promotion, strangled the emperor in his sleep. Eugenius immediately assuming the supreme authority in the Western parts of the empire, conducted himself in such a manner as might be expected from a usurper. When the Emperor Theodosius was made acquainted with these things, he was exceedingly distressed, because his defeat of Maximus had only prepared the way for fresh troubles. He accordingly assembled his military forces, and having proclaimed his son Honorius Augustus, on the 10th of January, in his own third consulate and which he bore with Abundantius, he again set out in great haste toward the Western parts, leaving both his sons invested with imperial authority at Constantinople. As he marched against Eugenius a very great number of the barbarians beyond the Danube volunteered their services, and followed him in this expedition. After a rapid march he arrived in the Gauls with a numerous army, where Eugenius awaited him, also at the head of an immense body of troops. Accordingly an engagement took place near the river Frigidus, which is [about thirty-six miles] distant [from Aquileia]. In that part of the battle where the Romans fought against their own countrymen, the conflict was doubtful: but where the barbarian auxiliaries of the Emperor Theodosius were engaged, the forces of Eugenius had greatly the advantage. When the emperor saw the barbarians perishing, he cast himself in great agony upon the ground, and invoked the help of God in this emergency: nor was his request unheeded; for Bacurius his principal officer, inspired with sudden and extraordinary ardor, rushed with his vanguard to the part where the barbarians were hardest pressed, broke through the ranks of the enemy, and put to flight those who a little before were themselves engaged in pursuit. Another marvelous circumstance also occurred. A violent wind suddenly arose, which retorted upon themselves the darts cast by the soldiers of Eugenius, and at the same time drove those hurled by the imperial forces with increased impetus against their adversaries. So prevalent was the emperor's prayer. The success of the struggle being in this way turned, the usurper threw himself at the emperor's feet, and begged that his life might be spared: but as he lay a prostrate suppliant at the feet [of the emperor] he was beheaded by the soldiers, on the sixth of September, in the third consulate of Arcadius, and the second of Honorius. Arbogastes, who had been the chief cause of so much mischief, having continued his flight for two days after the battle, and seeing no chance of escape, dispatched himself with his own sword.

5.66 Augustine of Hippo, *The City of God* 5.26 (ca. 413–426 C.E., concerning events in 392 C.E.)

. . . .Theodosius, having again received a response from the prophet [John of Egypt], and placing entire confidence in it, marched against the tyrant Eugenius, who had been unlawfully elected to succeed that emperor [Valentinian II], and defeated his very powerful army, more by prayer than by sword. . . . The sons of his own enemies, whose fathers had been slain not so much by his orders as by the vehemence of war, having fled for refuge to a church, though they were not yet Christians, he was anxious, taking advantage of the occasion, to bring over to Christianity, and treated them with Christian love. Nor did he deprive them of their property, but, besides allowing them to retain it, bestowed on them additional honors.

Theodosius died just three years after his victory over Eugenius. His reign had been one of great vigor and accomplishment, but he was the last emperor to rule over a unified Roman Empire. His successors proved unable either to build upon or preserve his military and political accomplishments and over the next two generations the Western half of the Roman Empire collapsed and the Eastern half was sorely pressed to survive. By the end of his reign, however, less than seventy-five years after the Council of Nicaea, Christianity had clearly replaced the thousand-year-old pagan religious tradition of the political and social elite of the Graeco-Roman world.[36] Although in 400 C.E. the majority of the Empire's population was probably still pagan—indeed, paganism lingered on into the eighth century among the rural populace[37]—the ultimate fate of paganism was sealed in the face of a unified political/economic/social elite willing and able to use moral persuasion, private violence, and state force to spread and enforce Christian belief.

5.67 Theodosian Code, 16.5.28 (September 3, 395 C.E.)

The Emperors Arcadius and Honorius to Aurelianus, Proconsul of Asia: Those persons who may be discovered to deviate, even in a minor point of doctrine, from the tenets and the path of the Catholic religion are included under the designation of heretics and must be subject to the sanctions which have been issued against them. . . .

36. Ramsay MacMullen, *Christianity & Paganism in the Fourth to Eighth Centuries* (New Haven: Yale University Press, 1997), 21–23.
37. Ibid., 25–29, 151–52, chapter 4 *passim*. It is commonly stated that the very word "pagan" derives from "*paganus*," or "rural person," and this was indeed the later meaning of the term. In its earliest form, however, "paganus" seems to have meant "civilian," as opposed to a "soldier of Christ." See, e.g., Robin Lane Fox, *Pagans and Christians* (New York: Alfred A. Knopf, 1986), 30–31 and Henry Chadwick, *The Early Church* (New York: Penguin Books, 1990), 152.

6 | THE SCOURING OF ALEXANDRIA
CA. 361–416 C.E.

The historian John Matthews has written that, "Imperial government in Ammianus [Marcellinus]'s time was unmatched in Greco-Roman history in its scale and complexity of organization, in its physical incidence upon society, the rhetorical extravagance with which it expressed itself, and the calculated violence with which it attempted to impose its will."[1] Nowhere is the "calculated violence" of the fourth-century C.E. Christian effort to suppress heretics, pagans, and Jews more fully documented for a single locale than for the city of Alexandria, Egypt. Over a period of approximately sixty years a succession of strong-willed Alexandrian bishops, with the support of the Christian emperors, strove vigorously to establish, even at the cost of many lives, the dominance of the Christian church in the political and religious life of Alexandria. The measures these bishops took and the price they were willing to exact of others to reach this goal speak eloquently of the ways in which the Christian church changed in the process of its rise to dominance in the Mediterranean world.

During the mid-fourth century C.E., the sons of Constantine issued a number of edicts directing that Roman civil officials take action against pagans and the pagan places of worship. The following are typical of these edicts.

> 6.1 Theodosian Code, 16.10.4 (December 1 of 346, 354 or 356 C.E.)
> Emperors Constantius and Constans Augustus to Taurus, praetorian prefect: It is Our pleasure that the temples shall be immediately closed in all places and cities, and access to them forbidden, so as to deny to all abandoned men the opportunity to commit sin. It is also Our will that all men shall abstain from sacrifices. But if perchance any man should perpetrate any such criminality, he shall be struck down with avenging sword. We also decree that the property of a man executed thus shall be vindicated to the fisc. The governors of the provinces shall be similarly punished if they should neglect to avenge such crimes.
>
> 16.10.6 (February 20, 356 C.E.)
> Emperor Constantius and Julian Caesar: If any persons should be proved to devote their attention to sacrifices or to worship images, We command that they shall be subjected to capital punishment.

---

1. John Matthews, *The Roman Empire of Ammianus* (Baltimore: John Hopkins University Press, 1990), 256.

Paganism was still the majority religion of the Roman Empire's peoples during the mid-fourth century C.E., and edicts of this nature were often simply ignored by the local officials and populaces in a display of passive resistance. The Christian emperors responded to such resistance by reiterating the edicts in ever harsher language with ever severer penalties. The people of Alexandria, Egypt, however, were well known in the ancient world for their volatility and propensity to riot, not for passive resistance, and during the attempted restoration of paganism by the emperor Julian (361–363 C.E.) mob violence broke out against the city's Christian leadership in 361 C.E.

6.2 Ammianus Marcellinus, *History* 22.11.3 (ca. 390 C.E.)

Now, however, they [the people of Alexandria] turned their rage upon their bishop George, a human snake who had often made them suffer from his poisonous fangs. George was born, they say in a fuller's shop in the Cilician town of Epiphania, and rose in the world to be the instrument of many people's ruin. Finally, against his own interest as well as the state's, he was consecrated bishop of Alexandria, a city given to frequent spontaneous and unmotivated outbreaks of violence. George himself acted as a powerful irritant to the savage temper of the populace by proceeding to denounce a number of people to Constantius, who was always ready to listen, on the ground that they had disobeyed his commands. In doing this he forgot the faith which he professed, which preaches only justice and mercy, and descended to the abominable trade of an informer. Among the other pieces of malicious information which he fed to Constantius, he was said to have told him that all the buildings on the soil of the said city which had been erected by its founder Alexander at great public expense ought in consequence to be a source of profit to the treasury. All these mischievous deeds were crowned by another, which in short time brought him to utter destruction. On his way back from the emperor's court, attended as usual by a large crowd, he looked in passing at the fine temple of the city's protecting deity [Serapis[2]] and remarked, "How long shall this sepulchre stand?" Many of his hearers were thunderstruck by these words, and, fearing that he would attempt to destroy the temple, devoted all their energies to plotting his downfall. Suddenly there arrived the glad tidings that Artemius [the former commander of the Roman army in Egypt] was no more. The whole population went wild with joy at this unexpected piece of good news. They fell upon George, howling and yelling, beat him about, trampled on him, and finally spread-eagled him and finished him off. Dracontius, the superintendent of the mint, and a certain Diodorus, who was thought to be in league with him, had ropes tied

---

2. The Serapeum of Alexandria honored the god Serapis and was probably the most renowned of all pagan religious sites in the Roman Empire at this time.

to their legs and were killed at the same time. The former had over-turned an altar recently set up in the mint which he controlled, and the latter, while directing the building of a church, had taken the liberty of cropping the curls of some boys, because he thought that long hair was a feature of the worship of the heathen. Not content with this, the brutal mob loaded the mutilated bodies on camels and took them to the beach, where they burned them and threw their ashes into the sea, for fear that the remains might be collected and have a church built over them. This had happened in other cases, when men prosecuted for their religion endured torture until they met a glorious death with their faith unspotted, and are now called martyrs. The wretched victims of these cruel sufferings might have been saved by the help of their fellow Christians had not the whole population been inflamed by universal hatred of George.

When news of this outrage reached the emperor [Julian] his anger was roused and he was on the point of exacting the supreme penalty from the authors of this abominable crime, but he was pacified by those nearest to him, who urged him to be lenient. So he issued a proclamation in which he expressed his horror in sharp terms, and threatened extreme measures if any similar breach of law and order were committed in the future.

6.3 Socrates, *Ecclesiastical History* 3.2–3 (ca. 440 C.E., concerning events ca. 362 C.E.)

[2] It is now proper to mention what took place in the churches under the same [Emperor Julian]. A great disturbance occurred at Alexandria in consequence of the following circumstance. There was a place in that city which had long been abandoned to neglect and filth, wherein the pagans had formerly celebrated their mysteries, and sacrificed human beings to Mithra. This being empty and otherwise useless, Constantius had granted to the church of the Alexandrians; and George wishing to erect a church on the site of it, gave directions that the place should be cleansed. In the process of clearing it, an adytum [sanctuary] of vast depth was discovered which unveiled the nature of their heathenish rites: for there were found there the skulls of many persons of all ages, who were said to have been immolated for the purpose of divination by the inspection of entrails, when the pagans performed these and such like magic arts whereby they enchanted the souls of men. The Christians on discovering these abominations in the adytum of the Mithreum, went forth eagerly to expose them to the view and execration of all; and therefore carried the skulls throughout the city, in a kind of triumphal procession, for the inspection of the people. When the pagans of Alexandria beheld this, unable to bear the insulting character of the act, they became so

exasperated, that they assailed the Christians with whatever weapon chanced to come to hand, in their fury destroying numbers of them in a variety of ways: some they killed with the sword, others with clubs and stones; some they strangled with ropes, others they cruci- fied, purposely inflicting this last kind of death in contempt of the cross of Christ: most of them they wounded; and as it generally hap- pens in such a case, neither friends nor relatives were spared, but friends, brothers, parents, and children imbrued their hands in each other's blood. Wherefore the Christians ceased from cleansing the Mithreum: the pagans meanwhile having dragged George out of the church, fastened him to a camel, and when they had torn him to pieces, they burnt him together with the camel.

[3] The emperor [Julian] being highly indignant at the assassination of George, wrote to the citizens of Alexandria, rebuking their violence in the strongest terms. A report was circulated that those who detested him because of Athanasius, perpetrated this outrage upon George: but as for me I think it is undoubtedly true that such as cher- ish hostile feelings against particular individuals are often found identified with popular commotions; yet the emperor's letter evi- dently attaches the blame to the populace, rather than to any among the Christians. George, however, was at that time, and had for some time previously been, exceedingly obnoxious to all classes, which is sufficient to account for the burning indignation of the multitude against him. That the emperor charges the people with the crime may be seen from his letter. . . .

By fortunate circumstance, the letter of Julian to the populace of Alexandria has survived. Julian's letter makes it clear that while Julian was sympathetic toward the pagan resentment of the Christian bishop, he would not tolerate private violence against Christians.

6.4 Julian the Apostate, *Epistle 21* (January, 362 C.E.)

The Emperor Julian Caesar, most Mighty Augustus, to the People of Alexandria. If you do not revere the memory of Alexander, your founder, and yet more than him the great god, the most holy Serapis, how is it that you took no thought at least for the welfare of your community, for humanity, for decency? Furthermore, I will add that you took no thought for me either, though all the gods, and, above all, the great Serapis, judged it right that I should rule over the world. The proper course was for you to reserve for me the decision con- cerning the offenders. But perhaps your anger and rage led you astray, since it often "turns reason out of doors and then does terri- ble things"; for after you had restrained your original impulse, you later introduced lawlessness to mar the wise resolutions which you had at the first adopted, and were not ashamed, as a community, to

commit the same rash acts as those for which you rightly detested
your adversaries. For tell me, in the name of Serapis, what were the
crimes for which you were incensed against George? You will doubt-
less answer: He exasperated against you Constantius of blessed
memory; then he brought an army into the holy city, and the general
in command of Egypt seized the most sacred shrine of the god and
stripped it of its statues and offerings and of all the ornaments in the
temples. And when you were justly provoked and tried to succor the
god, or rather the treasures of the god, Artemius dared to send his
soldiers against you, unjustly, illegally and impiously, perhaps
because he was more afraid of George than of Constantius; for the
former was keeping a close watch on him to prevent his behaving to
you too moderately and constitutionally, but not to prevent his acting far more like a tyrant. Accordingly you will say it was because you
were angered for these reasons against George, the enemy of the
gods, that you once more desecrated the holy city when you might
have subjected him to the votes of the judges. For in that case the
affair would not have resulted in murder and lawlessness but in a
lawsuit in due form, which would have kept you wholly free from
guilt, while it would have punished that impious man for his inexpi-
able crimes, and would have checked all others who neglect the gods,
and who moreover lightly esteem cities like yours and flourishing
communities, since they think that cruel behavior toward these is a
perquisite of their own power.

Now compare this letter of mine with the one that I wrote to you
a short time ago, and mark the difference well. What words of praise
for you did I write then! But now, by the gods, though I wish to praise
you, I cannot, because you have broken the law. Your citizens dare to
tear a human being in pieces as dogs tear a wolf, and then are not
ashamed to lift to the gods those hands still dripping with blood!
But, you will say, George deserved to be treated in this fashion.
Granted, and I might even admit that he deserved even worse and
more cruel treatment. Yes, you will say, and on your account. To this
I too agree; but if you say by your hands, I no longer agree. For you
have laws which ought by all means to be honored and cherished by
you all, individually. Sometimes, no doubt, it happens that certain
persons break one or other of these laws; but nevertheless the state as
a whole ought to be well governed and you ought to obey the laws,
not transgress those that from the beginning were wisely established.
It is a fortunate thing for you, men of Alexandria, that this trans-
gression of yours occurred in my reign, since by reason of my reverence for the god and out of regard for my uncle and namesake, who
governed the whole of Egypt and your city also, I preserve for you the
affection of a brother. For power that would be respected and a really

strict and unswerving government would never overlook an outrageous action of a people, but would rather purge it away by bitter medicine, like a serious disease. But, for the reasons I have just mentioned, I administer to you the very mildest remedy, namely admonition and arguments, by which I am very sure that you will be the more convinced if you really are, as I am told, originally Greeks, and even to this day there remains in your dispositions and habits a notable and honorable impress of that illustrious descent. Let this be publicly proclaimed to my citizens of Alexandria.

Julian's attempted revitalization of pagan worship was short-lived and ended with his death in 363 C.E. Julian was succeeded by a series of Christian emperors who again sought to repress paganism and spread the Christian faith among the peoples of the Roman Empire. Warfare against the Visigoths and other barbarian invaders preoccupied these Christian emperors during much of the 370s and 380s C.E., but by 391 C.E. there was a period of relative calm that allowed the emperor Theodosius I to turn his attention to the suppression of pagan worship. One of his edicts against paganism was addressed directly to the imperial officials in Egypt.

6.5 Theodosian Code 16.10.11 (June 16, 391 C.E.)
The Emperors Gratian, Valentinian and Theodosius Augustus to Evargrius, Augustal Prefect, and Romanus, Count of Egypt: No person shall be granted the right to perform sacrifices; no person shall go around the temples; no person shall revere the shrines. All persons shall recognize that they are excluded from profane entrance into temples by the opposition of Our law, so that if any person should attempt to do anything with reference to the gods or the sacred rites, contrary to Our prohibition, he shall learn that he will not be exempted from punishment by any special grants of imperial favor. If any judge also, during the time of his administration, should rely on the privilege of his power, and as a sacrilegious violator of the law, should enter polluted places, he shall be forced to pay into Our treasury fifteen pounds of gold, and his office staff a like sum, unless they opposed him with their combined strength.

The bishop of Alexandria at the time of this edict was Theophilus (bishop, 385–412 C.E.). In response to the edict's clear imperial support for the suppression of paganism, Theophilus sought and received from Theodosius permission to move against Alexandria's pagan temples of worship. The following passage describes Theophilus's seizure of the Serapeum in approximately 392 C.E.

6.6 Socrates, *Ecclesiastical History* 5.16 (written ca. 440 C.E.)
At the solicitation of Theophilus bishop of Alexandria, the emperor issued an order at this time for the demolition of the heathen temples in that city, commanding also that it should be put in execution

under the direction of Theophilus. Seizing this opportunity, Theophilus exerted himself to the utmost to expose the pagan mysteries to contempt. And to begin with, he caused the Mithreum to be cleaned out, and exhibited to public view the tokens of its bloody mysteries. Then he destroyed the Serapeum, and the bloody rights of the Mithraeum he publicly caricatured; the Serapeum also he showed full of extravagant superstitions, and he had the phalli of Priapus carried through the midst of the forum. The pagans of Alexandria, and especially the professors of philosophy, were unable to repress their rage at this exposure, and exceeded in revengeful ferocity their outrages on a former occasion, for with one accord, at a preconcerted signal, they rushed impetuously upon the Christians, and murdered every one they could lay hands on. The Christians also made an attempt to resist the assailants, and so the mischief was the more augmented. This desperate affray was prolonged until satiety of bloodshed put an end to it. Then it was discovered that very few of the heathens had been killed, but a great number of Christians; while the number of wounded on each side was almost innumerable. Fear then possessed the pagans on account of what was done, as they considered the emperor's displeasure. For having done what seemed good in their own eyes, and by their bloodshed having quenched their courage, some fled in one direction, some in another, and many quitting Alexandria, dispersed themselves in various cities. . . .

The next passage is an alternative account of these same events by another fifth-century Christian historian, Sozomen.

6.7 Sozomen, *Ecclesiastical History* 7.15 (after 440 C.E.)
    . . . . About this period, [Theophilus] the bishop of Alexandria, to whom the temple of Dionysus had, at his own request, been granted by the emperor, converted the edifice into a church. The statues were removed, the adyta were exposed; and, in order to cast contumely on the pagan mysteries, he made a procession for the display of these objects; the phalli, and whatever other object had been concealed in the adyta which really was, or seemed to be, ridiculous, he made a public exhibition of. The pagans, amazed at so unexpected an exposure, could not suffer it in silence, but conspired together to attack the Christians. They killed many of the Christians, wounded others, and seized the Serapion, a temple which was conspicuous for beauty and vastness and which was seated on an eminence. This they converted into a temporary citadel; and hither they conveyed many of the Christians, put them to the torture, and compelled them to offer sacrifice. Those who refused compliance were crucified, had both legs broken, or were put to death in some cruel manner. When the sedition had prevailed for some time, the rulers came and urged the

people to remember the laws, to lay down their arms, and to give up the Serapion. There came then Romanus, the general of the military legions in Egypt; and Evagrius was the prefect of Alexandria. As their efforts, however, to reduce the people to submission were utterly in vain, they made known what had transpired to the emperor. Those who had shut themselves up in the Serapion prepared a more spirited resistance, from fear of the punishment that they knew would await their audacious proceedings, and they were further instigated to revolt by the inflammatory discourses of a man named Olympius, attired in the garments of a philosopher, who told them that they ought to die rather than neglect the gods of their fathers. Perceiving that they were greatly dispirited by the destruction of the idolatrous statues, he assured them that such a circumstance did not warrant their renouncing their religion; for that the statues were composed of corruptible materials, and were mere pictures, and therefore would disappear; whereas, the powers which had dwelt within them, had flown to heaven. By such representations as these, he retained the multitude with him in the Serapion.

When the emperor [Theodosius I] was informed of these occurrences, he declared that the Christians who had been slain were blessed, inasmuch as they had been admitted to the honor of martyrdom, and had suffered in defense of the faith. He offered free pardon to those who had slain them, hoping that by this act of clemency they would be the more readily induced to embrace Christianity; and he commanded the demolition of the temples in Alexandria which had been the cause of the popular sedition. It is said that, when this imperial edict was read in public, the Christians uttered loud shouts of joy, because the emperor laid the odium of what had occurred upon the pagans. The people who were guarding the Serapion were so terrified at hearing these shouts, that they took to flight, and the Christians immediately obtained possession of the spot, which they have retained ever since. I have been informed that, on the night preceding this occurrence, Olympius heard the voice of one singing hallelujah in the Serapion. The doors were shut and everything was still; and as he could see no one, but could only hear the voice of the singer, he at once understood what the sign signified; and unknown to any one he quitted the Serapion and embarked for Italy. It is said that when the temple was being demolished, some stones were found, on which were hieroglyphic characters in the form of a cross, which on being submitted to the inspection of the learned, were interpreted as signifying the life to come. These characters led to the conversion of several of the pagans, as did likewise other inscriptions found in the same place, and which contained predictions of the destruction of the temple. It was thus that the Serapion was taken, and, a little while after, converted into a church; it received the name of the Emperor Arcadius. . . .

The two accounts by the fifth-century Christian historians Socrates and Sozomen provide an interesting example of the ways in which different versions of the "politically correct" story allow us to reconstruct a more probable account of what actually happened. During the course of the Christian action against the pagan temples of Alexandria, pagans gathered to defend the Serapeum against the Christian mobs and serious fighting broke out between the two groups. After the initial conflict, the two sides settled in to await the response of an appeal to the emperor, which because of the distances involved would have required at least a month or two, even if the message were sent by ship. Because Theodosius offered pardon to the pagans involved in the fighting, he likely was aware that the Christians instigated the violence, but nonetheless he granted possession of the temple to the Christians. The result was the scattering of a significant portion of Alexandria's pagan community and Bishop Theophilus obtained Alexandria's greatest structure for his use as a Christian church.[3]

For a generation afterwards, there was no further conflict in Alexandria of the magnitude surrounding the Christian seizure of the Serapeum, but the pagan and Jewish population continued to resist the efforts of Theophilus to strengthen the church's position in Alexandria. The political balance between the competing factions was ultimately broken by the vigorous efforts of Theophilus's successor as bishop, Cyril (bishop from 412–444 C.E.).

6.8 Socrates, *Ecclesiastical History* 7.7 (ca. 440 C.E.)

Shortly afterwards Theophilus bishop of Alexandria, having fallen into a lethargic state, died on the fifteenth of October, in the ninth consulate of Honorius, and the fifth of Theodosius [412 C.E.]. . . . Whereupon on the third day after the death of Theophilus, Cyril came into possession of the episcopate, with greater power than Theophilus had ever exercised. For from that time the bishopric of Alexandria went beyond the limits of its sacerdotal functions, and assumed the administration of secular matters.

Cyril first focused his efforts against the Christian heretics in the city, but he soon turned his attention toward the non-Christian population. Alexandria was a long-established center of Judaism and pagan philosophy, and the resistance of these groups to Cyril's plans for Christian dominance in the city ultimately culminated in an outbreak of violence in about 415 C.E. The resulting riots led to the destruction of Alexandria's Jewish quarter and the attempted assassination of the city's Roman governor by Christian monks.

---

3. Other sources confirm Sozomen's statement that the Serapeum was converted to a church, and Socrates's reference to the destruction of the Serapeum is thought to refer to the inner-most sanctum and not to the temple as a whole.

6.9 Socrates, *Ecclesiastical History* 7.13–14 (written ca. 440 C.E.).

[13] About this same time [ca. 415 C.E.] it happened that the Jewish inhabitants were driven out of Alexandria by Cyril the bishop on the following account. The Alexandrian public is more delighted with tumult than any other people: and if at any time it should find a pretext, breaks forth into the most intolerable excesses; for it never ceases from its turbulence without bloodshed. It happened on the present occasion that a disturbance arose among the populace, not from a cause of any serious importance, but out of an evil that has become very popular in almost all cities, a fondness for dancing exhibitions. In consequence of the Jews being disengaged from business on the Sabbath, and spending their time, not in hearing the Law, but in theatrical amusements, dancers usually collect great crowds on that day, and disorder is almost invariably produced. And although this was in some degree controlled by the governor of Alexandria, nevertheless the Jews continued opposing these measures. And although they are always hostile toward the Christians they were roused to still greater opposition against them on account of the dancers. When therefore Orestes the prefect was publishing an edict—for so they are accustomed to call public notices—in the theater for the regulation of the shows, some of the bishop Cyril's party were present to learn the nature of the orders about to be issued. There was among them a certain Hierax, a teacher of the rudimental branches of literature, and one who was a very enthusiastic listener of the bishop Cyril's sermons, and made himself conspicuous by his forwardness in applauding. When the Jews observed this person in the theater, they immediately cried out that he had come there for no other purpose than to excite sedition among the people. Now Orestes had long regarded with jealousy the growing power of the bishops, because they encroached on the jurisdiction of the authorities appointed by the emperor, especially as Cyril wished to set spies over his proceedings; he therefore ordered Hierax to be seized, and publicly subjected him to the torture in the theater. Cyril, on being informed of this, sent for the principal Jews, and threatened them with the utmost severities unless they desisted from their molestation of the Christians. The Jewish populace on hearing these menaces, instead of suppressing their violence, only became more furious, and were led to form conspiracies for the destruction of the Christians; one of these was of so desperate a character as to cause their entire expulsion from Alexandria; this I shall now describe. Having agreed that each one of them should wear a ring on his finger made of the bark of a palm branch, for the sake of mutual recognition, they determined to make a nightly attack on the Christians. They therefore sent

persons into the streets to raise an outcry that the church named
after Alexander was on fire. Thus many Christians on hearing this ran
out, some from one direction and some from another, in great anxiety to save their church. The Jews immediately fell upon and slew
them; readily distinguishing each other by their rings. At daybreak the
authors of this atrocity could not be concealed: and Cyril, accompanied by an immense crowd of people, going to their synagogues—for
so they call their house of prayer—took them away from them, and
drove the Jews out of the city, permitting the multitude to plunder
their goods. Thus the Jews who had inhabited the city from the time
of Alexander the Macedonian were expelled from it, stripped of all
they possessed, and dispersed some in one direction and some in
another. One of them, a physician named Adamantius, fled to Atticus
bishop of Constantinople, and professing Christianity, some time
afterwards returned to Alexandria and fixed his residence there. But
Orestes the governor of Alexandria was filled with great indignation
at these transactions and was excessively grieved that a city of such
magnitude should have been suddenly bereft of so large a portion of
its population; he therefore at once communicated the whole affair
to the emperor. Cyril also wrote to him, describing the outrageous
conduct of the Jews; and in the meanwhile sent persons to Orestes
who should mediate concerning a reconciliation: for this the people
had urged him to do. And when Orestes refused to listen to friendly
advances, Cyril extended toward him the book of gospels, believing
that respect for religion would induce him to lay aside his resentment. When, however, even this had no pacific effect on the prefect,
but he persisted in implacable hostility against the bishop, the following event afterwards occurred.

[14] Some of the monks inhabiting the mountains of Nitria, of a very
fiery disposition, whom Theophilus had some time before unjustly
armed against Dioscorus [bishop of Hermopolis] and his brethren,
being again transported with an ardent zeal, resolved to fight in
behalf of Cyril. About five hundred of them therefore quitting their
monasteries, came into the city; and meeting the prefect in his chariot, they called him a pagan idolater, and applied to him many other
abusive epithets. He supposing this to be a snare laid for him by Cyril,
exclaimed that he was a Christian, and had been baptized by Atticus,
the bishop at Constantinople. As they gave but little heed to his protes-
tations, and a certain one of them named Ammonius threw a stone at
Orestes which struck him on the head, and covered him with the
blood that flowed from the wound, all the guards with a few excep-
tions fled, plunging into the crowd, some in one direction and some
in another, fearing to be stoned to death. Meanwhile the populace of

Alexandria ran to the rescue of the governor, and put the rest of the monks to flight; but having secured Ammonius they delivered him up to the prefect. He immediately put him publicly to the torture, which was inflicted with such severity that he died under the effects of it; and not long after he gave an account to the emperors of what had happened. Cyril also on the other hand forwarded his statement of the matter to the emperor; and causing the body of Ammonius to be deposited in a certain church, he gave him the new appellation of Thaumasius ["wonderful"], ordering him to be enrolled among the martyrs, and eulogizing his magnanimity in church as that of one who had fallen in a conflict in defense of piety. But the more sober minded, although Christian, did not accept Cyril's prejudiced estimate of him; for they well knew that he had suffered the punishment due to his rashness, and that he had not lost his life under torture because he would not deny Christ. And Cyril himself being conscious of this suffered the recollection of the circumstance to be gradually obliterated by silence. But the animosity between Cyril and Orestes did not by any means subside at this point, but was kindled afresh by an occurrence similar to the preceding.

Socrates's account is clearly a one-sided Christian apologetic for the events surrounding the destruction of the Jewish quarter. Note, for example, that the Roman governor Orestes is called "jealous" because he objected to Bishop Cyril's encroachments on the governor's authority and efforts to plant spies in the governor's private council. Further, the governor's refusal to overlook the destruction of the Jewish quarter simply because Bishop Cyril "extended toward him a book of gospels" is characterized as "implacable hostility." It is also difficult to believe that it was an organized Jewish population who planned and carried out a night attack on the Christian population (depending on finger rings for identification of friend and foe in the night!) when at dawn it was a Christian mob léd by Bishop Cyril who swept through the Jewish quarter, destroying the synagogues and looting the residences.

While the last sentence of Socrates's account indicates that there was another incident between Cyril and Orestes soon after the destruction of the Jewish quarter, at this point Orestes disappears from the extant historical record. Because the "occurrence" to which Socrates referred was the murder of the eminent pagan philosopher and city leader Hypatia by a Christian mob under church leadership in circumstances suspiciously similar to the attempt on Orestes's life, historians believe that Orestes either died or fled Alexandria for a safer locale.[4] The following text describes the circumstances of Hypatia's murder in March of 415 C.E.

---

4. See, for example, Maria Dzielska, *Hypatia of Alexandria*, trans. F. Lyra (Cambridge: Harvard University Press, 1995), 104.

6.10 Socrates, *Ecclesiastical History* 7.15 (ca. 440 C.E.)

[15] There was a woman at Alexandria named Hypatia, daughter of the philosopher Theon, who made such attainments in literature and science, as to far surpass all the philosophers of her own time. Having succeeded to the school of Plato and Plotinus, she explained the principles of philosophy to her listeners, many of whom came from a distance to receive her instructions. On account of the self-possession and ease of manner which she acquired in consequence of the cultivation of her mind, she not infrequently appeared in public in the presence of the magistrates. Neither did she feel abashed in coming to an assembly of men. For all men on account of her extraordinary dignity and virtue admired her the more. Yet even she fell a victim to the political jealousy which at that time prevailed. For as she had frequent interviews with Orestes, it was calumniously reported among the Christian populace, that it was she who prevented Orestes from being reconciled to the bishop. Some of them, therefore, hurried away by a fierce and bigoted zeal, whose ringleader was a reader named Peter, waylaid her returning home, and dragging her from her carriage, they took her to the church called Caesareum, where they completely stripped her, and then murdered her with [pieces of roof] tiles.[5] After tearing her body in pieces, they took her mangled limbs to a place called Cinaron, and there burnt them. This affair brought not the least opprobrium, not only upon Cyril, but also upon the whole Alexandrian Church. And surely nothing can be farther from the spirit of Christianity than the allowance of such massacres, fights and transactions of that sort. This happened in the month of March during Lent, in the fourth year of Cyril's episcopate, under the tenth consulate of Honorius, and the sixth of Theodosius.

In addition to being the head of the pagan school of philosophy in Alexandria, Hypatia was a leading member of the city council of Alexandria. Her political influence with the Christian Roman governor Orestes was apparently seen by Bishop Cyril as an affront to his dignity and that of the church, and Cyril was widely thought at the time to have ordered her murder. Although there are modern historians who believe that Cyril (today Saint Cyril) was not involved in Hypatia's murder, the majority view holds Cyril guilty of at least inspiring the murder, if not actually ordering it. That is due to the similarity of the circumstances of Hypatia's murder to the attempted assassination of Orestes (intercepted in a public street by a waiting mob), the fact that Hypatia was taken to the grounds of a church before her gruesome murder (which

5. The Greek "ostrakois aneilon" can be read as either "clay roof tiles" or "oyster shells." Because the church at Caesareum was near the sea, some historians prefer to translate the phrase as "oyster shells."

undoubtedly was intended to be an example to others), and the fact that the church lector led the mob.[6]

The Alexandrian city council, apparently outraged by the Christian violence against the Jews, the Roman governor Orestes, and the city councilor Hypatia, seems to have protested to the Christian emperors.

6.11 Theodosian Code 16.2.42 (September 29, 416 C.E.)

The Emperors Honorius and Theodosius to Monaxius, Praetorian Prefect: Whereas, among other useless claims of the Alexandrian delegation, this request also was written in their decrees, that the Most Reverend bishop [Cyril] should not allow certain persons [not[7]] to depart from the City of Alexandria, and this claim was inserted in the petition of the delegation because of the terror of those who are called attendants of the sick (parabalani), it is the pleasure of Our Clemency that clerics shall have nothing to do with public affairs and with matters pertaining to the municipal council.

We further direct that the number of those who are called attendants of the sick shall not be more than five hundred. Moreover, the wealthy and those who would purchase this office shall not be appointed, but the poor from the guilds, in proportion to the population of Alexandria, after their names have been submitted, of course, to the Respectable Augustal Prefect and through him referred to Your Magnificence.

We do not grant to the aforesaid attendants of the sick liberty to attend any public spectacle whatever or to enter the meeting place of a municipal council or a courtroom, unless, perchance, they should appeal to a judge, separately in connection with their own cases and interests, when they sue someone in litigation or when they are themselves sued by another, or when they are official advocates appointed in a cause common to the entire group. The condition shall be observed that if anyone of them should violate the foregoing provisions, he shall be removed from the registers of the attendants of the sick and shall be subjected to due punishment, and he shall never return to the same office.

---

6. *The Oxford Classical Dictionary* (Oxford: Oxford University Press, 1996), reflects this split among historians: the entry for "Hypatia," at 736 by G. J. Toomer states that Hypatia was murdered "at the instigation" of Cyril, whereas the entry for "Cyril of Alexandria," at 422–23 by Henry Chadwick and John F. Matthews states that the monks "probably had not his approval." The recent study by Maria Dzielska, *Hypatia of Alexandria* (Cambridge: Harvard University Press, 1995), 97 holds that even if Cyril were not "legally responsible" for planning Hypatia's murder, he "must be held to account for a great deal" as chief instigator of the campaign against her.

7. The translator of this passage believes that "not" was inadvertently omitted here; the original text reads "should not allow certain persons to depart from the City." Clyde Pharr, *The Theodosian Code* (Princeton: Princeton University Press, 1952), 448 at note 123.

> Furthermore, We grant to the Respectable Augustal Prefect the
> power to appoint successors to the deceased attendants of the sick,
> under the condition that is designated above.

The *parabalani* who served the bishop of Alexandria were not unique; the
bishop of Antioch controlled the *lecticarri* (pallbearers for the urban poor) and
the bishop of Rome controlled the *fossores* (grave diggers who excavated the
tombs of the catacombs). Because ancient cities typically had neither police
forces nor militias, the control of large groups of often-times armed monks
and/or workers gave the bishops a decisive edge in the "battle for the streets"
and a useful weapon for intimidating municipal councils, imperial officials,
and even other bishops. From the complaint of the Alexandrian municipal
council and its "terror" of the *parabalani*, it appears that Cyril's *parabalani*
played a significant role in the events of 415–416 C.E.

The scouring of the non-Christian population of Alexandria during the late
fourth and early fifth centuries C.E. demonstrated the extent to which
Christianity had overturned the normalities of the Graeco-Roman world since
the time of Pliny and Trajan. Where once Roman officials punished the mere
profession of the Christian faith as a capital offense, now Christian bishops
expected that Roman officials would aid and abet the Christian intimidation,
pillaging, and murder of pagans, heretics, and Jews. In a real sense, the events
in Alexandria also demonstrated the extent of the changes in the way
Christianity's role in the ancient world was understood by the church and its
bishops, as one can readily imagine the puzzled reaction of bishops like
Theophilus or Cyril if anyone had asserted that their actions were not in accordance with the teachings of Jesus. Even at that time, however, a few Christians
recognized what had been gained and lost during Christianity's rise to dominance in the Roman world.

> 6.12 St. Jerome, *Life of Malchus the Captive Monk* 1 (ca. 390 C.E.)
> When Christ's church came into the hands of Christian princes, its
> power and wealth increased but its virtues were diminished.

APPENDIX A: ROME'S ACCOMMODATION WITH JUDAISM

Jews were a significant minority group within the Roman Empire, constituting perhaps as much as 10 percent of the population in the early first century C.E. However, Jews were never widely popular among the peoples of the Roman Empire and the ancient sources are filled with accounts of bloody conflicts between Jews and their neighbors. The pagan animosity toward Jews was the result of both the Jewish rejection of the pagan gods and the fact that Jews who maintained their religious traditions necessarily held themselves apart from much of the everyday social and civic life of the larger pagan communities. The Jewish refusal to participate in the many festivals and celebrations that revolved around or touched upon worship of the pagan gods, the maintenance of separate food customs, the practice of circumcision (which the Greeks saw as mutilation of the body), and the reluctance to intermarry with non-Jews all served to make Jews distinctive from the surrounding peoples and disliked for this separateness.

When the Romans expanded their political control into the eastern Mediterranean in the first century B.C.E., two of the more significant problems they faced were how to integrate Jewish Palestine into the Roman provincial system and how to prevent outbreaks of mob violence between Jews and non-Jews in the other Eastern provinces. This task was not made easier by the fact that the Romans themselves did not generally like or respect the Jews as a people, although the religion itself was tolerated by Romans because of its antiquity.

A–1 Cicero, *Pro Flacco* 69 (59 B.C.E.)
Even when Jerusalem was still standing and the Jews at peace with us, the demands of their religion were incompatible with the majesty of our Empire, the dignity of our name, and the institutions of our ancestors; and now that the Jewish nation has shown by armed rebellion what are its feelings for our rule, they are even more so; how dear it was to the immortal gods has been shown by the fact that it has been conquered, farmed out to the tax-collectors and enslaved.

A–2 Tacitus, *The Histories* 5.4–5 (ca. 106 C.E.)
[4] To establish his influence over this people for all time, Moses introduced new religious practices, quite opposed to those of all other religions. The Jews regard as profane all that we hold sacred; on the

243

other hand, they permit all that we abhor. They dedicated, in a shrine, a statue of that creature whose guidance enabled them to put an end to their wandering and thirst, sacrificing a ram, apparently in derision of Ammon. They likewise offer the ox, because the Egyptians worship Apis. They abstain from pork, in recollection of a plague, for the scab to which this animal is subject once afflicted them. By frequent fasts even now they bear witness to the long hunger with which they were once distressed, and the unleavened Jewish bread is still employed in memory of the haste with which they seized the grain. They say that they first chose to rest on the seventh day because that day ended their toils; but after a time they were led by the charms of indolence to give over the seventh year as well to inactivity. Others say that this is done in honor of Saturn, whether it be that the primitive elements of their religion were given by the Idaeans, who, according to tradition, were expelled with Saturn and became the founders of the Jewish race, or is due to the fact that, of the seven planets that rule the fortunes of mankind, Saturn moves in the highest orbit and has the greatest potency; and that many of the heavenly bodies traverse their paths and courses in multiples of seven.

[5] Whatever their origin, these rites are maintained by their antiquity: the other customs of the Jews are base and abominable, and owe their persistence to their depravity. For the worst rascals among other peoples, renouncing their ancestral religions, always kept sending tribute and contributions to Jerusalem, thereby increasing the wealth of the Jews; again, the Jews were extremely loyal toward one another, and always ready to show compassion, but toward every other people they feel only hate and enmity. They sit apart at meals, and they sleep apart, and although as a race, they are prone to lust, they abstain from intercourse with foreign women; yet among themselves nothing is unlawful. They adopted circumcision to distinguish themselves from other peoples by this difference. Those who converted to their ways follow the same practice, and the earliest lesson they receive is to despise the gods, to disown their country, and to regard their parents, children, and brothers as of little account. However, they take thought to increase their numbers; for they regard it as a crime to kill any late-born child, and they believe that the souls of those who are killed in battle or by the executioner are immortal; hence comes their passion for begetting children, and their scorn of death. They bury the body rather than burn it, thus following the Egyptians' custom; they likewise bestow the same care on the dead, and hold the same belief about the world below; but their ideas of heavenly things are quite the opposite. The Egyptians worship many animals and monstrous images; the Jews conceive of one god only, and that with the mind alone: they regard as impious those who

make from perishable materials representations of gods in man's image; that supreme and eternal being is to them incapable of representation and without end. Therefore they set up no statues in their cities, still less in their temples; this flattery is not paid to their kings, nor this honor given to the Caesars.

A–3 Juvenal, *Satires* 14.96–125 (ca. 127 C.E.)
Some who have had a father who reveres the Sabbath, worship nothing but the clouds, and the divinity of the heavens, and see no difference between eating swine's flesh, from which their father abstained, and that of man; and in time they take to circumcision. Having been wont to flout the laws of Rome, they learn and practice and revere the Jewish law, and all that Moses handed down in his secret tome, forbidding to point out the way to any not worshiping the same rites, and conducting none but the circumcised to the desired fountain. For all which the father was to blame, who gave up every seventh day to idleness, keeping it apart from all the concerns of life. All vices but one the young imitate of their own free will; avarice alone is enjoined on them against the grain. For that vice has a deceptive appearance and semblance of virtue, being gloomy of mien, severe in face and garb. The miser is openly commended for his thrift, being deemed a saving man, who will be a surer guardian of his own wealth than if it were watched by the dragon of the Hesperides or of Colchis. Moreover, such a one is thought to be skilled in the art of money-getting; for it is under workers such as he that fortunes grow. And they grow bigger by every kind of means: the anvil is ever working, and the forge never ceases to glow. Thus the father deems the miser to be fortunate; and when he worships wealth, believing that no poor man was ever happy, he urges his sons to follow in the same path and to attach themselves to the same school. There are certain rudiments in vice; and in these he imbues them from the beginning, compelling them to study its pettiest meannesses; after a while he instructs them in the unappeasable lust of money-getting. . . .

A–4 Ammianus Marcellinus, *History* 22.4.5 (ca. 390 C.E.)
Marcus [Aurelius, emperor 161–180 C.E.]'s complaint was uttered when he was passing through Palestine on his way to Egypt and was frequently disgusted by the disturbances made by the filthy Jews. What he is supposed to have said was, "Oh for the Marcomanni, the Quadi, and the Sarmatians![1] At last I have found a people more unruly than they!"

---

1. These are the three barbarian tribes along the Danube River frontier that Marcus Aurelius fought for so many years of his reign.

JUDAISM UNDER THE PAGAN EMPERORS

The Romans always demanded absolute obedience from their subject peoples. Because the Romans, like most other ancient peoples, did not recognize any meaningful distinction between religion and politics, the obedience of subject peoples required a recognition of both the political supremacy of the Romans and of the Roman gods that had granted such supremacy. In practice, most subject peoples acknowledged Roman supremacy by sacrificing to both the Roman gods and the Roman emperor, who was perceived as being at least the symbolic embodiment of the Roman people and state, and in much of the Eastern Empire as being a divine being himself. The Romans were well aware, however, that Jews were notorious for the violent defiance of any demand that they acknowledge the supremacy of any god other than their own. Thus the problem for the Romans was to find a compromise which publicly acknowledged Roman supremacy without offending Jewish sensibilities.

The Roman answer to the problem began with the decision to exempt Jews from civic duties that conflicted with Jewish religious belief. Thus, Jews were exempted from military service in the Roman legions and from civil service or judicial matters that might require an oath to a pagan god or service on the Jewish Sabbath.

> A–5 A Decree Of Caesar Augustus To The Jews as reported by Josephus in *Jewish Antiquities* 16.162–165
>
>> Caesar Augustus, Pontifex Maximus with tribunician power, decrees as follows: Since the Jewish nation has been found well disposed to the Roman people not only at the present time but also in time past, and especially in the time of my father the emperor Caesar,[2] as has their high priest Hyrcanus, it has been decided by me and my council under oath, with the consent of the Roman people, that the Jews may follow their own customs in accordance with the laws of their fathers, just as they followed them in the time of Hyrcanus, high priest of the Most High God, and that their sacred monies shall be inviolable and may be sent up to Jerusalem and delivered to the treasurers in Jerusalem, and that they need not give bond [to appear in court] on the Sabbath or on the day of preparation for it [Sabbath eve] after the ninth hour. And if anyone is caught stealing their sacred books or their sacred monies from a synagogue or an ark [of the Law], he shall be regarded as sacrilegious, and his property shall be confiscated to the public treasury of the Romans. . . .

This grant of rights followed upon earlier rights granted the Jews by Julius

---

2. Because Pompey had violated the sanctity of the Temple by entering the Holy of Holies, Jews generally supported Julius Caesar against Pompey during the Roman civil war of the 40s B.C.E.

Caesar and was itself followed by grants from Tiberius (14–37 C.E.), Claudius (41–54 C.E.), and other emperors. Despite these accommodations, however, Rome was not willing to excuse the Jews from all demonstrations of loyalty and so the very real issue remained as to the manner in which Jews would acknowledge Rome's supremacy. The solution that evolved is described by two Jewish writers, who unfortunately disagreed on the details.

A–6 Josephus, *Against Apion* 2.75–77 (late 90s C.E.)

On the other hand, our legislator, not in order to put, as it were, a prophetic veto upon honors paid to the Roman authority, but out of contempt for a practice profitable to neither God nor man, forbade the making of images, alike of any living creature, and much more of God, who, as is shown later on, is not a creature. He did not, however, forbid the payment of homage of another sort, secondary to that paid to God, to worthy men; such honors we do confer upon the emperors and the people of Rome. For them we offer perpetual sacrifices; and not only do we perform these ceremonies daily, at the expense of the whole Jewish community, but, while we offer no other victims in our corporate capacity, even for the [imperial] family, we jointly accord to the emperors alone this signal honor which we pay to no other individual.

A–7 Philo, *Embassy to Gaius* 157 (c.38 C.E.)

Another example no less cogent than this shows very clearly the will of Augustus. He gave orders for a continuation of whole burnt offerings every day to the Most High God to be charged to his own purse. These are carried out to this day. Two lambs and a bull are the victims with which he added luster to the altar, knowing well that there is no image there openly or secretly set up.

As part of the accommodation reached with Rome, the Jews offered sacrifice twice daily on behalf of the then reigning Roman emperor to the Jewish God in the Temple at Jerusalem. That the sacrifices on behalf of the Roman emperor to the Jewish God were the minimum acceptable act of allegiance was made clear at the start of the First Jewish War (66–70 C.E.), when the Jewish decision in 66 C.E. to stop such sacrifices was seen by both sides as constituting a declaration of war against Rome.

A–8 Josephus, *Jewish War* 2.409–410 (Aramaic c.73–75, Greek ca. 75–76 C.E.)

Eleazar, son of Ananias the high priest, a very daring youth, then holding the position of captain [of the Temple], persuaded those who officiated in the Temple services to accept no gift or sacrifice from a foreigner. This action laid the foundation of the war with the Romans; for the sacrifices offered on behalf of that nation and the emperor were in consequence rejected.

After the Romans captured Jerusalem in 70 C.E., the Temple was destroyed
and Jews were forbidden to live in the city. Thus, after the First Jewish War there
was no physical means to reinstate the Temple sacrifices on behalf of the
Roman emperors and so the Romans had to institute a new policy with respect
to the Jews.

> A–9 Josephus, *Jewish War* 7.216–218 (Aramaic ca. 73–75 C.E., Greek ca.
> 75–76 C.E.)
>
> About the same time, Caesar [Vespasian, emperor 69–79 C.E.] sent
> instructions to Bassus and Laberius Maximus, the procurator, to
> farm out all Jewish territory.... On all Jews wheresoever resident, he
> imposed a tax of two drachmas, to be paid annually in the Capitol as
> formerly contributed by them to the Temple at Jerusalem.

> A–10 Cassius Dio, *Roman History* 65.7.2 (ca. 214–226 C.E.)
>
> Thus was Jerusalem destroyed on the very day of Saturn, the day which
> even now the Jews reverence most. From that time forth it was ordered
> that the Jews who continued to observe their ancestral customs should
> pay an annual tribute of two denarii to Jupiter Capitolinus.

The annual tax instituted by the emperor Vespasian was used for the upkeep
of the Temple of Capitoline Jupiter in the city of Rome. A tax to support the
worship of a pagan god obviously served as a constant reminder to the Jews of
the penalties to be paid for rebelling against Rome in the First Jewish War. In
return for payment of this tax, however, a Jew was also allowed to enroll in a
synagogue, which by law carried an exemption from all obligations of Roman
religious observance, including the worship of the emperor. It is not clear how
firmly this tax was enforced in its early years, but less than a generation after its
establishment the emperor Domitian (81–96 C.E.) enforced stringent measures
for its collection. Domitian's measures must have created some further turmoil
because his successor Nerva issued imperial sestercii bearing the legend "the
elimination of the wrongful accusations concerning the fiscus Judaicus."[3]

Jewish hatred for Roman rule did not disappear during the decades after the
First Jewish War and a massive (but poorly documented) Jewish revolt broke
out in several Eastern provinces during the period 115–117 C.E., while the
emperor Trajan was campaigning against Persia. During the revolt, the Jewish
and Greek populations conducted ruthless massacres of one another as one
side or the other temporarily gained the upper hand, but the conflict turned
inevitably against the Jews when units of the Roman army were recalled from
the Persian campaign. As punishment for the revolt, Trajan's successor, Hadrian
(117–138 C.E.) banned circumcision and built a Roman city on the ruins of
Jerusalem, using discharged Roman veterans as the first colonists. As further
insult, Hadrian changed the city's name from Jerusalem to Aelia Capitolina.

---

3. *"Fisci Iudaici Calumnia Sublata."*

Within a few years of Hadrian's measures a third Jewish revolt, known as the Second Jewish War (ca. 132–136 C.E.), broke out in Judaea with the goals of defeating the Romans and reinstituting Temple worship in Jerusalem. It is not certain whether the Jews were able to capture Jerusalem during the war, and the rebellion was brutally suppressed by the Romans, who renamed the province "Syria-Palestina" and forbade Jews to enter the site of Jerusalem or its environs.[4] The Jewish religion itself was not prescribed, however.

The Second Jewish War was the last significant armed revolt by Jews against the Roman occupation of Palestine. Thereafter, Jewish religious aspirations turned inward during the late second and third centuries C.E. There was some further accommodation by Rome, as Hadrian's successor Antoninus Pius revoked Hadrian's edict forbidding the circumcision of Jewish males, but the prohibition remained in effect with respect to converts to Judaism. The result was that Jews were permitted to resume a custom that helped define their community but were restricted with respect to converting Gentiles to the faith.

THE STATUS OF JEWS UNDER THE CHRISTIAN EMPERORS

The position of Jews under Roman rule underwent significant change during the fourth century C.E., when Christians came to control the political apparatus of the state. Many Christians held a great animosity toward Jews and Judaism because of the belief that the Jews were responsible for the death of Jesus, but there was also a sense of frustration and anger over the fact that Jews, who were the living witnesses to God's first Covenant with mankind and who accepted the Old Testament as the holy word of God, adamantly denied that Jesus was the Messiah prophesied by the writings of the Old Testament. These attitudes shaped the actions of the Christian emperors, who were confronted with the difficult task of ending Jewish proselytism and bringing Jews into the Christian faith while acknowledging that Jews were people of the Covenant and the ancestors of the Christian faith. The Christian emperors' uncertainty as to the best way to carry out this policy is reflected in the twists and turns found in the imperial edicts of the period, beginning with edicts issued by Constantine in an effort to stop Jewish proselytism of Christians and subject Jews to the financial obligations required of the decurion order.

> A–11 Theodosian Code 16.8.1 (October 18, 315 C.E.)
> Emperor Constantine Augustus to Evagrius: It is Our will that Jews and their elders and patriarchs shall be informed that if, after the issuance of this law, any of them should dare to attempt to assail with stones or with any other kind of madness-a thing which we have learned is now being done—any person who has fled their feral sect and has resorted to the worship of God, such assailant shall be immediately delivered to the flames and burned, with all his accomplices.

---

4. Eusebius, *Ecclesiastical History* 4.6 and Tertullian, *An Answer to the Jews* 13.

Moreover, if any person from the people should betake himself to their nefarious sect and should join their assemblies, he shall sustain with them the deserved punishment.

16.8.3 (December 11, 321 C.E.)

Emperor Constantine to the Decurions of Koln: By a general law We permit all municipal senates to nominate Jews to the municipal council. But in order that something of the former rule may be left them as a solace,* We extend to two or three persons from each group the perpetual privilege of not being disturbed by any nomination.

> *"Solace" because such nominations made the Jews liable
> for the financial responsibilities of municipal counselors.

16.8.4 (December 31, 331 C.E.)

Emperor Constantine to the Priests, Rulers of the Synagogues, Fathers of the Synagogues, and all others who serve in the said place: We command that priests, rulers of the synagogues, fathers of the synagogues and all others who serve the synagogues shall be free from every compulsory public service of a corporal nature.

16.8.5 (October 22, 335 C.E.)

Emperor Constantine to Felix, Praetorian Prefect: Jews shall not be permitted to disturb any man who has been converted from Judaism to Christianity or to assail him with any outrage. Such contumely shall be punished according to the nature of the act which has been committed.

After Constantine's reign, the legal and social position of Jews continued to deteriorate as the emperors took steps to see that Jews were cut off from sources of converts and both the emperors and the Christian bishops undertook harsh measures to suppress the Jewish faith.

A–12 Theodosian Code, 16.8.7 (July 3, 352 C.E.)

Emperor Constantius Augustus and Julian Caesar to Thalassaius, Praetorian Prefect: In accordance with the venerable law which has been established, We command that if any person should be converted from Christianity to Judaism and should join their sacrilegious gatherings, when the accusation has been proved, his property shall be vindicated to the ownership of the fisc.

The extent of the open animosity toward Judaism by the last decade of the fourth century C.E., is reflected in a letter of Bishop Ambrose to the emperor Thedodosius.

A–13 Ambrose, *Epistle 40* (390 C.E.)

To the most august Emperor Theodosius, Ambrose, bishop
It was reported by a count of military affairs in the East that a synagogue [at Callinicum] was burned, and this at the instigation of a

bishop. You gave the order for those who were involved to be punished and the synagogue rebuilt at the bishop's expense. . . .

Let no one call the bishop to task for performing his duty: that is the request I make of your Clemency. And although I have not read that the edict was revoked, let us consider it revoked. What if other more timid persons should, through fear of death, offer to repair the synagogue at their expense, or the count, finding this previously determined, should order it to be rebuilt from the funds of Christians? Will you, O Emperor, have the count an apostate, and entrust to him the insignia of victory, or give the labrum, which is sanctified by Christ's name, to one who will rebuild a synagogue which knows not Christ? Order the labarum carried into the synagogue and. . . see if they do not resist.

Shall a place be provided out of the spoils of the Church for the disbelief of the Jews, and shall this patrimony, given to Christians by the favor of Christ, be transferred to the treasuries of unbelievers? We read that, of old, temples were revered for idols from the plunder taken from the Cimbrians and from the spoils of the enemy. The Jews will write on the front of their synagogue the inscription: "The Temple of Impiety, erected from the spoils of the Christians". . . .

There is really no adequate cause for all this commotion, people being punished so severely for the burning of a building, and much less so, since a synagogue has been burned, an abode of unbelief, a house of impiety, a shelter of madness under the damnation of God Himself. . . . God forbids us to make intercession for those that you think should be vindicated. . . .

Furthermore, into what false charges will they not break forth, when they even falsely accused Christ with their false witnesses. Into what false charges will men not break forth when they were liars even in matters divine? . . .

While Ambrose might argue that a bishop's "duty" encompassed the burning of Jewish synagogues, there were limits to the sort of unsanctioned, private violence that the emperors were willing to tolerate in society at large, particularly when the violence was directed at a not insignificant minority population concentrated in the provinces along the eastern frontier with Persia. By the end of the fourth century, the Christian emperors were willing to grant some minimal legal protections for Jews, although the emperors still sought to prohibit conversion to Judaism and any action that might lead to an increase in the numbers or prestige of Jews.

A–14 Theodosian Code 16.8.9
(September 29, 393 C.E.)
Emperors Theodosius, Arcadius, and Honorius Augustuses to Addeus, Count and Master of both branches of the Military Service

in the Orient: It is sufficiently established that the sect of Jews is forbidden by no law. Hence We are gravely disturbed that their assemblies have been forbidden in certain places. Your Sublime Magnitude will, therefore, after receiving this order, restrain with proper severity the excesses of those persons who, in the name of the Christian religion, presume to commit certain unlawful acts and attempt to destroy and to despoil the synagogues.

16.8.12 (June 17, 397 C.E.)

Emperors Arcadius and Honorius Augustuses to Anatolius, Praetorian Prefect of Illyricum: Your Exalted Authority shall direct that the governors shall be notified, so that they shall know on receipt of this notice that all the insults of persons attacking the Jews shall be averted and that their synagogues shall remain in their accustomed quietude.

16.8.14 (April 11, 399 C.E.)

Emperors Arcadius and Honorius Augustuses to Messala, Praetorian Prefect: It is characteristic of an unworthy superstition that the rulers of the synagogues or the priests of the Jews or those whom they themselves call apostles, who are dispatched by the patriarch at a certain time to collect gold and silver, should bring back to the patriarch the sums which has been exacted and collected from each of the synagogues. Wherefore, everything that We are confident has been collected, taking into the consideration the period of time, shall be faithfully dispatched to Our treasury. For the future, moreover, We decree that nothing shall be sent to the aforesaid patriarch. The people of the Jews shall know, therefore, that we have abolished the practice of such depredation. But if any persons should be sent on such a mission of collection by that despoiler of the Jews, they shall brought before the Judges, in order that a sentence may be pronounced against them as violators of Our laws.

16.8.17 (July 25, 404 C.E.)

The same Augustuses [Arcadius and Honorius] to Hadrianus, Praetorian Prefect: We had formerly ordered that what was customarily contributed by the Jews of these regions to the patriarchs should not be contributed. Now We revoke the first order in accordance with the statutory privileges granted by the early Emperors, and it is Our will that all men shall know that the privilege of sending this contribution is hereby conceded to the Jews by Our Clemency.

16.8.21 (August 6, 412 C.E.)

Emperors Honorius and Theodosius Augustuses to Philippus, Praetorian Prefect of Illyricum: No person shall be trampled upon when he is innocent, on the ground that he is a Jew, nor shall any religion cause any person to be exposed to contumely. Their synagogues and habitations shall not be burned indiscriminately, nor shall they be injured wrongfully without any reason, since, moreover, even if any person should be implicated in crimes, nevertheless, the vigor of Our courts and the protection of public law appear to have been established in Our midst for the purpose that no person should have the power to seek his own revenge.

But just as it is Our will that the foregoing provision shall be made for the persons of the Jews, so We decree that the Jews also shall be admonished that they perchance shall not become insolent and, elated by their own security, commit any rash act in disrespect of the Christian religion.

16.8.24 (March 10, 418 C.E.)

Emperors Honorius and Theodosius Augustuses to Palladius, Praetorian Prefect: Those persons who live in the Jewish superstition shall hereafter be barred from seeking entrance to the imperial service. To those persons who have undertaken the oaths of enlistment in the imperial service as members of the secret service or as palatines We grant the right to complete such service and to end it within the statutory periods, ignoring the fact rather than favoring it. But the regulations which We wish to be relaxed for a few at present shall not be permitted in the future.

We decree, however, that those persons who are bound to the perversity of this race and who are proved to have sought armed imperial service shall unquestionably be released from their cincture of office, and they shall not be protected by the patronage of their earlier merits.

Indeed, We do not prohibit Jews instructed in liberal studies from acting as advocates, and We permit them to enjoy the honor of compulsory public services of decurions, which they obtain through the prerogative of birth and splendor of family.

Since the aforesaid privileges ought to suffice them, they must not consider the prohibition of imperial service as a mark of infamy.

By the early fifth century a new policy of accommodation had taken shape. Jews would be given some minimal protection against private violence, but proselytizing by Jews was strictly forbidden in the hope and expectation that Judaism would slowly die away in a Christian empire. In light of this expectation, the Jews would be protected in their existing properties and houses of worship, but they would not be allowed to build new places of worship.

A–15 Theodosian Code

16.8.25 (February 15, 423 C.E.)

Emperors Honorius and Theodosius Augustuses to Asclepiodotus, Praetorian Prefect: It is Our pleasure that in the future no synagogue at all of the Jews shall be indiscriminately taken away from them or

consumed by fire, and that if, after the issuance of this law, there are
any synagogues which by recent attempt have thus been seized, vindicated to the churches, or at any rate consecrated to the venerable
mysteries, the Jews shall be granted compensation therefore, places
in which they can construct synagogues commensurate, of course,
with those that were taken away. . . . In the future no [new] synagogues shall be constructed, and the old ones shall remain in their
present condition.

16.16.27 (June 8, 423 C.E.)

The same Augustuses to Asclepiodotus, Praetorian Prefect: Our
recent decrees about Jews and their synagogues shall remain in full
force, namely, that they shall not be permitted to construct new synagogues and that they shall not fear that the old ones will be taken
from them. But they shall know that all other prohibitions must be
observed in the future, as the general rule of the constitution recently
issued declares.

APPENDIX B: ACCUSATIONS OF CHRISTIAN IMMORALITY

T he extant texts from the first four centuries C.E. contain a number of accusations that Christians engaged in the most immoral sorts of behavior,
including cannibalism and unrestrained sexual conduct, "Thystean feasts and
Oedipean intercourse," as it was commonly phrased. (See, e.g., Selections 3.21
and 3.29.) Many modern writers dismiss these accusations without any real
investigation, often asserting instead that such charges were mere slanders
brought against a group that challenged the norms of the larger society. In fact,
however, the early Christians themselves wrote rather frequently about the
problem of sexual misconduct among members of the faith. Some of these
Christian accounts can even be found in the works of the New Testament itself.

B–1 Jude 3–8, 12 (ca. 80 C.E.)
  [3] Beloved, being very eager to write to you of our common salvation,
  I found it necessary to write appealing to you to contend for the faith
  which was once for all delivered to the saints. For admission has been
  secretly gained by some who long ago were designated for this condemnation, ungodly persons who pervert the grace of our God into
  licentiousness and deny our only Master and Lord, Jesus Christ. Now
  I desire to remind you, though you were once for all fully informed,
  that He who saved a people out of the land of Egypt, afterward
  destroyed those who did not believe. And the angels that did not keep
  their own position but left their proper dwellings have been kept by
  Him in eternal chains in the nether gloom until the judgment of the
  great day; just as Sodom and Gomorrah and the surrounding cities,
  which likewise acted immorally and indulged in unnatural lust, serve
  as an example by undergoing a punishment of eternal fire. Yet in like
  manner these men in their dreamings defile the flesh, reject authority and revile the glorious ones. . . .
  [12] These [men] are blemishes on your love feast, as they boldly carouse
  together, looking after themselves. . . .

B–2 2 Peter 2:1–2, 13–14, 18–22 (late first or early second century C.E.)
  [1] But false prophets also arose among the people, just as there will be
  false teachers among you, who will secretly bring in destructive heresies, even denying the Master who bought them, bringing upon

themselves swift destruction. And many will follow their licentiousness, and because of them the way of the truth will be reviled. . . .
[13] They count it pleasure to revel in the daytime. They are blots and
blemishes, reveling in their dissipation, carousing with you. They
have eyes full of adultery, insatiable for sin. They entice unsteady
souls. They have hearts trained in Greed. Accursed children! . . .
[18] For, uttering loud boasts of folly, they entice with licentious pas-
sions of the flesh men who have barely escaped from those who live
in error. They promise them freedom, but they themselves are slaves
of corruption; for whatever overcomes a man, to that he is enslaved.
For if, after they have escaped the defilements of the world through
the knowledge of our Lord and Savior Jesus Christ, they are again
entangled in them and overpowered, the last state has become worse
for them than the first. For it would have been better for them never
to have known the way of righteousness than after knowing it to turn
back from the holy communion delivered to them.

The epistles of Jude and 2 Peter indicate that at least some members of the
first-century churches were teaching that the traditional prohibitions against
"free sex" and adultery were no longer applicable to the "new race" of Christians.
The abandonment of the old rules and ways of life were certainly a part of early
Christian teachings, and the problem of sexual promiscuity may be related to
Paul's teaching that people were saved by faith and not by deeds. As R. Joseph
Hoffman has written, "Without the constraint of the Jewish law, such
Christians reasoned, anything is possible; and as the Christian is saved by grace
and faith rather than by works, anything is permissible. Given the terms of his
message to the churches, Paul cannot really dispute such logic. But its practical
consequences in primarily gentile congregations must have been obvious to
him from an early date."[1]

The problems caused by such reasoning were still known to the Christian
communities of the early second century C.E.

B–3 Ignatius
Epistle to the Ephesians 16 (ca. 108 C.E.)
    Make no mistake, my brothers; adulterers will not inherit God's
    Kingdom. If, then, those who act carnally suffer death, how much
    more shall those who by wicked teaching corrupt God's faith for
    which Jesus Christ was crucified. Such a vile creature will go to the
    unquenchable fire along with anyone who listens to him.
Epistle to the Philadelphians 2 (ca. 108 C.E.)
    Since you are children of the light of truth, flee from schism and false
    doctrine. Where the Shepherd is, there follow like sheep. For there

---

1. R. Joseph Hoffman, *Celsus on the True Doctrine* (New York: Oxford University Press,
1987), 14.

are many specious wolves who, by means of wicked pleasures, capture those who run God's race. In the face of unity, however, they will
not have a chance. Keep away from bad pasturage.

Accusations of Christian immorality were apparently so common and
wide-spread by the mid-second century C.E. that Justin Martyr felt compelled
to address the accusations in his First Apology. However, instead of claiming
that such accusations were completely unfounded, Justin attempted to defend
the faith by arguing that such accusations could be true only of "heretical"
Christians and not of the "orthodox" congregations.

B–4 Justin Martyr, *First Apology* 26–29 (ca. 155 C.E.)
   [26] Then we know of a certain Menander, who was also a Samaritan,
   from the village of Capparetaea, who had been a disciple of Simon's,
   and was also possessed by the demons. He deceived many at Antioch
   by magic arts, and even persuaded his followers that he would never
   die; there are still some who believe this [as they learned] from him.
   Then there is a certain Marcion of Pontus, who is still teaching his
   converts that there is another God greater than the Fashioner. By the
   help of the demons he has made many in every race of men to blaspheme and to deny God the Maker of the universe, professing that
   there is another who is greater and has done greater things than he.
   As we said, all who derive [their opinions] from these men are called
   Christians; just as men who do not share the same teachings with the
   philosophers still have in common with them the name of philosophy, thus brought into disrepute. Whether they commit the shameful deeds about which stories are told—the upsetting of the lamp,
   promiscuous intercourse, and meals of eating human flesh—we do
   not know; but we are sure that they are neither persecuted nor killed
   by you, on account of their teachings anyway. I have compiled and
   have on hand a treatise against all the heresies which have arisen,
   which I will give you if you would like to consult it. . . .
   [29] To show you that promiscuous intercourse is not among our mysteries, just recently one of us submitted a petition to the prefect Felix
   in Alexandria a petition, asking that a physician be allowed to make
   him an eunuch, for the physicians there said they were not allowed
   to do this without the permission of the prefect. When Felix would
   by no means agree to endorse [the petition], the young man
   remained single, satisfied with [the approval of] his own conscience
   and that of his fellow believers.

Justin's reference to "meals of human flesh" is one of the earliest express references to the accusation that Christians engaged in cannibalism as part of
church ritual, but the existence of such accusation is implied by Pliny the
Younger's letter of approximately 111 C.E. to the emperor Trajan, in which Pliny

wrote "After which it was their custom to separate, and then later reassemble to partake of food—but food of an ordinary and innocent kind." It is understandable that outsiders, upon hearing that Christians gathered regularly in secret services to participate in eating and drinking the body and blood of Christ, might believe that Christians engaged in cannibalism. What is perhaps more surprising is that these accusations spread steadily throughout the Roman Empire during the second century C.E., even though Roman society lacked essentially all means of mass communication. Ignatius and Pliny wrote their respective letters in Asia Minor in approximately 108–111 C.E., Justin Martyr wrote his *First Apology* in Rome about 155 C.E., and by the 160s and 170s C.E. accusations of cannibalism and incest are found in sources from Gaul, Greece, and North Africa. By the end of the second century, another Christian writer believed it necessary to confront these accusations.

> B–5 Tertullian, *Apology* 2.4–5; 7.1 (197 C.E.)
>
> [2.4-5] Yet, if you are trying any other criminal, it does not follow at once from his confessing to the name of murderer, or temple robber, or adulterer, or enemy of the state (to touch on our indictments!), that you are satisfied to pronounce sentence, unless you pursue all the consequent investigation, such as the character of the act, how often, where, how, when he did it, his accessories, his confederates. In our case nothing of the kind! Yet it ought just as much to be wrung out of us (whenever that false charge is made) how many murdered babies each of us has tasted, how many acts of incest he had done in the dark, what cooks were there—yes, and what dogs. Oh! The glory of that magistrate who had brought to light some Christian who had eaten up to date a hundred babies!
>
> [7.1] We are said to be the most criminal of men, on the score of our sacramental baby-killing and the baby eating that goes with it and the incest that follows the banquet, where the dogs are our pimps in the dark, forsooth, and make a sort of decency for guilty lusts by overturning the lamps.

With the exception of Pliny's letter, all of the above sources were written by Christians and there are in fact few pagan sources that make such accusations—perhaps only the passage by Apuleius in his *Metamorphosis* (Selection 3.15) during the period up to the mid-third century C.E. However, many historians believe that a dialogue written by the Christian M. Minucius Felix preserved the substance of arguments presented in a famous speech by the pagan M. Cornelius Fronto against Christianity. Fronto was a close friend of the emperor Marcus Aurelius (161–180 C.E.) and Fronto's political influence and prominence were such that his attack on Christianity may have encouraged the growth of anti-Christian feelings in the years leading up to the outbreak of the persecutions of the 170s C.E.

B–6 M. Minucius Felix, *Octavius* 8–9.1–13 (written ca. 230– 240 C.E.)

[8] Why is it not a thing to be lamented, that men (for you will bear with my making use pretty freely of the force of the plea that I have undertaken)—that men, I say, of a reprobate, unlawful, and desperate faction, should rage against the gods? Who, having gathered together from the lowest dregs the more unskilled, and women, credulous and, by the facility of their sex, yielding, establish a herd of a profane conspiracy, which is leagued together by nightly meetings, and solemn fasts, and inhuman meats—not by any sacred rite, but by that which requires expiation—a people skulking and shunning the light, silent in public, but garrulous in corners. They despise the temples as dead-houses, they reject the gods, they laugh at sacred things; wretched, they pity, if they are allowed, the priests; half naked themselves, they despise honors and purple robes. Oh, wondrous folly and incredible audacity! They despise present torments, although they fear those which are uncertain and future; and while they fear to die after death, they do not fear to die for the present: so does a deceitful hope soothe their fear with the solace of a revival.

[9] And now, as wickeder things advance more fruitfully, and abandoned manners creep on day by day, those abominable shrines of an impious assembly are maturing themselves throughout the whole world. Assuredly this confederacy ought to be rooted out and execrated. They know one another by secret marks and insignia, and they love one another almost before they know one another. Everywhere also there is mingled among them a certain religion of lust, and they call one another promiscuously brothers and sisters, that even a not unusual debauchery may by the intervention of that sacred name become incestuous: it is thus that their vain and senseless superstition glories in crimes. Nor, concerning these things, would intelligent report speak of things so great and various, and requiring to be prefaced by an apology, unless truth were at the bottom of it. I hear that they adore the head of an ass, that basest of creatures, consecrated by I know not what silly persuasion—a worthy and appropriate religion for such manners. Some say that they worship the genitals of their pontiff and priest, and adore the nature, as it were, of their common parent. I know not whether these things are false; certainly suspicion is applicable to secret and nocturnal rites; and he who explains their ceremonies by reference to a man punished by extreme suffering for his wickedness, and to the deadly wood of the cross, appropriates fitting altars for reprobate and wicked men, that they may worship what they deserve. Now the story about the initiation of young novices is as much to be detested as it is well known. An infant covered over with meal [flour], that it may deceive

the unwary, is placed before him who is to be stained with their rites; this infant is slain by the young pupil, who has been urged on as if to harmless blows on the surface of the meal, with dark and secret wounds. Thirstily—O horror!—they lick up its blood; eagerly they divided its limbs. By this victim they are pledged together; with their consciousness of wickedness they are covenanted to mutual silence. Such sacred rites as these are more foul than any sacrileges. And of their banqueting it is well known all men speak of it everywhere; even the speech of our Cirtensian [Marcus Cornelius Fronto] testifies to it. On a solemn day they assemble at the feast, with all their children, sisters, mothers, people of every sex and age. There, after much feasting, when the fellowship has grown warm, and the fervor of incestuous lust has grown hot with drunkenness, a dog that has been tied to the chandelier is provoked, by throwing a small piece of offal beyond the length of the line by which he is bound, to rush and spring; and thus the conscious light being overturned and extinguished in the shameless darkness, the connection of abominable lust involve them in the uncertainty of fate. Although not all in fact, yet in consciousness all are alike incestuous, since by the desire of all of them everything is sought for which can happen in the act of each individual.

These are harsh accusations, but they are clearly the same charges presented in the earlier Christian sources. However, many of the Christian accounts of sexual immorality and the like are found in the writings of "orthodox" Christians who were attacking other Christian sects as heretical and so it is difficult to separate truth from slander intended to discredit theological opponents. An example can be found in the writings of Clement, bishop of Alexandria.

B–7 Clement of Alexandria, *Miscellanies* 3.2.5, 10; 4.27 (ca. 200 C.E.)

3.2.5 But those who are descended from Carpocrates and Ephiphanes think it proper that wives be shared in common, from which emanates the most shameful acts against the name of Christ. . . .

2.10 These then constitute the doctrines of the excellent Carpocratians. These, they say, and some other imitators of similar evil, gather together for meals (I would not call the gatherings of these people an Agape), men and women at the same time. After sating themselves with the meal they bring forth desire, extinguishing the light that reveals the shame of their "righteous" fornication, and they have intercourse wherever they wish and with whomever they wish. Moreover, after they have practiced communion of that kind in their love feast, during the day they demand of whatever women they wish that they obey the law of Carpocrates—it would not be right to say the law of God. . . .

[4.27] There are some, moreover, who proclaim physical love a mystical communion. . . . Even the words of the Lord are falsified by these debauched communicants, the brothers of lust, a shame not only to philosophy but even to all life, who corrupt the truth or destroy it, as far as they are able. These most wretched men consecrate carnal and sexual communion, and they think that it will bring them to the kingdom of God.

Although Christians clearly were accusing one another of sexual immorality and cannibalism, by the mid-third century C.E. some orthodox Christians were beginning to argue that such stories were in fact attributable to the slanders of Jews.

B–8 Origen, *Against Celsus* 6.27 (240s C.E.)
He [Celsus] appears to me, indeed, to have acted like those Jews who, when Christianity began to be first preached, scattered abroad false reports of the Gospel, such as that "Christians offered up an infant in sacrifice, and partook of its flesh"; and again, "that the professors of Christianity wishing to do the work of darkness, used to extinguish the lights (in their meetings), and each one to have sexual intercourse with any woman he chanced to meet." These calumnies have long exercised, although unreasonably, an influence over the minds of very many, leading those who are aliens to the Gospel to believe that Christians are men of such a character, and even at the present day they mislead some, and prevent them from entering even into the simple intercourse of conversation with those who are Christians.

During the early fourth century C.E., the same charges were being repeated against the "heretical" Christians of the second and third centuries C.E.

B–9 Eusebius, *Ecclesiastical History* 4.7.9–13 (ca. 311–323 C.E.)
Irenaeus also writes that Carpocrates was a contemporary of these, the father of another heresy which was called that of the Gnostics. These did not, like Basilides, desire to transmit the magic of Simon secretly but openly, as though it was some great thing, speaking almost with awe of their magical ceremonies, of love charms, of the bringers of dreams and familiar spirits, and of other similar performances. In accordance with this they teach that those who purpose coming to initiation in their mysteries, or rather in their obscenities, must perform all the shocking deeds because in no other way can they escape the "rulers of the world," as they would say, except by fulfilling to all of them what was necessary through their mysteries. By using these ministers the demon who rejoices in evil accomplished the piteous enslavement to perdition of those who were thus deceived by them and brought much weight of discredit

upon the divine word among the unbelieving Gentiles, because the
report which started from them was scattered calumniously on the
whole race of Christians. It was especially in this way that it came to
pass that a blasphemous and wicked suspicion concerning us was
spread among the heathen of those days, to the effect that we practiced unspeakable incest with mothers and sisters and took part in
wicked food. Yet this did not long succeed, for the truth vindicated
itself and as time went on shone ever more brightly.

The extremes to which the conduct of certain Christian sects, or at least the
Christian accusations against other Christians, might go are best exemplified in
the work of the fourth-century Christian writer Epiphanius, the bishop of
Constantia in Cyprus. His account of the forms of worship of a Gnostic-
Christian sect known as the Phibionites has been described as one of the most
repulsive stories in all of ancient literature.[2]

B–10 Epiphanius, *Panarion* (*The Medicine Chest*, a/k/a *Refutation of All
the Heresies*) 26.4–6 (ca. 374 C.E.)

[4] I will now come to the place of depth of their deadly story (for they
have various false teachings about pleasure). First they have their
women in common. And if a stranger appears who is of the same
persuasion, they have a sign, men for women and women for men.
When they extend the hand for greeting at the bottom of the palm
they make a tickling touch and from this they ascertain whether the
person who appeared is of their faith. After they have recognized
each other, they go over at once to eating. They serve rich food, meat
and wine even if they are poor. When they thus ate together and so
to speak filled up their veins to an excess they turn to passion. The
man leaving his wife says to his own wife: Stand up and make love
with the brother [literally, "Perform the Agape with the brother"].
Then the unfortunates unite with each other, and as I am truly
ashamed to say the shameful things that are being done by them,
because according to the holy apostle the things that are happening
by them are shameful even to mention nevertheless, I will not be
ashamed to say those things which they are not ashamed to do, in
order that I may cause in every way a horror in those who hear about
their shameful practices. After they have had intercourse in the passion of fornication they raise their own blasphemy toward heaven. The
woman and the man take the fluid of the emission of the man into
their hands, they stand, turn toward heaven, their hands besmeared

---

2. Stephen Benko, *Pagan Rome and the Early Christians* (Bloomington: Indiana University
Press, 1984), 66.

with the uncleanness, and pray as people called "Stratiotikoi" and "Gnostikoi," bringing to the father who is the nature of all that which they have on their hands, and they say: "We offer to thee this gift, the body of Christ." And then they eat it, their own ugliness, and say: "This is the body of Christ and this is the Passover for the sake of which our bodies suffer and are forced to confess the suffering of Christ." They do the same with what is of the woman, when she has the flow of blood: collecting the monthly blood of impurity from her, they take it and consume it together in the same way. "This [they say] is the blood of Christ."

[5] So also when they read in the apocryphal books, "I saw a tree bearing twelve fruits a year and he said to me: this is the tree of life," they interpret it as referring to the monthly female flow. They have intercourse with each other but they teach that one may not beget children. The infamy is committed by them not for the sake of begetting children, but for the sake of pleasure, because the devil plays with them and mocks the image formed by God. They bring the pleasure to its end, but they take to themselves the sperm of their uncleanness, not for the purpose of begetting children, but to eat their shame themselves. And if someone from among them is detected to have let the natural emission of semen go in deeper and the woman becomes pregnant, then hear, what even worse they do; they pull out the embryo in the time when they can reach it with the hand. They take out this unborn child and in a mortar pound it with a pestle and into this mix honey and pepper and certain other spices and myrrh, in order that it may not nauseate them, and then they come together, all this company of swine and dogs, and each communicates with a finger from the bruised child. And after they have finished this cannibalism finally they pray to God, saying, "We did not let the Archon of lust play with us but collected the mistake of the brother." And this they consider to be the perfect Passah. Many other horrible things are done by them. For when they again get into this rage among themselves, they smear their hands with their own emission. They stretch them out and pray with the besmeared hands naked in the whole body that through this practice they may find with God free conversation. But they take care of their bodies day and night, women and men, with creams, washings and foods, and devote themselves to the bed and to wine. They curse the man who fasts because they say that one should not fast, for fasting is the work of the Archon who made this aion. Rather one should nourish himself in order that the bodies may be strong, so that they may give the fruit in its time.

[6] They use both the Old Testament and the New Testament, but reject the one who spoke in the Old Testament. . . .

As the historian Stephen Benko has noted,[3] these accusations against the Phibionites were so spectacular that Epiphanius felt obligated to lend some credence to his statements by admitting that in his youth he had been approached to join a Phibionite church and had only escaped by the power of God. It is therefore of interest that Ephiphanius claimed that the Phibionites were expelled from the orthodox Christian churches in Egypt only after he had exposed the sect,[4] as this indicates that such groups were able to participate in the orthodox communities until sometime in the mid-fourth century C.E.

As gruesome as Ephiphanius's account of Phibionite practices is, his description of their practices are consistent with what is known about the sect's doctrine. Phibionites apparently believed that the primordial unity of the universe had been disrupted by the creation of the world, with the result that every living thing had within it a portion of the Creator's power. Jesus' mission had been to restore this unity and the duty of every Christian was to help gather together the generative substances of life that contained this power. As a consequence, procreation was prohibited since this only divided further the Creator's power. On the basis of such doctrine, it is certainly possible to believe that Phibionites engaged in abortion and perhaps in the cannibalism of fetuses.

Epiphanius also wrote that the Phibionites were descended from an early Christian sect called the Nicolaitans, which according to Christian tradition was founded by Nicolaus, "a proselyte of Antioch" and one of the seven Hellenistic deacons of the first Christian congregation in Antioch.[5] While Epiphanius wrote his account during the late fourth century C.E., there are texts from the third century C.E. by other Gnostic sects strongly condemning the Phibionites.[6] Thus, the Phibionites can be traced back to at least the time of Minucius Felix and less than a century from the time of Justin Martyr and Marcus Cornelius Fronto. It may well be that the even earlier stories of cannibalism and sexual licentiousness can be traced to early forms of the Phibionites and other Gnostic sects.[7]

THE HOLY KISS

The specter of sexual misconduct was ever present even in the congregations of the orthodox churches and many a sermon was preached on the topic. One of the more curious issues that the orthodox congregations faced in this connection was the potential danger associated with the exchange of the sign of peace in a mixed sex congregation.

3. Stephen Benko, *Pagan Rome and the Early Christians* (Bloomington: Indiana University Press, 1984), 66–67. The following discussion is adapted from his book, 68–69.

4. *Panarion* 26.17.1.

5. *Panarion* 25.2.1; see Revelation 2:6, 15, and Acts 6:5. See also Eusebius's *Ecclesiastical History* 3.29.1–3.

6. Pistis Sophia, 147 and *The Second Book of Jeu*, 43.

7. See Stephen Benko, *Pagan Rome and the Early Christians* (Bloomington: Indiana University Press, 1984), 64–74 and the sources cited therein for a more detailed examination of the Phibionites.

B–11 Paul (ca. 63 or 64 C.E.) 1 *Thessalonians* 5:26[8]
"Greet all the Brethren with a holy kiss."

B–12 Athenagoras of Athens, *Plea on Behalf of the Christians* 32 (ca. 177 C.E.)
We feel it a matter of great importance that those, whom we thus
think of as brother and sister and so on, should keep their bodies
undefiled and uncorrupted. For the Scripture* says again, "If one
kisses a second time, because he found it enjoyable . . . [passage miss-
ing from manuscript]. . . . Thus the kiss, or rather the religious salu-
tation, should be very carefully guarded. For if it is defiled by the
slightest evil thought, it excludes us from eternal life."

This reference is to an unknown "Scripture."

B–13 Clement of Alexandria, *The Instructor* 3.11.81 (ca. 190–192 C.E.)
And if we are called to the Kingdom of God, let us walk worthy of the
kingdom, loving God and our neighbor. But love is not proved by a
kiss, but by kindly feeling. But there are those that do nothing but
make the churches resound with a kiss not having love itself within.
For this very thing, the shameless use of a kiss, which ought to be
mystic, occasions foul suspicions and evil reports. (The Apostle calls
the kiss holy.) When the Kingdom is worthily tested, we dispense the
affection of the soul by a chaste and closed mouth, by which chiefly
gentle manners. . . . "And this is the love of God," says John, "that we
keep the commandments," not that we stroke each other on the mouth.

B–14 John Chrysostom, *Homily on 2 Corinthians 13:10* 30.2 (ca. 400 C.E.)
What is "holy," not hollow, not treacherous, like the kiss which Judas
gave to Christ. For therefore is the kiss given, that it may be fuel unto
love, that it may kindle the disposition, that we may so love each
other, as brothers brothers, as children parents, as parents children;
yea, rather even far more. For those things are a disposition
implanted by nature, but these by spiritual grace. Thus our souls
bound unto each other. And therefore when we return after an
absence we kiss each other, our souls hastening unto mutual intercourse. For this is that member which most of all declares to us the
workings of the soul. But about this holy kiss somewhat else may yet
be said. To what effect? We are the temple of Christ; we kiss then the
porch and entrance of the temple when we kiss each other. See ye not
how many kiss even the porch of this temple, some stooping down,
others grasping it with their hand, and putting their hand to their
mouth. And through these gates and doors Christ both had entered
into us, and doth enter, whensoever we communicate. Ye who partake of the mysteries understand what I say. For it is in no common
manner that our lips are honored, when they receive the Lord's Body.
It is for this reason chiefly that we here kiss. Let them give ear who

---

8. See also 1 Corinthians 16:20, 2 Corinthians 13:12, and Romans 16:16.

speak filthy things, who utter railing, and let them shudder to think what that mouth is they dishonor; let those give ear who kiss obscenely. Hear what things God hath proclaimed by thy mouth, and keep it undefiled.

In response to these problems, many orthodox Christian congregations eventually switched to a kiss on the cheek or seated men and women in separate groups.

APPENDIX C: THE WORSHIP
OF THE ROMAN EMPEROR

D uring the period of the Roman Republic, Romans did not generally believe that a living person could be a god. However, during the last century B.C.E. the Republic's expanding empire came into contact with many peoples, such as the Egyptians, who did hold such beliefs. The growing acceptance of such beliefs within Roman society was evidenced by the fact that when Julius Caesar was assassinated in 44 B.C.E., many Romans were willing to believe that he had undergone apotheosis at death, being raised up as a god. The first emperor Augustus (27 B.C.E.–14 C.E.), while rejecting divine honors from Romans during his lifetime, deliberately encouraged the belief that he, too, would undergo such an apotheosis upon his death.[1] After Augustus's death, the Roman Senate did indeed proclaim that Augustus had become a god of the state, citing in support of this measure the testimony of a senator that at Augustus's funeral he had seen Augustus ascending into the heavens. With the example thus set, the subsequent Roman emperors and the senate generally followed a similar pattern during the rest of the first century C.E.: a living emperor was not a god, but once the emperor was safely dead the Roman Senate might vote to confer divinity on a "good" emperor.

While this accommodation satisfied Roman sensibilities, there still remained the issue of treating with the many peoples of Rome's Empire who, as the result of long-held traditions of worshiping their native rulers as gods, looked upon the Roman emperors as divine figures, too. In practice, the early Roman emperors generally tolerated such worship among the peoples of the Eastern provinces, but in the Western provinces the emperors encouraged instead the worship of Roma, the divine spirit of Rome. This dual policy was reflected in a speech in 25 C.E. by the second emperor, Tiberius (14–37 C.E.).

C–1 Tacitus, *Annals of Imperial Rome* 4.37–38 (ca. 115–120 C.E.)
> [37] About the same time, Further Spain sent a deputation to the senate, asking leave to follow the example of Asia by erecting a shrine to Tiberius and his mother. On this occasion, the Caesar, sturdily disdainful of compliments at any time, and now convinced that an

---

1. The evidence is summarized by John Ferguson in *The Religions of the Roman Empire* (Ithaca: Cornell University Press, 1970), 90–95.

answer was due to the gossip charging him with a declension into vanity, began his speech in the following vein: "I know, Conscript Fathers, that many deplored my want of consistency because, when a little while ago the cities of Asia made this identical request, I offered no opposition. I shall therefore state both the case for my previous silence and the rule I have settled upon for the future. Since the deified Augustus had not forbidden the construction of a temple at Pergamum to himself and the City of Rome, observing as I do his every action and word as law, I followed the precedent already sealed by his approval, with all the more readiness that with worship of myself was associated veneration of the senate. But, though once to have accepted may be pardonable, yet to be consecrated in the image of deity through all the provinces would be vanity and arrogance, and the honor paid to Augustus will soon be a mockery, if it is vulgarized by promiscuous experiments in flattery.

[38] As for myself, Conscript Fathers, that I am mortal, that my functions are the functions of men, and that I hold it enough if I fill the foremost place among them—this I call upon you to witness, and I desire those who shall follow us to bear it in mind. For they will do justice, and more, to my memory, if they pronounce me worthy of my ancestry, provident of your interests, firm in dangers, not fearful of offenses in the cause of the national welfare. These are my temples in your breasts, these my fairest and abiding effigies: for those that are reared of stone, should the judgement of the future turn to hatred, are scorned as sepulchers. And so my prayer to allies and citizens and to Heaven itself is this: to Heaven, that to the end of my life it may endow me with a quiet mind, gifted with understanding of law human and divine; and to my fellow men, that, whenever I shall depart, their praise and kindly thoughts may still attend my deeds and the memories attached to my name." And, in fact, from now onward, even in his private conversations, he persisted in a contemptuous rejection of these divine honors to himself: an attitude by some interpreted as modesty, by many as self-distrust, by a few as degeneracy of soul: "The best of men," they argued, "desired the greatest heights: so Hercules and Liber among the Greeks, and among ourselves Quirinus, had been added to the number of the gods. The better way had been that of Augustus—who hoped! To princes all other gratifications came instantly: for one they must toil and never know satiety—the favorable opinion of the future. For in the scorn of fame was implied the scorn of virtue!"

Most of the first-century emperors were content to wait for death to be recognized as divine. A down-to-earth emperor like Vespasian (69–79 C.E.) could even find humor in the thought of his prospective divinity.

C–2 Suetonius, *Life of Vespasian* 23 (ca. 122 C.E.)

He [Vespasian] did not cease his jokes even when in apprehension of death and in extreme danger... and as death drew near, he said, "Woe's me! Methinks I'm turning into a god!"

However, even during the first century C.E., emperors like Caligula (37–41 C.E.) and Domitian (81–96 C.E.) seem to have demanded recognition that each was indeed a living god on earth.

C–3 Suetonius, *Life of Caligula* 22.2–3 (written ca. 122 C.E.)

But on being reminded that he [Caligula] had risen above the elevation of both princes and kings, he began from that time on to lay claim to divine majesty; for after giving orders that such statues of the gods as were especially famous for their sanctity or their artistic merit, including that of Jupiter of Olympia, should be brought from Greece, in order to remove their heads and put his own in their place, he built out a part of the Palace as far as the Forum, and making the temple of Castor and Pollux its vestibule, he often took his place between the divine brethren, and exhibited himself there to be worshipped by those who presented themselves; and some hailed him as Jupiter Latiaris. He also set up a special temple to his own godhead, with priests and with victims of the choicest kind.

C–4 Suetonius, *Life of Domitian* 13–14 (ca. 122 C.E.)

[13] When he [Domitian] became emperor, he did not hesitate to boast in the Senate that he had conferred their power on both his father [Vespasian, Emperor 69–79 C.E.] and his brother [Titus, Emperor 79–81 C.E.], and that they had but returned him his own; nor on taking back his wife after their divorce, that he had "recalled her to his divine couch." He delighted to hear the people in the amphitheater shout on his feast day, "Good fortune attend our Lord and mistress".... With no less arrogance he began as follows in issuing a circular letter in the name of his procurators, "Our Master and our God [*Dominus et deus noster*] bids that this be done." And so the custom arose henceforth of addressing him in no other way even in writing or in conversation. . . .

[14] In this way he became an object of terror and hatred to all, but he was overthrown at last. . . .

While Caligula and Domitian were hated by the senatorial order for their pretensions and overbearing conduct, by the early second century C.E. the tendency to treat a living emperor as partaking of the divine was evident even in the conduct of an educated Roman administrator like Pliny the Younger. During his examination of Christians brought before him for trial (Selection 3.3), Pliny tested the accused by requiring that they offer sacrifice to statutes of both the gods and the emperor Trajan (98–117 C.E.). Although in his response to Pliny Trajan wrote that it was sufficient that homage be given just to the statutes of the gods, it is telling that statutes of both the Roman gods and Trajan were readily available for Pliny's use even in a quiet corner of the Empire like Bithynia-Pontus and that Pliny would require homage to the emperor as well as the gods.

The emperor's cult served as both a convenient expression of provincial loyalty to Rome and as a means of centering provincial loyalty to the Roman Empire around religious devotion to the emperor's own person, which strengthened the emperor's political power as a whole. It is therefore not surprising that most emperors encouraged the growth of such cult worship and that the cult of the emperor acquired increasing prominence during the second century C.E. Such religious devotion of course caused great difficulties for Christians. As early as the late first century C.E., Pergamon's great cult temple to Augustus so offended the Christian author of the Book of Revelation that Pergamon was described as the site of "Satan's throne" (Revelation 2:13). By the mid-second century C.E., Christians encountered increasing suspicion and distrust for their refusal to honor the emperors. The explanations offered for such refusal did not satisfy either the Romans or the provincials.

C–5 Tertullian, *Apology* 10.1, 29.4–5, 32.1–3 (197 C.E.)

> [10.1] "You do not," say you, "worship the gods; you do not offer sacrifice for the Emperors." It follows by parity of reasoning that we do not sacrifice for others because we do not sacrifice for ourselves—it follows from our not worshipping the gods. So, we are accused of sacrilege and treason at once. That is the chief of the case against us—the whole of it, in fact. . . .
>
> [29.4] So, after all, our crime against the majesty of the Emperors comes to this: that we do not subordinate them to their property; that we do not make a jest of our care for their safety, and do not think it really lies in hands soldered on with lead. But it is you who are the really religious people—you who seek Caesar's safety where it is not, who pray for it from those by whom it cannot be given, who pass by Him in whose power it is. Yes, and more than that, you wage war on those who know how to pray for it, and who can obtain it too, since they know how to pray for it.
>
> [32.3] There is another need, a greater one, for our praying for the Emperors, and for the whole estate of the empire and the interests of Rome. We know that the great force which threatens the whole world, the end of the age itself with its menace of hideous suffering, is delayed by the respite which the Roman empire means for us. We do not wish to experience all that; and when we pray for its postponement are helping forward the continuance of Rome. We make our oaths, too, not by "the genius of the Caesar," but by his health, which is more august than any genius. Do you not know that genius is a name for demon, or in the diminutive daemonium? We respect

the judgment of God in the Emperors, who has set them over the nations. We know that to be in them which God wished to be there, and so we wish that safe, which God wished; and we count that a great oath. But demons, or geniuses, we are accustomed to exorcise, in order to drive them out of men—not to swear by them and so give them the honor of divinity.

During the troubled years of the third century C.E., the Roman emperors generally placed even more emphasis on their association with divine powers in an effort to establish a basis of political legitimacy to combat the frequent challenges for the throne. In general, however, the emperors still observed the tradition that deification came only after death, although Aurelian (270–275 C.E.) apparently claimed divine honors during his lifetime, styling himself "Lord and God."

The most complete account of the deification ceremonies for a deceased emperor is found in the work of the pagan Herodian.

C–6 Herodian, *Histories of the Empire after Marcus* 4.2 (ca. 238 C.E.)

It is the custom of the Romans to deify those of their emperors who die, leaving successors, and this rite they call apotheosis. On this occasion a semblance of mourning, combined with festival and religious observances, is visible throughout the city. The body of the dead they honor after human fashion with a splendid funeral, and making a wax image resembling him in all respects, they expose it to view in the vestibule of the palace, on a lofty ivory couch of great size, spread with cloth of gold. The figure is made pallid, like a sick man. During most of the day senators sit round the bed on the left-hand side, clothed in black, and noblewomen on the right, clothed in plain white dress, like mourners, wearing no gold or necklaces. These ceremonies continue for seven days, and the doctors severally approach the bed, examine the patient, and declare him to be growing steadily worse. When they have made believe that he is dead, the noblest of the equites, and young men, carefully selected, of senatorial rank, pick up the bed, carry it along the Sacred Way, and lay it in the open in the old forum. Platforms, rather like steps, are erected on either side. On one stands a choir of young nobles, on the other a choir of noblewomen; they sing hymns and songs of praise to the dead, modulated in a solemn, mournful strain. After this they carry the bed through the city to the Campus Martius. Here, in the broadest portion, a square erection is constructed entirely of gigantic timber logs, in the shape of a room, filled with faggots, and decorated outside with hangings interwoven with gold and ivory pictures. Upon this a similar but smaller chamber is built, with open doors and windows, and above it a third and fourth, still diminishing to the top, so that one might compare it to the lighthouses which go by the name of

Pharos. In the second story they place a bed, and collect all sorts of aromatics and incense, and every kind of fragrant fruit, herb or juice; for all cities, nations and eminent individuals emulate one another in contributing these last gifts in honor of the emperor. When a vast heap of aromatics is collected, there is a procession of horsemen and chariots around the pile, with the drivers wearing robes of office, and masks made to resemble the most distinguished Roman emperors and military commanders. When all this is done, the others fire the pile from all sides; the fire easily catches hold of the faggots and aromatics. Then from the smallest story at the very top, as from a pinnacle, an eagle is let loose to mount into the sky as the fire ascends. This is believed by the Romans to carry the soul of the emperor from earth to heaven, and from that time he is worshipped with the other gods.

It would seem logical to suppose that the cult of the emperor and the associated divine honors would have come to an end with the triumph of Christianity, but in fact the political uses of the cult were such that Christian emperors of the fourth century continued the association of their person with the divine power.[2]

---

2. Ramsay MacMullen, *Christianity & Paganism in the Fourth to Eighth Centuries* (New Haven: Yale University Press, 1997), 34–36. Constantine's cult worship is discussed in chapter 5, above.

APPENDIX D: THE FORMULATION OF THE NICENE CREED

T he fiercest theological disputes among Christians of the fourth century C.E. concerned the nature of the relationship between the Son and the Father. The most significant controversy involved the views of Arius (ca. 250–336 C.E.), a priest of Alexandria, Egypt. Arius believed that God was a pure Spirit who could have no direct contact with the material world and that the Son was a being created by God before time began to act as the intermediary between God and the material world. Because the Son was a created being, Arius believed that the Son was inferior to God and was divine only through participation in the Divinity of the Father.[1]

The bishop of Alexandria saw Arius's theology as heretical and called for Arius's excommunication. Arius's supporters rallied to his defense and his views spread among Christians, gaining many supporters. The emperor Constantine, troubled by this evident disunity within the church, urged the leaders of the two factions to reconcile their differences, but these efforts failed. Constantine then summoned a great council of bishops in 325 C.E. to meet at Nicaea in the province of Bithynia to resolve this and other disputes confronting the faith.

D–1 Eusebius of Caesarea, *Life of Constantine* 3.6–8 (ca. 338–339 C.E.)
> Then as if to bring a divine array against this enemy, he [Constantine] convoked a general council, and invited the speedy attendance of bishops from all quarters, in letters expressive of the honorable estimation in which he held them. Nor was this merely the issuing of a bare command but the emperor's good will contributed much to its being carried into effect: for he allowed some the use of the public means of conveyance, while he afforded to others an ample supply of horses for their transport. The place, too, selected for the synod, the city Nicaea in Bithynia (named from "Victory"), was appropriate to the occasion. As soon then as the imperial injunction was generally made known, all with the utmost willingness hastened thither, as though they would outstrip one another in a race; for they were impelled by the anticipation of a happy result to the conference, by

---

1. Joan O'Brady, *Early Christian Heresies* (New York: Barnes & Noble, 1985), 91.

273

the hope of enjoying present peace, and the desire of beholding something new and strange in the person of so admirable an emperor.

But that assembly was less, in that not all who composed it were ministers of God; but in the present company, the number of bishops exceeded two hundred and fifty, while that of the presbyters and deacons in their train, and the crowd of acolytes and other attendants was altogether beyond computation.

The Council of Nicaea, which was composed almost entirely of Greek-speaking bishops from the Eastern provinces of the Roman Empire, sought to formulate a creed that would summarize the orthodox faith. Eusebius, the bishop of Caesarea, put forward the formula used by his church as a basis for such a creed.

D–2 The Creed of the Church of Caesarea quoted in Socrates, *Ecclesiastical History* 1.8.

We believe in one god, the Father All-Sovereign, the maker of things visible and invisible; And in one Lord Jesus Christ, the Word of God, God of God, Light of Light, Life of Life, Son only-begotten, Firstborn of all creation, begotten of the Father before all the ages, through whom also all things were made; who was made flesh for our salvation and lived among men, and suffered, and rose again on the third day, and ascended to the Father, and shall come again in glory to judge the living and dead; We believe also in one Holy Spirit.

The creed of Caesarea, while orthodox, did not expressly address the issues of dispute with the Arian belief. The creed was therefore modified by the bishops.

D–3 The Creed Adopted by the Council of Nicaea (marked to show changes from the Creed of Caesarea)

We believe in one god, the Father All-Sovereign, ~~the~~ maker of all things visible and invisible; And in one Lord Jesus Christ, the ~~Word~~ Son of God, begotten of the Father, only-begotten, that is, of the substance [literally, "from the inmost being"] of the Father, God of God, Light of Light, ~~Life of Life, Son only-begotten, firstborn of all creation, begotten of the Father before all the ages,~~ true God of true God, begotten not made, of one substance with the Father, through whom ~~also~~ all things were made, things in heaven and things on the earth, ~~who was made flesh for our salvation and lived among men, and~~ who for us men and for our salvation came down and was made flesh, and became man, ~~and~~ suffered, and rose ~~again~~ on the third day, ~~and~~ ascended into the heavens, ~~Father, and shall come again in glory~~ is coming to judge ~~the~~ living and dead. ~~We believe also~~ And in ~~the one~~ Holy Spirit. And those that say, "There was when he was not," and, "Before he was begotten he was not," and that, "He came into being from what-is-not," or those that allege that the son of God is "of

another substance or essence" or "created" or "changeable" or "alterable," these the Catholic and Apostolic church anathematizes.

The creed adopted by the Council of Nicaea quickly circulated among the
churches of the Eastern provinces, but the creed did not circulate widely in the
Western provinces. Very few bishops at the Council of Nicaea were from the Western
provinces and the Latin-speaking Western bishops as a whole were less concerned with doctrinal disputes of this nature, perhaps because Latin did not
lend itself to the subtle distinctions in meaning that underlay the theological
debates of the Greek-speaking bishops of the Eastern Empire. Moreover,
because of a general decline in education, very few Western bishops could read
the Greek in which the creed was written. As a result of these factors, the Nicene
Creed was generally unknown in the Western churches for at least a generation
after the Council of Nicaea.

The adoption of the creed was a major triumph for the orthodox position, but
many orthodox bishops, even though hostile to Arian belief, were troubled by the
council's use of the word *homoousios* ("of the same substance") in the creed
because this term was not found anywhere in either the Old or the New
Testament. In fact, the use of *homoousios* was the first time fundamental Christian
doctrine was based on a theological construct rather than on scriptural text.

The Arian controversy was not resolved by the Council of Nicaea. Arius
refused to accept the verdict of the Council of Nicaea and he was sent into exile
by Constantine, but many of Arius's followers continued to argue his beliefs
and even Arius's exile proved temporary, as just three years after the council,
Constantine recalled Arius from exile. Many of the fourth-century Christian
emperors after Constantine held Arian or semi-Arian beliefs and accepted a
formula that stated that the "Son was like unto the Father" or "of like substance
but not the same." The word used to describe the Arian position was *homoiousios*,
as opposed to the orthodox *homoousios*. Although these two words varied only
by a single letter, the iota or "jot," the debate between the supporters of each
was one of the utmost fierceness, particularly since few of the fourth-century
Christian emperors refrained from attempting to push the church toward
adopting the emperor's own personal views on the issue. It was only much later,
after Arianism had been finally defeated, that Christians would devise the
ironic saying that an insignificant point of dispute was one which "doesn't
make a jot's/iota's worth of difference."

D–4 St. Hilary, Bishop of Potiers, *Second Epistle to the Emperor Constantius*
1.2.c 4, 5 (ca. 360 C.E.)

It is a thing equally deplorable and dangerous, that there are as many
creeds as opinions among men, as many doctrines as inclinations, and
as many sources of blasphemy as there are faults among us; because
we make creeds arbitrarily, and explain them as arbitrarily. The
Homoousion is rejected, and received, and explained away by successive
synods. The partial or total resemblance of the Father and of the Son

is a subject of dispute for these unhappy times. Every year, nay, every moon, we make new creeds to describe invisible mysteries. We repent of what we have done, we defend those who repent, we anathematize those whom we defended. We condemn either the doctrine of others in ourselves, or our own in that of others; and reciprocally tearing one another to pieces, we have been the cause of each other's ruin.

As a result of the continuing controversy over the Arian position, another church council was called to address the issue. This council, which met during the late spring and early summer of 381 C.E. in Constantinople, was attended by approximately one hundred and fifty bishops. The bishops eventually ratified a modified version of the Creed of Nicaea.

D–5 The Creed of the Council of Constantinople (marked to show the changes from the Creed of Nicaea)

The Bishops out of different provinces assembled by the grace of God in Constantinople, on the summons of the most religious Emperor Theodosius, have decreed as follows:

Canon One: The Faith of the Three Hundred and Eighteen Fathers assembled at Nice in Bithynia shall not be set aside, but shall remain firm. And every heresy shall be anathematized, particularly that of the Eunomians or [Anomoeans, the Arians or] Eudoxians, and that of the Semi-Arians or Pneumatomachi, and that of the Sabellians, and that of the Marcellians, and that of the Photinians, and that of the Apollinarians.

We believe in one god, the Father All-Sovereign, ~~the~~ <u>maker of heaven and earth, and of all</u> things visible and invisible; And in one Lord Jesus Christ, the <u>only-begotten</u> Son of God, begotten of the Father <u>before all the ages,</u> ~~only-begotten, that is, of the substance, God of God,~~ Light of Light, ~~Life of Life,~~ true God of true God, begotten not made, of one substance with the Father, through whom all things were made, ~~things in heaven and things on earth,~~ who for us men and for our salvation came down <u>from the heavens</u> and was made flesh <u>of the Holy Spirit and the Virgin Mary,</u> and became man, <u>and was crucified for us under Pontius Pilate, and</u> suffered, and was buried, and rose <u>again</u> on the third day <u>according to the Scriptures, and</u> ascended into the Heavens, <u>and sitteth on the right hand of the Father, and cometh again with glory</u> ~~is coming~~ to judge ~~the~~ living and dead, <u>of whose kingdom there shall be no end.</u>

And in the Holy Spirit, <u>the Lord and the Life-Giver, that proceedeth from the Father, who with Father and Son is worshiped together and glorified together, who spake through the prophets. In one holy Catholic and Apostolic church; We acknowledge one baptism unto remission of sins. We look for a resurrection of the dead, and the life of the age to come.</u> ~~And those that say, "There was when he was not," and "Before he was begotten he was not," and that, "He~~

~~came into being from what is not," or those that allege that the son of God is "of another substance or essence" or "created" or "changeable" or "alterable", these the Catholic and Apostolic church anathematizes~~.

The Council of Constantinople was again dominated by Greek-speaking bishops of the Eastern Empire, and a council of Western bishops meeting at Aquilia, Italy at approximately the same time essentially ignored the issue of the Nicene Creed. Although the support for the Arian position was weakened after the Council of Constantinople, the revised Nicene Creed had to be revisited and reaffirmed again in the mid-fifth century C.E.

D–6 The Creed Approved by the Council of Chalcedon 451 C.E. (Extracts from the Acts of Session II)

Cecropius, the most reverend bishop of Sebastopol, said, "The faith has been well defined by the 318 holy fathers and confirmed by the holy fathers Athanasius, Cyril, Celestine, Hilary, Basil, Gregory, and now once again by the most holy Leo: and we pray that those things which were decreed by the 318 holy fathers, and by the most holy Leo be read." The most glorious judges and great Senate said, "Let there be read the expositions of the 318 fathers gathered together at Nice." Eunomius, the most reverend bishop of Nicomedia, read from a book The Exposition of Faith of the Council held at Nice. "In the consulate of Paul and Julian," etc. "We believe in one God," etc. "But those who say," etc. The most reverend bishops cried out: "This is the orthodox faith; this we all believe: into this we were baptized; into this we baptize; Blessed Cyril so taught: this is the true faith; this is the holy faith; this is the everlasting faith; into this we were baptized; into this we baptize; we all so believe; so believes Leo, the Pope; Cyril thus believed; Pope Leo so interpreted it." The most glorious judges and great senate said, "Let there be read what was set forth by the 150 holy fathers." Aetius, the reverend deacon of Constantinople, read from a book the holy faith which the 150 fathers set forth as consonant to the holy and great Synod of Nice. "We believe in one God," etc. All the most reverend bishops cried out: "This is the faith of all of us; we all so believe."

The Nicene Creed affirmed at Constantinople stated that the Son is "begotten" of the Father while the Spirit "proceeds" from the Father. St. Augustine was concerned that this distinction allowed for the possibility of Arianism and in his book *On the Trinity* he proposed that the Spirit proceeded from both the Father and the Son. This doctrine of "double procession" was adopted into the Athanasian form of the Nicene Creed and eventually the Latin word *filioque* ("and the Son") was added to the Latin translations of the Nicene Creed. In the seventh and eighth centuries C.E. the use of *filioque* became a significant point of dispute between the Eastern and Western branches of Christianity, as the Eastern church refused to accept this interpolation to the creed by the Western church.

APPENDIX E: DETERMINING THE
DATES OF THE LIFE OF JESUS

M ost people today are aware that the Western system of identifying years by reference to "B.C." and "A.D." dates was based on the birth of Jesus Christ, with B.C. meaning "Before Christ" and A.D. (*anno Domini*) meaning "In the year of the Lord"; in scholarly works these are often referred to as B.C.E. (before the common era) and C.E. (of the common era). However, many people are surprised and puzzled to learn that essentially all modern historians date the birth of Jesus to sometime between 4 B.C.E. and 12 B.C.E. The explanation of how historians have come to date the year of Jesus' birth "Before Christ" is one of the more curious aspects of ancient history and provides an excellent opportunity to practice some of the historical methodology presented in Chapter 1.

THE PROBLEMS WITH ANCIENT CALENDARS

During the period of the Roman Empire, a wide variety of different calendar systems were in use throughout the Mediterranean world. These calendars varied greatly as to both the beginning point of each new year and the number and length of the months and thus greatly complicated the task of translating dates from one calendar system into another. The resultant confusion is still a problem to modern historians because the dates given in any particular ancient text are not always easily calculable with reference to our modern system.

The problems caused by the existence of so many different calendars might have been resolved if the Romans, the one people to have held such lengthy political dominance over the ancient Mediterranean world as to have had any chance of imposing a universal calendar system, had not used a method of numbering the years that was so terribly inefficient that it was never widely adopted by the subject peoples of the Roman Empire. Under the traditional Roman calendar, the years were designated by reference to the names of the two Roman consuls then in office.[1] (For example, the year of a famous battle would be described as having occurred "in the year of the consulship of A and B.") The

---

1. From approximately the fifth century B.C.E., the Roman year consisted of 366 ¼ days and began with the consuls' assumption of office on March 1. In 158 B.C.E., the date on which consuls took office was moved to January 1. In 46 B.C.E., Julius Caesar undertook a reform of the calendar, which involved changing the year to 365 ¼ days, with a leap day added every fourth year.

Roman system was obviously cumbersome and frustrating, if one wished to determine the relative order of events or the number of years between events, since the names of the consuls were useless in determining chronological relationships without additional information. The Romans themselves attempted to address this problem by maintaining long lists of the sequential order of their consuls and modern historians are fortunate that significant portions of various stone inscriptions of these lists have survived. As clumsy as it was, however, the Roman system of dating managed to survive even the collapse of the Western Roman Empire, for while no Western Roman Emperor was ever recognized after 476 C.E., consuls continued to be appointed in the West through 534 C.E. and in the Eastern Roman Empire through 541 C.E. For a brief period thereafter the years were designated as *post consulatum Paulini* in the West and *post consulatum Basilii* in the East; but by 566 C.E. the Eastern Roman Empire had adopted a system that dated events with reference to the regnal year of the then-reigning emperor. (That is, the date of an event would be expressed as "the fifth year of the emperor So-and-So.")

From time to time in the ancient world more universal systems of dating had been proposed, mostly based on numbering the years from a fixed point in time such as the founding of the city of Rome or the beginning of the Greek Olympic Games. None of these systems gained universal acceptance, however, and in light of the many competing calendars, most Christians quite naturally used whatever system was in effect for their local community. From the fourth century C.E., for example, the important Christian community in Alexandria, Egypt used an Egyptian calendar system based on numbering the years from the accession of Diocletian as Roman emperor (August 29, 284 C.E., by the modern Western calendar). The intellectual and theological preeminence of the Alexandrian Christians in the Christian church was such that the Alexandrian calendar enjoyed rather wide-spread use among Christians, even though many Christians found it distasteful to use a calendar based on the ascension of the emperor who initiated the most severe of all Roman persecutions, the "Great Persecution" of 303–311 C.E.

EASTER, DIONYSIUS EXIGUUS, AND THE ORIGINS OF THE B.C./A.D. (B.C.E./C.E.) CALENDAR

The series of events that led to the B.C./A.D. (B.C.E./C.E.) calendar can be traced back to the problems the ancient Christians faced in setting a date for Easter. The celebration that modern Christians call Easter was known as "the Passover of the Lord" among the early Christians.[2] The "Christian Passover" was the most

---

2. See, for example, *Letter to Diognetus* 12.9, written by an unknown Christian in the early second century C.E. In Greek, "Passover" is *pascha*, and this is the root word for both the modern English "paschal" and the "Pesah" used in most modern European languages to name the Easter celebration. The word "Easter" is derived from the German "Oster," which is a form of "Eostre," the Germanic god of spring.

important celebration of the early church and its date was used as the basis for calculating the dates of a number of other important liturgical events. However, the proper date for the Easter celebration was a point of dispute among Christians from at least the first half of the second century C.E. Because the Synoptic Gospels of Matthew, Mark, and Luke indicated that the Last Supper was the Jewish Passover meal held on Nisan 14 under the Jewish calendar, many Christians celebrated Easter on Nisan 14, regardless of the particular day of the week that Nisan 14 happened to fall on during any given year.[3] The ancient Jews, who used a lunar calendar, normally set Passover and Nisan 14 to fall on the first full moon after the spring equinox. Other Christians preferred to celebrate Easter always on a Sunday, the day of the Resurrection, and adopted the Sunday following Nisan 14 as the date of the Easter celebration.

Over the course of the second and third centuries C.E., most, but not all, Christians came to observe Easter on the first Sunday after the first full moon after the spring equinox. The adoption of the Sunday after Nisan 14 rather than Nisan 14 itself for the Easter observance seems in large part attributable to the Christian desire to distinguish the "Passover of the Lord" from the Jewish Passover.[4] Regardless of the individual preferences concerning the proper day on which to celebrate Easter, however, all Christians found it difficult to use the Roman calendar or any other calendar to calculate the date of the spring equinox and the appropriate full moon. As a result, the actual date of the Easter celebration could and often did vary rather widely even among churches that agreed on the same theoretical date for Easter.

In 325 C.E., the Council of Nicaea attempted to adopt a uniform method of calculating Easter. The council decided to set Easter as the first Sunday following the fourteenth day of the paschal moon, where the paschal moon was the first moon whose fourteenth day would fall on or after the spring equinox.[5] This formula insured that Easter would never fall on or before the Jewish Passover, but it did not in practice establish a uniform date for Easter because the time of the spring equinox varies according to the observer's longitude. Thus, the calculations of the spring equinox by the Christians of Rome and Alexandria would not always agree because of the different longitudes for the two cities, and in the next year after the council, in 326 C.E., the churches of

---

3. The Nisan 14 date had a particularly strong following among the Christians of Asia Minor, who claimed that this was the date observed by the Apostle John. See, e.g., Eusebius, *Ecclesiastical History* 5.23–24; and Irenaeus, fragment 3 in *Ante Nicene Fathers* (Grand Rapids: Eerdmans, 1884), volume 1, 1140–41.

4. See, e.g,. Eusebius, *Life of Constantine* 3.18–20.

5. While no mention of the formula appears in the extant record of the council itself, letters by the council to the Church at Alexandria and by Constantine confirm that the council did decide that the East would celebrate Easter at the same time as the churches of Rome and Alexandria. The texts of these letters may be found at *The Nicene and Post Nicene Fathers* (Grand Rapid: Eerdmans, 1991), volume 14, 53–55 and Eusebius, *Life of Constantine* 3.18–20.

Rome and Alexandria celebrated Easter on different dates, as happened again in 330, 333, 340, 341, and 343 C.E.[6]

Because of the difficulty the individual churches encountered in calculating the date of Easter, by the second half of the fourth century C.E. the Christians of Alexandria began calculating and circulating tables of the Easter dates for general use. One of the most important of these tables was that prepared in the early fifth century C.E. for Cyril, the bishop of Alexandria. The tables prepared for Cyril set forth the dates of Easter for the years 437 through 531 C.E. and were adopted by the Church in Rome for its observance of Easter. In 525 C.E. Pope John I, realizing that Alexandrian Easter tables were about to run out, asked the Scythian monk Dionysius Exiguus ("Dennis the Little," c.500–560 C.E.) to prepare a continuation of the Alexandrian tables for the years after 531 C.E.

In calculating new Easter tables, Dionysius Exiguus used an Alexandrian system based on a nineteen-year cycle of dates, with the intent of calculating the date of Easter for the next five cycles after 531 C.E. During the course of his work, in approximately 532 C.E., Dionysius noted that he lived in what was the twenty-eighth of these cycles after the then commonly accepted date for the year of Jesus' birth. Dionysius suddenly realized that the year of Jesus' birth could be used to establish a method of numbering the years that would have a universal meaning throughout Christendom. All that needed to be done was to date the events of history with reference to the date of Jesus' birth, which Dionysius computed to be during the reign of King Herod the Great, on December 25 of the 753rd year after the founding of the city of Rome (*ab urbe condita*, or "A.U.C."). Rather than use December 25 as the fixed point in his system, however, Dionysius shifted his reference point from the birth of Jesus to the Feast of Circumcision on the eighth day of Jesus' life, because (under the Roman method of counting both the first and last numbers of a numerical sequence, as further discussed below) that latter date fell on January 1, the first day of the first month of the Roman year. Thus, January 1, 754 A.U.C. was the date designated by Dionysius as January 1 of the year 1 C.E.

Dionysius was pleased with his new calendar, especially because it meant that the reign of the persecutor Diocletian would no longer be the basis of the Christian calendar: "We have been unwilling to connect our cycle with the name of an impious persecutor, but have chosen rather to note the years from the incarnation of our Lord Jesus Christ."[7] However, because of an anti-Greek reaction in Rome after the death of Pope John, the system devised by the Greek

6. Henry R. Percival, *The Seven Ecumenical Councils of the Undivided Church* (Grand Rapids: Eerdmans, 1991), 55. In 387 C.E., Easter was celebrated in Gaul on March 21, in Rome on April 8, and in Alexandria on April 25. Geoffrey Moorhouse, *Sun Dancing* (New York: Harcourt Brace, 1997), 216.

7. Qtd. in Jack Finegan, *Handbook of Biblical Chronology* (Peabody: Hendrickson Publishing, 1998), 113.

Dionysius did not find immediate acceptance in the Western provinces. Dionysius' system was, however, adopted by Bede of England in the preparation of his *Ecclesiastical History of the English People*, completed in 731 C.E. In the same book, Bede also dated events by reference to years numbered "Before Christ" as well as "Anno Domini," and many eighth century chronicles adopted this dual system of styling the years. This "B.C.–A.D." (B.C.E.–C.E.) system of dates spread further when Charlemagne of France used it in some of his imperial decrees and eventually the system came into widespread use throughout Western Europe.

While Dionysius's system was certainly easier to use than the old Roman system and had the advantage of being acceptable in principle to all Christians, his designation of 754 A.U.C. as "1 A.D." (C.E.) had several unfortunate consequences. One such consequence is that because there was no year "0," one cannot make an arithmetic computation of the interval of years between events dated B.C.E. and C.E.: December 31, 1 B.C.E. and January 1, 1 C.E. are consecutive days under Dionysius's system, whereas arithmetically the difference between -1 and +1 is 2. While it may seem strange that Dionysius began his system with the year 1 rather than the year 0, we should remember that in Dionysius's day the concept of zero as a mathematical placeholder had not yet been recognized in Western Europe.

A less significant consequence, but one contrary to the understanding of a great many people, is that because Dionysius's system began with the year 1 C.E., the first year of the second century was 101 C.E., the first year of the third century was 201 C.E., and so on down through the centuries, with the result that January 1, 2001 is the first day of the third millennium. A further unfortunate fact about Dionysius's 1 C.E. date, however, and the answer to the question of why most historians date Jesus' birth prior to 1 C.E., is that Dionysius erred in calculating that Jesus was born in 753 A.U.C.

In reviewing Dionysius's calculation of 753 A.U.C. as the year of Jesus' birth, it appears that Dionysius accepted the statement of Clement of Alexandria (writing ca. 200 C.E.) that Jesus was born in the twenty-eighth year of the reign of Caesar Augustus and believed that Augustus's reign began in the year 727 A.U.C. (27 B.C.E.), when the Roman Senate bestowed upon him the title "Augustus."[8] Unfortunately, however, Augustus himself always dated the start of his reign from his famous naval victory at Actium over Anthony and Cleopatra in 723 A.U.C. (September 2, 31 B.C.E.) and there is no evidence that Clement had any certain knowledge concerning the year of Jesus' birth, although Clement's date would coincide with the generally accepted year for the date of Herod the Great's death. Modern historians, who have access to both a wider range of archaeological and historical evidence than Dionysius and the assistance of modern astronomers in calculating the dates of solar and lunar

---

8. E. G. Richards, *Mapping Time* (Oxford: Oxford University Press, 1998), 218.

eclipses mentioned in the ancient texts, have determined that if Jesus were born during the reign of Herod the Great, then the time of his birth could be no later than the death of Herod in the spring of 4 B.C.E. However, the dates of Western history have been determined with respect to the year set by Dionysius as 1 C.E. for so long that it would be extremely impractical to insist that everyone learn new dates counted from a different base year, particularly since modern historians now recognize that the extant evidence does not allow for an exact determination of the year of Jesus' birth.

As a final matter, we should note that the fact that Dionysius miscalculated the year of Jesus' birth has an interesting implication for the recent celebration of the millennium: regardless of whether one accepts that the new millennium begins on January 1, 2001 rather than January 1, 2000, the celebration pertained to the passage of 2000 years from the year Dionysius's picked to be 1 C.E. and not to the two-thousandth anniversary of the birth of Jesus, which had already come and gone some years before.

INTERPRETING THE EVIDENCE FOR THE YEAR OF JESUS' BIRTH

The study of the ancient sources pertinent to the determination of the year of Jesus' birth provides both an excellent example of the "nuts and bolts" of historical investigation and an interesting view of the political relationships between Rome and its Jewish client states in Palestine during the period of the early Roman Empire. The modern historian begins the determination of the year of Jesus' birth by first seeking to establish a reliable date for an event reasonably close in time to Jesus' birth year and then attempting to link together references in the extant sources to construct a chain of dates leading from the "base date" to the birth year. Because the Gospel of Matthew and the Gospel of Luke both indicate that Jesus was born late in the reign of Herod the Great of Judaea,[9] most historians undertake first to establish the year of Herod's death and then attempt to use the extant sources to calculate from that date to the year of Jesus' birth. Because the ancient Jewish historian Josephus wrote fairly extensively about the reign of Herod the Great, his works are usually the starting point for determining the date of Herod's death.

E–1 Jospehus,
The Jewish War 1.665 (Aramaic ca. 73 C.E.; Greek ca. 75–76 C.E.)

> Herod [the Great] survived the execution of his son but five days. He expired after a reign of thirty-four years, reckoning from the date when, after putting Antigonus to death, he assumed control of the state; of thirty-seven years, from the date when he was proclaimed king by the Romans.[10]

---

9. Matthew 2:1–2 (Selection E.13, below) and Luke 1:5; 2:1 (Selection E.12, below).
10. This same passage is quoted almost verbatim in Josephus's Jewish Antiquities 17.191.

Jewish Antiquities 14.388–389, 487 (ca. 93–94 C.E.)

[388] Now when the Senate was adjourned, Antony and Caesar went out with Herod between them, and the consuls and other magistrates leading the way, in order to sacrifice and to deposit the decree in the Capitol. Then Antony entertained him on the first day of his reign. Thus did Herod take over royal power, receiving it in the hundred and eighty-fourth Olympiad, the consuls being Gnaeus Domitius Calvinus for the second time, and Gaius Asinius Pollio. . . .

[487] This calamity [Herod's capture of Jerusalem and execution of Antigonus] befell the city of Jerusalem during the consulship at Rome of Marcus Agrippa and Caninus Gallus, in the hundred and eighty-fifth Olympiad, in the third month, on the day of the Fast, as if it were a recurrence of the misfortune which came upon the Jews in the time of Pompey, for they were captured by Sossius on the very same day, twenty-seven years later.

With their precise statements as to the interval of years, the text of *The Jewish Wars* relates the year of Herod's death to both the year of his ascension to power and the year Rome granted Herod the title of king, and the text of *Jewish Antiquities* relates these events to specific events in Roman history. If the year of any one of these events were known with respect to a fixed point in time, such as 1 C.E., then the years of the other events could also be calculated with respect to that fixed point. If none of the events had previously been dated with respect to 1 C.E., then the historian would search for a text that tied one of these events to either 1 C.E. itself or to an event or series of events whose dates were known with respect to 1 C.E. Such a series of events might, for example, consist of determining that Herod was made king in the same year as Event "A," which Event "A" was known to be ten years before Event "B," which Event "B" was known to be thirteen years before Event "C," which Event "C" was known to be seventeen years before 1 C.E. An important side benefit of calculating the dates of these events in Herod's life would be that these dates would then become part of an ever-larger "database" of established historical dates that would in theory make it progressively easier and easier to calculate the dates of still other events found in the historical sources.

In constructing a chronology of dates in this manner, there are two important points to consider. The first point is that the relative time intervals between the events must be related to a fixed point in time—any arbitrarily chosen date may serve as the base date—before a date like "753 A.U.C," "4 B.C.E.," or "2000 C.E." can be assigned. The second point is that the reliability of the date calculated for any specific historical event is dependent upon the accuracy of the statements of time intervals found in the historical sources. Thus, the historian would like to have independent evidence to confirm Josephus's statements of the intervals of years between the events described in Selection E.1. The most obvious way to confirm Josephus's statements would be to find different historical sources that allowed for an independent determination of the relative dates of the events. In this respect, Josephus's reference to specific Roman consuls and the Greek Olympiads in the *Jewish Antiquities* passage is extremely useful because it cross-references the events described in the passage from *The Jewish War* to the Roman and Greek calendar systems and thus allows his statements to be checked for consistency against independent sources.

Unfortunately, the fragmentary and often obscure historical sources that have survived from antiquity do not always permit the cross-checking of dates through the use of independent sources. For this reason the degree of reliability of the date assigned by modern historians to any event in antiquity is dependent upon both the number of independent historical sources that refer to the event and the relative reliability of these historical sources.[11] The only real exception to this general rule occurs when an historical source mentions a regularly occurring astronomical event, such as an eclipse or a periodic comet, in association with an event, because modern astronomers can calculate the date of the astronomical event to verify the date indicated by the historical source.

The extant historical sources concerning the life of Herod the Great are fairly numerous by ancient standards and allow us to calculate a reasonably reliable date for the year of the death of Herod the Great. These sources collectively indicate that if we use Dionysius Exiguus's 1 C.E. as our fixed reference point, then Herod was declared king by the Romans in 40 B.C.E.[12] and Antigonus died in 37 B.C.E.[13] To relate these dates properly to the information given by Josephus and to make a preliminary calculation of the year of Herod's death, however, the historian must be aware of a particular nuance of Roman culture: unlike Americans, the Romans included both the first and last number in counting a numerical sequence. This Roman cultural characteristic is reflected in the New Testament's accounts of the death and resurrection of Jesus, which uniformly report that Jesus died on a Friday and rose again on Sunday, "the third day." Accordingly, once the historian has confirmed that Josephus did in fact use the Roman method of counting years, it is possible to calculate that, according to Josephus, Herod died in 4 B.C.E., not 3 B.C.E.

This date of 4 B.C.E. for Herod's death is supported by a number of other historical sources and by various dated coins issued by Herod's successors, his sons Archelaus, Philip, and Antipas, that indicate that they dated their own reigns as beginning in 4 B.C.E.[14] Thus, there is strong literary and numismatic evidence for the belief that Herod died in 4 B.C.E. By good fortune, this 4 B.C.E.

---

11. Because multiple sources do exist for many events, modern historians have been able to determine that some ancient writers were generally much more accurate than others in their accounts of dates and events.

12. Strabo, *Geography* 16.2.46; Tacitus, *Histories* 5.9; Appian, *Civil War* 5.75.

13. Tacitus, *Histories* 5.9; Cassius Dio 49.22.

14. The literary and numismatic evidence is summarized by T. D. Barnes in "The Date of Herod's Death," *Journal of Theological Studies* 19 (1968), 204–209. See also, Jack Finnegan, *Handbook of Biblical Chronology* (Peabody, Mass.: Hendrickson, 1998), 300. Some historians have suggested that the dates of these coins are misleading in that Herod did not die in 4 B.C.E. but rather allowed his sons to jointly rule with him in a co-regency after that date, but there is little if any evidence to support such a theory. See Footnote 17 and the sources cited therein.

date is supported by a reference in Josephus's text to a lunar eclipse associated with Herod's death.

> E–2 Josephus, *Jewish Antiquities* 17.167–168 (ca. 93–94 C.E.)
> Herod then deposed Matthias from the high priesthood. As for the other Matthias, who had stirred up the sedition, he burnt him alive along with some of his companions. And on that same night there was an eclipse of the moon. But Herod's illness became more and more acute, for God was inflicting just punishment upon him for his lawless deeds.

This eclipse is the only lunar eclipse mentioned by Josephus in all of his *Jewish Antiquities*. The text of *Jewish Antiquities* 17.168–190 goes on to state that Herod died shortly after the eclipse. A reference in Josephus's *The Jewish War* to the events surrounding Herod's death provides further information about the time of Herod's death.[15]

> E–3 Josephus, *The Jewish War* 2.1–2, 4–6, 8–10 (Aramaic ca. 73 C.E.; Greek ca. 75–76 C.E.)
> [1] The necessity under which Archelaus found himself of undertaking a journey to Rome was the signal for fresh disturbances. After keeping seven days' mourning for his father [Herod the Great] and providing the usual funeral banquet. . . he changed into white raiment and went forth to the Temple, where the people received him. Speaking from a golden throne on a raised platform he greeted the multitude. He thanked them for the zeal which they had displayed over his father's funeral and for the marks of homage shown to himself, as to a king whose claim to the throne was already confirmed. He would, however, he said, for the present abstain not only from the exercise of authority, but even from the assumption of the titles, of royalty, until his right to the succession had been ratified by Caesar, to whose ruling everything had been submitted under the terms of the will. . . .
> [4] Delighted at these professions, the multitude at once proceeded to test his intentions by making large demands. One party clamored for a reduction of the taxes, another for the abolition of the duties, another for the liberation of prisoners. To all these requests, in his desire to ingratiate himself with the people, he readily assented. Then after offering a sacrifice, he regaled himself with his friends. Toward evening, however, a large number of those who were bent on revolution assembled on the same spot, and, now that the public mourning for the king was ended, began a lamentation on their own account, bewailing the fate of those whom Herod had punished. . . .

---

15. The same events are related in *Jewish Antiquities* 17.213.

[8] Archelaus, exasperated by these proceedings, but in haste to depart, wished to defer retaliation from fear that, if he provoked the hostility of the people, he would be detained by a general uprising. He, accordingly, endeavored to appease the rebels by persuasion, without resort to force, and quietly sent his general to entreat them to desist. . . . To all remonstrances they replied with anger, and it was evident that, given any accession to their numbers, they had no intention of remaining inactive. And now the feast of the unleavened bread, which the Jews call Passover, came round; it is an occasion for the contribution of a multitude of sacrifices, and a vast crowd streamed in from the country for the ceremony. . . .

Modern astronomers have calculated that in 4 B.C.E. Passover would have occurred on approximately April 11.[16] Collectively, therefore, Selections E.1, E.2, and E.3 can be read to indicate that Herod's death occurred (1) after the start of his thirty-fourth year of reign, a date known to fall in the summer or autumn of 5 B.C.E.,[17] (2) before the Passover of April 11, 4 B.C.E., and (3) after a lunar eclipse that preceded the Passover. The historian can use astronomical calculations to determine whether there was any lunar eclipse in Judaea that fits the foregoing para-meters. In this instance, astronomers have determined that there was in fact only one lunar eclipse visible in Palestine during 4 B.C.E., a partial eclipse that occurred on the night of March 12–13, 4 B.C.E.[18] The astronomical support for the 4 B.C.E. date indicated by the historical sources and the numismatic evidence thus allows the historian to place a relatively high degree of confidence in a 4 B.C.E. date for the death of Herod the Great, and it is this date that will be used as our starting point in constructing a chronology of events that lead to the birth of Jesus.

After Herod's death in 4 B.C.E., a dispute arose among his sons as to the proper division of his kingdom. The dispute was resolved by the Roman emperor Caesar Augustus.

---

16. Jack Finegan, *Handbook of Biblical Chronology* (Peabody, Mass.: Hendrickson, 1998), 294.

17. Josephus, *Jewish Antiquities* 14.487 and Jack Finegan, *Handbook of Biblical Chronology* (Peabody, Mass.: Hendrickson, 1998), 299. But see Cassius Dio, *Roman History* 49.22–23.

18. Jack Finegan, *Handbook of Biblical Chronology* (Peabody, Mass.: Hendrickson, 1998), 299; Raymond Brown, *The Birth of the Messiah* (New York: Doubleday, 1977), 167. Astronomers have also determined that in Palestine there was total lunar eclipse on September 15/16 of 5 B.C.E. and no lunar eclipses during 3 B.C.E. or 2 B.C.E. Finegan at 299. Because the eclipse in March of 4 B.C.E. allows only a maximum of 29 days for all of the events described by Josephus, whereas the September eclipse of 5 B.C.E. would allow approximately 7 months for the same events, some historians have questioned whether the 5 B.C.E. eclipse is not in fact the eclipse described by Josephus. An eclipse in the fall of 5 B.C.E. would not change the 4 B.C.E. date for the next following Passover, but it is conceivable that Herod could have died late in 5 B.C.E., so occasionally one sees Herod's death stated at "5/4 B.C.E." Other historians have argued that an eclipse of 1 B.C.E. would better fit the sources, although this involves the assumption that Herod allowed his sons to participate in a joint reign during the last years of his life. The arguments for the alternative dates for the death of Herod are summarized by John P. Meier in *A Marginal Jew: Rethinking the Historical Jesus* (New York: Doubleday, 1991), volume 1, 414–18, note 18.

E–4 Josephus, *The Jewish War* 2.93–97

[93] Caesar, after hearing both parties, dismissed the assembly. His decision was announced a few days later: he gave half the kingdom to Archelaus, with the title of ethnarch, promising, moreover, to make him king, should he prove his deserts; the

[95] other half he divided into two tetrarchies, which he presented to two other sons of Herod, one to Philip, the other to Antipas, who had disputed the throne with Archelaus. Antipas had for his province Peraea and Galilee, with a revenue of two hundred talents. Batanaea, Trachonitis, Auranitis and certain portions of the domain of Zeno in the neighborhood of Panias, producing a revenue of a hundred talents,

[96] were allotted to Philip. The ethnarchy of Archelaus comprised the whole of Idumaea and Judaea, besides the district of Samaria, which had a quarter of its

[97] tribute remitted in consideration of its having taken no part in the insurrection. The cities subjected to Archelaus were Strato's Tower, Sebaste, Joppa and Jerusalem; the Greek towns of Gaza, Gadara and Hippos were, on the other hand, detached from his principality and annexed to Syria.

The division of Herod's kingdom among his surviving sons is reflected in the New Testament Gospels, which refer to Antipas as the ruler of Galilee during Jesus' lifetime and to Archelaus as the ruler of Judaea when Jesus was a small child.[19]

A few years after the events of 4 B.C.E. another controversy arose concerning Archelaus, which again had to be resolved by the Roman authorities.

E–5 Josephus, *The Jewish War* 2.111 (Aramaic ca. 73 C.E.; Greek ca. 75–76 C.E.)

Archelaus, on taking possession of his ethnarchy, did not forget old feuds, but treated not only the Jews but even the Samaritans with great brutality. Both parties sent deputies to Caesar to denounce him, and in the ninth year of his rule he was banished to Vienna, a town in Gaul, and his property confiscated to the imperial treasury. . . .

E–6 Josephus, *Jewish Antiquities* 17.342–344 (ca. 93–94 C.E.)

[342] In the tenth year of Archelaus' rule, the leading men among the Jews and Samaritans, finding his cruelty and tyranny intolerable, brought charges against him before Caesar the moment they learned that Archelaus had disobeyed his instructions to show moderation in dealing with them. . . .

[344] And when Archelaus arrived, Caesar gave a hearing to some of his accusers, and also let him speak, and then sent him into exile, assigning him a residence in Vienna, a city in Gaul, and confiscating his property.

---

19. Luke 3:1–2 and 23:6–12 for Antipas as ruler of Galilee, and Matthew 2:19–22 for Archelaus as ruler of Judaea.

Calculating the date of Archelaus's removal is obviously complicated by the conflict between Josephus's two works as to the length of Archelaus's reign: *The Jewish War* indicates 5 C.E. and *Jewish Antiquities* indicates 6 C.E. (In counting the years remember to use the inclusive numbering of the Romans and that there is no year zero, so that 1 C.E. immediately follows 1 B.C.E.) This discrepancy in the sources might have proved irresolvable, if the date of the removal of Archelaus were not mentioned in an independent Roman source.

> E–7 Cassius Dio, *Roman History* 55.25, 27 (ca. 214–226 C.E.)
>
> [25] After this, in the consulship of Aemilius Lepidus and Lucius Arruntius, when no revenues for the military fund were being discovered that suited anybody. . . .
>
> [27] Those were the events which took place in the City [of Rome] that year. In Achaea the governor died in the middle of his term, and instructions were given to his quaestor and assessor (whom as I have explained we call envoy) for the former to administer the province as far as the Isthmus [of Corinth] and the other the remainder. Herod of Palestine [i.e., Herod Archelaus], who was accused by his brothers of some wrongdoing or other, was banished beyond the Alps, and his portion of the domain was confiscated to the [Roman] state.

The "year during the consulship of Aemilius Lepidus and Lucius Arruntius" is known from other evidence to have been 6 C.E.[20] Thus the text of the Roman historian Cassius Dio supports the ten-year reign described by Josephus in *Jewish Antiquities*. However, we should here make note that the "fact" that Archelaus's reign lasted ten years is not conclusively established simply because a majority of the extant historical sources favor the 6 C.E. date over the 5 C.E. date; it is possible that the two sources indicating 6 C.E. are wrong and the one source indicating 5 C.E. is correct. The consensus of modern historians that Archelaus was removed by the Romans in 6 C.E. should therefore be understood as meaning that 6 C.E. is the date best supported by the relatively fragmentary evidence which has survived from antiquity. It is unfortunate that modern historians, as a matter of convention, normally use the dates established by consensus within the profession without any statement of the underlying degree of reliability or probability of the date because the non-historian, who is typically unaware of both the professional convention and the fragmentary nature of the evidence, has no real concept of the degree of uncertainty that may underlie a historian's casual recitation of historical dates.[21] Most

---

20. Tables of the Roman Consuls are preserved in the *Chronographus Anni CCCLIIII*, which is reproduced in chart form in Jack Finegan, *Handbook of Biblical Chronology* (Peabody, Mass.: Hendrickson, 1998), 84–85.

21. In defense of the professional convention, it should be acknowledged that the dates of most of the significant historical events during the period of the Roman Empire are in fact relatively well established, give or take a small margin of error. For the great majority of events, knowing the exact date of the event is not nearly so important as placing the event in the correct relative order with respect to the other events of the period.

historians would also acknowledge that the same professional convention is applied to the "what happened" aspect of historical reconstruction as well as the "when," and it is a rare history book indeed that examines and evaluates the degree of certainty underlying more than a small proportion of all the historical "facts" stated in the book.[22]

Rome's removal of Archelaus in 6 C.E. presented the Romans with the choice of either taking over direct rule of his territories or appointing a successor to his position. The Romans decided to establish direct rule of his territories. From the Roman perspective, one of the first tasks to be performed when a new province was brought under direct rule was to set up an *ad valorem* tax system, as the taxes would be used to offset the costs of administration and defense incurred in governing the province. Setting up an *ad valorem* tax system required both the registration of the taxable property in the province and the identification of the owner of property, who would be personally responsible for the payment of the taxes. The novelty of the Roman tax system shocked many Jews and led to a minor revolt that was quickly suppressed by the Romans.

E–8 Josephus, *Jewish War* 2.117–118 (Aramaic ca. 73 C.E.; Greek ca. 75–76 C.E.)

[117] The territory of Archelaus was now reduced to a province,[23] and Coponius, a Roman of the equestrian order, was sent out as procurator, entrusted by Augustus with full power, including the infliction of capital punishment.

[118] Under his administration, a Galilaean, named Judas, incited his countrymen to revolt, upbraiding them as cowards for consenting to pay tribute to the Romans and tolerating mortal masters, after having God for their lord.

E–9 Josephus, *Jewish Antiquities* 18.1–4, 26 (ca. 93–94 C.E.)

[1] [P. Sulpicius] Quirinius, a Roman senator who had proceeded through all the magistracies to the consulship and a man who was extremely distinguished in other respects, arrived in Syria, dispatched by Caesar to be governor of the nation and to make an assessment of their property.
[2] Coponius, a man of equestrian rank, was sent along with him to rule over the Jews with full authority. Quirinius also visited Judaea, which had been annexed to Syria, in order to make an assessment of the property of the Jews and to liquidate the estate of Archelaus.

---

22. At this point, it is only fair to alert the reader that in this book I have generally followed without comment the consensus as to "what happened" and "when" and discuss the underlying evidentiary problems for only a few of the more interesting historical problems, such as the issues in this appendix. I have placed greater emphasis on alerting the reader to the significant historical problems in reconstructing the history of Christianity's relationship to the Roman world and in presenting a fair sampling of the most important primary source materials on these issues.

23. "Now" refers to and follows the events of *The Jewish War* 2.111, Selection E–5 above.

³ Although the Jews were at first shocked to hear of the registration of property, they gradually condescended, yielding to the arguments of the high priest Joazar, the son of Boethus, to go no farther in opposition. So those who were convinced by him declared, without unnecessary delay, the value of their property.

⁴ But a certain Judas, a Gaulanite from a city named Gamala, who had enlisted the aid of Saddok, a Pharisee, threw himself into the cause of rebellion. They said that the assessment carried with it a status amounting to downright slavery, no less, and appealed to the nation to make a bid for independence. . . .

²⁶ Quirinius had now liquidated the estate of Archelaus; and by this time the registrations of property that took place in the thirty-seventh year after Caesar's defeat of Antony at Actium were complete.

The battle of Actium can be reliably dated to September 2, 31 B.C.E. by a variety of independent sources.[24] Accordingly, a quick calculation indicates that Quirinius's registration of property took place in 6 C.E., which coincides with the earlier calculation of 6 C.E. for the removal of Archelaus and the imposition of direct Roman rule over the province of Judaea. The fact that Quirinius was governor of Syria at this time has been confirmed by the discovery of coins issued by Quirinius as governor of Syria that bear the date "the thirty-sixth year of Caesar [Augustus]," a year that equates to 5/6 C.E. when counting from the Battle of Actium. That Quirinius conducted a census of Syria has been confirmed by the discovery near Venice, Italy, of the tombstone of a Roman officer who served in Syria under Quirinius.

E–10 The Tombstone of Q. Aemilius (*Inscriptiones Latinae Selectae* 2683). This tombstone dates to shortly after 14 C.E.

Quintus Aemilius Secundus, son of Quintus
of the Palatina tribe, in
military service to the Divine Augustus under
P. Sulpicius Quirinius, legate of
Caesar for Syria, decorated with honors,
Prefect of the Cohort I Augustus and Prefect
Of the Cohort II of the Fleet,
By order of the same Quirinius I took
A census of the city of Apamea,
A town of 117,000 citizens.
By the same Quirinius I was sent to fight
The Ituraeans in the Libanus Mountains
And I captured their citadel. . . .

---

24. Vellius Paterculus, *Roman History* 2.84; Cassius Dio, *Roman History* 50.31; Plutarch, *Life of Anthony* 65.

Josephus wrote that a certain Judas led a brief revolt against the Romans at the time of Quirinius's census. The revolt of Judas at the time of "the census" is mentioned in the New Testament's Acts of the Apostles in a speech attributed to the Pharisee Gamaliel before the Council concerning the danger posed by Peter and the Apostles.

E–11 The Acts of the Apostles 5:35–37
> And he said to them, "Men of Israel, take care what you do with these men. For before these days Theudas arose, giving himself out to be somebody, and a number of men, about four hundred, joined him; but he was slain and all who followed him were dispersed and came to nothing. After him Judas the Galilean arose in the days of the census, and drew away some of the people after him; he also perished, and all who followed him were scattered.

The biblical text clearly indicates that "the census" was a well-known and singular event needing no further identification or explanation to a Jewish audience. It was almost certainly for that reason that the Gospel of Luke referred to the census of Quirinius in dating the year of Jesus' birth.

E–12 The Gospel of Luke 1:5, 2:1–6
> [1:5] In the days of Herod, king of Judaea, there was a priest named Zechariah of the division of Abijah. . . .
> [2:1] In those days a decree went out from Caesar Augustus that all the world should be enrolled. This was the first enrollment, when Quirinius was governor of Syria.* And all went to be enrolled, each to his own city. And Joseph also went up from Galilee, from the city of Nazareth, to Judaea, to the city of David, which is called Bethlehem, because he was of the house and lineage of David, to be enrolled with Mary, his betrothed, who was with child. And while they were there, the time came for her to be delivered. And she gave birth to her first-born son. . . .
>
> > * *aute apographe prote egeneto hegemoneuontos tes Syrias Kureniou.*
> > *This enrollment first was [when] governing Syria Quirinius*

While the text of the Gospel of Luke appears to present a precise date, our earlier calculation of the dates of 4 B.C.E. for the death of Herod the Great and 6 C.E. for the census of Quirinius indicates that the text of the Gospel is in fact inconsistent with the other historical evidence. In searching for other evidence to resolve this inconsistency, one quickly comes across the account of the birth of Jesus set forth in the Gospel of Matthew.

E–13 The Gospel of Matthew 2:1–2, 14–16, 19, 21 and 22
> [1-2] Now when Jesus was born in Bethlehem of Judaea in the days of Herod the king, behold, wise men from the East came to Jerusalem, saying, "Where is he who has been born king of the Jews? For we have seen his star in the East, and have come to worship Him." . . .

> [14] And he [Joseph] rose and took the child and his mother by night, and departed to Egypt, and remained there until the death of Herod. . . . Then Herod, when he saw that he had been tricked by the wise men, was in a furious rage, and he sent and killed all the male children in Bethlehem and in all that region who were two years old or under, according to the time which he had ascertained from the wise men. [19] But when Herod died. . . he [Joseph] rose and took the child and his mother, and went to the land of Israel. But when he heard that Archelaus reigned over Judaea in place of his father Herod, he was afraid to go there, and being warned in a dream he withdrew to the district of Galilee.

The Gospel of Matthew expressly states that the birth of Jesus was during the reign of Herod the Great and that Jesus was a "child" when Archelaus succeeded Herod as ruler of Judaea. Thus, even though the Gospel of Matthew does not actually mention the census of Quirinius, its account contradicts the Gospel of Luke and is consistent with the belief that Jesus was born some years before 6 C.E., when Rome removed Archelaus from his office and Quirinius conducted his census of Archelaus's territory as part of the establishment of direct Roman rule.

The apparent conflict between the dates given in the Gospel of Luke for Herod's death and the census of Quirinius and the dates indicated by all the other extant sources has greatly agitated those Christians who hold to a doctrine of strict biblical inerrancy and much inventive argument has been put forth to resolve the discrepancy. In general, the arguments made in support of the accuracy of the Gospel of Luke revolve around the theories that either (i) the Greek of the Gospel has been mistranslated, or (ii) Quirinius conducted a census during the reign of Herod the Great, which census has either been misdated to 6 C.E. or was a second census separate from the census in 6 C.E.

While there has been some dispute concerning the proper translation of the Greek text of the Gospel of Luke, the majority opinion is accurately summarized by the historian Robin Lane Fox:

> Since the nineteenth century, there have been attempts to evade the meaning of the third Gospel's Greek: "This census was the first, while Quirinius was governor of Syria" is twisted into "This census was held before the one which Quirinius, governor of Syria, held." Nobody has ever entertained this translation for non-doctrinal reasons: it is not true to the Greek, let alone the clear Greek of the Third Gospel.[25]

To reach the "doctrinal" translation, "*prote*" must be used in the comparative sense of "former" or "prior," which would then govern the following genitive "*hegemoneuontos*." However, the genitive in the Greek text is a genitive absolute

---

25. Robin Lane Fox, *The Unauthorized Version: Truth and Fiction in the Bible* (New York: Alfred A. Knopf, 1992), 30–31.

and thus the comparative form of "prote" would not be a proper translation. The overwhelming majority of modern historians and all major Bible translations accept the "non-doctrinal" translation as correct, and it is fair to say that no real dispute exists concerning the proper translation of this passage, notwithstanding the occasional assertion to the contrary by conservative Christian writers.[26]

More frequently encountered than the argument concerning the translation of the Gospel text are the arguments that (i) Quirinius's census in 6 C.E. has been misdated and actually occurred during the reign of Herod the Great, or (ii) Quirinius conducted two censuses of Judaea, one being the 6 C.E. census described by Josephus and the other being the census described in the Gospel of Luke. It is beyond the scope of this book to examine each and every one of these arguments, but the interested reader will find most of these arguments, and the reasons for rejecting them, summarized in Raymond E. Brown's *The Birth of the Messiah*,[27] and in *The Anchor Bible Dictionary*, "Chronology."[28] From a methodological perspective, however, it is useful to examine in detail one of the more famous arguments in favor of the "two censuses" theory. This argument is based upon the text of a damaged inscription found near Rome, which was translated by some individuals as indicating that P. Sulpicius Quirinius served twice as governor of Syria.

E–14 The Inscription from Tibur (*Inscriptiones Latinae Selectae* 918).

[....................]
Publius Sulpicius son of Publius Quirinius consul
[....................]
praetor proconsul obtained the Province Crete and Cyrene
[....................]
legate propraetor of the divine Augustus obtaining Syria and Phoenicia waged war with the nation of the Homonadenses which had killed Amyntas the King. Which having been restored to the power of the Emperor, Caesar Augustus, and of the Roman People, the Senate decreed to the immortal gods double supplications because of affairs prosperously completed by him and to him triumphal insignia
[....................]
proconsul obtained the Province Asia, legate propraetor* of the divine Augustus obtained again [or "again, obtained"] Syria and Phoenicia**.

Proconsul Asiam Provinciam Optinvit Legatus PR. PR.
**Divi Augustus Iterum Syriam et Phoenicen Optinvit*

26. For examples of support for the "doctrinal translation," see, Harold W. Hoehner, *Chronological Aspects of the Life of Christ* (Grand Rapids: Zondervan, 1977), 20–23, and A. J. B. Higgins, "Sidelights on Christian Beginnings in the Graeco-Roman World," *The Evangelical Quarterly* 41 (1969), 198–200.
27. Raymond E. Brown, *The Birth of the Messiah* (New York: Doubleday, 1977), 546–55.
28. *Anchor Bible Dictionary* (New York: Doubleday, 1997), volume I, 1012–13.

The major problems with interpreting this partial inscription are the gaps in the text and the identity of the person to whom the inscription refers. While some historians have argued that the text refers to P. Sulpicius Quirinius,[29] the greater weight of opinion is that the inscription does not refer to Quirinius[30] and may refer to the career of L. Calpurnius Piso.[31] Even if one were to accept, however, that the inscription referred to Quirinius, there would still be the question of the proper translation of the text: does the word "again" (*iterum*) modify "legate" or "obtained Syria and Phoenicia"? The generally accepted rules of Latin grammar indicate that "again" modifies "legate" and such is the majority opinion today.[32] ("Propraetorial legate of the Divine Augustus for the second time, he received Syria and Phoenicia.") Over the last century, however, a number of reputable historians have translated the text as reading "obtained again Syria," and thus have concluded that Quirinius served twice as governor of Syria.[33] On this basis, these historians have concluded that either Quirinius conducted two censuses (the one in 6 C.E. described by Josephus and an otherwise unknown census during the reign of Herod described by the Gospel of Luke) or that the census dated to 6 C.E. by Josephus was really conducted during Herod's reign. This conclusion is quite literally a "leap of faith" as its logic is obviously flawed. Even if one accepted that Quirinius was in fact twice governor of Syria, such a fact is not evidence that Quirinius conducted two censuses of Judaea, that such a second governorship occurred during the reign of Herod the Great (or for that matter, was either earlier or later than the governorship in 6 C.E.), or that the one census known to have been conducted by Quirinius was actually conducted in a year other than 6 C.E. In other words, while the hypothesis that Quirinius conducted a census during Herod's reign is in theory "conceivable," if one accepts that Quirinius was twice governor of Syria, such a hypothesis must still be tested against all of the extant evidence and not be deemed established merely because such a conclusion would support the veracity of one piece of evidence out of the many pieces available. Good historical methodology tests the conclusion against the evidence, rather than interpreting the evidence to fit a predetermined conclusion.

29. Raymond E. Brown *The Birth of the Messiah* (New York: Doubleday & Co., 1977), 546–55.

30. Raymond E. Brown, a conservative Catholic scholar, has acknowledged that an article by R. Syme has "devastatingly" exposed the weakness of the Quirinius attribution. *The Birth of the Messiah* (New York: Doubleday & Co., 1977), 551, note 11.

31. *The Oxford Classical Dictionary* (Oxford University Press, 1997), 1455; Raymond Brown, *The Birth of the Messiah* (New York: Doubleday, 1977), 551, note 11.

32. *The Anchor Bible Dictionary*, "Chronology" (New York: Doubleday, 1992), volume 1, 1012.

33. D. S. Potter, "Quirinius," *Anchor Bible Dictionary* (New York: Doubleday, 1992), V.587–588. See, for example, William M. Ramsay, *Was Christ Born at Bethlehem* (Grand Rapids: Baker Books, 1979), 227–28; Ben Witherington III, "Birth of Jesus," *Dictionary of Jesus and the Gospels* (Downers Grove, Ill.: InterVarsity Press, 1992), 67–68.

The problems that arise from not using proper historical methodology can be seen with regard to the argument that Quirinius conducted a census during the reign of Herod the Great. This argument begins with the presumption that the Gospel of Luke is correct in stating that Quirinius conducted a census during the reign of Herod the Great. To avoid contradicting this presumption, the text of the inscription from Tibur must then be translated to indicate that Quirinius was twice governor of Syria, because such a second governorship makes possible the presumption that this second governorship was during the reign of Herod the Great, which in turn makes possible the presumption that Quirinius conducted a census during Herod's reign, which in turn "supports" the text presented in the Gospel of Luke. The argument does not address the other extant evidence on this issue, which indicates that there was not any time when Quirinius could have been governor of Syria during the latter years of Herod's reign.

From a variety of literary sources and dated coins issued by the various Roman governors of Syria, we can reconstruct the following chronology for the Roman governors of Syria:[34]

23–13 B.C.E.	M. Agrippa
ca. 10 B.C.E.	M. Titius
9–6 B.C.E.	S. Sentius Saturninus
6–4 B.C.E. or later	Quintilius Varus
1 B.C.E.–4 C.E.	Gaius Caesar
4–5 C.E.	L. Volusius Saturninus

The only open dates for a second governorship of Syria by Quirinius are 12–11 B.C.E. and 4/3–1 B.C.E. The later dates are after Herod's death, however, and in 12 B.C.E. Quirinius was consul in Rome.[35] Moreover, in all the extant literary references to the career of Quirinius, there is no suggestion that he served as the legate of any province between 12 B.C.E. and 6 C.E. These inconvenient facts have not stopped those who wish to preserve the accuracy of the Gospel of Luke, however, as some writers have asserted that Quirinius "must" have held an unprecedented "dual governorship" with Quintilius Varus in Syria during the period 6–4/3 B.C.E.

The arguments made in favor of two censuses and dual governorships clearly indicate the real methodological issues in controversy here. Because a particular statement of fact is made in the Gospel of Luke, those people who begin with the assumption that the Gospel is inerrant are willing to presume the existence of however many censuses, governorships, or other "facts" as may be necessary to make the known evidence fit with the Gospel text. These proponents are not at all dismayed by the fact that the logic and reasoning that must be applied to the extant evidence to reach this conclusion are extremely

34. Raymond E. Brown, *The Birth of the Messiah* (New York: Doubleday, 1977), 550.
35. Tacitus, *Annals* 3.48.

tortured.[36] The dubiousness of such a methodology from a logical perspective is made even clearer by the fact that the various passages of Luke and Acts that refer to the census contain a variety of other mistakes with respect to the relevant dates and sequence of the events described. Thus, we find that in Acts 5:34–40, the author of Luke/Acts mistakenly dated Judas's uprising at the time of Quirinius's census after Theudas's uprising in the mid-40s C.E., and committed the anachronism of having Gamaliel, in a speech made in approximately 35 C.E., refer to Theudas's revolt from the following decade.[37] Even the Gospel's description of the nature of the census itself, with families having to leave their homes to travel to ancestral towns of an extraordinarily remote past for the purposes of the census registration is without support in the extant evidence and defies the logic of a census designed to enroll property, not people.[38]

At its most fundamental level, historical methodology consists of reasoning from the known evidence to the conclusion and not reasoning backwards from the conclusion to the interpretation of the evidence. Thus, the modern historian, who does not begin the analysis with an assumption of the inerrancy of the Gospel text, believes that the reconstruction of events with the greatest degree of logic, simplicity, and evidentiary support is that Quirinius conducted a single

---

36. The historian John P. Meier has written that "Attempts to reconcile Luke 2:1 with the facts of ancient history are hopelessly contrived." *A Marginal Jew: Rethinking the Historical Jesus* (New York: Doubleday, 1991), volume 1, 213. For a fine example of the convoluted logic and historically unsupported presumptions which have been used to argue in favor of the "two census" theory, see *Dictionary of Jesus and the Gospels*, "Birth of Jesus" (Downers Grove, Ill.: InterVarsity Press, 1992), 67–68.

37. Josephus, *Jewish Antiquities* 20.97–103.

38. The historical problems with the Gospel of Luke's account of the census are notorious and have been recounted by many historians. See, for example, E. P. Sanders, *The Historical Figure of Jesus* (New York: Penguin Press, 1993), 86–87; Raymond E. Brown, *The Birth of the Messiah* (New York: Doubleday, 1977), 412–18, 547–56; John P. Meier, *A Marginal Jew: Rethinking the Historical Jesus* (New York: Doubleday, 1991), 212–213. Occasional reference is made to an early second-century papyrus, British Museum Papyrus No. 904 (lines 18–38), as support for the belief that the Romans might require people to return to their ancestral homes for a census, but in fact the text of the papyrus states only that people temporarily absent from their homes were to return to their "hearths" (not their ancestral homes) for the census and resume "the farming incumbent upon them":

> Gaius Vibius Maximus, prefect of Egypt, declares: The house-by-house census having begun, it is essential that all persons who for any reason at all are absent from their nomes [an administrative unit of the Egyptian province] be notified to return to their own hearths in order that they may fulfill the customary procedure of registration and apply themselves to the farming incumbent upon them. Knowing, however, that our city [Alexandria] has need of some of the people from the country, I desire all who think they have a satisfactory reason for remaining here to register their reasons with Bul [. . .] Festus, squadron prefect, whom I have appointed for this purpose. Those showing their presence to be necessary will receive signed permits from him in accordance with this edict before the 30th of the present month of Epeiph, and all others shall return home within [. . .] days. Anyone found without a permit thereafter [?] will be severely punished; for I know well [. . .]

Naphtali Lewis and Meyer Reinhold, *Roman Civilization Sourcebook II: The Empire* (New York: Harper & Row, 1955), 389.

census of Judaea in 6 C.E. in connection with the establishment of direct Roman rule over Archelaus's territories. While some no doubt will wish to argue for the ultimate superiority of the religious perspective over the historical perspective, it is well to remember E. P. Sander's comments at the end of Chapter 1 concerning the problems created by such personal bias when interpreting history, and each reader should at least recognize the difference between the two methodologies and be aware of which methodology he or she brings to the historical sources.

In view of the strong evidence in favor of the 6 C.E. date for the census of Quirinius, historians have suggested a variety of explanations for the error in the Gospel of Luke. One suggestion is that the Gospel mistakenly referred to Quirinius when a census by a different Roman governor was intended. This explanation occurred to at least a few early Christians. Thus it was that Tertullian wrote in about 207 to 211 C.E. that there was "historical evidence" of an unspecified nature that a census was conducted in Judaea by S. Sentius Saturninus, the Roman governor of Syria from 9–6 B.C.E.[39] The nature of this evidence has been entirely lost, if in fact it ever existed, but the point is that Tertullian recognized that there was no evidence of a census of Palestine by Quirinius during the reign of Herod the Great and was trying to save the essentials of the Gospel text by arguing for an alternative account of the census, even while implicitly admitting that the precise details of the Gospel were incorrect.

Other historians have suggested that the author of the Gospel confused the census of Roman citizens conducted by Caesar Augustus in 8 B.C.E.[40] with Quirinius's enrollment of Judaea. Dating the birth of Jesus to around the time of 8 B.C.E. would be consistent with the tradition that Jesus was born late in Herod's reign and not terribly inconsistent with the tradition that Jesus was about thirty when he began his ministry, as his ministry must have begun between 26–30 C.E. It is conceivable that the author of the Gospel of Luke, writing some seventy to ninety years after Jesus' birth, might have confused the census of Quirinius with the census of Roman citizens by Augustus, but there is no evidence to support this speculation and it is difficult to understand why Jesus' family would have remembered the year of the birth of their son with reference to a census of Roman citizens at a time when Judaea and Galilee were still part of Herod's kingdom.

Other historians have suggested that the error in the Gospel of Luke resulted from a confusion of names arising out of the fact that while P. Sulpicius Quirinius was governor of Syria in 6 C.E., the legate of Syria from approximately 6–4 B.C.E. was P. Quintilius Varus. However, even if one concedes that the confusion of names was possible, a confusion of names is not evidence that P. Quintilius Varus conducted a census of Judaea during Herod the Great's reign.

---

39. Tertullian, *Against Marcion* 4.19.
40. *Res Gestae Divi Augusti* 8.3.

The problems experienced by the author of the Gospel of Luke in determining the year of Jesus' birth were not unknown to other ancient Christian writers who attempted to calculate the year of Jesus' birth and made similar errors in their conclusions. About 180 C.E., Irenaeus wrote that Jesus was born in the forty-first year of the reign of Augustus (*Against Heresies* 3.21.3), a date that, using the Julian calendar, would be 4 B.C.E. if using a nonaccession-year system or 3 B.C.E. by the accession-year system. About 198 C.E., Tertullian wrote that Jesus was born in the forty-first year of Augustus's reign, twenty-eight years after the death of Cleopatra (*An Answer to the Jews* 8), a date that would fall in 3/2 B.C.E. About 200 C.E., Clement of Alexandria wrote that Jesus was born in the twenty-eighth year of the reign of Augustus, exactly one hundred and ninety-four years, one month, and thirteen days before the death of the Emperor Commodus (*Miscellanies* 1.21.145), a date that calculates to November 18, 3 B.C.E. In the early third century C.E., Julius Africanus calculated a date of 3/2 B.C.E. for Jesus' birth (*Chronographies* 235), while Origen followed Tertullian in stating that Jesus was born in the forty-first year of Caesar Augustus (*Homilies on Luke*, fragment 82), or 3 B.C.E. In the first quarter of the fourth century C.E., Eusebius of Caesaria wrote that Jesus was born in the forty-second year of Augustus's reign and in the twenty-eighth year after Cleopatra's death (*Ecclesiastical Histories* 1.52), or 3/2 B.C.E. In the last half of the fourth century, Epiphanius wrote that Jesus was born in the consulship of Silvanius and Octavian (*Panarion* 51.22.3), or 2 B.C.E. Other Christian writers proposed other dates, but the general idea is the same: no ancient Christian was sure exactly when Jesus was born and almost invariably the Christian writers dated Jesus' birth after the death of Herod in 4 B.C.E.

Most modern historians are willing to accept the statements in the Gospels of Matthew and Luke that Jesus was born during Herod's reign precisely because these two accounts, which vary so greatly in most of their details, agree on the detail of Herod's reign.[41] However, there is no indication in either Gospel that indicates clearly when the birth occurred during Herod's reign. Because Matthew 2:11 states that Jesus was a "very young child" (*to paidion*) when the three Magi came to honor him and Matthew 2:19 uses the same "very young child" to describe Jesus at the time of Herod's death, many people interpret the Gospel as indicating that Jesus was born late in the reign of King Herod. Some support for this argument can also be found in the story at Matthew 2:16 that Herod, after learning of the birth of the Messiah from the Magi, ordered the massacre of all male children in Bethlehem who were "two years old or under," but many historians dismiss this story as mere legend. All in all, however, the Gospel of Matthew would seem to indicate that Jesus was born late in Herod's reign, within a few years of Herod's death in the spring of 4 B.C.E. This is consistent with

41. John P. Meier, *A Marginal Jew: Rethinking the Historical Jesus* (New York: Doubleday, 1991), volume 1, 213.

the Luke 3:23's statement that Jesus was "about thirty" when he began his ministry, an event that occurred sometime between 26 to 30 C.E. Thus, while the Gospels of Matthew and Luke indicate an approximate time for the birth of Jesus, it is also evident that no single year can be fixed with certainty. Arguments can and are made for a range of dates from as late as 2 B.C.E. to as early as 10 or 12 B.C.E., but the majority of modern historians favor just prior to 4 B.C.E.

Because the literary evidence does not provide any certain answer to this question, from time to time people have attempted to use the Matthew 2:1–2 description of a "star" in the sky at Jesus' birth to calculate the year of birth. Any such argument must presume that Mathew's "star" was a regularly recurring natural phenomenon rather than an undatable supernatural miracle, but it is an area worth examining. Unfortunately, astronomers have determined that there are many possible candidates, as there are in fact a fair number of novas, comets, and/or planetary conjunctions that can be dated to the approximate period of 10–4 B.C.E.

If Matthew's "star" were a nova, it would be impossible to date the event unless the nova were mentioned in an ancient source because a nova is a non-repeating event. If the "star" were a comet, however, then a determination of the date might be possible, depending on whether the comet was a periodically repeating event like Haley's Comet, which is calculated to have appeared in 12–11 B.C.E., or a one-time visitor to the solar system. The extant Chinese astronomical records indicate that there were at least two such events during the period under investigation.[42] The first was a comet, or "sweeping star," which appeared in March of 5 B.C.E. and was visible for a period of seventy days.[43] The second was a "comet without a tail," which could be either a nova or a comet, which appeared in April of 4 B.C.E. for an unspecified period of time.[44]

If Matthew's "star" were instead a conjunction of planets, then possible dates can be calculated by modern astronomers because planetary conjunctions are regular, repeating events. However, it turns out that there were several such conjunctions during the period in question. For example, astronomers have determined that in 7 B.C.E. there were conjunctions of Jupiter and Saturn on May 27, October 6, and December 1,[45] and that in February of 6 B.C.E. Mars moved into a triangular configuration with these two planets in the constellation Pisces.[46] While these three planets and the constellation Pisces have astrological

---

42. In addition to the two events discussed in the text, the Chinese records also reflect comets in 12 B.C.E. and 13 C.E. See Jack Finnegan, *Handbook of Biblical Chronology* (Peabody: Hendrickson, 1998), 315.

43. Ma Tuan-Lin 380; and Pan Ku, *Ch'ien-Han Shu*, 26.

44. Tung Keen Kang Muh; Pan Ku, *Ch'ien-Han Shu* 11. (Note that this comet seems too late in Herod's reign to fit the events in the Gospel of Matthew discussed above.)

45. Jack Finnegan, *Handbook of Biblical Chronology* (Peabody: Hendrickson, 1998), 313.

46. Ibid., 316. Finnegan discusses a cuneiform text originally from Sippan, Mesopotamia and now in the Berlin Museum, which predicted the May conjunction of Jupiter and Saturn in 7 B.C.E., thus indicating the ability of ancient astronomers to forecast such events. Id. at 316–317. The interpretation of this text has been disputed, however.

connotations that some might think appropriate for heralding the birth of Jesus, the pseudo-science of astrology is hardly a firm basis for making historical judgments of fact. We must remember also that the Gospel of Matthew spoke of a star, not a conjunction of planets, and modern astronomers do not calculate that the three planets were so close together in the sky as to appear to be a single star.

In summary, our review of the extant sources indicates that Dionysius Exiguus should not be unduly criticized for erring in his calculation of Jesus' birth year. Dionysius lived more than five centuries after the events in question and had access to far fewer sources of evidence and astronomical resources than the modern historian. Moreover, Dionysius's calculation was not materially different than the dates computed by earlier Christian writers.

DETERMINING THE DATE OF THE DEATH OF JESUS

As with the birth of Jesus, the extant sources do not allow an exact determination of the year of Jesus' crucifixion, but an approximate range of dates can be established. Again, we begin the investigation by establishing a fixed date as beginning point and cross-referencing the other evidence to that date.

> E–18 Josephus, *Jewish Antiquities*, 18.32–35, 89 (ca. 93–94 C.E.)
>
> [32] Ambivulus's successor was Annius Rufus, whose administration was marked by the death of Caesar [Augustus on August 19, 14 C.E.], the second emperor of the Romans, who had ruled for fifty-seven years, six months and two days. Antony had shared authority with him for fourteen years of this period. He was seventy-seven years old when he died. Caesar's successor in authority was the third emperor, Tiberius Nero, the son of his wife Julia. He dispatched Valerius Gratus to succeed Annius Rufus as procurator over the Jews. . . . After these acts Gratus retired to Rome, having stayed eleven years in Judaea. It was Pontius Pilate who came as his successor.
>
> [89] Vitellius thereupon dispatched Marcellus, one of his friends, to take charge of the administration of Judaea, and ordered Pilate to return to Rome to give the emperor his account of the matters with which he was charged by the Samaritans. And so Pilate, after having spent ten years in Judaea, hurried to Rome in obedience to the orders of Vitellius, since he could not refuse. But before he reached Rome Tiberius had already passed away.

We know from other sources that the emperor Tiberius died March 16, 37 C.E.[47] and so, allowing for the travel time involved, *Jewish Antiquities* 18.89 indicates that Pontius Pilate most likely left for Rome in December of 36 C.E. or January of 37 C.E. In conjunction with *Jewish Antiquities* 18.32–35, one can therefore determine the terms of several Roman governors for Judaea and the

---

47. Suetonius, *Life of Tiberius* 73.

fact that Pontius Pilate was governor from 26 C.E. until very late 36 C.E. or very early 37 C.E. The unanimous Christian tradition that Jesus died while Pilate was governor of Judaea at the time of a Passover celebration[48] therefore indicates that the range of possible dates for the crucifixion runs from the spring of 26 C.E. through the spring of 36 C.E.

From this point, we must look for additional evidence to narrow the range of possible dates. One obvious cross-reference would be to Caiaphas, the high priest at the time of Jesus' death, but unfortunately it appears that Caiaphas held the position of high priest from 18 C.E. to not later than the Passover of 37 C.E.,[49] a term of office that does not narrow the range of dates indicated by Pilate's governorship. A potentially more useful date can be computed from two passages in the Gospel of Luke.

E–19 The Gospel of Luke 3:1–2, 23
¹ In the fifteenth year of the reign of Tiberius Caesar, Pontius Pilate being governor of Judaea, and Herod being tetrarch of Judaea, and his brother Philip tetrarch of the region of Ituraea and Trachonitis, and Lysanias Tetrarch of Abilene, in the high-priesthood of Annas and Caiaphas, the Word of God came to John the son of Zechariah in the Wilderness. . . .
²³ Jesus, when he began his ministry, was about thirty years of age. . . .

According to the Gospel of Luke, the ministry of Jesus began after the Word of God came to John the Baptist "in the fifteenth year of the reign of Tiberius Caesar." Tiberius held a co-regency with Caesar Augustus during the years 12–14 C.E. and after the death of Caesar Augustus in 14 C.E. Tiberius served as sole emperor from his election by the senate on September 17, 14 C.E. The first issue in interpreting the passage is thus whether the "fifteenth year of the reign of Tiberius" should be counted from 12 C.E. or 14 C.E. We know from inscriptions that Tiberius himself calculated his reign as emperor from 14 C.E. and 14 C.E. was described as the first year of his reign by the Roman historians Tacitus, Suetonius, and Cassius Dio.[50] If one assumes that the author of the Gospel of Luke used the Roman Julian calendar (and not the Jewish, Syrian-Macedonian or Egyptian calendars) and began the count when Tiberius became sole emperor in September of 14 C.E., then the fifteenth year of Tiberius's reign would corre-spond to roughly September of 28 C.E. through August of 29 C.E., although 27 C.E. and the later part of 29 C.E. would be possible dates under the other three cal-endars. If the Gospel of Luke began its count with 12 C.E., then the earliest date for the start of John's ministry would fall in 26 C.E. under the Roman calendar and 25 C.E. or 27 C.E. under the other calendars. Most historians believe that the

---

48. Matthew 27:1–2; Mark 15:1; Luke 23:1; John 18:29; Acts 3:13.
49. Josephus, *Jewish Antiquities* 18.35, 95.
50. Harold W. Hoehner, *Chronological Aspects of the Life of Christ* (Grand Rapids: Zondervan, 1977), 31–32 and notes 11, 12, and 13.

author of the Gospel of Luke began his count with the year 14 C.E. and therefore accept 28/29 C.E. as the approximate starting date for the ministry of John,
but all of the possible dates under any of the four different calendars are consistent with the idea that first John and then Jesus conducted their respective
ministries after the start of Pontius Pilate's governorship in 26 C.E.

The next potential piece of evidence concerning the year of the crucifixion
comes from another Gospel text.

E–20 The Gospel of John 2:19–20
Jesus answered them, "Destroy this temple and in three days I will
raise it up." The Jews then said, "It has taken forty-six years to build
this temple, and will you raise it up in three days?"

In his writings Josephus gave two different dates for the start of construction of the Second Temple: *Jewish Antiquities* 15.380 states that construction
began in the eighteenth year of Herod the Great's reign (20–19 B.C.E.) and *The
Jewish War* 1.401 states Herod's fifteenth year (23–22 B.C.E.). Most historians,
using the additional evidence given by Cassius Dio at *Roman History* 54.7.4–6
and by Josephus at *Jewish War* 1.399, accept 20–19 B.C.E. for the start of the
rebuilding of the Temple and thus the passage from John would indicate a date
of about 26 C.E., a time just possibly within Pontius Pilate's governorship of
Judaea. However, the four Gospels of the New Testament do not agree whether
Jesus' cleansing of the Temple occurred at the beginning of Jesus' ministry or at
the end.[51] Moreover, since Pilate's governorship began sometime in 26 C.E. a
crucifixion in the spring of 26 C.E. would seem to telescope the events of Jesus'
ministry into a few months at most, which strikes most historians as extremely
improbable within the context of the Gospel accounts. Thus, the date indicated
by John 2:19–20 seems doubtful.

The most significant additional pieces of information to be found in the
Gospels concerning the date of the crucifixion are the references to the connection between the Last Supper, Passover, and the Friday crucifixion. If the
relationship of these events could be precisely determined, then in theory
astronomers could calculate the possible dates for a Friday crucifixion in conjunction with Passover during the period 26 to 36 C.E. Unfortunately, not only
are the four Gospel accounts inconsistent, but two other issues relevant to the
Jewish calendar cannot be resolved with certainty.

E–21 The Gospel of Mark 14:12–17
And on the first day of Unleavened Bread, when they sacrificed the
Passover lamb, his disciples said to him, "Where will you have us go
and prepare for you to eat the Passover?" And he sent two of his disciples, and said to them, "Go into the city, and a man carrying a jar

---

51. The Gospel of John places the incident early in Jesus' ministry, while Mark, Matthew, and
Luke place it in the last week of Jesus' life.

of water will meet you; follow him, and wherever he enters, say to the householder, 'The Teacher says, Where is my guest room, where I am to eat the Passover with my disciples?' And he will show you a large upper room furnished and ready; there prepare for us." And the disciples set out and went to the city, and found it as he had told them; and they prepared the Passover. And when it was evening he came with the twelve.

E–22 The Gospel of Luke 22:7–15

Then came the day of Unleavened Bread, on which the Passover lamb had to be sacrificed. So Jesus sent Peter and John, saying, "Go and prepare the Passover for us, that we may eat it." They said to him, "Where will you have us prepare it?" He said to them, "Behold, when you have entered the city, a man carrying a jar of water will meet you; follow him into the house which he enters, and tell the householder, 'The Teacher says to you, Where is the guest room, where I am to eat the Passover with my disciples?' And he will show you a large upper room furnished; there make ready. And they went, and found it as He had told them; and they prepared the Passover. And when the hour came, He sat at table, and the apostles with Him. And He said to them, "I have earnestly desired to eat this Passover with you before I suffer. . . ."

E–23 The Gospel of Matthew 26:17–20

Now on the first day of Unleavened Bread the disciples came to Jesus, saying, "Where will you have us prepare for you to eat the Passover?" He said, "Go into the city to a certain one, and say to him, 'The Teacher says, My time is at hand; I will keep the Passover at your house with my disciples.'" And the disciples did as Jesus had directed them, and they prepared the Passover. When it was evening, he sat at the table with the twelve disciples;

E–24 The Gospel of John 13:1-4; 18:28; 19:12-14

13:1 Now before the feast of the Passover, when Jesus knew that his hour had come to depart out of this world to the Father, having loved his own who were in the world, he loved them to the end. And during supper, when the devil had already put it into the heart of Judas Iscariot, Simon's son, to betray him, Jesus, knowing that the Father had given all things into his hands, and that he had come from God and was going to God, rose from supper, laid aside his garments, and girded himself with a towel. . . .

18:28 Then they led Jesus from the house of Caiaphas to the praetorium. It was early. They themselves did not enter the praetorium, so that they might not be defiled, but might eat the Passover. . . .

19:12 Upon this Pilate sought to release him, but the Jews cried out, "If you release this man, you are not Caesar's friend; every one who makes himself a king sets himself against Caesar." When Pilate heard these words, he brought Jesus out and sat down on the judgment seat at a place called The Pavement, and in Hebrew Gabbatha. Now it was the day of Preparation of the Passover; it was about the sixth hour.

The conflict between the Synoptic Gospels of Mark, Luke, and Matthew on the one hand and the Gospel of John, on the other, as to whether the Last Supper was the Passover meal obviously complicates the calculation of the year of Jesus' crucifixion. Exodus 12 indicates that the Passover lambs were sacrificed during daylight hours on Nisan 14 and were eaten that day after sunset, on Nisan 15. Thus, the discrepancy between the Synoptic Gospels and the Gospel of John concerns whether the crucifixion occurred on Friday, Nisan 15 (Passover began at Thursday sunset), or on Friday, Nisan 14 (Passover began at Friday sunset). Historians are divided over whether to accept the Gospel of John's chronology, as some believe the author of the Gospel has intentionally re-dated events to create a parallel between the Passover sacrifice and the crucifixion of Jesus.[52] It is possible, however, that the account of the release of Barabbas found in the Gospels supports the dating found in the Gospel of John.

E–25 The Gospel of Matthew 27:15
Now at the feast the governor was accustomed to release for the crowd any one prisoner whom they wanted.

This custom is not attested by any source outside of the Gospels (See also, Mark 15:6, Luke 23:17, and John 18:38–40) and many historians do not accept the custom as factual.[53] If the custom was genuine and one presumes that the intent was to allow the prisoner to participate in the feast of Passover, then the custom supports the dating of the Gospel of John. This argument unfortunately rests on an *a priori* assumption as to the timing of the release of the prisoner. None of the Gospels state that the practice was to release the prisoner on the Passover as opposed to in conjunction with the celebrations associated with Passover. Moreover, while Pontius Pilate might have released a prisoner before the Passover to permit participation in the meal, Pilate might just as likely have released the prisoner after the Passover to symbolize that death had "passed over" the prisoner.[54]

Often lost in the arguments concerning the choice of Nisan 14 or Nisan 15 for the crucifixion is the fact that two other problems exist because of the

---

52. See, for example, E. P. Sanders, *The Historical Figure of Jesus* (New York: Penguin, 1993), 285–286. Raymond E. Brown rejects such arguments in *The Death of the Messiah* (New York: Doubleday, 1994), II.1372.

53. John Dominic Crossan, *Who Killed Jesus?* (San Francisco: HarperSanFrancisco, 1995), 111; S. G. F. Brandon, *The Trial of Jesus of Nazareth* (New York: Dorset Press, 1968), 94–102; Paula Fredriksen, *Jesus of Nazareth, King of the Jews* (New York: Alfred A. Knopf, 1999), 222–223; Michael Grant, *Jesus: An Historian's Review of the Gospels* (New York: Charles Scribner's Sons, 1977), 164–65. Raymond E. Brown believes that Barabbas was a real person, but does not accept the custom of releasing a prisoner at Passover as authentic. *The Death of the Messiah* (New York: Doubleday, 1994), 814–820. See *Ibid.* at I.814, footnote 51 for a summary of historians on either side of this issue.

54. John P. Meier, *A Marginal Jew* (New York: Doubleday, 1991), 400 argues the opposite view.

nature of the Jewish calendar. The Jewish month of Nisan (March/April) began on the evening of the 29th day of the prior month only if two reliable witnesses could attest to the calendar committee in Jerusalem that they had seen the light of the new moon after sunset. Accordingly, rain, fog, or clouds could result in a postponement of the start of the new month for one day. (Under the then-current Jewish religious law, months could only be twenty-nine or thirty days in length.) Moreover, we know that a leap month was added to the Jewish calendar every two or three years to keep the Jewish lunar year in synchronization with the seasons of the solar year and there seems to have been no regular cycle of making this adjustment during the early first century C.E.—leap months were simply added as needed to match up the seasons under the solar and lunar calendars. Leap months might also be added to the calendar for a more practical reason: barley was needed for the Festival of Unleavened Bread that followed the Passover and if unseasonably cool temperatures had delayed the maturing of the barley crops the priests of the Temple could insert a month to allow the crop to ripen.[55] Unfortunately, there is simply no evidence at all as to whether a leap month was added to any year in the Jewish calendar between 26 and 36 C.E. or whether during that period the start of Nisan was ever delayed a day because of the weather.

Still, if one accepts the unanimous Christian tradition that the crucifixion occurred during Pontius Pilate's governorship on a Friday that was Nisan 14 or 15 and allows for the possible combinations of leap months and/or delays in the start of Nisan, it is possible to calculate a number of potential dates for the crucifixion:[56]

	No Leap Month No One Day Delay	No Leap Month One Day Delay	Leap Month No One Day Delay	Leap Month One Day Delay
26 C.E.				
27 C.E.	Nisan 15–April 11	Nisan 14–April 10		
28 C.E.				Nisan 15–April 29
29 C.E.				
30 C.E.	Nisan 14–April 7			
31 C.E.				Nisan 15–April 26
32 C.E.				
33 C.E.	Nisan 14–April 3			
34 C.E.			Nisan 15–April 23	Nisan 14–April 22
35 C.E.		Nisan 15–March 25		
36 C.E.	Nisan 14–March 30			

---

55. E. P. Sanders, *The Historical Figure of Jesus* (New York: Penguin, 1993), 285.

56. Adapted from Jack Finegan, *Handbook of Biblical Chronology* (Peabody: Hendrickson Publsihers, 1998), 363.

The 36 C.E. date is generally seen by most historians as being too late in light of the general circumstances of Jesus' life, although it has its supporters.[57] In an interesting example of an apparent inconsistency that arises from following good methodology, most historians prefer either 30 or 33 C.E. as the year of the crucifixion (i.e., Nisan 14 dates consistent with the Gospel of John) even though the same historians may reject the Gospel of John's identification of Jesus' crucifixion with the sacrifice of the Passover lamb as a theological construct rather than a historical fact.[58] This inconsistency perhaps arises in part as the result of applying the "Occam's Razor" theorem discussed in chapter one— since the 30 and 33 C.E. dates fit without making unprovable assumptions about the weather or the insertion of a leap month necessary for the other dates, historians prefer the Nisan 14 dates, notwithstanding the simultaneous belief that the Gospel of John is wrong in its dating.

We can see that, as with the birth of Jesus, a determination of the precise year of Jesus' death has eluded the best efforts of modern historians and that it is probably insolvable with the available sources. It is also evident that the same general problem with determining the date existed in antiquity, as the early Christian sources gave a variety of inconsistent dates for the year of the crucifixion.

E–26 Clement of Alexandria, *Miscellanies* 1.21.46 (ca. 200 C.E.)
> Accordingly, in fifteen years of Tiberius and fifteen years of Augustus; so were completed the thirty years till the time He suffered. And from the time that He suffered till the destruction of Jerusalem [September of 70 C.E.] are forty-two years and three months; and from the destruction of Jerusalem to the death of Commodus [192 C.E.], a hundred and twenty-eight years, ten months, and three days. From the birth of Christ, therefore, to the death of Commodus are, in all, a hundred and ninety-four years, one month, thirteen days. And there are those who have determined not only the year of our Lord's birth, but also the day; and they say that it took place in the twenty-eighth year of Augustus, and in the twenty-fifth day of Pachon.

Clement's calculations reflect the difficulty that the ancients had in dating past events: as we have just seen, the assertion that Jesus died in the fifteenth year of Tiberius (28 C.E.) is not one of the possible years for the crucifixion and certain of Clement's stated intervals of years are inaccurate.

E–27 Origen, *Against Celsus* 4.22 (240s C.E.)
> And any one who likes may convict this statement of falsehood, if it be not the case that the whole Jewish nation was overthrown within

---

57. Nikos Kokkinos, "Crucifixion in A.D. 36: The Keystone for Dating the Birth of Jesus," *Chronos, Kairos, Christos* (n.2) 133–63; Robin Lane Fox, *The Unauthorized Version* (New York: Alfred A. Knopf, 1991), 33–34 and note on p. 423.

58. See, for example, E. P. Sanders, *The Historical Figure of Jesus* (New York: Penguin Press, 1993), 285–86.

one single generation after Jesus had undergone these sufferings at their hands. For forty and two years, I think, after the date of the crucifixion of Jesus, did the destruction of Jerusalem take place [70 C.E.].

Origen's date does not correspond with any of the possible years indicated by the modern astronomical calculations. The same is true of other Christian writers who gave very precise dates for the crucifixion.

E–28 Tertullian, *An Answer to the Jews* 8 (ca. 208–217 C.E.)
And the suffering of this "extermination" was perfected within the times of the 70 hebdomads, under Tiberius Caesar, in the consulate of Rubellius Geminus and Fufius Geminus, in the month of March, at the times of the Passover, on the eighth day before the kalends of April, on the first day of unleavened bread, on which they slew the lamb at even, just as had been enjoined by Moses. . . .

E–29 Lactantius, *On the Death of the Persecutors* 2 (ca. 317–318 C.E.)
In the latter days of the Emperor Tiberius, in the censorship of Rubellius Geminus and Fufius Geminus, and on the tenth of the kalends of April, as I find it written, Jesus Christ was crucified by the Jews.

E–30 Augustine, *The City of God* 18.54.1 (ca. 413–416 C.E.)
Now Christ died when the Gemini were consuls, on the eighth day before the kalends of April.

The texts of Augustine and Tertullian indicate that Jesus was crucified on the "eighth day before the calends of April" during the consulship of Rubellius Geminus and Fufius Geminus, or March 25, 29 C.E., while Lactantius refers to the "tenth day," or March 23, 29 C.E. As indicated by the chart above, neither of these dates are consistent with the Gospel accounts.

THE ACTS OF JESUS

Having spent some time examining the date of the crucifixion of Jesus, it would seem appropriate to mention one of the more curious historical questions concerning the crucifixion of Jesus: the early Christian tradition that Pontius Pilate forwarded to the Emperor Tiberius an account of the trial and punishment of Jesus and that the account survived until at least the second century C.E.

E–31 Justin Martyr, *The First Apology* 35, 48 (ca. 155 C.E.)
[35] After fastening Him to the cross, those who crucified Him cast lots for His clothing, and divided it among themselves. That these things really happened, you can learn from the Acts* of what was done under Pontius Pilate.

> *(In the second century C.E., when this account was written, Christians referred to the records of the trial and martyrdom of Christians as "Acts.")*

[48] How it was prophesied that our Christ would heal all diseases and raise the dead, hear what was spoken as follows: "At His coming the lame will leap like a hart, and the stammering tongue will be clear;

blind will see and lepers be cleansed, and the dead will arise and walk." That He did these things, you can learn from the Acts of what took place under Pontius Pilate.

E–32 Tertullian, *Apology* 5.2; 21.24 (ca. 197–98 C.E.)

[5.2] It was in the age of Tiberius, then, that the Christian name went out into the world, and he referred to the Senate the news which he had received from Syria Palestine, which had revealed the truth of Christ's divinity; he did this exercising his prerogative in giving it his endorsement. The Senate had not approved beforehand and so rejected it. Caesar held to his opinion and threatened dangers to accusers of the Christians.

[21.24] The whole story of Christ was reported to Caesar (at that time it was Tiberius) by Pilate, himself in his secret heart already a Christian.

These two second-century texts clearly cannot refer to the "Acts of Pilate," which were forged and circulated in the early fourth century C.E. in conjunction with the "Great Persecution" of Christianity under the Emperor Diocletian. Most historians reject the idea that such Acts existed because it is extremely difficult to believe that an official Roman record of the trial of Jesus could have existed as late as the second half of the second century C.E. and not been preserved by Christian writers. However, Justin Martyr and Tertullian clearly believed that such an account existed. This is just one more unanswerable question concerning the life and death of Jesus.

SOURCES AND TRANSLATIONS

ACTS OF CYPRIAN
> J. Stevenson, trans. *A New Eusebius*. (revised by W. H. C. Frend) London: SPCK, 1997, 247–250, slightly altering E. C. E. Owen. *Some Authentic Acts of the Early Martyrs*. London: SPCK, 1933, 95–99. Used by permission of SPCK Publishing.

ACTS OF FRUCTUOSUS
> Herbert Musurillo, trans. *The Acts of the Christian Martyrs*. Oxford: Oxford University Press, 1972, 177–79. © 1972 Oxford University Press. Used by permission of Oxford University Press.

ACTS OF THE APOSTLES
> Revised Standard Version of the Bible. ©1946, 1952, 1971 by the Division of Christian Education of the National Council of the Churches of Christ in the United States of America. Used by permission. All rights reserved.

ACTS OF THE SCILLITAN MARTYRS
> J. Stevenson, trans. *A New Eusebius*. (revised by W. H. C. Frend) London: SPCK, 1987, 44–45, slightly altering E. C. E. Owen. *Some Authentic Acts of the Early Martyrs*. London: SPCK, 1933, 71–73. Used by permission of SPCK Publishing.

AELIUS ARISTIDES (Publius Aelius Aristides Theodorus, ca. 117 or 128–181 C.E.) A famous rhetorician, Aristides retired to Smyrna because of a series of serious illnesses. Cured of his illnesses at the Asclepium in Pergamum, he became a devoted follower of the god Asclepius and wrote "Sacred Teachings" in honor of the god.
> Stephen Benko, trans. "Speech on the Four" 2.394ff in *Pagan Rome and the Early Christians*. Bloomington: Indiana University Press, 1984, 46. Used by permission of Indiana University Press.

AMBROSE (Ambrosius, ca. 339–397 C.E.) Bishop of Milan from 373–397 C.E., Ambrose was chaplain and advisor to several Christian emperors. As bishop of the imperial capital of the Western Roman Empire, Ambrose wielded tremendous influence in the affairs of both the church and the civil government. He used his power and influence to vigorously prosecute heretics and non-Christians. On the basis of his writings and actions, Ambrose is ranked with Augustine, Gregory I, and Jerome as one of the "Four Fathers of the Church."
> Mary M. Beyenka, trans. *Epistles 40, 41, 51* and *82* in *Saint Ambrose:*

Letters. Vol. 26 of *Fathers of the Church.* Washington, D.C.: Catholic
University of America Press, 1954, 6–19, 20–26, 37–51, 385–395. Used by
permission of Catholic University of America Press.

H. De Romestin, trans. *Epistle 81 in The Nicene and Post-Nicene Fathers.*
Second Series. Grand Rapids: Eerdmans, 1955, 808–12. Used by permission of Wm. B. Eerdmans Publishing Co.

AMMIANUS MARCELLINUS (ca. 330–395) Ammianus, a Greek from
Antioch, wrote the last great Latin language history of Rome. Volumes
14–31 have survived, covering the years 354–378 C.E. As a pagan, Ammianus
was a strong supporter of Julian the Apostate, but he maintained a neutral
stance towards the Christians in his history.

Walter Hamilton, trans. *The Later Roman Empire* 21.2.4–5, 21.16.18,
22.4.5, 22.5.1–4, 22.10.6, 22.11.3, 27.3.12–13. London: Penguin Classics,
1986, 209–10, 232, 238–39, 239, 246, 246–47, 335–36. © Walter
Hamilton 1986. Used by permission of Penguin Classics.

APULEIUS (Lucius Apuleius, ca. 125–170 C.E.) Apuleius studied Platonic philosophy in Athens and practiced law in Rome, but is most famous today for his
novels. He returned to his native Africa ca. 155 C.E., where he was appointed
chief priest of the province and apparently spent the rest of his life there.

Stephen Benko, trans. *The Golden Ass* 9.14 in *Pagan Rome and the Early
Christians.* Bloomington: Indiana University Press, 1984, 104. Used by
permission of Indiana University Press.

ATHENAGORAS OF ATHENS (fl. ca. 180 C.E.) A Christian from Athens, he
wrote an apology in defense of Christianity to the emperor Marcus Aurelius
in about 177 C.E.

Cyril C. Richardson, ed. *Plea on Behalf of the Christians* 1–3, 32 in *Early
Christian Fathers.* Library of Christian Classics. New York: Collier Books,
1970, 301–3, 337. Used by permission of Westminster John Knox Press
and SCM Press.

AUGUSTINE (Aurelius Augustinus, 354–430 C.E.) Baptized by Ambrose,
Augustine was the most important ancient figure in the development of
early Christian philosophy and is known today as one of the "Four Fathers
of the Church." His most famous books are *The City of God* and *The
Confessions of St. Augustine.*

Marcus Dods, trans. *The City of God* 5.26; 10.24, 32; 18.54; 19.23 in *The
Nicene and Post-Nicene Fathers.* First Series. Grand Rapids: Eerdmans,
1956, 240–41; 425, 441, 840, 881, 884. Used by permission of Wm. B.
Eerdmans Publishing Co.

J. G. Pilkington, trans. *The Confessions of St. Augustine* 8.12.28–29 in *The
Nicene and Post-Nicene Fathers.* First Series. Grand Rapids: Eerdmans,
1956, 224–25. Used by permission of Wm. B. Eerdmans Publishing Co.

J. G. Cunningham, trans. *Epistle 102* in *The Nicene and Post-Nicene
Fathers.* First Series. Grand Rapids: Eerdmans, 1896, 416. Used by permission of Wm. B. Eerdmans Publishing Co.

CANONS OF THE COUNCIL OF ANCYRA
> Henry R. Percival, trans. *The Nicene and Post-Nicene Fathers*. Second Series. Grand Rapids: Eerdmans, 1991, 63–65. Used by permission of Wm. B. Eerdmans Publishing Co.
> British Museum Papyrus, No. 904 (lines 18–38) 28, p. 389.

CANONS OF THE COUNCIL OF NICAEA
> Henry R. Percival, trans. *The Nicene and Post-Nicene Fathers*. Second Series. Grand Rapids: Eerdmans, 1991, 10, 24, 27, 31, 36, 42. Used by permission of Wm. B. Eerdmans Publishing Co.

CASSIUS DIO (Cassius Dio Cocceianus, ca. 163–after 229 C.E.) Born in Bithynia, Cassius Dio came to Rome as a young man and entered the senate under the emperor Commodus (emperor 180–192 C.E.). Twice consul, he also served as pro–consul of Africa and governor of Dalmatia and Pannonia.
> Earnest Cary, trans. *Roman History* 55.25, 55.27, 67.14, 68.1–2 and 78.9. Loeb Classical Library. Cambridge: Harvard University Press, 1955, 349–51, 361, 459, 465–67. Used by permission of the publishers and the Trustees at the Loeb Classical Library. The Loeb Classical Library® is a registered trademark of the President and Fellows of Harvard College.

CELSUS (active third quarter of the second century C.E.) Because Celsus's works were ordered destroyed by order of the Christian emperors Constantine and Theodosius II, we know little about Celsus other than for the meager information contained in the book *Contra Celsus* by the Christian writer Origen (ca. 185–254). Celsus's *True Doctrine* was published around 177–80 C.E., and Origen's *Contra Celsus* was written about seventy years later. Historians estimate that approximately 70 percent of *True Doctrine* can be reconstructed from the passages quoted by Origen in *Contra Celsus*.
> Frederick Crombie, trans. *True Doctrine* passages are reproduced from *Contra Celsus* in *The Nicene and Post-Nicene Fathers*. Grand Rapids: Eerdmans, 1994. Used by permission of Wm. B. Eerdmans Publishing Co.

CERTIFICATE OF SACRIFICE
> Henry Bettenson, ed. *Documents of the Christian Church*. 2nd ed. Oxford: Oxford University Press, 1963, 13. Used by permission of Oxford University Press, Inc.

CHRYSOSTOM, JOHN (ca. 347–407 C.E.) Educated in Antioch, Chrysostom served there as a deacon, priest and educator. In 398 C.E. he became bishop of Constantinople. Chrysostom, "the golden mouthed," reflects the eloquent speech for which he was most famous.
> Talbot W. Chambers, trans. *Homily on 2nd Corinthians 13.12* 30.2 in *The Nicene and Post-Nicene Fathers*. First Series. Grand Rapids: Eerdmans, 1956, 905. Used by permission of Wm. B. Eerdmans Publishing Co.

CICERO (Marcus Tullius Cicero, 106–143 B.C.E.) One of the most important orators, authors, philosophers and political leaders of the Late Roman Republic.
> C. MacDonald, trans. *Pro Flacco*, 69. Loeb Classical Library. Cambridge: Harvard University Press, 1989, 517–19. Used by permission of the

publishers and the Trustees at the Loeb Classical Library. The Loeb Classical Library® is a registered trademark of the President and Fellows of Harvard College.

CLEMENT OF ALEXANDRIA (Titus Flavius Clemens, ca. 150–215 C.E.) An Athenian and pagan who converted to Christianity as an adult, Clement became head of the catechetical school in Alexandria, Egypt and wrote several notable books on Christian belief and theology.

A. Cleveland Coxe, trans. *The Instructor* 3.11.81 in *The Ante-Nicene Fathers*. Grand Rapids: Eerdmans, 1951, 571. Used by permission of Wm. B. Eerdmans Publishing Co.

A. Cleveland Coxe, trans. *Miscellanies* 1.21.46 in *The Ante-Nicene Fathers*. Grand Rapids: Eerdmans, 1951, 659–60. Used by permission of Wm. B. Eerdmans Publishing Co.

Ralph Martin Novak, Jr., trans. *Miscellanies* 3.2.5, 10; 4.27.

CONSTANTINE'S LETTER TO ARIUS

Ernest Cushing Richardson, trans. Eusebius's *Life of Constantine* in *The Nicene and Post-Nicene Fathers*. Second Series. Grand Rapids: Eerdmans, 1952, 720–21, 723. Used by permission of Wm. B. Eerdmans Publishing Co.

CONSTITUTIO ANTONINIANA

Naphtali Lewis and Meyer Reinhold. Giessen Papyrus No. 40 column 1, as quoted in *Roman Civilization—Sourcebook II: The Empire*. New York: Columbia University Press, 1955, 427–28. Used by permission of Columbia University Press.

CREED APPROVED BY THE COUNCIL OF CHALCEDON, THE

Henry R. Percival, trans. *The Nicene and Post-Nicene Fathers*. Second Series. Grand Rapids: Eerdmans, 1991, 249. Used by permission of Wm. B. Eerdmans Publishing Co.

CREED OF THE CHURCH OF CAESAREA, THE

Henry Bettenson, trans. *Documents of the Christian Church*. 2nd ed. Oxford: Oxford University Press, 1963, 24–25. Used by permission of Oxford University Press, Inc.

CREED OF THE COUNCIL OF CONSTANTINOPLE, THE

Henry R. Percival, trans. The Introduction and Canon One in *The Nicene and Post-Nicene Fathers*. Second Series. Grand Rapids: Eerdmans, 1991, 173. Used by permission of Wm. B. Eerdmans Publishing Co.

Henry Bettenson, trans. *The Creed in Documents of the Christian Church*. 2nd ed. Oxford: Oxford University Press, 1963, 26. Used by permission of Oxford University Press, Inc.

CREED OF THE COUNCIL OF NICAEA, THE

Henry Bettenson, trans. *Documents of the Christian Church*. 2nd ed. Oxford: Oxford University Press, 1963, 25. Used by permission of Oxford University Press, Inc.

CYPRIAN (Thescius Caecilius Cyprianus, ca. 200–258 C.E.) Cyprian was bishop of Carthage from 248–258 C.E. Cyprian successfully hid from arrest during the persecution of Trajan Decius, 249–251 C.E., but during the subsequent persecution of 257–260 C.E. under the emperor Valerian, he turned himself in and refused "to curse the Christ"; he died a martyr on September 13, 258.

A. Cleveland Coxe, trans. *The Unity of the Church* 20–21 in *The Ante-Nicene Fathers*. Grand Rapids: Eerdmans, reprinted 1981, 877. Used by permission of Wm. B. Eerdmans Publishing Co.

A. Cleveland Coxe, trans. *Epistles* 81 and 82 in *The Ante-Nicene Fathers*. Grand Rapids: Eerdmans, 1951, 841–43. Used by permission of Wm. B. Eerdmans Publishing Co.

CYRIL OF ALEXANDRIA (d. 440 C.E.) Bishop of Alexandria from 412–444 C.E., Cyril was a vigorous opponent of Nestorius and other perceived heretics.

Robert L. Wilken, trans. *Patrologia graeca* 76.508c in *The Christians as the Romans Saw Them*. New Haven: Yale University Press, 1984, 177–78. © 1984. Used by permission of Yale University Press.

DECREE OF CAESAR AUGUSTUS TO THE JEWS

Ralph Marcus and Allen Wikgren, trans. Josephus's *Jewish Antiquities* 16.162. Loeb Classical Library. Cambridge: Harvard University Press, 1963, 271–73. Used by permission of the publishers and the Trustees at the Loeb Classical Library. The Loeb Classical Library® is a registered trademark of the President and Fellows of Harvard College.

THE DIDACHE

Cyril C. Richardson, ed. *Early Christian Fathers*. Library of Christian Classics. New York: Collier Books, 1970, 171–78. Used by permission of Westminster John Knox and SCM Press.

DIONYSIUS (d. 264 C.E.) Bishop of Alexandria.

J. E. L. Oulton, trans. *Letter to Fabius* reproduced from Eusebius, *Ecclesiastical History* 6.41.1, 8–13. Loeb Classical Library. Cambridge: Harvard University Press, 1932, 99–101, 103–5. Used by permission of the publishers and the Trustees at the Loeb Classical Library. The Loeb Classical Library® is a registered trademark of the President and Fellows of Harvard College.

J. E. L. Oulton, trans. *Letter to Hermammon* reproduced from Eusebius, *Ecclesiastical History* 7.10.1–4. Loeb Classical Library. Cambridge: Harvard University Press, 1932, 151–53. Used by permission of the publishers and the Trustees at the Loeb Classical Library. The Loeb Classical Library® is a registered trademark of the President and Fellows of Harvard College.

EDICT OF GALERIUS, THE

A. Cleveland Coxe, trans. Reproduced from Lactantius's *On the Deaths of the Persecutors* 34 in *The Ante-Nicene Fathers*. Grand Rapids: Eerdmans, 1951, 659–60. Used by permission of Wm. B. Eerdmans Publishing Co.

EDICT OF MILAN, THE

Sister Mary Francis McDonald, trans. Reproduced from Lactantius's *On the Deaths of the Persecutors* 48 in *Lactantius: The Minor Works*. Washington,

D.C.: The Catholic University of America Press, 1965, 197–99. Used by permission of The Catholic University of America Press.

EPICTETUS (ca. 55–ca. 135) Stoic Philosopher. Born in Phrygia, Epicetus grew up as a slave of Nero's freedman Epaphroditus. After being freed, he taught in Rome until the emperor Domitian expelled all philosophers from the city in 89 C.E. He spent the remainder of his life in Nicopolis, in Epirus. While he wrote no books during his life, his teachings were collected and published after his death by his student Arrian (Flavius Arrianus).

Reprinted from Whitney J. Oates, ed. *Discourses* 4.7.1–6 in *The Stoic and Epicurean Philosophers*. Cyril Bailey, trans. New York: Random House, 1940, 297–98.

EPIPHANIUS (ca. 315–403 C.E.) Epiphanius was the bishop of Salamis from 367–403, and author of *Panarion* (*The Medicine Chest*), also known as *Refutation of All the Heresies*.

Stephen Benko, trans. *Panarion* 26.4–6 in *Pagan Rome and the Early Christians*. Bloomington: Indiana University Press, 1984, 65–66. Used by permission of Indiana University Press.

Philip R. Amidon, trans. *Panarion* 6.1; 68.1.1, 4, 8; 68.2.1–3; 68.3.1–4 in *The Panarion of St. Epiphanius, Bishop of Saints: Selected Passages*. Oxford: Oxford University Press, 1990, 77, 247–48. © 1990 by Philip R. Amidon. Used by permission of Oxford University Press.

EPISTLE OF THE EMPERIOR GALLIENUS TO THE CHRISTIAN BISHOPS

J. E. L. Oulton, trans. Reproduced from Eusebius's *Ecclesiastical History* 7.13. Loeb Classical Library. Cambridge: Harvard University Press, 1932, 169. Used by permission of the publishers and the Trustees at the Loeb Classical Library. The Loeb Classical Library® is a registered trademark of the President and Fellows of Harvard College.

EPISTLE OF THE GALLICAN CHURCHES

Kirsopp Lake, trans. Reproduced from Eusebius's *Ecclesiastical History* 5.1.3–61. Loeb Classical Library. Cambridge: Harvard University Press, 1932, 407–37. Used by permission of the publishers and the Trustees at the Loeb Classical Library. The Loeb Classical Library® is a registered trademark of the President and Fellows of Harvard College.

EPITAPH OF MARCELLUS AVIRCIUS, THE

J. Stevenson, ed. *A New Eusebius* (rev. by W. H. C. Frend) London: SPCK, 1997, 110. Used by permission of SPCK Publishing.

EUSEBIUS of Caesarea (ca. 260–340 C.E.) Bishop of Caesarea (314–340 C.E.), Eusebius was one of the signers of the Nicene Creed and a friend of the emperor Constantine I.

Kirsopp Lake, trans. *Ecclesiastical History* Books I–V. Loeb Classical Library. Cambridge: Harvard University Press, 1926; J. E. L. Oulton, trans. Books VI–X. Loeb Classical Library. Cambridge: Harvard University Press, 1932. Used by permission of the publishers and the

Trustees at the Loeb Classical Library. The Loeb Classical Library® is a registered trademark of the President and Fellows of Harvard College.

Ernest Cushing Richardson, trans. *Life of Constantine* in *The Nicene and Post-Nicene Fathers*. Second Series. Grand Rapids: Eerdmans, 1952. Used by permission of Wm. B. Eerdmans Publishing Co.

J. Stevenson, ed. *On the Martyrs of Palestine* 3.1 in *A New Eusebius*. (rev. by W. H. C. Frend) London: SPCK, 1997, 275. Used by permission of SPCK Publishing.

FIRST PETER

Revised Standard Version of the Bible. © 1946, 1952, 1971 by the Division of Christian Education of the National Council of the Churches of Christ in the United States of America. Used by permission. All rights reserved.

GALEN THE PHYSICIAN (Claudius Galenus, 129–199 C.E.) One of the ancient world's most important physicians and medical authors. A prolific writer, his works became the mainstays of medieval medicine in both the European and Arabic worlds. For a time, he served as the personal physician of the emperor Marcus Aurelius.

Richard Walzer, trans. *On the Pulse* 2.4, 3.3 in *Galen on Jews and Christians*. Oxford: Oxford University Press, 1949, 46, 14. Used by permission of Oxford University Press, Inc.

Richard Walzer, trans. On *The Prime Mover* in *Galen on Jews and Christians*. Oxford: Oxford University Press, 1949, 15. Used by permission of Oxford University Press, Inc.

Richard Walzer, trans. *Summary of Plato's Republic* in *Galen on Jews and Christians*. Oxford: Oxford University Press, 1949, 15. Used by permission of Oxford University Press, Inc.

Richard Walzer, trans. *On the Usefulness of the Parts of the Body* 11.14 in *Galen on Jews and Christians*. Oxford: Oxford University Press, 1949, 12. Used by permission of Oxford University Press, Inc.

GALLIO INSCRIPTION AT DELPHI, THE

W. Dittenberger. *Sylloge Inscriptionum Graecarum*. 3d ed. 801D, as presented in *The New Testament Background*. Edited by C. K. Barrett. San Francisco: HarperSanFrancisco, 1987, 51–52, quoting F. J. F. Jackson and K. Lake, *The Beginnings of Christianity*. London: Macmillan, 1933, V. 461.

GESTA APUD ZENOPHILUM

A. H. M. Jones. *Constantine and the Conversion of Europe*. Rev. 2nd ed. Toronto: University of Toronto Press, 1978. © 1962 by A. H. M. Jones. Used by permission of Scribner, a division of Simon & Schuster.

GOSPEL OF JOHN

Revised Standard Version of the Bible. © 1946, 1952, 1971 by the Division of Christian Education of the National Council of the Churches of Christ in the United States of America. Used by permission. All rights reserved.

GOSPEL OF LUKE

Revised Standard Version of the Bible. © 1946, 1952, 1971 by the Division of Christian Education of the National Council of the Churches of Christ in the United States of America. Used by permission. All rights reserved.

GOSPEL OF MARK

Revised Standard Version of the Bible. © 1946, 1952, 1971 by the Division of Christian Education of the National Council of the Churches of Christ in the United States of America. Used by permission. All rights reserved.

GOSPEL OF MATTHEW

Revised Standard Version of the Bible. © 1946, 1952, 1971 by the Division of Christian Education of the National Council of the Churches of Christ in the United States of America. Used by permission. All rights reserved.

HERODIAN (d. after 238 C.E.) A Syrian rhetorician from Antioch who wrote a Greek history of the Roman Empire for the reigns of Marcus Aurelius through Gordian III (180–238 C.E.).

John Ferguson, trans. *Histories of the Empire after Marcus* 4.2 in *The Religions of the Roman Empire*. Ithaca: Cornell University Press, 1970, 96–98. © 1970 by John Ferguson. Used by permission of Cornell University Press.

IGNATIUS (d. ca. 108 C.E.) By tradition the second bishop of Antioch, Ignatius was arrested as a Christian during a local persecution and taken under guard to Rome for execution. The seven letters he wrote to various churches while being transported to Rome indicate that, in spite of the Roman guards, during the journey Christians were allowed relatively free access to visit with Ignatius and no effort was made to arrest them. Our sources vary as to whether Ignatius was executed in 108 C.E. (per Eusebius, writing in the early fourth century) or 115 C.E. (per a source written ca. 600 C.E.).

Cyril C. Richardson, ed. *Epistle to the Ephesians* 16 in *Early Church Fathers*. Library of Christian Classics. New York: Collier Books, 1970, 92. Used by permission of Westminster John Knox and SCM Press.

Cyril C. Richardson, ed. *Epistle to the Romans* 4.1, 5.1–2 in *Early Church Fathers*. Library of Christian Classics. New York: Collier Books, 1970, 104. Used by permission of Westminster John Knox and SCM Press.

Cyril C. Richardson, ed. *Epistle to the Philadelphians* 2, 10.1.2 in *Early Church Fathers*. Library of Christian Classics. New York: Collier Books, 1970, 108, 111. Used by permission of Westminster John Knox and SCM Press.

INSCRIPTION ON THE ARCH OF CONSTANTINE, THE

J. Stevenson, ed. *A New Eusebius*. (rev. by W. H. C. Frend) London: SPCK, 1997, 286. Used by permission of SPCK Publishing.

INSCRIPTION FROM TIBUR, THE

W. M. Ramsay. *The Bearing of Recent Discovery on the Trustworthiness of the New Testament*. Grand Rapids: Eerdmans, 1953, 228–30, as quoted in Daniel J. Theron, trans. *Evidence of Tradition*. London: Bowes & Bowes, 1957, 21–22.

JEROME (Eusebius Sofronius Hieronymous, 342–420 C.E.)

Ralph Martin Novak, Jr., trans. *Life of Malchus the Captive Monk* 1.

Robert L. Wilken. *Commentary on Daniel* "Prologue" in *The Christians as the Romans Saw Them*. New Haven: Yale University Press, 1984, 140–41. © 1984. Used by permission of Yale University Press.

JOSEPHUS (a/k/a Flavius Josephus, ca. 37–100 C.E.) Born in Jerusalem, Josephus was the Jewish commander in charge of Galilee during the First Jewish War against Rome (66–70 C.E.). Captured by Vespasian (Emperor, 69–79 C.E.) in 67 C.E., he remained with Vespasian and Vespasian's son Titus (Emperor, 79–81 C.E.) for the rest of the campaign, and witnessed the destruction of Jerusalem in 70 C.E. After the war, he traveled to Rome, where he became a client of the Flavius family of Vespasian and Titus.

H. St. J. Thackeray, trans. *Against Apion* 2.75–77. Loeb Classical Library. Cambridge: Harvard University Press, 1926. Used by permission of the publishers and the Trustees at the Loeb Classical Library. The Loeb Classical Library® is a registered trademark of the President and Fellows of Harvard College.

Ralph Marcus and Allen Wikgren, trans. *Jewish Antiquities*. Books XIV–XVII. Loeb Classical Library. Cambridge: Harvard University Press, 1963; Louis H. Feldman, trans. Books XVIII–XX. Loeb Classical Library. Cambridge: Harvard University Press, 1965. Used by permission of the publishers and the Trustees at the Loeb Classical Library. The Loeb Classical Library® is a registered trademark of the President and Fellows of Harvard College.

H. St. J. Thackeray, trans. *The Jewish War*. Books I–III. Loeb Classical Library. Cambridge: Harvard University Press, 1927; H. St. J. Thackeray, trans. Books IV–VII. Loeb Classical Library. Cambridge: Harvard University Press, 1928. Used by permission of the publishers and the Trustees at the Loeb Classical Library. The Loeb Classical Library® is a registered trademark of the President and Fellows of Harvard College.

Shlomo Pines, trans. An Arabic Version of the Testimonium Flavianum and Its Implications. Jerusalem: Israel Academy of Science and Humanities, 1971. © Israel Academy of Science and Humanities 1971. All rights reserved. Used by permission of Israel Academy of Science and Humanities. Reprinted from Zvi Baras, "The *Testimonium Flavianum* and the Martyrdom of James." *Josephus, Judaism and Christianity*. Edited by Louis H. Feldman and Gohei Hata. Tokyo: Yamamoto Shoten Publishing House, 1987. Published by Wayne State University Press, 340.

JUDE

Revised Standard Version of the Bible. © 1946, 1952, 1971 by the Division of Christian Education of the National Council of the Churches of Christ in the United States of America. Used by permission. All rights reserved.

JULIAN THE APOSTATE (Flavius Claudius Julianus, ca. 332–363 C.E.) Emperor of Rome, 361–363 C.E. A small boy at the time of Constantine death, Julian was spared during the massacre of potential claimants to the throne conducted by Constantine's sons. Julian was raised as a Christian and trained at the church school run by Eusebius, bishop of Caesarea. Julian converted to paganism about age twenty, but did not publicly announce his apostasy until becoming sole emperor. Cyril of Alexandria (ca. 370–444 C.E.), the bishop of Alexandria (412–444 C.E.), wrote in his book *Against Julian* (ca. 435–440 C.E.) that of all "the foes of Christ," Julian was especially to be feared because "before he became emperor he was numbered among the believers; he was worthy of holy Baptism, and he was trained in the Holy Scriptures." Julian's intimate familiarity with Christian doctrine made his attacks particularly effective, since, unlike many pagan critics, he was familiar with the standard Christian rebuttals to pagan arguments. Manuscripts of Julian's *Against the Galilaeans* were ordered burned by the Christian Emperor Theodosius II in 448 C.E.

> Wilmer C. Wright, trans. *Against the Galilaeans* in *Julian* volume III. Loeb Classical Library. Cambridge: Harvard University Press, 1923, 319, 379–81, 395–97, 409–11, 413. Used by permission of the publishers and the Trustees at the Loeb Classical Library. The Loeb Classical Library® is a registered trademark of the President and Fellows of Harvard College.
> Wilmer C. Wright, trans. *Epistles* 21, 22, 36, 37, 40, 41, 51 in *Julian* volume III. Loeb Classical Library. Cambridge: Harvard University Press, 1923, 61–67, 67–73, 117–23, 123, 127–29, 129–35, 177–81. Used by permission of the publishers and the Trustees at the Loeb Classical Library. The Loeb Classical Library® is a registered trademark of the President and Fellows of Harvard College.

JUSTIN MARTYR (ca. 100 or 114–165 C.E.) Born in Samaria, and probably of Roman descent, Justin is known to have taught in Ephesus and Rome. While his *First Apology* was not the first apology composed in defense of Christianity, it is the earliest complete example of the genre. After being arrested as a professed Christian, Justin Martyr refused to make sacrifice to the emperor Marcus Aurelius and died a martyr in 165.

> Cyril C. Richardson, ed. *The First Apology* 1–5, 26, 29, 31, 35, 48 in *Early Christian Fathers*. Library of Christian Classics. Translated by Edward Rochie Hardy. New York: Collier Books, 1970, 242–44, 258–59, 260, 261, 264, 273. Used by permission of Westminster John Knox and SCM Press.

JUSTINIAN'S CODE 3.12.3

> Henry Bettenson, ed. *Documents of the Christian Church*. 2nd ed. Oxford: Oxford University Press, 1963, 18–19. Used by permission of Oxford University Press, Inc.

JUVENAL (Decimus Junius Juvenalis, flourished late first and early second centuries C.E.)

> G. G. Ramsay, trans. *Satires* 14.96–125. Loeb Classical Library. Cambridge: Harvard University Press, 1918, 271–73. Used by permission of the publishers and the Trustees at the Loeb Classical Library. The Loeb Classical Library® is a registered trademark of the President and Fellows of Harvard College.

LACTANTIUS (Lucius Caecilius Firmianus Lactantius, ca. 245–323) Latin apologist from Proconsular Africa who taught rhetoric at Nicomedia in Asia until ca. 305. He later moved to Gaul, where he was a tutor to Crispus, the eldest son of Constantine.

Sister Mary Francis McDonald, trans. *On the Deaths of the Persecutors* 10–12, 33, 34, 36, 38, 44 in *Lactantius: The Minor Works*. Washington, D.C.: The Catholic University of America Press, 1965. Used by permission of The Catholic University of America Press.

LAST ORACLE OF APOLLO AT DELPHI, THE

Ralph Martin Novak, Jr., trans. *The Last Oracle of Apollo at Delphi*.

LETTER OF THE CHURCH OF ROME TO THE CHURCH AT CORINTH, THE (1st Clement) 5

Cyril C. Richardson, trans. *Early Christian Fathers*. New York: Collier Books, 1970, 45–46. Used by permission of Westminster John Knox and SCM Press.

LETTER TO DIOGNETUS 5.11–17 (written ca. 120s C.E.) Of uncertain authorship, the letter is thought to combine portions of works by Quadratus of Asia Minor and Hippoltus of Rome.

Cyril C. Richardson, ed. *Early Christian Fathers*. Translated by Eugene R. Fairweather. New York: Collier Books, 1970, 217. Used by permission of Westminster John Knox and SCM Press.

LIBANIUS (314–393 C.E.) A pagan rhetorician from Antioch in Syria, Libanius was one of the leading defenders of paganism in the last decades of the fourth century C.E.

Ramsay MacMullen and Eugene N. Lane, trans. *Oration 30* 26–29 in *Paganism and Christianity 100–425 C.E.* Minneapolis: Fortress Press, 1992, 283–84, quoting (with alterations) A.F. Norman, trans. *Libanius*. Loeb Classical Library. Cambridge: Harvard University Press, 1989. Used by permission of the publishers and the Trustees at the Loeb Classical Library. The Loeb Classical Library® is a registered trademark of the President and Fellows of Harvard College.

LUCIAN (a/k/a Lucian of Samosata, ca. 125–190 C.E.) Born in Samosata, on the Euphrates River in Commagene, Lucian was one of the most prolific Greek language writers and satirists of the second century.

A. M. Harmon, trans. *On the Death of Peregrinus* 9–14, 16. Loeb Classical Library. Cambridge: Harvard University Press, 1955, 11–17, 19. Used by permission of the publishers and the Trustees at the Loeb Classical Library. The Loeb Classical Library® is a registered trademark of the President and Fellows of Harvard College.

A. M. Harmon, trans. *Alexander the False Prophet* 25, 38. Loeb Classical Library. Cambridge: Harvard University Press, 1925, 209, 225. Used by permission of the publishers and the Trustees at the Loeb Classical Library. The Loeb Classical Library® is a registered trademark of the President and Fellows of Harvard College.

M. MINUCIUS FELIX (?–240 C.E.) A Christian lawyer active during 200–240 C.E., he wrote a book in defense of Christianity, set as a conversation between a Christian and a pagan.

Robert Ernest Wallis, trans. *Octavius* 8–9.1–3 in *The Ante-Nicene Fathers*. Grand Rapids: Eerdmans, 1994, 177–78. Used by permission of Wm. B. Eerdmans Publishing Co.

MARA BAR SARAPION (active last third of the first century C.E.)

F. Schulthess. *Letter to his Son.* "Der Brief des Mara bar Sarapion. Ein Beitrag zur Geschichte der syrischen Literatur," *Zeitschrift der deutschen morgenlandischen Gesellschaft* 51, 1897. As quoted in *The Historical Jesus.* Gerda Theissen and Annette Merz. Minneapolis: Fortress Press, 1998,77.

MARCUS AURELIUS (121–180 C.E.) Emperor of Rome from 161 to180 C.E., Marcus Aurelius was one of the last notable Stoic philosophers of the ancient world. In an irony of history, this "philosopher-king" spent almost his entire reign in warfare against the Germanic tribes threatening Rome's border on the Danube River. While on campaign he kept a personal diary. Published after his death, the diary is now known as "The Meditations of Marcus Aurelius."

Whitney J. Oates, ed. "Meditations" 11.3 in *The Stoic and Epicurean Philosophers*. Translated by George Long. New York: Random House, 1940, 571. Used by permission of Oxford University Press, Inc.

MARTYRDOM OF JUSTIN, THE

M. Dods, trans. *The Ante-Nicene Fathers*. Grand Rapids: Eerdmans, 1956, 611–14. Used by permission of Wm. B. Eerdmans Publishing Co.

MARTYRDOM OF PERPETUA AND FELICITAS, THE

Rosemary Rader. "The Martyrdom of Perpetua and Felicitas" in *A Lost Tradition: Women Writers of The Early Church*. Edited by Patricia Wilson Kastner. New York: University Press of America, 1981, 19–30. Used by permission of G. Ronald Kastner.

MARTYRDOM OF POLYCARP, THE

Cyril C. Richardson, ed. *Early Christian Fathers*. Library of Christian Classics. Translated by Massey Shepherd, Jr. New York: Collier Books, 1970, 149–58. Used by permission of Westminster John Knox Press and SCM Press.

MELITO (died ca. 190 C.E.) Bishop of Sardis in Lydia.

Kirsopp Lake, trans. *To Antoninus* reproduced from Eusebius's *Ecclesiastical History* 4.26.5–11. Loeb Classical Library. Cambridge: Harvard University Press, 1926, 389–91. Used by permission of the publishers and the Trustees at the Loeb Classical Library. The Loeb Classical Library® is a registered trademark of the President and Fellows of Harvard College.

ORACLES OF THE PROPHETS OF APOLLO AND HECATE

Marcus Dods, trans. Reproduced from St. Augustine's *The City of God* 19.23. *The Nicene and Post-Nicene Fathers*. First Series. Grand Rapids: Eerdmans, 1956, 881–83. Used by permission of Wm. B. Eerdmans Publishing Co.

ORIGEN (Origenes Adamantius, ca. 185–254 C.E.) Born and raised in
Alexandria, Egypt, Origen was trained there at the famous catechism school
under Clement of Alexandria. He was perhaps the greatest of the pre-Nicene
Christian intellectuals. Origen became caught up in the dispute between the
Christians of Egypt and Judaea when he accepted ordination from the
bishops of Jerusalem and Caesarea, and was exiled from Alexandria by the
bishop there. He moved to Caesarea and taught there. Arrested as a Christian
in 250 during the persecution of Trajan Decius (emperor 249–251), he was
severely tortured, and upon his release in 251 lived for only three more years.
     Frederick Crombie, trans. *Contra Celsus* in *The Ante-Nicene Fathers.*
     Grand Rapids: Eerdmans, reprinted 1994. Used by permission of Wm. B.
     Eerdmans Publishing Co.
PANEGYRIC TO CONSTANTINE
     C. E. V. Nixon and Barbara Saylor Rogers, trans. Panegyrici Latini
     6(7).21.3–6, 12.2.1–5, 12.4.1, 12.13.1–2, 12.26.1 in *In Praise of Later
     Roman Emperors.* Berkeley: University of California Press, 1994, 295–96,
     299, 313–14, 332–33. © 1994. Used by permission of The Regents of The
     University of California.
PAUL
     First Thessalonians 5:26. Revised Standard Version of the Bible. © 1946,
     1952, 1971 by the Division of Christian Education of the National
     Council of the Churches of Christ in the United States of America. Used
     by permission. All rights reserved.
PAULINUS OF FLORENCE (active ca. 394–422 C.E.) Paulinus served as private
     secretary to Ambrose during the period of approximately 394–397 C.E. Later
     he became a deacon of Milan.
     Reprinted from Frederick R. Hoare, trans. *Life of Ambrose* 5–9, 22, 24 in
     The Western Fathers. New York: Sheed and Ward, 1954, 152–54, 165–68.
PETITION AGAINST THE CHRISTIANS, A
     Robert L. Wilken, trans. *The Christians as the Romans Saw Them.* New
     Haven: Yale University Press, 1984, 157. © 1984. Used by permission of
     Yale University Press.
PHILO (Philo Judaeus, ca. 20 B.C.E.–50 C.E.)
     F. H. Colson, trans. *Embassy to Gaius* 157 Loeb Classical Library.
     Cambridge: Harvard University Press, 1962, 159. Used by permission of
     the publishers and the Trustees at the Loeb Classical Library. The Loeb
     Classical Library® is a registered trademark of the President and Fellows
     of Harvard College.
PLINY'S MEMORIAL STELE
     Robert L. Wilken, trans. *The Christians as the Romans Saw Them.* New
     Haven: Yale University Press, 1984, 29–30. © 1984. Used by permission
     of Yale University Press.
PLINY THE YOUNGER (G. Plinius Caecilius Secundus, 61 or 62–ca. 113)
     Pliny was adopted by his uncle (the famous Pliny the Elder) and raised in

Rome, where he obtained an excellent education. Consul in 100, he also sat on Trajan's imperial advisory council.

> Reprinted from John D. Lewis, trans. *Letters of Pliny* 10.96–97 in *The Letters of Pliny the Younger*. London, 1879, as quoted in *History of Western Civilization: Selected Readings*. Chicago: University of Chicago Press, 1970, 68–70. Modified by R. M. Novak.

PORPHYRY (ca. 233–305 C.E.) Porphyry was a neo-Platonist philosopher from Tyre in Phoenicia, and a student of Plotinus. While much of his philosophic teachings are known, we know little of Porphyry's anti-Christian works, because they were destroyed by orders of the Christian emperors Constantine I and Theodosius II. What has survived of his anti-Christian writings are fragments appearing as scattered quotations and references in the works of about a half-dozen Christian authors. St. Augustine called Porphyry "the most learned of philosophers." As a young man, Porphyry met and knew the Christian writer Origen. [Eusebius, *Ecclesiastical History*, VI.xix.2–3]

> Robert L. Wilken, trans. *Against the Christians.* Reproduced from Jerome's Summary of Book XII in *Commentary on Daniel* in *The Christians as the Romans Saw Them.* New Haven: Yale University Press, 1984,140–41. © 1984. Used by permission of Yale University Press.
>
> Marcus Dods, trans. *Philosophy From Oracles* fragments reproduced from *The City of God* XIX.23. New York: The Modern Library, 1950, 701–3.
>
> Fragment 63 from Adolf von Harnack, "Porphyrius gegen die Christen, 15 Buchen, Zeugnisse, Fragmente und Referate" in *A New Eusebius.* Edited by J. Stevenson. (rev. W. H. C. Frend) London: SPCK, 1997, 270. Used by permission of SPCK Publishing.

RABBINIC ACCOUNT OF THE DEATH OF JESUS, A (Babylonian Talmud Sanhedrin 43a)

> G. Dalman, trans. *Jesus Christ in the Talmud, Midrash, Zohar, and the Liturgy of the Synagogue* (1893) as reproduced in *The Historical Jesus.* Gerda Theissen and Annette Merz. Minneapolis: Fortress Press, 1998, 75.

RESCRIPT OF ANTONINUS PIUS

> Kirsopp Lake, trans. Reproduced from Eusebius's *Ecclesiastical History* IV.xiii.1–7. Loeb Classical Library. Cambridge: Harvard University Press, 1932, 333–35. Used by permission of the publishers and the Trustees at the Loeb Classical Library. The Loeb Classical Library® is a registered trademark of the President and Fellows of Harvard College.

RESCRIPT OF CONSTANTINE I (Selection 5.19)

> J. E. L. Oulton, trans. Reproduced from Eusebius's *Ecclesiastical History* X.vi.1–5. Loeb Classical Library. Cambridge: Harvard University Press, 1932, 461–63. Used by permission of the publishers and the Trustees at the Loeb Classical Library. The Loeb Classical Library® is a registered trademark of the President and Fellows of Harvard College.

RESCRIPT OF CONSTANTINE I (Selection 5.31)

> A. C. Zenos, trans. Reproduced from Socrates' *Ecclesiastical History* I.9 in

Nicene and Post-Nicene Fathers. Second Series. Grand Rapids: Eerdmans, 1989, 64–65. Used by permission of Wm. B. Eerdmans Publishing Co.

RESCRIPT OF THE EMPEROR HADRIAN

Kirsopp Lake, trans. Reproduced from Eusebius's *Ecclesiastical History* IV.ix. Loeb Classical Library. Cambridge: Harvard University Press, 1932, 325. Used by permission of the publishers and the Trustees at the Loeb Classical Library. The Loeb Classical Library® is a registered trademark of the President and Fellows of Harvard College.

RESPONSE OF MAXIMINAS TO THE PETITION OF TYRE, THE

J. E. L. Oulton, trans. Reproduced from Eusebius's *Ecclesiastical History* IX.vii.11–12. Loeb Classical Library. Cambridge: Harvard University Press, 1932, 347–49. Used by permission of the publishers and the Trustees at the Loeb Classical Library. The Loeb Classical Library® is a registered trademark of the President and Fellows of Harvard College.

SCRIPTORES HISTORIAE AUGUSTAE

David Magie, trans. *Life of Septimus Severus* 17. Loeb Classical Library. Cambridge: Harvard University Press, 1924, 409. Used by permission of the publishers and the Trustees at the Loeb Classical Library. The Loeb Classical Library® is a registered trademark of the President and Fellows of Harvard College.

David Magie, trans. *Life of Severus Alexander* 29.1–3. Loeb Classical Library. Cambridge: Harvard University Press, 1924, 235. Used by permission of the publishers and the Trustees at the Loeb Classical Library. The Loeb Classical Library® is a registered trademark of the President and Fellows of Harvard College.

SECOND PETER

Revised Standard Version of the Bible. © 1946, 1952, 1971 by the Division of Christian Education of the National Council of the Churches of Christ in the United States of America. Used by permission. All rights reserved.

SOCRATES (ca. 380–after 440 C.E.) A Christian historian from Constantinople, who wrote to continue the *Ecclesiastical History* of Eusebius down to 439 C.E. Very little is known about his life, but there is some evidence that he was an advocate before the courts and thus he is often given the cognomen "Scholasticus." His writings indicate that he had little information concerning events in the Western Empire.

A. C. Zenos, trans. *Ecclesiastical History* in *The Nicene and Post-Nicene Fathers*. Second Series. Grand Rapids: Eerdmans, 1989. Used by permission of Wm. B. Eerdmans Publishing Co.

SOZOMEN (Salaminius Hermias Sozomen, active in the early fifth century C.E.) A Christian historian thought to be from Gaza. Very little is known about his life. He relied heavily on the history of Socrates, but had good independent sources for events in the Western Empire.

Chester D. Hartranft, trans. *Ecclesiastical History* in *The Nicene and Post-Nicene Fathers*. Second Series. Grand Rapids: Eerdmans, 1989. Used by permission of Wm. B. Eerdmans Publishing Co.

ST. HILARY Bishop of Potiers (ca. 300–368 C.E.)

> Edward Gibbon, trans. *Second Epistle to the Emperor Constantius* 1.2.c 4, 5 in *The Decline and Fall of the Roman Empire*. Chapter 21. New York: Washington Square Press, 1960, 394–95.

SUETONIUS (Caius Suetonius Tranquillas, ca. 69–ca. 130 C.E.) Suetonius was a Roman of the senatorial order. He served as a member of the staff of Pliny the Younger in Bithynia-Pontus, as director of Imperial Libraries under the emperor Trajan, and as secretary of correspondence under the emperor Hadrian.

> John C. Rolfe, trans. *Life of Caligula* 22.2–3. Loeb Classical Library. Cambridge: Harvard University Press, 1997, 435–37. Used by permission of the publishers and the Trustees at the Loeb Classical Library. The Loeb Classical Library® is a registered trademark of the President and Fellows of Harvard College.

> John C. Rolfe, trans. *Life of Claudius* 25.4. Loeb Classical Library. Cambridge: Harvard University Press, 1997, 51. Used by permission of the publishers and the Trustees at the Loeb Classical Library. The Loeb Classical Library® is a registered trademark of the President and Fellows of Harvard College.

> John C. Rolfe, trans. *Life of Nero* 16.2. Loeb Classical Library. Cambridge: Harvard University Press, 1997, 107. Used by permission of the publishers and the Trustees at the Loeb Classical Library. The Loeb Classical Library® is a registered trademark of the President and Fellows of Harvard College.

> John C. Rolfe, trans. *Life of Vespasian* 23. Loeb Classical Library. Cambridge: Harvard University Press, 1997, 301. Used by permission of the publishers and the Trustees at the Loeb Classical Library. The Loeb Classical Library® is a registered trademark of the President and Fellows of Harvard College.

> John C. Rolfe, trans. *Life of Domitian* 13–14. Loeb Classical Library. Cambridge: Harvard University Press, 1997, 347–49. Used by permission of the publishers and the Trustees at the Loeb Classical Library. The Loeb Classical Library® is a registered trademark of the President and Fellows of Harvard College.

SULPICIUS SEVERUS (ca. 360–420 C.E.) Sulpicius Severus was born in Aquitania, Gaul about 360 C.E. to a prominent family. He studied law at Bordeaux, and converted to Christianity about 389 C.E. His *Chronicle* was an attempt to present history written from the Christian point of view.

> Alexander Roberts, trans. *Chronicle* ii.29 in *The Nicene and Post-Nicene Fathers*. Second Series. Grand Rapids: Eerdmans, 1978, 110–11. Used by permission of Wm. B. Eerdmans Publishing Co.

SYMMACHUS (Quintus Aurelius Symmachus, ca. 340–402) In 382 C.E., the Christian emperor Gratian removed the Altar of Victory from the Roman Senate, where Caesar Augustus had placed it in 30 B.C.E. Symmachus, a most distinguished Roman senator and the leader of the pagan faction in the senate, was sent by the senate to plead with Gratian for the restoration of the altar, but Gratian would not grant a hearing. In 384 C.E., after Gratian's death, Symmachus presented the petition of the senate to the emperor Valentinian II, asking for restoration of the Altar of Victory.

H. De Romestin, trans. *Dispatches to the Emperor in The Nicene and Post-Nicene Fathers.* Second Series. Grand Rapids: Eerdmans, 1955, 813–18. Used by permission of Wm. B. Eerdmans Publishing Co.

TACITUS (Publius Cornelius Tacitus, 60–ca. 120 C.E.) Tacitus was consul of Rome in 97 C.E., and served as proconsul of Asia in 112–113 C.E., during which time his friend Pliny the Younger was serving as Trajan's emissary in the neighboring province of Bithynia-Pontus. Tacitus was conservative and a supporter of the ideal, if not the practice, of the Roman Republic.

J. Jackson, trans. *Annals of Imperial Rome* 4.37–38, 13.32, 15.44. Loeb Classical Library. Cambridge: Harvard University Press, 1937. Volume IV, 65–67; Volume V, 53–54, 283–85. Used by permission of the publishers and the Trustees at the Loeb Classical Library. The Loeb Classical Library® is a registered trademark of the President and Fellows of Harvard College.

C. H. Moore, trans. *The Histories* 5.4–5, 9. Loeb Classical Library. Cambridge: Harvard University Press, 1925. Volume III, 179–83, 191. Used by permission of the publishers and the Trustees at the Loeb Classical Library. The Loeb Classical Library® is a registered trademark of the President and Fellows of Harvard College.

TERTULLIAN (Quintus Septimius Florens Tertullianus, 160–ca. 220 C.E.) Tertullian is the first "Latin Father" of the Christian church, the first Christian author to write exclusively in Latin. Born in Carthage as the son of a Roman centurion, he converted to Christianity about 195–196 C.E. By 207 C.E., in disillusionment with the Christianity practiced by the African church, which he saw as too worldly and unspiritual, he first turned to the Christian Montanist Movement, and then formed his own strict Christian sect, the Tertullianists. Tertullian exercised a very strong influence on Christian belief, especially with regards to his development of the doctrines of the Trinity and of the nature of the person of Christ. His main literary output was from 196/197–212 C.E.

S. Thelwall, trans. *An Answer to the Jews* 8 in *The Ante-Nicene Fathers.* Grand Rapids: Eerdmans, 1980, 160. Used by permission of Wm. B. Eerdmans Publishing Co.

T. R. Glover, trans. *Apology.* Loeb Classical Library. Cambridge: Harvard University Press, 1984. Used by permission of the publishers and the Trustees at the Loeb Classical Library. The Loeb Classical Library® is a registered trademark of the President and Fellows of Harvard College.

S. Thelwall, trans. *On Idolatry* 17, 19 in *The Ante-Nicene Fathers.* Grand Rapids: Eerdmans, 1994, 72–73. Used by permission of Wm. B. Eerdmans Publishing Co.

S. Thelwall, trans. *To Scapula* 5 in *The Ante-Nicene Fathers.* Grand Rapids: Eerdmans, 1994, 107, as modified by Ralph Martin Novak. Used by permission of Wm. B. Eerdmans Publishing Co.

Dr. Peter Holmes, trans. *To the Peoples* (Ad nationes) I.3 in *The Ante-Nicene Fathers*. Grand Rapids: Eerdmans, 1980, 111. Used by permission of Wm. B. Eerdmans Publishing Co.

GREGORY THAUMATURGUS (205–265 C.E.) Born in the town of Neo-Caesareia in the province of Pontus to a pagan family of some wealth and standing, Gregory was converted to Christianity by Origen, and in 240 C.E. he became bishop of the Christian church in his home town.

> S. D. F. Salmond, trans. *Canonical Epistle* in *The Ante-Nicene Fathers*. Grand Rapids, Eerdmans, 1975, 19–20. Used by permission of Wm. B. Eerdmans Publishing Co.

THEODORET (Theodoretus, ca. 393–466 C.E.) Bishop of Cyrrhus (east of Antioch) from 423–466 C.E., Theodoret was a prolific writer. His *Ecclesiastical History* and some 230 surviving letters provide important information about the history of his own time.

> Bloomfield Jackson, trans. *Ecclesiastical History* 5.17, 5.21 in *The Nicene and Post-Nicene Fathers*. Second Series. Grand Rapids: Eerdmans, 1989. Used by permission of Wm. B. Eerdmans Publishing Co.
>
> R. M. Price, trans. *A History of the Monks of Syria* XVII.1–4. Kalamazoo, Mich.: Cistercian Publications, 1985, 120–21. Used by permission of Cistercian Publications.

THEODOSIAN CODE Issued in 448 C.E. under the emperor Theodosius II, emperor of the Eastern Roman Empire from 408 to 450 C.E., this is the first of the great compilations of Roman law.

> Clyde Pharr, trans. *The Theodosian Code and Novels and the Sirmondian Constitutions*. Princeton: Princeton University Press, 1952. © 1952 by Princeton University Press. Used by permission of Princeton University Press.

TOMBSTONE OF QUINTUS AEMILIUS (ILS 2683)

> Ralph Martin Novak, Jr., trans. Based on the Latin text found in *Was Christ Born in Bethlehem?* by William Ramsay. London: Hodder & Stoughton, 1905, 274.

TWELFTH BENEDICTION, THE

> Reprinted from Everett Ferguson, *Backgrounds of Early Christianity*. Grand Rapids: Eerdmans, 1987. Used by permission of Wm. B. Eerdmans Publishing Co.

INDEX OF ANCIENT TEXTS

INDEX OF SUBJECTS